The Hebrew Portuguese Nations in Antwerp and London at the Time of Charles V and Henry VIII

New documents and interpretations

By

Aron di Leone Leoni

Published in cooperation with
The American Sephardi Federation with Sephardic House

KTAV PUBLISHING HOUSE
Brooklyn, NY

In memory of

my Father Rabbi Yehudah Gavriel Leoni Z.Z.L.
and my Mother Margalit Berukha Ravenna Z.L.
from whom I derived the love for our history

לזכרין ולעב

אבי מורי כמוהר"ר יהודה גבריאל ליאני זצ"ל
ואמי מורתי מרת מרגלית ברוכה ראוינא ז"ל

This work was made possible by a grant
from the Memorial Foundation for Jewish Culture
which enabled me to widen and complete the research
in several archives and libraries throughout different States.

This book was published with the support of
Monique and Serge Benveniste of Portugal in memory of
their parents Alberto and Sara Benveniste and sponsored by
The American Sephardi Federation with Sephardic House.

Table of Contents

Introduction

The details of what happened to thousands of the Jews on the Iberian Peninsula who were either forced or coerced into converting to Catholicism during the final years of the 15th century is not a story that fires the imagination of many Jewish scholars. Relative to other topics in Jewish history, only a minimal amount of research has been done on the lives of these people – known as New Christians, conversos or marranos – at least during the period immediately following their conversions when they became victims of widespread ethnic cleansing.

And that is a pity because the story of how they schemed and plotted to survive and also reach a land where they could openly practice and perpetuate their ancestral faith once more is well worth telling. In addition, it is an object lesson in the depth of feeling that many of these people (also known euphemistically as members of the Portuguese Nation) retained for their Jewish faith, despite the hardships and setbacks.

It is important for another reason: many were brilliant merchants whose skill in international commerce helped to enrich the great Renaissance cities of Antwerp, Venice and Ferrara; something that is rarely mentioned when Renaissance history is discussed. And it shows how they leveraged those financial skills and worked closely together to enable as many of them as possible to survive.

Aron di Leone Leoni, the author of this work and an Italian scholar of fine repute, spent years digging in archives to piece together at least a portion of this story – particularly the part that touches upon the colorful individuals who helped organize and fund an escape network that brought the less fortunate among them by ship from Lisbon to Antwerp and then onwards by foot, barge and cart, over the Alps to friendlier city-states of Italy and the Ottoman Empire.

He provides us with a wealth of documents in an appendix that should permit future scholars to read primary material that might be otherwise unobtainable. The prohibitive cost, language barriers and logistics of doing this sort of research in archives that are scattered across the face of Europe has all but placed such material off limits, at least to the American research community. While some of it has appeared in French and Italian journals, this is one of the first attempts to make the comprehensive story accessible to all English-speaking scholars, along with information and a rich trove of source notes that were never before available.

Having spent over six years researching and writing the life of Doña Gracia Nasi, one of the leaders of this escape network, I can attest to the fact that Professor Leoni has plucked some remarkable documents from the archives; giving us names, families and details that put flesh on the bone of this dynamic community and add immeasurably to our knowledge. I can also vouch for the fact that locating the documents is only the first of many hurdles. Leoni must be praised as well for undertaking the Herculean task of deciphering the 16th century script and the archaic forms of the languages in which they were written, as well as figuring out the acronyms widely used at the time.

Every university library that is serious about its commitment to Mediterranean Jewish history, and especially the Renaissance period, should have at least one copy on its shelves.

Andrée Aelion Brooks*

* Andrée Aelion Brooks, a noted journalist and lecturer and Associate Fellow, Yale University, is the author of "The Woman who Defied Kings: the Life and Times of Doña Gracia Nasi, a Jewish woman leader during the Renaissance."

Preface

A few years ago, I began to research archives and libraries in Portugal, Belgium and England in order to gather information on the Portuguese New Christians[1] who established an important "Nation" in Ferrara. I had the good fortune to find a vast array of documents that throw new light on the Portuguese settlements in Antwerp and London, and on the policies followed by Emperor Charles V and King Henry VIII that, in my opinion, deserve a reappraisal.

This book is devoted mainly to the study of the Portuguese Nation of Antwerp, its internal structure and organization, its juridical position and its frequently strained relations with Emperor Charles V and the Regents who governed the Low-Countries on his behalf.

The Portuguese of Antwerp were linked by family and commercial relationships with the members of the smaller, but equally important, Portuguese colony of London. The events related to the two settlements are so strictly interwoven that it is impossible to study the history of the settlement of Antwerp without dealing with its sister-community in London. Therefore, we shall describe both groups.

After the establishment of the Inquisition in Portugal, there was a dramatic increase in the immigration of *conversos*[2] of Jewish origin to Northern Europe. This influx reached important proportions when Duke Ercole of Este invited the Portuguese exiles to settle in Ferrara and offered them the opportunity to return to the Jewish faith. A complex rescue organization was set up to plan and finance the flight of *conversos* from the Iberian Peninsula to London and Antwerp, where some of them

---

1. New Christians (*Christianos Nuevos* in Spanish, *Christãos Novos* in Portuguese): this term was usd to designate the victims of the (more or less) forced conversions in Spain and in Portugal. Their descendants were referred to by this same appellative for several centuries.
2. Conversos (lit.: converted people). The term is generally used as a synonym of "New Christians".

found shelter while others continued their journey to Italy and the Levant. A vast amount of information has been found on the procedures adopted by the rescue organization and their attempts to smuggle *conversos* from Portugal to England and Flanders and, from there, to Italy and the Levant. Several documents provide a simple but extremely dramatic description of the itinerary followed by the émigrés from Antwerp to Italy along the rivers and the roadways of Germany, across secondary Swiss Alpine passes and narrow pathways, and then following the rivers of Lombardy down to Ferrara.

According to the existing literature, Diogo Mendes, an important businessman in Antwerp, was the major force behind these operations, using his commercial network to this end. The effort, however, did not come from him alone. A number of other *conversos* devoted their energies and finances for this purpose. I have attempted to gather information on the leaders of the rescue organization, as well as on the many people who helped at a lower level. As we shall see, Charles V was fiercely opposed to this migratory movement and set up special police corps to prevent the flight of the Portuguese New Christians towards Italy and to seize their property. At some point, the imperial police blocked the Brenner Pass and imposed an economic boycott against Ferrara.

The writing of the history of Low Countries – and of the Portuguese settlement in Antwerp – has been influenced by the erroneous assumption that Charles V introduced an ecclesiastic Spanish-styled Inquisition into this particular hereditary dominion of his. This was not the case. Contrary to accepted interpretations, the task of enforcing the persecutory policy against various forms of heresy was entrusted to civil courts. As we shall see, the Portuguese of Antwerp were often persecuted by the imperial police and high-ranking court officers, and not by ecclesiastical tribunals. We shall study this aspect of the history of New Christians in Antwerp, on the basis of both published and unedited documents, local legislation, and existing historiography.

The Emperor was more concerned with considerations of financial rather than religious nature. By examining the files of the Police of Brabant at the General Archives of the Kingdom in Brussels, it was possible to ascertain that only cursory attention was paid to the religious observance of the New Christians of Antwerp. The accusations of heresy and apostasy were often used as a pretext for the imprisonment of some rich merchant who would eventually be released on payment of a large sum. The prosecution of heresy was turned into a financial tool for the benefit of the Emperor.

Most of the New Christians of Antwerp and London moved to Italy where they established new Portuguese Nations in several cities. In many cases we could follow their tracks and describe their communal and commercial activities.

I conclude these notes with a clarification. During the last few decades, there has been a lively debate between those who maintain that the majority of New Christians of Jewish origin remained true to the religion of their ancestors and those who sustain that a "Judaizing heresy" did not exist in the Iberian Peninsula. I do not want to use the documents published in this study to draw general conclusions on the religious behavior of New Christian living in Portugal around the middle of the 16th century. However, I am convinced that only a strong leaning towards Judaism could have swayed so many people to adopt such a risky and otherwise unimaginable step, as the flight from remote regions of Portugal to London and Antwerp and the subsequent hazardous *caminho* (journey) from there to Ferrara using secondary routes and hidden paths through the Alps.

The thesis of the non-existence of *marranism*[3] is, *per se*, indemonstrable. It is impossible to provide proof of the non-existence of a sentiment that, by its very nature, had to be clandestine and could not leave documentary traces other than those of Inquisitorial papers, or documents of the Flemish police. Recent research conducted by various scholars from several countries has produced mounting evidence of the persisting attachment to the Jewish faith on the part of vast segments of the population of Jewish origin. Recent investigations into the Inquisitorial papers throw new light on the persistent messianic expectations of most New Christians. The overwhelming enthusiasm generated by the invitation extended by the Duke of Ferrara to the *conversos*, and the vastness of the ensuing migratory movement, are meaningful and revealing.

Some scholars have questioned whether those New Christians who moved to Italian cities were more attracted to the economic importance of these places than to the possibility of returning to Judaism. These scholars have adopted the same position held at the beginning of the past cen-

---

3. *Marranism* = crypto Judaism; (*marranos* = crypto Jews). This word was originally tainted with derogatory meanings and allusions. Today it is used as a technical term to designate those New Christians who remained faithful to their ancestral religion and practiced Jewish rites in the privacy of their homes or in secret synagogues.

tury by many Iberian-Catholic historians who tried to attach an illicit and unethical connotation to the economic prosperity obtained by many Portuguese *conversos* in London, Antwerp and various Italian cities, which they referred to, with a certain disdain, as *gañancia*.

According to the Protestant ethic, honestly obtained wealth is a prize bestowed by God, rewarding the industriousness of man, and there is nothing reprehensible in that. According to the Jewish ethic, wealthy people have the obligation to help the less fortunate. It is a fact that the Portuguese of Antwerp and London dedicated a large part of their resources to help their persecuted brethren, some of whom lost their fortunes to the Inquisition, the Imperial police, or during their perilous journey to safe havens. It is known that the Sephardic Communities dedicated their energy to charitable works, known in Hebrew as tzedaka (loosely translated as charity).

In my opinion, the thesis of those scholars who suggest that the Portuguese merchants were motivated exclusively by economic considerations is completely groundless. No Italian prince or government would have accepted immigrants who were not gifted with business or artisan skills, or who could not offer important economic contributions to their domain. No Christian state would have offered asylum to the New Christians persecuted in Portugal simply on humanitarian considerations. Even Ercole II, in 1550, inserted a clause in the safe-conduct for the Jews of the Portuguese and Spanish Nations, in which he stated that the poor and the lazy ones were excluded from his invitation. The case of Ferrara is emblematic because this city, run by an enlightened dynasty, was the seat of a fabulous court but had little or no economic importance and certainly could not be described as a mercantile center before Ercole II was able to attract the Portuguese merchants from Antwerp and London, offering them the possibility to freely return to Judaism. It was precisely for this reason that so many merchants from London and Antwerp settled in this city, even though it offered fewer economic advantages than other Italian localities.

By comparing the results of research conducted in Portugal in England and in Belgium with the outcome of parallel investigations carried on in different Italian cities it was possible to identify several merchants of London and Antwerp (hitherto known only by their Portuguese names) with prominent personalities of the Sephardic Settlements of Ferrara, Ancona, Pesaro and Venice (who, in different circumstances, used alternatively their Portuguese name and their newly assumed Jewish appellation). In our essay we used "alias" as a technical term to indicate the acquired [or resumed] Jewish name.

The rendering of names has presented a number of peculiar problems as the present essay is based essentially on documents drawn up in different languages and dialects and preserved in several archives scattered in different countries.

During the period examined in this essay, notaries, chancellors and public officers did not follow any orthographic rules in whatever language they used. The rendering of words, even of common use, was not uniform not only in different documents preserved in the same archive but even in a single document drawn up by the same notary.

In Flanders and in England as well as in Italy, notaries and scribes were unfamiliar with Iberian languages and encountered some difficulty in writing the Portuguese names. They generally transcribed these names phonetically, using the combination of letters which, in their own language, could render the sound of foreign names.

In French as well as in Latin and Italian texts, several letters, or groups of letters were used interchangeably. For instance "c" was frequently transcribed as "qu[i,e]" and was often replaced by "g" and vice-versa. For instance: Micas/Miques/Migues; Enrique/Enrico/Enrigo (whence the famous diminutive *Righetto*).

Final "s" was often replaced by "z" and even by "x" and vice-versa. That is why in the original documents we find both Fernandez and Fernandes, Alvarez and Alvares, Dinis or Diniz.

In French, Latin and Italian texts the diptychs "si", "se" (i.e the consonant "s" followed by the vowels i or e) is frequently rendered as "ci" or "ce" or even as "sci" and "sce". That is why in notarial deeds drawn up in Italy we find side by side the forms Naci, Nasci or Nasi.

French and Flemish speaking chancellors in Brussels and in Antwerp encountered particular difficulties in transcribing the Portuguese surname Ronha (= *Roña* in Spanish) which they variously rendered as *Ronia*, *Ronija*, *Rongha* or *Roigne*. Public notaries in Ferrara adopted the form *Rogna* while in Hebrew documents the form רונייה was used.

I did not try to estabilish a fixed set of rules in order to unify the various forms of the names in the essay but I decided to adopt a case by case solution. For instance, it was possible to ascertain that Micas (from the Latin *e-micare* = to excel) was the surname given at the court of Lisbon to Doctor Agostinho Anriques (Ioão Micas' s father) who excelled in his knowledge and ability. I decided to use the form Micas and to repudiate all the spurious forms derived from an imperfect pronounciation of this name.

As I have already pointed out, another problem was posed by the transcription into Latin letters of the family name נשיא adopted in Istambul by Doña Gracia, which in contemporary documents is transcribed in several different ways. I decided to adopt the spelling already in use among the English speaking scholars who have written about this family.

For the Jewish names the anglicized form was adopted, whenever it existed.

I obviously did not modify the orthography of the archival documents published in appendix, which remain in their original form .

Dates marked with the letters "S.d.C." (Style de la Court) indicate that the original document was dated according to the use of the Roman Imperial Court (followed also in the Court of the Low Countries, in Brussels) with the year starting on the day of the Christian Easter.

Acknowledgements

I have greatly benefited from the bibliographical suggestions and guidance of Prof. Gustav Janssens, Librarian of the Bibliothèque du Palace Royal in Brussels; I am deeply indebted to Seth Jerchouer of the Library of the Jewish Theological Seminary, N.Y.; Umberto Fortis of the Biblioteca della Comunità Ebraica, Venice; Monsignor P. Francesco Fumagalli of the Biblioteca Ambrosiana, Milan, Jack Lunzer and Pauline Malkiel of the Valmadonna Trust Library, London; Dominique Morillon and Chantal Ritz of the Bibliothéque Nationale de France, Paris; Michel Oosterbosch of the Archives Gènérales du Royaume, Bussels; Angelo Mordechai Piattelli of the Bibliographic Institute of the Hebrew University of Jerusalem; Ilana Tahan of the British Library, London; Professors António Lopes de Andrade of the University of Aveiro, Portugal; Benjamin Arbel of the Tel Aviv University; Roberto Bonfil of the Hebrew University of Jerusalem; Iacob M. Hasssàn and Elena Romero of the Consejo Superior de Investigaciones Cientifícas, Madrid; Pier Cesare Ioly Zorattini of the State University of Udine; Bice Migliau, Director of the Jewish Cultural Center in Rome; Rav Elia Ricchetti, Chief Rabbi of Venice; Herman Prins Salomon of the New York State University in Albany; Miriam Silvera, Università La Sapienza, Rome; Ariel Toaff of the Bar Ilan University.

I am particularly grateful to Ms. Marcia Haddad Ikonomopoulos who provided invaluable suggestions, and edited my English text with great competence and knowledge enhancing it with an elegant form.

The ancient Benveniste family, with whom I have dealt in this book, is extant and some of its members living in Portugal, still faithful to their traditions, created in honor of their father the Chair "Cátedra de Estudos Sefarditas Alberto Benveniste" in the University of Lisbon to promote Sephardic Culture. I am grateful to Monique and Serge Benveniste who supported the publication of this book.

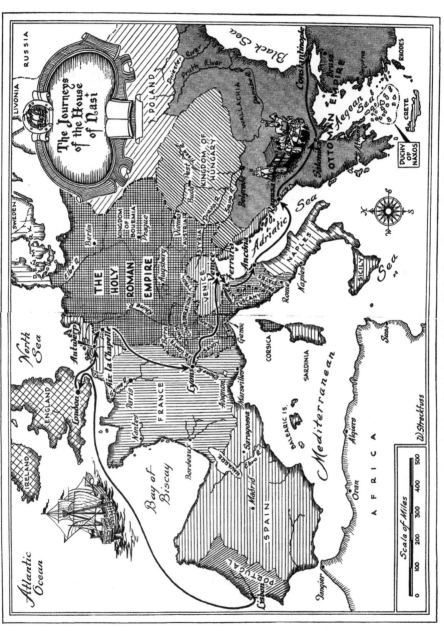

The route followed by Doña Beatriz Mendes de Luna in her flight from Portugal to London and Antwerp and from there to Italy and the Levant. Scores of fugitive marranos covered the same or similar route.

§ 1. The Portuguese Settlement of Antwerp in the first half of the XVIth Century

At the beginning of the 16th Century, a small group of Portuguese merchants of Jewish origin settled in Antwerp. They played a substantial role in the development of the city as a primary center of trade, and obtained important commercial privileges. In 1511, the Burgomasters of Antwerp extended special concessions to the Portuguese Merchants living in their city, including the right to be represented by a commercial consul.[1] The *Men of the Nation*[2] availed themselves of these prerogatives to facilitate the entry of other newcomers.

In his *Description of the Low Countries,* Lodovico Guicciardini stated that the development of Antwerp as a commercial *emporium*[3] must be

---

1. A. B. FREIRE, *Noticias da Feitoria de Flandres*, Doc. XXVII, pp. 170-171.
2. The expressions *Homens da Nação* [Men of the (Jewish) Nation] and *Homens de nego-cio* [businessmen] were widely used to designate the Portuguese conversos of Jewish origin. See Y.H. YERUSHALMI, *From Spanish Court to Italian Ghetto, Isaac Cardoso, A Study on Seventeenth Century Marranism and Jewish Apologetics*, Columbia University Press 1971, [Reprint 1981], pp. 12-21; Cf. A.J. SARAIVA, *Inquisição e Cristãos Novos*, Porto 1969.
3. On the development of Antwerp as the main European commercial metropolis in the XVIth century see F.H. MERTENS and K.L.TORFS, *Geschiedenis van Antwerpen*, Vol. IV, 1846 [Reprint 1975]; DENUCÉ, Jean, *L'Afrique au XVIe siècle et le commerce anversois*, Anvers, 1937; H. VAN der WEE, *The Growth of the Antwerp Market and the European Economy (Fourteenth-Sixteenth Centuries)*, the Hague 1963; IDEM, *The Low Countries in the Early Modern World*, Alderhot 1993, pp. 101-111, 115-125; E. COORNAERT, *Les Français et le Commerce international à Anvers à la fin du XVe et au XVIe siècle*, Paris, 1961; W. BRULEZ, *Le commerce international des Pays-Bas au XVIe siècle: essai d'appreciation quantitative*, in «Belgisch Tijdschrift voor Filologie en Geschiedenis», XLVI, 1968, pp. 1205-21; R. BAETENS and B. BLONDE, *À la recherche de l'identité sociale et de la culture matèrielle de la bourgeoisie anversoise aux temps modernes*, «Histoire, Economie et Société», XIII, Asnière 1994 pp. 531-541.

ascribed to its flourishing spice trade.[4] Beginning in 1503, the entire harvest of pepper and other spices[5] was shipped from the Portuguese East Indies to the northern city of Antwerp via Lisbon. Other "colonial" products dispatched from the Lusitanian empire included: precious stones, Brazilian wood and pigments, sugar, tin and silver. Portugal also exported huge quantities of salt, wines, dry fruits, olive oil and other agricultural products to the northern emporium.[6]

By the 1520's, the spice trade had passed under the control of a consortium led by a Portuguese merchant, Diogo Mendes, and his associate, Giancarlo Affaitati, an Italian. Among their partners were other Portuguese merchants, as well as the Italian, Luca Giraldi.[7] Through their associates in Lisbon, they bought all the *"colonial"* products from the King of Portugal and distributed them to other countries in Europe.

On March 31, 1526, an imperial ordinance allowed all Portuguese New Christians to remain in the Low Countries for commercial reasons.

---

4. L. GUICCIARDINI, *Descrittione di tutti i Paesi Bassi*, Antwerp 1567, pp. 83-84: «Il secondo augumento de più notabili che ha fatta questa città tanto grande, ricca e famosa comincia ... circa l'anno MDIII & quattro che i Portoghesi avendo poco avanti ... occupato Calicut ... comminciarono a condurre le spetierie & le drogherie d'India in Portoghallo poi di Portogallo condurle in questa terrra».

5. L. GUICCIARDINI, *ibid.*, p. 124, provided a list of these products: «Di Portogallo ci mandano gioie et perle orientali perfette, oro ... spetierie, drogherie, ambra, musco zibetto, avorio ... (From Portugal they deliver to Antwerp jewelry, genuine oriental pearls, spices and groceries, amber, musk-oil, civet, ivory... »; A.B. FREIRE, *Noticias da Feitoria de Flandres,* Lisboa 1920, pp. 76-78; J. DENUCÉ, *Rapports économiques anciens entre le Portugal et la Belgique*, «BCP», numéro spécial, 1935 pp. 9-13; J.A. Goris, *La Nation Portugaise à Anvers de 1488 à 1587,* published in two instalments in the «BCP» 1936-1937: n.4 , n.6 pp. 7-12; O. SMEDT, *De Engelse Natie te Antwerpen in de 16ᵉ EEUW, (1496-1582),* II , Anvers 1954; R. Van ANSWAARDEN, *Les Portugais devant le Grand Conseil des Pays-Bas (1460-1580)*, Paris 1991, p. 50.

6. AMATUS LUSITANUS, *Curationum medicinalium centuria tertia*, Curatio 61; A. B. FREIRE, *Lista das mercadorias permutadas com os estados de Flandres e Brabante no reinado de Dom Manuel*, in appendix to *Maria Brandoa, a do Crisfal*, «AHP» VI, 1908, p. 408.

7. On the Italian merchants in Antwerp see JEAN-ALBERT GORIS, *Étude sur les colonies marchandes meridionales (Portugaises, Espagnoles, Italiennes) à Anvers, de 1488 à 1567. Contribution à l'histoire des débuts du capitalisme moderne*, Louvain 1925; C. BECK, *Elements sociaux et economiques de la vie des marchands genois a Anvers entre 1528 et 1555*, «Revue du Nord», Lille 1982, pp. 759-784.

The provision was reconfirmed in 1529.[8] In a short time the Portuguese colony grew apace. The Margrave and burgomasters of Antwerp looked upon the new arrivals as extremely useful for their city's economy and they valued their integrity, spirit of enterprise and special contributions in commercial and financial techniques.[9] The local bourgeoisie did not oppose the rapid expansion of these activities because the Portuguese merchants imported mainly exotic and colonial goods without competing with any pre-existing interests.

Prominent in the Portuguese colony was Diogo Mendes[10] who lived in a palace of his own with dozens of commercial agents, clerks, and stewards, many of whom were *conversos* of Jewish origin. In a country where Jews were not permitted to reside, they had no choice but to declare themselves to be Christians. It soon became evident that their practice of Catholicism was not overly devout. They were suspected of adhering to Judaism and were frequently persecuted on this pretext.

We shall attempt to analyze the Emperor's varying policies towards the New Christians of Antwerp within the general framework of his struggle against various forms of heresy.

---

8. C.H. LAURENT et J. LAMEERE, *Ordonnances des Pays-Bas, deuxième série, règne de Charles Quint,* Vol. II, Bruxelles 1893, p. 583.

9. H.I. BLOOM, *Economic Activities of the Jews of Amsterdam in XVII and XVIII Centuries*, New York and London, 1937, p. 2, note 8; C. ROTH, *Doña Gracia of the House of Nasi*, Philadelphia 1947 [Reprint 1977], p. 26; S.W. BARON, *A Social and Religious History of the Jews*, XIII: *Inquisition, Renaissance and Reformation*, New York and Philadelphia 1969, pp. 119-121; R. Van ANSWAARDEN, *Le Grand Conseil*, p. 48 and *passim.*

10. Amato Lusitano called him «o mais abastado dos mercadores do seu tempo (the richest merchant of his time)», *Amati Lusitani In Dioscoridis Anarzabei de medica materia libros quinque narrationes eruditissimae ...Cum rerum ac vocum memorabilium indice locupletissimo, Venetijs : ex officina Iordani Zilleti, 1557 cum privilegio Ill.mi Senati,* Liber I, n.120. See MAXIMIANO LEMOS, *Amato Lusitano, A sua vida e a sua obra*, Porto 1907, p. 79.

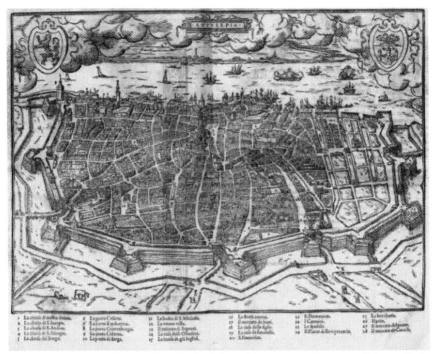

A map of Antwerp in the first half of the 16th century. From L. Guicciardini, *Descrittione di tutti Paesi Bassi*, Reprint, Antwerp 1567.

§ 2. Charles V's struggle against heresy in the Low Countries

Charles V is well known for his unwavering Catholic zeal, his determination in the struggle against the infidels, his commitment to the preservation of Catholic hegemony in Europe and his unconditional support of the Inquisition in Spain and Portugal[1] [after a period of initial diffidence][2]. Nevertheless, he did not introduce a similar institution into the Low Countries. This territory [not contiguous with the other lands of the House of Habsburg] was the first,[3] the most prosperous and densely populated, and the most cherished among all of Charles V' s dominions. It was neither a part of the Holy Roman Empire nor an appendage of the Spanish Crown, but an independent [even if not unitary] State. It comprised an aggregation of Provinces and Cities and a variety of duchies, counties and feudal *signories* that enjoyed separate statutes and privileges with [or without] a special relationship with the central

---

1. J.L. DE AZEVEDO, *História dos christãos-novos portugueses*, Lisboa 1975[2], pp. 106-109; Y. H. YERUSHALMI, *Prolegomenon* to ALEXANDRE HERCULANO, *History of the Origin and Establishment of the Inquisition in Portugal*, [Original title: *História da Origem e estabelecimento da Inquisição em Portugal*, translated by J.C.BRANNER) Ktav Publishig House New York 1972], pp. 25-26; H. RABE, *Karl V* in *Theologische Realenziklopädie*, Band XVII, 1988, pp. 635-644: 638-639; H. SCHILLING, *The Cold Heart of the Retreat*, «Journal of Early Modern History», IV, 2000 pp. 431-441.
2. M. F. ALVAREZ, *Historia de España (dirigida por R. M. Pidal)*, XX, *La España del Emperador Carlos V, 1500-1558, El Hombre, la politica Española, la politica europea*, Madrid 1989, pp. 106-107, 125, 874;
3. Charles V (1500-58) was born in Ghent. He was Duke of Burgundy (1506-1555), King of Castile and of Aragon (1516-1556), Holy Roman Emperor (1519-1556). He inherited the Netherlands from his father, Philip le Bel, and Spain from his mother Joanna the Mad. His mother tongue was French. On his education and linguisitic proficiency see L. de GRAUWE, *Welke taal sprak Keizer Karel (Which language did Emperor Charles speak?)*, «Handelingen der Maatschappij voor Geschiedenis en Oudheidkunde te Gent» LIV, Ghent 2000 pp. 17-29.

government.[4] As it is well known, Charles V's attempts to adopt a firm policy against the Lutheran heresy in the Holy Roman Empire were frustrated by the opposition of Protestant Princes who compelled him to adopt a conciliatory approach.[5] In the Netherlands, by contrast, the Emperor felt himself free to perform his role as protector of Catholicism and, starting from the 1520's onwards, he began to issue severe edicts against the Lutheran and Anabaptist heretics.

The writing of the history of Low Countries – and of the Portuguese settlement in Antwerp – has been heavily dominated by the assumption that, in 1522, Charles V began to introduce a Spanish styled Inquisition into this territory. However, the task of enforcing the persecutory policy against the heretics was entrusted to local civil courts. As Tracy has clearly stated, in Holland the supervision of local tribunals was entrusted to the Regional Council of The Hague, which represented the Emperor in his capacity as Count of Holland.[6] Similar Councils were operating in Brabant, Flanders and other Provinces, and acted on Charles' behalf as Duke of Burgundy and Count of Flanders. The highest judicial authority of the Low Countries was embodied by the *Grote Raad van Mechelen* (Grand Conseil de Malines).[7]

---

4. H. PIRENNE, *Histoire de Belgique des origines à nos jours*, Tome II, *De la mort de Charles le Téméraire à la paix de Munster,* Brusselles s.d. [1950 ?]. II, pp. 74-75; C. WILSON, *Rebellion, Liberty and Nationhood* in H. Trevor-Roper, Ed., *The Age of Expansion, Europe and the World, 1559-1660,* London 1968, pp. 75-108: 95; On provincial administrations see H.C.C. de SCHEPPER, *De Burgerlijke overheden en hun permanente kaders 1480-1579,* «Nievwe Algemene Geschiedenis der Niederlanden» V, Haarlem 1980, pp. 337-343; J.D. TRACY, *Heresy Law and Centralisation under Mary of Hungary: Conflict between the Council of Holland and the Central Government over the Enforcement of Charles V's Placards,* «ARG» 1982, 284-307, pp. 284-285.

5. H. KAMEN, *Spain, a Society of Conflict, 1469-1714*, London and New York 1986[4], p. 72; R. BONNEY, *The European Dynastic States, 1494-1660,* Oxford 1991, pp. 22-23; H. SCHILLING, *Veni, vidi, Deus vixit. Karl V zwischen Religionskrieg und Religionsfrieden* «ARG» 89, 1998, pp. 144-166: 155-166; I. NEW, *Die Spanische Inquisition und die Lutheraner im 16. Jahrhundert,* «ARG» 90, 1999, pp. 289-320; H. DUCHHARDT, *Das Tunisunternehmen Karls V, 1535,* «MÖS», XXVII, 1984 pp. 35-72.

6. J.D. TRACY, *Heresy Law and Centralisation,* pp. 285-86 and *passim.* The Council of Holland was seated in The Hague. It was composed of eight Councilors-Ordinary and presided by the Stadholder or Provincial Governor (*Ibid.*).

7. H.C.C. De SCHEPPER, *De Groote Raad van Mechelen: Hoogste Rechtcollege van der Nederlanden?* «Bijdragen en Mededelingen betreffende de Geschiedenis van de Nederlanden», XCIII 1978, pp. 389-411; R. Van ANSWAARDEN, *Le Grand Conseil,* pp. 7-11 and *passim.*

The first edict issued by Charles V concerning heresy in the Low Countries was published on September 28, 1520, when the Emperor upheld a resolution by the theologians of the University of Louvain[8] prescribing the destruction(s) of Luther's writings.[9] On March 20, 1521, in Mechelen, Charles issued an ordinance against the dissemination of Luther's works and all heterodox books. A few weeks later [on May 8, 1521] a new general *placard* (posted public notice), the so-called *Edict of Worms*, confirmed and extended the previous ordinances.[10]

These first edicts[11] already contained all the basic principles of the religious policy that would be developed in the following years by the Emperor and the Regents who governed the Low Countries in his name.[12] Heresy was equated with *lèse majesté,* a crime lying within the exclusive competence of civil and, only later, imperial[13] courts. A new crime was configured: the non-observance of imperial edicts against heresy. Failure to comply with imperial edicts[14] was equated with high treason, an offence usually dealt with by lay tribunals. By means of a simple equation, the prosecution of heresy was transferred to the competence of the

---

8. P. FRÉDÉRICK, *Corpus Documentorum Inquisitionis Haereticae Pravitatis Neederlandicae,* in five Vols., Ghent 1897-1902, IV, pp. 12-14. Cf. L.van der ESSEN, *Le rôle de l'Université de Louvain au XVIe Siècle,* «Revue Générale Belge», XXIV, Bruxelles 1929, p. 8; ALINE GOOSENS, *Les Inquisitions modernes dans les Pays-Bas Meridionaux 1520-1633,* Tome I, *La Legislation,* Bruxelles 1997, pp. 47-48.

9. FRÉDÉRICK, *Corpus Documentorum,* IV, pp. 33-34 ; H. HALKIN *Le plus ancien texte d'édit promulgué contre les Luthériens,* «Revue d'Histoire Ecclésiastique» XXIV, Louvain 1929, p. 8, A. GOOSENS, *Les Inquisitions,* p. 75.

10. FRÉDÉRICK, *Corpus Documentorum,* IV, pp. 43-45, 58-76; LAURENT and LAMEERE, *Ordonnances des Pays-Bas,* II, pp. 70-71, 73-83. See also J.D. TRACY, *Heresy Law,* pp. 288-290.

11. For other, subsequent ordinances and placards see J.D. TRACY, *Heresy Law,* pp. 289-290: A. GOOSENS, *Inquisitions,* pp. 50-52.

12. Margaret of Savoy, Charles' aunt, governed the Low Countries from 1519 to 1530. After her death, Mary of of Habsburg, Charles' sister, the so called Queen of Hungary, was appointed Regent of the Low Countries in 1531.

13. The *crimen lesæ mayestatis* was later described as a «geprivilegiëerd misdriif (crime privilégé)» lying within the exclusive competence of the Emperor (and beyond the jurisdiction of regional courts).

14. Even if he acted as Duke of Burgundy, Charles V signed his decrees as Charles, Roman Emperor.

State. These offences were to be punished by death[15] and by confiscation of all properties. The Emperor was to take advantage of the seized properties. Informers were to be rewarded.

In 1522 Charles V attempted to set up a State Inquisition and appointed General Inquisitor François Van der Hulst, a member of the Council of Brabant.[16] In order to maintain some semblance of ecclesiastic authority over the new institution, Pope Adrian VI hastened to designate Van der Hulst «universalem et generalem inquisitorem et investigatorem» by special designation, in spite of the fact that he was a lay-person.[17]

The Emperor issued severe edicts enjoining the officers of every province to assist the newly appointed inquisitor in the fulfillment of his task.[18] However, city magistrates and local courts were generally lax in enforcing the imperial edicts: in part because many officers were in sympathy with the new religious ideas and, to a larger extent, because local authorities were generally opposed to any regulation that might infringe on their privileges. Several magistrates conveyed their reservations to the central government about the feasibility and efficacy of religious persecutions.[19]

In 1522, when the Inquisitor General transferred a prisoner from The Hague to a fortress in Brabant, the provincial authorities saw in this move an attempt to override their privilege not to have their cases "evoked for trial" outside the territory of Holland.[20] The incautious move caused a general uproar. In the end, Van der Hulst set the prisoner free in order to calm the protesters down but, in so doing, he lost the Emperor's confidence and was dismissed from office. Cardinal Campeggi, the papal

15. The death penalty was not specifically mentioned in the 1521 *placard*: however, it was traditionally inflicted on offenders guilty of *lèse majesté* and/or of high treason.
16. AGR, PEA 1177, ff. 640-644, Jan. 27 1522: *lettres patentes* entrusting François van der Hulst, councillor of Brabant, with the task of prosecuting the Lutheran heresy in the Low Countries.
17. H. PIRENNE, *Histoire du Belgique*, II, pp. 202-203.
18. LAURENT and LAMEERE, *Ordonnances des Pays-Bas*, II, pp. 171-173, 188-191; P. FRÉDÉRICQ, *Corpus Documentorum*, IV, pp. 101-105, 118-120, 123-127: April 23 1522, *lettres patentes* appointing François van der Hulst *Inquisiteur Général* of the Low Countries; April 29 1522, imperial *placard* instructing all the magistrates and officers of the Low Countries to assist the Inquisitor; May 7 1522: Charles V's instructions to the Inquisitor.
19. J.D.TRACY, *Heresy Law*, pp. 287-288.
20. *Ibid.*, p. 285.

envoy, was quick in following Charles' example and divested Van der Hulst of every dignity.[21]

This episode made it evident that local privileges offered the most serious obstacle to the enforcement of the edicts against heresy. Charles V and the Regents who governed the Low Countries on his behalf became engaged in a continuous struggle with the various Provinces in order to compel the local authorities to enforce the new legislation.[22] This was not an easy task.

In 1523, Charles V tried to circumvent the opposition of urban and provincial councils by entrusting the repression of the Lutheran heresy to bishops.[23] He did so in a provisional way and managed to keep these inquiries under his direct control. In fact, the bishops were compelled to act in pursuance of the imperial ordinances [rather than the Canon Law].[24] In a subsequent development, even if the Pope maintained representatives nominally entrusted with the task of prosecuting the heretics, Charles V and his aunt, Margaret of Savoy, the Regent-Governor of the Low Countries, gradually divested them of every authority.

Henceforth, the task of enforcing edicts was transferred to the complete competence of local (lay) courts under the supervision of provincial councils. In 1524[25], and again in 1525 and 1526, Margaret of Savoy enacted new edicts reiterating all the former prohibitions and contemplating new offences such as the study of vernacular translations of the Scriptures and their discussion by laymen in secret conventicles. Violations were to be punished by fines ranging from a minimum of 20 carolus gulden to 80 gulden.[26] A much sterner edict issued in 1529 con-

---

21. H. PIRENNE, *Histoire du Belgique*, pp. 202-203.

22. See H.C.C. de SCHEPPER, *De Burgerlijke overheden*, pp. 337-343; J.D. TRACY, *Heresy Law*, p. 284-85.

23. The Inquisitors were chosen by Margaret of Savoy, the Governor of the Low Countries, and approved by the Pope. H. PIRENNE, *Histoire du Belgique*, pp. 202-203. This author observed that, in this period, the Inquisition was *half political and half religious*.

24. A. GOOSENS, *Les Inquisitions*, p. 50.

25. See: *Ordonancien, Statuten, Edicten ende Plakkaten ghepubliceert in den Landen ... der Keyserlicker ende Conijnglicker Majesteyten ende haerlieder zeer edele Voorsaeten,* Ghent 1559, pp. 88-127 (quoted by J.D. TRACY, *Heresy Law*, p. 288, note 16).

26. J.D. TRACY, *Heresy Law*, p. 289; Cf. C. AUGUSTIJN, *Niederlande* in «TRE», XXIV, pp. 474-502: 478-79.

templated, besides the death penalty, the confiscation of goods, to be executed at will by local officers, as a preventive measure.[27]

In 1531, after Margaret of Savoy's death, Mary of Habsburg[28] took her place as Regent-Governor of the Low Countries. Charles V decided to reshape the central government of this dominion in order to implement a policy of greater severity and to compel provincial and city authorities to comply with his edicts.[29] The new Regent and the Emperor became engaged in a continuous struggle to subject, not only the lay authorities, but also the clergy, to a firm central control. Emblematic are the patent letters by which, on June 18, 1531, Charles V instructed the law officers of Flanders to prosecute any churchmen who violated the imperial[30] ordinances against Lutheranism and other heresies.[31]

A *placard* issued on October 7, 1531, confirmed all the previous edicts, and extended the range of application of a specific penalty: the confiscation of the offenders' properties for the profit of the Emperor. Not only was the prosecution of heresy to be carried out by lay judicial officers,[32] but also– as we shall see in the following pages – it was turned into a financial instrument. This was to become a constant factor in Charles V's policy, especially in the case of Portuguese *Marranos*.

Strangely enough, many historians did not take into consideration this aspect of the imperial policy. This lack of attention can be partially explained by the fact that, in the past, several scholars were mainly interested in studying the Protestant martyrology, perpetrated by a (supposedly) ecclesiastical Inquisition and, in so doing, overlooked the role

---

27. LAURENT and LAMEERE, *Ordonnances des Pays-Bas*, II, pp. 578-583. On this placard see E. POULLET, *Histoire du droit pénal dans le Duché de Brabant*, II, Bruxelles 1870, p. 70; P. FRÉDÉRICQ, *Les placards du 14 Octobre 1529 et du 31 decembre 1529 contre le protestants des Pays-Bas* in *Melanges Godefroid Kurth,* I, Liège 1908, pp. 255-60.
28. Mary of Habsburg, also called Mary of Hungary, was the widow of king Loys II of Bohemia and Hungary. See E. de SEYND, *Dictionnaire de l'Histoire du Belgique*, Liege 1958, *sub voce*.
29. J.D. TRACY, *Heresy Law*, pp. 289-290.
30. It is perhaps worth remembering that, even when he acted in his capacity as Duke of Burgundy (or as Count of Flanders), Charles V signed his edicts: L'*Empereur*. All his other titles were listed in the text of the edicts.
31. A. GOOSENS, *Les Inquisiteurs modernes*, p. 204.
32. Strangely enough, it was only in 1950 that a Belgian scholar, H. PIRENNE (*Histoire du Belgique*, pp. 202-203), described the repressive machinery set up by Charles V as *Civil-* or *State-Inquisition*.

played by the Emperor, the Queen-Governor, their officers and local courts in general.

It was only recently that scholars[33] realized that a Spanish-styled Inquisition was never introduced into the Low Countries. We shall try to examine this historical problem, with special regard to Portuguese New Christians, viewing local legislation, existing literature, published and newly discovered documents.

---

33. E. BURMAN (*The Inquisition, the Hammer of Heresy*, Williamsborgh 1984, p. 194) was among the first historians who did not consider the Low Countries as belonging to and conquered by Spain and consequently subject to an [Iberian styled] Inquisition. Cf. A. GOOSENS' remarks in *Les Inquisiteurs modernes*, pp. 14-14, 63-65. See H. P. SALOMON, A di LEONE LEONI, *Mendes, Benveniste, De Luna, Micas, Nasci, the State of the Art"* «JQR» LXXXVIII, 1998, pp. 135-211: 143-145. Cf. J.P. DIDIEU, R. MILLAR CARVACHO, *Entre Histoire et Mémoire, L'Inquisition à l'époque moderne: dix ans d'Historiographie*, «*Annales, Histoires, Sciences Sociales*», Paris 2000, pp. 349-372: 371.

The "Bursa" Building in Antwerp where trading, banking, maritime transport and insurance were negotiated. From L. Guicciardini, *Descrittione di tutti i Paesi Bassi*, Reprint, Antwerp 1567.

§ 3. Charles V's unorthodox attitude towards the New Christians of Antwerp

Charles V adopted a pragmatic approach towards the New Christians, in sharp contrast to the Catholic doctrine and the policy that he himself had followed in the Iberian Peninsula. It is well known that, according to Canon Law, baptism is sacred, indelible and irreversible, even if imposed under threat or fear of death. The Church considered those *conversos* who practiced Jewish rites as clear-cut heretics and apostates.[1]

The Emperor was not familiar with theological subtleties and, in any case, he was more concerned with financial problems than with religious considerations. Unlike the Spanish inquisitors, he did not recognize baptism imposed on the New Christians as valid and, consequently, he did not regard those *Conversos* who practiced Jewish rites as clear-cut heretics and apostates. In his eyes, they were simply *mentiti et simulati christiani*, or «secret Jews» posing as Christians.[2] According to the Emperor, the Portuguese merchants of Antwerp were Jews who disguised their true identity *"sub habitu et specie christiana"*. Under this mask, they were able to reach high social and economic positions, thus depriving local merchants of important opportunities. In fact, their success and wealth had aroused great jealousy in government circles.

Charles V knew that many Portuguese *Conversos* had immigrated to countries where they could openly revert to Judaism. Some of them had transferred all their assets to the lands of the Ottoman Empire, strength-

---

1. For a broad and detailed discussion on this point see Y. H. YERUSHALMI, *The Inquisition and the Jews of France in the Time of Bernard Gui*, «Harvard Theological Review» LXIII, 1970, pp. 340 ff.; IDEM, *Prolegomenon*.
2. See Document 3 in Appendix

ening it to the detriment of Christian Nations.[3] The Portuguese remaining in Antwerp were suspected of waiting for a better opportunity to leave the country. In the meanwhile, they facilitated the flight of *Conversos* from Portugal to Flanders and, from there, to Italy and the Levant.

Only minor attention was paid to the religious observance of the New Christians of Antwerp who were subject, as a matter of fact, only to civil jurisdiction. To the best of my knowledge, in the period taken into consideration, not one of them was summoned to an ecclesiastical court. The charge of practicing Jewish rites could be used as a formal pretext to arrest wealthy New Christians and drag them off into prison. Even if they were formally charged with heresy and apostasy of the Catholic faith, this did not imply the same terrible consequences as similar accusations had in the Iberian Peninsula. The charge was usually dropped after a certain period of reclusion, without adjudication, by means of a huge *appointement*:[4] The punishment of heresy was turned into a tool to line the pockets of the Emperor.

Charles V was obsessed by the idea that many merchants had fled to the lands of the Grand Sultan or were planning to do so. He suspected them of banding together to move all their goods, and those of other *Conversos*, to the detriment of his States, his hereditary dominions and the whole of Christendom. Other merchants were suspected of trading with the Levant and supplying the infidels with all kinds of goods, including "offensive armaments". He even surmised that, for these deliveries, they branded their merchandise with the trademarks of Christian accomplices.

This state of affairs threatened the welfare and the security of his states. In 1530, he set up a special police corps *contra mentitos et simulatos christianos*. Corneille Scepperurs, councillor and secretary of Emperor, was appointed as general commissioner[5] to investigate those merchants who, *sub habitu et specie christiana*, shipped merchandise and

---

3. «Cum audiamus quam plures, Christianam religionem similantes, Christianosque sub christiana specie atque habitu decipientes, partim collectis rebus suis omnibus atque etiam alienis …» See Document 3 in Appendix.

4. *Appointement* = extra judiciary financial agreement.

5. AGR,Bx, PEA 1540, See Document 3 in Appendix. Cf. P.Génard, *Personen te Antwerpen in de XVIe eeuw voor het feit van religie gerechterlijk vervorlgt, lijst en ambtelijke bij-hoorige stukken*, «Antwerpsch Archievenblad» . VII [undated, *circa* 1870], pp. 190-289, pp. 191-194.

armaments to the Turks. Special attention was to be paid to the Old-Christian merchants who assisted the Portuguese to disguise their deliveries and allowed them to use their trademarks to smuggle goods out of the country. The offenders were to be arrested and prosecuted, and all their assets were to be confiscated and turned over to the Emperor.

The infamous Johannes de la Foia (Johannes Vuysting)[6] was appointed general sub-commissioner. The Emperor Charles V and his sister Mary entrusted him with the charge of ambushing and intercepting the Portuguese émigrés on their way from Antwerp to Italy. He accomplished this mission with great efficiency and cruelty. He dispossessed the prisoners of all their belongings, imprisoned them, and submitted them to torture in order to discover who had provided them with money for their journey. It appeared, in fact, that some Portuguese Merchants in Lisbon and Antwerp had created a special fund to cover these enormous expenses. The Emperor and his sister Queen Mary were haunted by the idea of identifying the managers of the Rescue Committee in the almost obsessive hope of laying their hands on the supposedly fabulous treasures of this organization.[7]

---

6. SAMUEL USQUE, *Consolaçam as Tribulações de Israel Composto por Samuel Usque, Empresso en Ferrara en casa de Abraham aben Usque 5313 da criaçam, am d. 7 de setembro* [Reprint, Fundação C. Gulbenkian, Lisbon 1989], f. 209v, described João de la Foya [in *Flemish*: Johannes Vuysting] as «o mais cruel perseguidor que desque perdeo a casa teve Ysrael (the most cruel persecutor Israel has had since the loss of the Temple)».
7. A. di LEONE LEONI, *Manoel Lopes Bichacho a XVIth Century Leader of the Portuguese Nation in Antwerp and in Pesaro*, «Sefarad » LIX, 1999, pp. 77-100: p. 80.

§ 4. A Diplomatic move of the Imperial State Secretary towards the Duke of Ferrara

It was perhaps in 1529, that the imperial Secretary of State had his first opportunity to announce Charles V's doctrine on the New Christians to the representatives of a foreign State. Probably, it was also the first time that the new terminology shaped by the Emperor was officially used in the course of diplomatic negotiations.

Charles V had convened the "Conference for Peace among the Italian States" in Bologna, where he was to be crowned Emperor by the Pope.[1] When the Ferrara delegate paid his respects to *Monseigneur* de Granvelle (the imperial Secretary of State *in pectore*),[2] the latter asked to have a «Jew now living in Ferrara» delivered to the imperial police. According to M. de Granvelle, the wanted man had lived in Antwerp, where he had pretended to be a good Christian and merchant, but in reality he was a Jew. He had left the city without settling some of his debts and had found asylum in Ferrara, where he was living under the ducal protection. The Secretary of State maintained that his safe-conduct[3] should not grant

---

1. On the «Spanish Peace» imposed on the Italians States and Segnories see M.F. ALVAREZ, *La España del Emperador Carlos V*, p. 453; K. EISENBICHLER, *Charles V in Bologna: the Self-fashioning of a Man and a City*, «Renaissance Studies», XIII. Oxford 1999, pp. 430-439.
2. On Nicolas Perrenot Seigneur de Granvelle [as the name is transcribed in Dutch, French and German documents] or Granvela [in Latin, Spanish and Italian documents], see the recent study by M.Van DARME, *Les Granvelle au Service des Hasbourg* in K. de JONGE and G. JANSSENS, *Les Granvelle et les anciens Pays-Bas*, pp. 11-82. Cfr. *Brockhaus Enziklopädie*, VII Wiesbaden 1969, p. 562.
3. We carefully consulted the Registers of Ducal Laws and Decrees at the State Archives in Modena where we could not find the safe-conduct mentioned by M. de Granvelle. Probably the wanted man had benefited by the Ducal Decree issued by Ercole I in 1493 in favour of the Spanish Jews who settled in Ferrara in 1492. This privilege was confirmed by Duke Alfonso I in 1506 and extended to all the Iberian Jews «who already lived in

immunity against the charge of "robbery" so that the Duke could extradite the wanted man without difficulties.[4] The Ferrarese delegate politely asked for the name of the sought-after merchant, because in Ferrara there were many Jews and it was difficult to find the wanted man without knowing his identity. The envoy reported this detail to the Duke and noted that the lack of this information provided the opportunity to play for time. In the meantime, the Duke consulted a renowned jurist on the legal position of the Iberian Jews in his states.

A few days later M. de Granvelle pressed his request more urgently and stated that he had received written instructions from the Emperor.[5] The diplomatic move was apparently unsuccessful. In all likelihood, Duke Alfonso did not break his word and did not withhold the protection granted by an official decree. We know neither the name of the émigré nor the continuation of this story.[6] In all probability the wanted man was discretely advised to leave the city.

Ferrara or would come in the future». See the text of the decree in A. di LEONE LEONI, *Documents inédits sur la Nation Portugaise de Ferrare,* «REJ» CLII, 1993, pp.137-176: 158-161.

4. ASMO, Cancelleria Estero, Ambasciatori Roma, Busta 33, December 29 1529.

5. *Ibid.*, January 4, 1530. See Documents 1, 2 in Appendix.

6. This episode was reported by Renata Segre, *La formazione di una Comunità Marrana: I Portoghesi di Ferrara* in *Storia d'Italia, Annali,* Vol. XI: *Gli Ebrei,* Torino, Einaudi Editore 1996, pp. 789-834: p. 785. Perhaps this authoress did not fully comprehend the significance of the term "false Christians" as it was used by the imperial minister. R. Segre also mistook "Monseigneur" de Granvelle for a Cardinal. She was also unaware of the fact that, at the time, the word "Marrano" was commonly used in Ferrara to designate any persons of Spanish or Iberian origins, regardless of their religious allegiance. She consequently assumed that a Jewish merchant had moved (from Ferrara!) to Antwerp, where he presented himself as a Christian in order to carry out his business. R. Segre proposed to identify the wanted man as Leone (Yehuda) NigroYaḥia, a banker at Massa Fiscaglia (not far from Ferrara) and she mistook him for Gabriel de Negro, a Portugese merchant who escaped from Antwerp in 1540 (not in 1529). On the meaning of the word *Marrano* in XVIth century Italy see G. REZASCO, *Dizionario del linguaggio storico ed amministrativo,* Firenze 1881 [Reprint, Bologna 1882], *sub voce.* On Gabriel de Negro's flight from Antwerp see J. DENUCÉ, *L'Inventaire des Affaitati banquiers italiens à Anvers de l'année 1568,* Anvers 1934, p. 23. See also § 7, below, and Documents 16 and 22 in Appendix. Perhaps I am stressing this point too much. I am doing so in order to provide a clear example of how frequently even experienced scholars, unaware of the particular terminology used by Charles V, could not grasp the real nature of events.

§ 5. The First Campaign waged by Charles V and Mary of Habsburg against the Portuguese Merchants of Antwerp

In 1531, the recently appointed commissioner *contra malos christianos*[1] and his aides arrested four Portuguese newcomers on several accounts, including the secret practice of Judaism and illegal immigration. They were detained for several months. The charges were finally dropped by means of an extra judiciary settlement negotiated directly with the Emperor.[2]

In (or about) 1531, a disillusioned young man left Salonika, where he had lived with his mother and brothers, and moved to Italy. In Rome he presented himself before the local Inquisitors and was received into the arms of the Catholic Church. They instructed him not to return directly to Portugal but to go first to Flanders. In Bruges, he reported to Fra Diego de San Pedro, the Emperor's confessor, and declared that a few years earlier, Manoel Serrano [Serrão], Gabriel de Negro, Diogo Mendes and Loys Perez, had provided his mother with funds to move to Salonika with her children. They had also instructed her as to the itinerary to follow.[3]

The name of the young man is not mentioned in the statement written by the Antwerp Pensionary. All we know about this spy is that, in Lisbon, his father had an influential position: the personal doctor of the

---

1. The term «malos Christianos» was also frequently used in reference to Lutherans. Cf. F. EDELMAYER, *Cristianos buenos y Cristianos malos – Carlos V y Fernando I y la Reforma* in B.J. GARCÍA GARCÍA, Edit., *El Imperio de Carlos V. Procesos de agregación y conflictos*, [Madrid] 2002, pp. 287-299.
2. GORIS, *Colonies marchandes*, pp. 561, 651. The prisoners were Antonio and Adam Vas, Diego Lopez and Alfonso Fourco.
3. SAA, V[ierschaar = Tribunal], 316, nr.3: undated fragment of an explanatory statement drawn up by Adriaan Herbouts, the Pensionary of Antwerp; Cfr. P.GÉNARD, *Personen te Antwerpen*, pp. 201-205.

King.[4] Strangely enough, in 1540, one Loys Garces, another (or possibly the same)[5] young man presented himself to Fray Diego and told him an almost identical story.[6]

In 1532, the imperial police had already piled up information on the "illegal" activities of Diogo Mendes, who was suspected of sheltering the Portuguese expatriates in his palace, and planning and financing their departure from there towards Italy and the Levant. The young fugitive provided new evidence of Diogo's guilt.

From a new document located at the General Archives of Brussels,[7] we learn that, in July 1532, Charles V dispatched some of his officers [8] to Antwerp. This group was under the command of Pierre Boisot[9] and included a provost marshal and several sergeants of the Imperial Palace. They had the task of intercepting and arresting all the New Christian [residents as well as newcomers] they could find in the city and other parts of Brabant. The goods of the prisoners were to be seized, to the Emperor's advantage. The reference to this episode is extremely brief. Neither the number nor the names of the prisoners is stated. Another, even shorter, mention of several new Christians rounded up in Antwerp is found in a letter sent by Ruy Fernandez, the Portuguese *Feitor* in Antwerp, to the Emperor.[10] Pierre Boisot was *commissioned* to hold an inquiry on the persons denounced by the young fugitive.

Manoel Serrano was arrested and imprisoned. Another «young man», one of Manoel's servants, also denounced him. However, the accusations were contradictory and Manoel was acquitted and set free without even having to pay the expenses of the proceedings.

---

4. *Ibid.*
5. According to J. VROMAN (*L' Affaire Diogo Mendez, Mésaventures d'un traficant du XVIe siècle*, «BCP» III, Janvier 1938, pp. 9-18: 13) the young fugitive who returned to Flanders in 1532 was named Loys Garces: he was therefore the same person who denounced Diogo Mendes and other Portuguese merchants in 1540 (see § 7 below). Unfortunatly Vroman did not state which documents he had perused.
6. See Document 11 in Appendix.
7. AGR, PEA 1504, August 24, 1532, Official statement by Queen Mary. See Document 4 in Appendix.
8. *Ibid.*, f. 1r: «certains ses officiers».
9. Pierre Boisot was *Procureur Géneral* of the Council of Brabant. Cf. J. VROMAN, *L' Affaire Diogo Mendez*, p. 13.
10. Ruy Fernandez' undated [August 1532] letter to the emperor: «... et que au dit Anvers estoient aussi arrestez, en corps et bien plusieurs Nouveaulx Christiens». See P. GÉNARD, *Personen te Antwerpen*, p. 212.

Gabriel Negro went into hiding. His goods and his books were seized. The merchant Erasmus Schetz was entrusted with the task of evaluating his assets and liabilities. He later maintained that the balance was in deficit and there was no advantage for the Emperor in appropriating Gabriel's estate. Thus, Erasmus succeeded in saving Gabriel de Negro. At this point, the imperial officers turned their attention to Diogo Mendes.

On July 19, 1532, Diogo was arrested and charged with Judaism. His palace ("hostel") and his warehouses were seized. The Burgomaster of Antwerp and the Portuguese *Feitor* claimed that Diogo's capture infringed on the city's privileges and they lodged a protest with the Emperor. They prevented the imperial officers from transferring the prisoner to Brussels and proclaimed his right to be tried by the magistrates of the city. The Queen Regent relinquished the pretension of having Diogo extradited to Brussels, but dispatched three of her highest officers[11] to Antwerp with the task of conducting a trial independent of the local authorities. In fact, according to the imperial edicts,[12] all the forms of heresy, including Judaizing (*Heresie en Judaïsering*), were equated to *crimen lesæ majestatis,* a so-called *geprivilegiëerd misdrijf*[13], the prosecution of which lay in the exclusive domain of the Emperor. Diogo was charged not only with practicing Judaism in secret, but also with promoting the return of *conversos* to their ancient faith, with helping and abetting the immigration of New Christians to the Levant, with transferring their goods and merchandise to the lands of the Sultan, the great enemy of Catholic Faith,[14] and with monopolizing the spice trade to the exclusion of local merchants, not to mention other minor offences.[15]

---

11. They were: «Maistres Loys de Heylwegen, Jehan van der Beken et Josse van der Dusschen», all members of the Council of Brabant.
12. See above § 3.
13. *Geprivilegiëerd misdrijf:* a "privileged" criminal offence that, according to the definition given in the *placards*, could be dealt with only by the Emperor or the Queen-Regent [and the officers expressly *commissioned* by them].
14. AGR,PEA, 1504, August 24, 1532. See Document 4 in Appendix.
15. Records of the proceedings against Diogo Mendes from the Antwerp Municipal Archives were published by P. GÉNARD, *Personen te Antwerpen*, pp. 205-236. See the précis by J.A. GORIS, *Colonies marchandes*, pp. 563-568; cfr. I. PRINS, *De Vestiging der Marranen in Noord-Nederland in de Zestiende eeuw*, Amsterdam 1927, pp. 58-66. New evidence was provided by SALOMON and LEONI, *Mendes Benveniste,* pp. 136-148, 182-189. See in Appendix. Document 4, providing new information on the development of the debate.

In a written statement[16], Diogo Mendes rejected all the accusations. However, Jasper Stinen, the defense lawyer, did not concentrate on the discussion of the different accounts but adopted an aggressive stance and contested the competence of the commissioners appointed by Queen Mary. He accepted the principle that a trial on the charge of heresy was a *cause privilégée*, but he argued that they were unable to deal with problems related to faith, as the matter was not in the area of their personal expertise. The lawyer suggested transferring the trial to some ecclesiastic judge who might better understand the reasons and nature of Diogo's behavior. It was an astute move. In theory, having recourse to a religious tribunal could be a very dangerous event. However, the lawyer pretended that his client had nothing to fear from it. In reality, Master Stinen knew very well that Queen Mary and Charles V were jealous of their dynastic prerogatives and too interested to keep the trial – and the properties eventually seized – for the Emperor, without sharing them with other authorities.

As for the charge of helping the New Christians to move their goods to Turkey, both the defense lawyer and the Antwerp authorities argued that this offence had nothing to do with religion: therefore the case fell within the competence of the city magistrates and could not be regarded as a *cause privilégée*.

The imperial officers were very impressed by these arguments and returned immediately to Brussels to report to the Queen. She decided to withdraw the charge of heresy and to maintain the other accusations. Diogo was to remain imprisoned and his property seized.

On August 14, 1532, the Emperor forbade any further immigration of Portuguese New Christians into the Low Countries.[17] The ordinance was enacted when Diogo Mendes had already been charged with promoting the immigration of *Conversos*. The prohibition remained in force until 1537, when it was (provisionally) revoked.[18]

In the meantime Ruy Fernandez, the Portuguese *Feitor* in Antwerp, protested against the seizure of Diogo's merchandise and claimed that most of these goods belonged to his King as they had been entrusted to

---

16. P. GÉNARD, *Personen te Antwerpen*, pp. 217-234.
17. LAURENT and LAMEERE, *Ordonnances des Pays-Bas*, III, p. 343; P.GÉNARD, *Personen te Antwerpen* pp. 236-237.
18. See below § 11.

Francisco Mendes, Diego Rodrigues Pinto[19] and other Lisbon merchants who had not yet paid for these deliveries.

On August 28, 1532, King João III of Portugal wrote to the Emperor and asked him to see that Diogo's case «be dispatched promptly and his rights fully respected ... [according to] the principles of justice and equity.» The King was to consider this as an «immense personal favor» as most of the seized goods belonged to him. King Henry VIII of England also pleaded with Charles V on behalf of Diogo Mendes, and claimed that English subjects had entrusted money and goods to him.[20]

These interventions brought a rapid resolution of Diogo's case. On September 17, 1532, he was "provisionally" set free upon payment of bail,[21] on condition that he would remain available for (improbable) further investigations. It was a mere formality, as the Queen could not admit having kept Diogo prisoner for two months without good reasons. However, the King of Portugal was concerned that, as long as the case was still pending, Diogo should not be sent large amounts of merchandise, for fear that the Emperor might have them seized.[22] In November 1532, the Portuguese ambassador at the imperial court conveyed the request that the Antwerp merchants dealing with spices and with other products of the "Indian House" be granted complete immunity against any charge of monopolistic activities. João III was concerned that his own business might be adversely affected by any action taken against these merchants. The Emperor agreed to the request and instructed his sister not to interfere with the King's commercial activities. The Queen was to show every special favor to the Portuguese *Feitor*, agents and merchants. Furthermore Charles V stated that no person was to be persecuted or bothered in any way for any matter linked to the spice trade.[23] As we shall see, Mary of Hapsburg did not follow these instructions.

In (or around) 1532, another Portuguese merchant, António de la Ronha,[24] was arrested, locked up in the fortress of Cogel and entrusted to

---

19. Diego was the elder brother of Duarte and of Bastião Pinto. See below.
20. See the official summary of conditions for the release of Diogo Mendes, in SALOMON-LEONI, *Mendes, Benveniste*, pp. 185-189.
21. AGR, PEA 1177, September 10 1532. See Document 5 in Appendix.
22. SALOMON-LEONI, *Mendes, Benveniste*, pp. 147-148.
23. P. GÉNARD, *Personen te Antwerpen*, pp. 251-252: November 27, 1532: Charles V to Mary.
24. From other sources we know that [in or around 1540] he was a tall, one eyed man, about 32 years old. He was a successful merchant and «magister in Theologia Hebrea».

the infamous Johannes Vuysting.[25] António was suspected of playing a major role as a leader of the organization that planned and financed the escape of *Marranos* from Portugal to Flanders and, from there, to Italy and the Levant. He was also accused of an even greater crime: the shipment of merchandise to the lands of the Turk. The Emperor attached the greatest importance to this offence, which, in his belief, threatened the welfare of his states. Charles V appointed one of his most distinguished officers, Francisco de Castelo Alto, as extraordinary commissioner with the assignment to inquire into this case along with Johannes Vuysting.[26] Don Francisco was to examine all the documents relating to the prisoner, and to interrogate all those who had ever dealt with him, from the captain of the fortress to the lowest soldier. The commissioner had to discover how the flight of the "Jews" was organized and by which routes their goods were transferred to the Levant.[27] The Emperor was determined to seize the leaders of this organization in the almost obsessive hope of laying his hands on their supposedly immense treasures.

At this point in the research, we know very little about the results of the inquiry and the conditions under which António de la Ronha was released from prison. At some point, he left Antwerp and moved to London where he continued his activity in favour of the *Marranos* fleeing the Iberian Peninsula.

A year later, Queen Mary opened a new inquiry into the activities of Portuguese merchants, whom she accused (again!) of monopolizing the spice trade and performing Jewish rites. In December 1533, orders were given for the arrest of António Fernandes, a member of the pepper consortium, on a charge of monopolistic practices. The unfortunate merchant was ambushed while traveling to Lyons on horseback, arrested and transferred to a fortress outside the territory of Brabant.

---

25. In 1530 Johannes Vuysting (or Vuystinck, *alias* de la Foia, Foilla, Foix) had been appointed deputy-commissioner (subordinate to Corneille Scepperus). P. GÉNARD, *Personen te Antwerpen*, pp. 195-196; AGR,OFB, 160/1233/2, *Codazzi File,* f. 19v. See Document 13 in Appendix.
26. UCL,ML,London, *Wolf Papers,* box "CC" folder 4 with an abbreviated transcription of Charles V's decree of September 17 1532. Cf. A. Æ. BROOKS, *The Woman who defied Kings, The life and times of Doña Gracia Nasi, A Jewish Leader during Renaissance,* St. Paul, Minnesota, 2002, p. 129.
27. AGR, PEA B. 1625, August 8, 1532: Patent Letters appointing Francisco de Castelo Alto.

The magistrates of Antwerp saw in this move a violation of their privileges, issued a fierce protest to the Queen and charged her Secretary of State with abuse of power. António's stewards (Francisco Alvares, Emanuel Nuñes and Fernando d'Espanha) were given the opportunity to conceal the accounts of their master and, probably, to smuggle a part of his patrimony out of the country.

Nevertheless, António Fernandes was detained for a few years. At a certain point the Queen-Regent consulted the Grote Raad van Mecheln (Grand Conseil de Malines). This Court expressed the opinion that monopolistic practices were *de facto* widespread and tolerated in many countries. Furthermore, the King of Portugal had stipulated these contracts according to the laws of his own country. The Grote Raad dropped the charges of Judaizing because they did not fall under the jurisdiction of this Court. The Councilors suggested, however, submitting this case to an ecclesiastical tribunal. Mary of Habsburg did not follow up on this proposition.

On June 17, 1534, the Council advised the Queen to refrain from any further action against foreign merchants who might be induced to leave the country depriving it of their indispensable services.[28] It was a respectful but clear contradiction of Queen Mary's evaluation of the role of the Portuguese merchants. António was not set free until 1536, when the Regent finally desisted from any further prosecution.[29]

As an outcome, Queen Mary was compelled to accept the existence of the spice monopoly.[30] A minor result of this episode was that a list of most of the members of the pepper consortium was made available to scholars.[31]

---

28. AGR, GRM, reg. 145, pp. 515-541: Cfr. P.GÉNARD, *Personen te Antwerpen*, pp. 265-273, 282-89, 330-345, 355-356, 393-425; R. ANSWAARDEN, *Le Grand Conseil*, Cause 38, pp. 259-268; GORIS, *Colonies Marchandes*, pp. 104-105, 199-201, 562-570.

29. R. ANSWAARDEN, *Le Grand Conseil*, p. 261

30. *Ibid.*, pp.259-60.

31. The list includes the names of Diogo Mendes, Luis Fernandis, Ruy Perus, Diego de Camergo, Steven Perus [Estevão Pires], Fernando d' España, Manoel Serano [Serão], the sons of Gonçalo Fernandis, Rodrigo de Peris, Diego Dies, and Luis de Sevilla, all described as «Jews or New Christians». The Italian merchants Jehan Charles [Affaitati] and Luca Giraldi, who were also members of the consortium, were called «Christians». Other partners, living in Portugal were: Francisco Mendes, António Martines and his son Diego, Nuño Henriques, his brother Henriquo Nuñes , Alonço de Torris, Diego de Torres, Giorgio Vixorda [Bixorda], Thomas Serrano «and others».

In 1537, shortly after Antonio Fernandes' acquittal, The Portuguese Nation petitioned the Emperor to revoke the provisions enacted on August 14, 1532[32] forbidding any further immigration of New Christians. Charles V agreed to the request (for a price) and issued a decree welcoming all Portuguese *conversos* willing to settle in Flanders and live there as genuine Christians. They were granted complete immunity for all crimes and transgressions committed before the safe-conduct was granted while, for crimes eventually committed after their arrival, they could be summoned only to local Courts. They would enjoy the same privileges granted to the merchants of other foreign nations. They were free to leave Antwerp at any time with their families and their belongings, either to return to Portugal or move to any other Christian State.[33] The decree provided the Portuguese colony of Antwerp with a few months of respite.

On July 18, 1538, Mary of Habsburg appointed Guillaume de Lare, the provost marshal of her Palace, as extraordinary-commissioner with the task of intercepting the New Christians on their way from Antwerp to Italy and the Levant. He had to post himself and his men out of the city and set ambushes along the routes departing from Antwerp.[34]

---

32. See above, at the beginning of this same chapter.
33. AGR, PEA, reg. 1177, ff. 23r-25r; copy in OFB 160/1233/2.
34. LAURENT and LAMEERE, *Ordonnances des Pays-Bas*, Tome IV, p. 77. A GOOSENS, *Les Inquisitions*, p. 72.

§ 6. The 1540 legislation for the eradication of all the heresies

After crushing the revolt of Ghent (1539-40),[1] Charles V was resolved to eradicate all forms of heresy from the Low Countries and to impose, once and for all, a firm central control on the provincial authorities. The Emperor was convinced that the two issues were strictly interwoven. The Queen Governor had been receiving many warnings that local Councils were not sufficiently zealous in implementing the *placards*.[2]

A new *placard*, issued on September 22, 1540, confirmed and enlarged the validity of the existing legislation. All previous prohibitions were repeated: draconian measures were taken against the circulation of forbidden books. Attending secret "conventicles" and the discussion of the sacred texts by laypersons were equated to heresy. The offenders were to be punished by loss of life and property. Not only were penalties hardened, but jurists were instructed to apply the maximum punishments in all cases without taking into account the "personal [extenuating] circumstances" of the transgressor".

The *placard* introduced the definition of new offences. Law officers were instructed to implement the *placard* with due zeal, according to its wording [i.e. by applying the decree in its full rigor]. "Non-conscientious" magistrates and uncooperative officers would be convicted of "negligence in enforcing the *placards*", stripped of their ranks, and considered "heretics" in every way. A new legal concept was introduced: heretics were declared "incapable individuals"; deprived of their faculties and

---

1. M. Boone, *Ledict mal s'est espandu comme peste fatale (The evil edict spread around like a deadly plague): Karel V en Gent, stedelijke identiteit en staatsgeweld*, «Handelingen der Maatschappij voor Geschiedenis en Oudheidkunde te Gent», LIV, Ghent 2000, pp. 31-63.
2. J.D. Tracy, *Heresy Law*, p. 287.

considered unable to perform any legal action. This was retroactive and became valid the very moment when the offender had first started to be a heretic. Those who gave hospitality to heretics, or hid their goods, should be regarded and prosecuted as heretics.[3]

On October 4, 1540, the Emperor issued a new decree confirming the previous *placard* and enjoining its strict and immediate enforcement without any dispensation or moderation.[4]

The new legislation was not specifically aimed against Judaizers, however, it provided a general frame of reference according to which any zealous and malicious officer could arrest new immigrants, pillage their property and seize the goods shipped to the Portuguese merchants of Antwerp.

---

3. LAURENT and LAMEERE, *Ordonnances des Pays-Bas,* IV, pp. 226-227; GENARD, *Personen te Antwerpen*, p.449.
4. LAURENT and LAMEERE, *Ordonnances des Pays-Bas,* IV, pp. 232-233. A. GOOSENS, *Les inquisitions,* p. 61.

§ 7. A New Wave of Persecutions Against the New Christians (1540-1541)

In November 1540, Charles V and his sister launched a new attack against the New Christians. Charles Boisot, a prominent member of the Privy Council, was sent to Antwerp with the task of arranging for the arrest of three well known Portuguese merchants and having them handed over to the imperial police. They were Gabriel de Negro,[1] Manoel Serrano (Serrão), and Manoel Manriques,[2] "particularly suspected" of belonging to the "Jewish sect" and of other "infamous crimes" (such as promoting and financing the escape of New Christians to Italy and the Levant). Loys Garces, a young man who had lived a few years in Salonika and had then returned to Flanders,[3] had denounced them.

From other sources, we know that Gabriel de Negro [later known as Moshe Yahia] was, in fact, one of the leaders of the Portuguese Nation. He was also a *mohel* (circumciser) and performed the function of rabbi.[4] Gabriel was married to Violante Henriques [Gracia Benveniste], the sis-

---

1. «Negro» was not a baptismal name. In the 12th century, Rabbi Yahia ibn haYsh distinguished himself during the war against the Moors. King Affonso V of Portugal rewarded him with a fief: the Aldeia dos Negros. The rabbi assumed the name of this territory and called himself Yahia Negro. The episode is reported by GEDALIA Ibn IAHIA in his *Sefer divrè ha-yamim le-toledot benè Yahia.* See M. KAYSERLING, *Geschichte der Juden in Portugal, sub indice;* J.V. SERRÃO, *História de Portugal,* Vol. I, Lisbon 1980², p. 193; LJTS, N.Y., «vellum broadside which is a family tree of the Ibn Yahia family, copied in 1603» currently located in the Rare Books Room, in Drawer no. 22; A. DAVID, *Gedaliah ibn Yahia, auteur de Shalshelet ha-Qabbalah,* «REJ», CLIII 1994, pp. 101-132: 105 and 123.
2. AGR, PEA 128, ff. 283r-284v, November 24, 1540.
3. SAA, V[ierschaar = Tribunal], 316, nr.3: undated fragment of an explanatory statement drawn up by Adriaan Herbouts, the Pensionary of Antwerp; P. GÉNARD, *Personen te Antwerpen,* p. 449; A. GOOSENS, *Les inquisitions modernes,* pp. 59-63.
4. P.C. IOLY ZORATTINI, *Processi 1570-1572,* Firenze, 1984, p. 28.

ter of Nuño Henriques [Senior Benveniste].[5] At the time, Gabriel was sixty years old, heavy-set, not very tall, and his beard was whitening.[6]

Both Gabriel and Manoel Serrão were partners of the pepper consortium. The Margrave of Antwerp described Gabriel as «a rich and mighty merchant who could count on many friendly associations».[7] Manoel Serrano (Serrão) was also one of the Nation's leaders and a member of the Rescue Committee, which planned and financed the escape of Marranos from Portugal to Flanders and from there to Italy.[8] Manoel Manriques was suspected of being responsible for the reception of the new immigrants in Antwerp: it was he who found them accommodations, provided for their needs and organized their departure.[9] He was obviously wealthy: otherwise he would not have attracted the Emperor's attention.

Doctor Boisot was provided with documents directing the local authorities to comply with any request he might present. However, when he asked to have Gabriel de Negro imprisoned, the Burgomasters raised many objections and reluctantly promised to have him summoned. The éscoutète[10] was entrusted with this task. As it turned out, the officer let Gabriel know about the impending threat and Gabriel managed to go into hiding. He was believed to be in some friend's house in the city.[11] In fact the imperial police had blocked all the routes out of the city.[12]

Manoel Serrano presented himself to the Margrave. The city authorities arranged summary proceedings against him but, in this case we

---

5. On Nuño Henriques, his brother Henrique Nuñes and their family see: P.C. Ioly Zorattini, *Processi 1570-1572*, pp. 18-19, 57-59, 219-232 and *passsim*; A. di Leone Leoni, *Documenti e Notizie Sulla Famiglie Nassì e Benvenisti*, «RMI». LVIII, 1992. For a genealogical tree of the family see: Salomon-Leoni, *Mendes, Benveniste*, pp. 210-211.
6. AGR, OFB,160/1233/2, *Codazzi File*, December 20, 1540: witness deposition of Odoardo Roderico, prisoner in Pavia.
7. AGR, OFB, 160/1233/2 November [19, *circa*] 1540 Charles Boisot's report to the Emperor. See Document 16 in Appendix.
8. A. di Leone Leoni, *Manoel Lopez Bichacho*, p. 81 and Doc. 1, p. 95.
9. AGR,OFB, 160/1233/2, *Enquete faite sur les nouveaux Christiens*, October 1540, witness testimony of Nicolas Fernandes.
10. *Escoutète/ écoutète* (from the Dutch "schout") = local justice officer.
11. AGR, PEA 1504, undated [end of November 1540] letter of Charles V to the Magistrates of Antwerp: «Pour ce que nous avons entendu que Gabriel de Negro et Manoel Menrique, grandement suspects de l'heresie judaique, se sont rendu fugitifs ou de moins latitans en nostre ville danveres, comme est le plus vraysemblable».
12. See *infra*.

should say *in his favor*. He was immediately declared "not-guilty" and set free.[13] In any case, he found it safer to go into hiding.[14] Manoel Manriques managed to leave his house unharmed and nothing more was heard of him.

The Emperor had dispatched a provost marshal of his Palace to Antwerp. He had to stay in the outskirts of the city, from where he organized ambushes to seize all people suspected of belonging to the Jewish Sect.[15] He had been instructed to apprehend any New Christian on whom he could lay his hands. When the marshal arrested an [unnamed] merchant and had him transferred to a distant fortress, the Antwerp magistrates saw in this move an infringement of the privileges of their city and, in turn, placed the marshal under house arrest and kept him in strict custody. In vain, Charles Boisot tried to intercede on his behalf, offering to assure the marshal's future behavior.[16] All he could do was to send a report to Charles V, who became extremely enraged.[17] This was the beginning of a long controversy between the Emperor, the Queen-Regent and the city elders.

The Emperor summoned the Margrave and the *Escoutète* to justify their behavior.[18] They explained that they were worried that the course of trading activities might be adversely affected by these actions. The life of

---

13. S. ULLMAN, *Studien zur Geschichte der Juden in Belgien*, Antwerp 1909, p. 30;

14. See Document 16 in Appendix.

15. AGR, OFB, 160/1233/2: November [19, *circa*] 1540 Charles Boisot's report to the Emperor: «Le prevost des marischaulx ma dit ce mesme matin avoir mis ses gens hors de la ville sur les passaiges tant ordonnaires que autres chemins ... pour ce donner garde sur la fuyte ou emport des personnes et biens des nouveaulx chrestiens». See Document 16 in Appendix.

16. AGR, OFB, 160/1233/2, March 12, 1540 [= 1541, Style de la Court]: Queen's Mary explanatory statement to the General Attorney of Brabant. See Document 22 in Appendix. On the dating of the documents issued by the imperial court see H. GROTENFEND and T. ULRICHT, *Taschenbuch der Zeitrechnung des deutschen Mittelalters und der Neuzeit*, Hannover 1960.

17. AGR, PEA 73, 24 and 25 November 1540, Charles V to the Margrave, burgomasters and echevins [local judges]: the Emperor issued a placard [copy not found in the file] directing the authorities to denounce the hidden Jews and hand them over to his officers.

18. AGR,OFB,160/1233/2, March 12, 1540 [=1541, Style de la Court], Explanatory statement presented by Queen Mary against the Margrave and éscoutète of Antwerp, f. 1v: «l'empereur adverti de la dite apprehention, et dicelle tres mal content, mandat jncontinent ausdits danvers denvoyer vers sa Majesté leurs deputéz pour declairer par quelle auctorité et occasion ilz avoient constitué prisonnier ledict prevost». See Document 22 in Appendix

Antwerp was founded precisely on the freedom of trade. In the recent past, the city had already suffered because of similar problems. They reported that foreign merchants were becoming more and more worried about their own future.[19]

When Charles Boisot asked to get all the assets of Gabriel seized, he received a flat refusal from the city authorities. The Margrave objected, stating that both Gabriel Negro and Manoel Serrano had settled in Antwerp long before 1537, had been living in the city for many years and were fully entitled to enjoy the privilege granted to their Nation. Rumors had spread among the merchants that these proceedings were based solely on greed and had nothing to do with religious zeal.[20] There was a widespread fear among the merchants that the Emperor, after accomplishing his attack against the New Christians, would turn his attention towards the Lutherans.[21] Some of them had already discussed the idea of leaving the city.[22]

A clear suggestion that Charles V was moved by greed is found in a report of the Venetian ambassador in Brussels. On November 21, 1540, he wrote to the *Signoria*:

> «In Antwerp, a number of Portuguese who lived as Christians and were in reality Jews have been arrested. Their synagogue and other similar evidence to that effect have been discovered, so they

---

19. AGR, PEA, 1177, ff. 28r-29r: undated [Febr. 21, 1541] *remonstrance de Jan van de Uberne, Eschoutet et Guillaume van Halmalc, Amman de la Ville d'Anverse à la Royne Marie*, February 21 1540, [Style de la Court =1541] : «... ce que a esté par eux dict ou faict procedoit par ung vray zele quilz avoient vers le train de la marchandise de quoy ladicte ville dependt, et pour la grande poursuite et protestations a eulx et encontre eulx faitz par les marchans, dont a cause des semblables protestations eulx et ladicte ville ont souffert autreffois grand dommaige».

20. AGR, Bx, OFB, 160/1233/2, undated [Novembrer 1540] report of Charles Boisot to the Emperor: « ...Le Margrave replica que l'apprehensions dedicts biens feroit murmurer tous marchans estrangiers que la presente poursuyte se fait plus pour les biens que pour chastier les personnes.» See document 16 in Appendix.; AGR,PEA 1552, Loys de Heylwegen («Conseiller du Conseil de Brabant ») to Queen Mary, February 19, 1541.

21. LAURENT et LAMEERE, *Ordonnances des Pays-Bas,* IV, pp. 226-227: placard against the Lutherans issued on september 22, 1540. Cfr. P. GÉNARD, *Personen te Antwerpen,* p. 449; A. GOOSENS, *Les inquisitions modernes*, pp. 59-63.

22. AGR, Bx, OFB, 160/1233/2, undated [November 1540] report of Charles Boisot to the Emperor. See Document 16 in Appendix; AGR,PEA 1552, Loys de Heylwegen (conseiller du Conseil de Brabant) to Queen Mary, February 19, 1541.

can scarcely excuse themselves. Their purses will be cut, especially that of some of their leaders, and it is believed that 100,000
crowns will thus be obtained».[23]

On December 17, 1540, the Emperor issued a new *placard* directing
the authorities and the inhabitants of Antwerp to denounce all persons
"infected by the Judaic fallacy".[24] As we have seen, in the bureaucratic
language of the Court the term "Jews" was frequently used as a synonym
for "New Christians". The wording of the decree lent itself to equivocal
interpretation. In theory, malevolent state officers could target any
Portuguese. However, the city authorities did not enforce the imperial
decree and fiercely opposed it.

At this point, Queen Mary ordered Charles Boisot to wait some time
before inquiring about other "Jews" and apprehending all those belonging to this sect.[25] Charles V and Mary of Habsburg had delivered a severe
blow to the Portuguese Nation: three outstanding merchants had been
compelled to leave their houses and estates. The other New Christians,
and especially the richest ones, were worried, distressed and felt threatened. Some of them left their homes and looked for shelter in the houses
of some friends. Others locked themselves in their dwellings and avoided
being seen.

In the same period, many Portuguese refugees reached the port of
Middleburg in Zeeland on board ships of the Royal Fleet transporting

23. BNM,Ve, *Manoscritti Italiani,* Cl. 7, N.802 [=8219], *Copialettere di Francesco
Contarini,* Venetian ambassador in Brussels, November 21, 1540: «In Anversa sono stati
ritenuti molti Portoghesi, quali vivevano da Christiani, et in effetto erano giudei, et è sta
trovato la Sinagoga, et molti altri inditii, che quasi non possono escusarsi, a questi se li
taglierà la borsa et massime ad alcuni principali et si crede che se li caverà da centomille
scudi.» The document was translated into English by R. BROWN, Edit., *Calendar of State
Papers and Manuscripts relating to English Affairs existing in the Archives... of Venice
and ... Northern Italy,* V, *(1434-1554),* London 1873, p. 88, Doc. 229. Cfr. LEONI, *La
Diplomazia Estense e l'immigrazione dei Cristiani Nuovi a Ferrara al tempo di Ercole II,*
«Nuova Rivista Storica» LXXVIII, 1994, pp. 294-326: p. 308.
24. AGR, PEA, reg 820, ff. 31r-32v, Dec. 17, 1540: *Ordonnance de declarer ceulx qui sont
infectéz de l'erreur judaique.* Copy in AGR, OFB 160/1633/2. See Document 17 in
Appendix.
25. AGR,PEA 1177, ff. 79-80: [undated] *Summaire ...en laffaire des Juifs qui se disent
nouveaulx christiens en Anvers* : (f. 80) «aussi est mande audict [conseiller Charles]
Boisot de se jnformer plus avant des aultres juifz residens en anvers et faire apprehender
tous ceulx quil trouvera estre de ceste secte».

"East Indian" spices to Flanders. When it appeared that none of them were provided with a royal license,[26] Jerome Sandelin, the *Rentmeester*[27] of Bewesterschelt in Zeeland, arrested and detained them.[28] He also confiscated all the goods dispatched by sea to the New Christians of Antwerp.[29] In vain, the representatives of the Portuguese merchants reminded the officer that they enjoyed special privileges. They were routinely told that Jews, *Marranos* and heretics[30] could not avail themselves of any prerogative; therefore, the 1537 patent letters were to be considered null and void.[31]

Many Portuguese refugees travelling to Flanders interrupted their journey in England to wait for more propitious times.[32] They could count on the support and advice of their countrymen in London, who often

26. On July 18, 1532, king João III issued an *Alvará* forbidding the emigration of New Christians from Portugal. The decree is published *in extenso* in the collection *As Gavetas da Torre do Tombo*, Vol. I, Lisbon 1960, Doc. 245, pp. 280-285. From witness depositions of several captains of the Portuguese Royal Navy we learn that it was re-enacted several times. See Documents 38, 39, 44, 55 in Appendix.

27. *Rentmeester* (Dutch) = Fiscal receiver serving also as regional law-officer. Cfr. R. Answaarden, *Le Grand Conseil*, p. 349.

28. AGR, PEA 1177/2, ff.63r-68v, 125r-145v. Cfr. A. di Leone Leoni, *Manoel Lopes Bichacho*, pp. 81, 95 and Doc.1 therein.

29. Among his booty there were two shiploads of sugar and other products dispatched to Gabriel de Negro.

30. This was an evident reference to the imperial *placard* of September 22, 1940. See above § 6.

31. There can hardly be any doubt that Sandelin acted according to precise directions from Queen Mary. The Rentmeester's behavior was later the subject of a *doléance* submitted by the New Christians to the Emperor. It is widely quoted in the decree by which, on March 10, 1541 [1542], Charles V reinstated the validity of the 1537 privilege. See Document 31 in the Appendix.

32. AGR, PEA 1177/2, ff 63r-68v: *Enquete faite en la ville de Middelbourg le 15e et le 16e jour de mars 1540 [=1541] pardevant le rentmaister assisté de l'advocat fiscal du Grand Conseil* where account is given of the journey of a certain Cristoforo Fernandes who, in March 1541, rushed from Antwerp to England to forewarn some Portuguese travellers arriving in Southampton that they should not continue their journey to Flanders. Lucien Wolf, (*Jews in Tudor England*, in Idem, *Essays in Jewish History,* edited by C. Roth, London 1934, pp. 73-90: p. 77) stated that Cristoforo was «at the service of Diego Mendes in London». This might well be true but it still lacks documentary evidence. Cristoforo however did not live in England but in Antwerp. L. Wolf (*Ibid.* p. 78) also assumed that António de la Ronha, an important merchant in London, was Mendes' representative and «financial agent» in England. Cfr. Roth, *Doña Gracia,* p. 30 (based on Wolf).

helped the travellers sell their merchandise and provided them with bills of credit on Antwerp, in order to avoid the danger of confiscations.[33]

Ship captains often robbed passengers of their goods, counting on the fact that their victims were unlikely to present official claims. In the ports of arrival, the Flemish policemen often took advantage of the situation as well. On October 8, 1541, Gerome Sandelin (the *Fiscal Receiver* of Bewesterschelt) could not conceal his disappointment when he learned from the crew of a Portuguese vessel that a certain Pedro Lopes had landed in England with his wife and children when the ship called at the port of [South] Hampton. According to the sailors, these passengers were "loaded with gold and silver". The officer was also distressed to find that a trunk addressed to Diogo Mendes had been broken into, and opened, and that he could only find items of no value together with a letter of exchange drawn in Diogo Mendes' name.[34]

In spite of all their machinations, at the beginning of 1541, the omnipotent Emperor and his sister had not acheived their main purpose, and were still unable to lay their hands on the property and assets of the three fugitive merchants. This was not an easy task as the city magistrates had raised every sort of legal obstacle and managed to delay the manoeuvres of the imperial agents.[35]

The ordinary administration of the Negro estate had been entrusted to Agostinho Henriques (Gabriel's nephew-in-law[36]), and Fernando Pires

---

33. In many cases the bills of exchange were drawn on the House of Diogo Mendes. Wide evidence is provided by documents in AGR, PEA, 1177/2 and PEA 1504, *passim*.

34. AGR, PEA 1177/2, October 8, 1541: Gerome Sandelin, *Rentmeester de Bewesterschelt* to Luys de Schorr, president du Privé Conseil. See Doc. 27 in Appendix. See also AGR, PEA 1177/2, ff. 15r-16r.

35. AGR, Bx, PEA, 1177, ff. 79r-80r; PEA 1504, February 2, 1541: *La Royne a ceulx de la loy denvers*; OFB, 160/1233/2, February 9, 1540 [=1541, Style de la Court]; AGR, PEA 1552, February 19, 1540 [1541]: (unidentified) officers' report to the Queen-Regent; *Ibid.*, March 22 1540 [= 1541]: the Queen to Loys de Heylwegen; AGR,PEA 1540, February 22, 1540 [= 1541]: the Queen to Corneille Scepperus ; PEA 1560, February 11, 1540 [1541], the Queen directs the burgomaster and city officers to comply with the Emperor's orders; PEA 1560, March 12, 1540 [1541]: the Queen directs the *Conseil de Brabant* to have the Amman and the Sheriff prosecuted and removed from their offices. See Document 22 in Appendix.

36. As we have seen, Gabriel was Nuño Henriques' brother-in-law. Agostinho Henriques had married Beatriz (Simḥa) one of Nuño 's daughters. See A. di LEONE LEONI, *I marrani di Coimbra denunciati al Papa dall' Inquisizione Portoghese nel 1578. Il loro status giuridico in diversi Stati italiani,* «Zakhor» II, 1998, pp. 73-109: 94; IDEM, *La presenza sefardita a Venezia intorno alla metà del Cinquecento. I Libri e gli Uomini,* «RMI» . LVVII, 2001, pp. 35-108. 62-64.

(probably one of Gabriel's sons in law). At a certain point, Queen Mary had them both arrested and indicted on charges of hiding part of Negro's estate. João Rebello, the Portuguese royal *feitor* in Antwerp, interceded several times on their behalf. They were set free on bail in May 1541.[37]

At a certain point, the Queen-Regent submitted the case to the Council of Brabant, which eventually ruled that all the belongings of Gabriel Negro and Manoel Manriques had to be transferred to the Emperor.[38] Gabriel succeeded in escaping to London and, from there, to Venice. Among his seized assets was an invaluable library.[39]

---

37. AGR, PEA 1627, April 13, 1541, Queen Mary to João Rebello: the Queen accepts a 100.000 florins guarantee; AGR, PEA 1560, f. 52, May 13, 1541: João Rebello to Loys de Schorr, president of the Privy Council, AGR, OFCB, 160/1233/2, February 2, 1536 [= 1537, Style de la Court]: four merchants: Jean Charles [Affaitati], Diogo Mendes, Erasmus Schetz and Jerome Sayler are prepared to provide a guarantee of 25,000 florins each. See Document 24 in Appendix.On Erasmus Schetz see R. EHRENBERG, *Das Zeitalter der Fugger, Geldkapital und Kreditverkehr im 16. Jahrhundert*, Vol. I, Jena 1922[3], pp. 333 ff.
38. AGR, Conseil du Brabant, reg. 586, February 2, 1540 [= 1541, Style de la Court] ; AGR,Bx,PEA 1504, February 9, 1540 [1541], Queen Mary's official statement.
39. S.W. BARON, *A Social and Religious History*, XIII, p. 121.

§ 8. The Results of the 1540-1541 Inquiries in Middelbourg and in Pavia

T he interrogations of Portuguese émigrés imprisoned in Zeeland,[1] and different localities of Lombardy,[2] provide important information on the social and religious background of these immigrants,[3] as well as the Portuguese already living in Antwerp. Most of the refugees had no knowledge of the Christian Faith. When questioned about the reasons for their departure from Portugal, they invariably answered that they were poor workmen affected by the economic crisis in Portugal, and were seeking employment opportunities in Antwerp or other European cities. They hoped that their countrymen in Antwerp would help them. It was, however, evident that before starting their journey they had been instructed to provide this justification.

The King of Portugal had prohibited the emigration of New Christians from his realm. The ports were strictly guarded. Fares from Lisbon to Antwerp had consequently skyrocketed and the refugees had to pay much more than "normal" passengers for their journey. It was clear that they could not afford these expenses and that somebody had planned their journey and paid for it.[4]

---

1. AGR, PEA 1177/2, especially ff. 63r-68v, 125r-145v.
2. Excerpts of interrogations conducted in Pavia are published in appendix as document 4.
3. A list of the prisoners held in Middelbourg in 1540-1541 was published by M. GINZBURGER, *Marie d'Hongrie, Charles V, les veuves Mendes et les néo chrétiens*, «REJ» 89, 1930, pp. 179-192: 189-92. Cfr. SALOMON-LEONI, *Mendes, Benveniste*, p. 145, note 22; A. di LEONE LEONI, *Manoel Lopes Bichacho*, pp. 78-80. A full transcription of all the documents (in French and Flemish) concerning the Portuguese immigrants arrested in Middelburg in 1540 and 1541 will be published by HERMAN PRINS SALOMON in the near future.
4. A. di LEONE LEONI, *Manoel Lopes Bichacho*, pp. 78-81.

João Rebello, the Portuguese Royal Feitor, interceded with the Queen-Regent on behalf of the prisoners. In the end, all but two of them were released upon payment of bail. Most of them were expelled from the country and had their belongings seized. Others were acquitted on condition that they would provide their children with a religious education.[5] To the best of my knowledge, this was only the second time that the Emperor, or his sister Mary, inflicted "spiritual" penances on New Christians in the Low Countries. Two old men, Luis and Marco Fernandes, refused to profess belief in the "divine nature" of Christ and denied that the Jews had crucified him. They were burnt at the stake at the beginning of 1541 on order of the Queen.[6]

In the meantime, other groups of immigrants succeeded in safely reaching the Flemish shores and continued their journey from Antwerp to Ferrara and Ancona. They started their difficult itinerary by carriage, along secondary roads, to Cologne where they travelled on barges on the Rhine River to Basel and, from there, by carriage and horse, or even on foot, across the Alps. Then, they continued by boat along the rivers of Lombardy towards Ferrara (located on the Po River).

Some of these refugees were taken prisoner by squads of guards led by Johannes Vuysting, the infamous "commissioner" *contra falsos christianos* who had been transferred to Milan.[7] In 1540, about ten refugees travelling by boat with their families were arrested and kept prisoner for many months. Vuysting had established his headquarters in Pavia, close to the city's port. It was here that most of the interrogations took place. Johannes and his guards were cruel, violent and pitiless. They continuously mistreated the prisoners, calling them "Jewish dogs" and "renegades".[8] The émigrés came from a country where this charge had already brought dozens of people to the stake and they believed that they were facing the same fate. They were no heroes: they confessed under torture that they had received money from merchants in Antwerp and denounced

---

5. AGR, PEA 1504, February 21 1540 [1541].
6. *Ibid.*, Cfr. A. di LEONE LEONI, *Manoel Lopez Bichacho*, p. 80.
7. According to L. WOLF (*Tudor England*, pp. 75, 82) a "Commission" was set up in Milan in 1540. Despite repeated searches I did not find in the Archives of Brussels, Milan and Pavia any reference to such a commission. From documents kept at the ASPv (Notary G.B. Codazzi, February 7, 1541) it appears that [sub] commissioner Vuysting performed his activities in Lombardy on the basis of the *commission* (appointment) received in 1532. See alco Document 13 in Appendix.
8. AGR, OFB 160/1233/2, *Lavezzoli File*, *passim*.

Diogo Mendes Benveniste, Manoel Serrão, Manoel Lopes, Lopo de Provincia, Gabriel de Negro, Domingo Mendes and others.[9]

Diogo Mendes was suspected of being the principal trustee and administrator of the fabulous relief fund, the so-called *Bôlsa* [or *Caixa*] *das Esmolas* that the Emperor and his sister Mary were longing to seize. Strangely enough, the official reports of interrogations conducted in Lombardy, mainly in Pavia, were delivered to Queen Mary only in 1542.[10] She contemplated using these documents to press charges against Diogo Mendes. The councilors who examined these papers came to the conclusion that there was not enough evidence and that they did not have a case. In fact, the declarations against Diogo Mendes were partially pre-fabricated and had evidently been extorted by torture. Furthermore, Vuysting had set all the prisoners free after depriving them of all their possessions. Nobody knew where these testimonies could be found; thus their depositions could not be reconfirmed before a court.[11] Vuysting's piratical operations had separate, clamorous developments leading to a diplomatic struggle between the Duke of Ferrara and the imperial court. Before we deal with these developments, we shall try to draw a picture of the Portuguese Nation of Ferrara.

---

9. AGR, *Codazzi file*, Dec. 20, 1540: deposition of Michael Nuñes.

10. AGR, PEA 53, July 15, 1542: the Emperor reminds Queen Mary that he had recently sent authenticated copies of the interrogations held in Lombardy. See Documents 33 and 34 in Appendix.

11. AGR, PEA 53, f. 209: July 12, 1542, The Emperor to Queen Mary. See J. Reznik, *Le Duc Joseph de Naxos*, Paris 1936, pp. 235-236. AGR. PEA 1177/2 f. 90v.

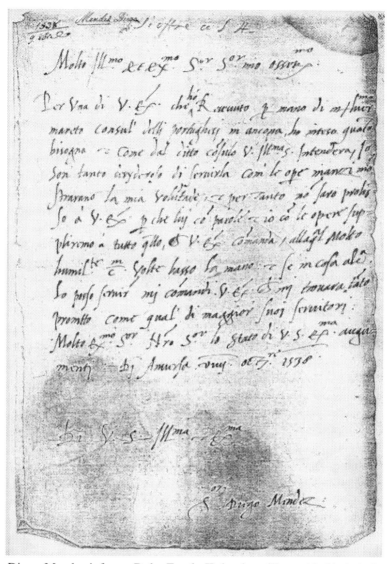

Diogo Mendes informs Duke Ercole II that he will provide his help in order to organize the emigration of New Christians from Antwerp to Ferrara – October 9, 1538.
Source: ASMo, CD, *Lettere particolari*, B. 885.

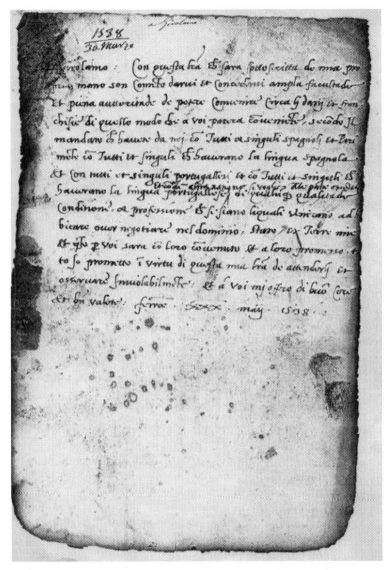

The invitation issued by Ercole II on May 30, 1538 to "each and every Spaniard and Portuguese."
ASMo, *Minutario Generale Cronologico*, Folder 9. Copies in ASMo, *Cancelleria Ducale*, EBREI folders 6 and 15.

§ 9. The Portuguese Nation of Ferrara (1538-1541)

Thanks to the protection of the Dukes of the House of Este, in the first half of the 16th century Ferrara was the most important center of Jewish life in Northern Italy.[1] In 1534, from the very moment of his ascent to the ducal throne, Ercole II d'Este confirmed the rights enjoyed by the Jews of his capital city. He also approved[2], in the most generous terms, the charter by which, in 1493,[3] his grandfather Ercole I had invited twenty-one Spanish exiles to settle in Ferrara with their families. These émigrés could establish an autonomous community: they were allowed to engage in every sort of trade, craft and profession, thus enjoying a special concession which other Italian Jews had not yet obtained owing to the exclusionist attitude of the Catholic craft guilds.

---

1. See C. Roth, *The History of the Jews of Italy*, Philadelphia 1946, pp. 187-189; A. Milano, *Storia degli Ebrei in Italia*, Torino 1963, pp. 267-269; David Ruderman, *The Founding of a Gemilut Hasadim Society in Ferrara in 1515*, «Association for Jewish Studies Review» I, 1976; idem, *The World of a Renaissance Jew: The Life and Thought of Abraham Farissol*, Cincinnati 1981; R. Bonfil, *Rabbis and Jewish Communities in Renaissance Italy*, The Oxford University Press, Oxford 1990, pp. 235-239 and *passim*; Idem, *The History of the Spanish and Portuguese Jews in Italy*, in H. Beinart, Edit., *Moreshet Sepharad, The Sephardi Legacy*, pp. 217-39: 219-23; E. Horowitz, *Membership and its Rewards: The Emergence and Decline of Ferrara's Gemilut Hasadim Society (1515-1603)* in E. Horowitz and M. Orfali, *Editors, The Mediterranean and the Jews, Society, Culture and Economy in early Modern Times*, Bar Ilan University, Ramat Gan 2002, pp. 27-66.
2. The validity of every law and decree expired with the death of the prince who had issued it. At least in theory the new prince had to approve and reconfirm all the laws of the country.
3. The charter was granted on February 1st, 1493, a few months after the actual arrival of the Spanish Jews. See the discussion in A. di Leone Leoni, *Gli Ebrei Sefarditi a Ferrara da Ercole I a Ercole II: nuove ricerche ed interpretazioni*:«RMI» LII, 1987 pp. 407-446: 407-410.

Unlike the *condotte*[4] of the Italian Jewish Bankers, the privileges of the Spanish Jews were not subject to expiration. The *eternal* validity of their charter was extended *forever*, not only to the offspring of the first émigrés, but also to any other Jews of Spanish origin who wanted to settle in Ferrara. The *Sephardim* were exempted from paying the taxes and tributes imposed on local Jews but were expressly forbidden to open new loan-banks, this activity being reserved for *local* (Italian and Ashkenazi) Jews.

Between 1493 and 1534, the initial group of Spanish settlers was reinforced by several new arrivals. Most of them were Portuguese *Marranos* who could join the Sephardic Community without any difficulty. The ducal government regarded them as Jews without taking into account the baptism they had received at some point in their life.

Since his accession, Ercole II took a more active and explicit stand. In 1535, when he allowed the Italian Jews to carry on the *arte strazzaria* and every other form of trade and craftwork, he took special care to state that this concession was extended to the Spanish Jews living in his state and to all the other Jews of Iberian origin who would later move to Ferrara.[5] In fact, the young Duke was eager to attract Sephardic merchants in the hope that they could introduce new trade and mercantile. In 1534, the rate of economic development in Ferrara was very minimal and the town was far from being a center of commercial activity. The few local merchants were engaged in supplying the ducal court with luxury goods and the city with basic foodstuffs. The only items of exportation were salt and eels from the Comacchio Lagoon. Concidering these conditions, the arrival of foreign merchants would by no means be in conflict with the interests of the native population.

Ercole II was well aware of the fact that, in the early 1530s, several merchants of Antwerp had opened a new trade route with Ancona and Ragusa, thus bypassing the Venetian *emporium*. The Portuguese of Antwerp established contacts with the Levantine merchants of Ancona, who became their partners and agents. Several Portuguese merchants settled in the Adriatic city where they exchanged *ultra-fine* woollen cloth for products from the Balkans. They become engaged, not only in the trade with Ragusa, but also in the distribution of Balkan products (mainly leather, skins and raw wool) in the inland towns and villages of the Papal States and the surrounding regions.

---

4. The *condotta* was the contract stipulated between the Prince (or the Municipality of a town) and the Jewish bankers.
5. ASMo, CD, Ebrei, Busta XX, May 20, 1535.

Gomes Rodrigues,[6] who settled in Ancona when the city was still an independent Republic, deserves special mention. In 1532, when the papal army occupied the city, he succeeded in obtaining a liberal safe conduct for the Spanish and Portuguese merchants.[7] Several New Christians from Antwerp and London started to make regular visits to the Adriatic entrepôt and stayed in the city for long periods. Duarte and Bastião Pinto, and Estevão Vas, were the most active in initiating this trade, and delivered huge quantities of "western ultra-fine" clothes to Ancona.[8]

In the late 1530s, when the war against Turkey disrupted the Venetian links with the Levant, most of the commercial traffic between Northern Europe and the Balkans was rerouted through Ancona.[9] Duke Ercole was especially eager to attract a portion of this trade and transform his city into a transit entrepôt between Northern Europe and the Adriatic ports. For this purpose, he tried to induce Sephardic Jews, especially the Portuguese of Antwerp, to settle in his State. In 1538, Duke Ercole appointed Gerolamo Maretta as Consul of the [non-existing] *Levantine Nation of Ferrara* and dispatched him to Antwerp with the task of inviting the Portuguese merchants to settle in Ferrara.[10] As we have already stated, the economical importance of the ducal town was somewhat negligible. In order to compensate for these shortcomings, and make his offer

6. A. di LEONE LEONI, *Per una storia della Nazione Portoghese ad Ancona ed a Pesaro* in IOLY ZORATTINI, Edit., *La Identità Dissimulata, Giudaizzanti Iberici nell'Europa Cristiana dell'Età Moderna*, Firenze 2000, pp. 27-97: 29-31.

7. B.D. COOPERMAN, *Venetian Policy towards Levantine Jews and its broader Italian Context* in G. COZZI, *Gli Ebrei e Venezia, Secoli XIV-XVIII*, Milano 1987; IDEM, *Portuguese Conversos in Ancona: Jewish Political Activity in Early Modern Italy* in Idem, Ed., *In Iberia and Beyond, Hispanic Jews between Cultures*, University of Delaware Press 1998 pp. 297-352: 301-303; A. di LEONE LEONI, *Per una storia della Nazione Portoghese ad Ancona ed a Pesaro* in Ioly Zorattini, Edit., *La identità dissimulata, Giudaizzanti Iberici nell'Europa Cristiana dell'Età Moderna*, Firenze 2000.

8. A. di LEONE LEONI, *Ancona e Pesaro*, pp. 29-32; V. BONAZZOLI, *Una identità ricostruita. I Portoghesi ad Ancona dal 1530 al 15472*, «Zakhor» V, 2001-2002, pp. 9-38: 32-33. Through António Fernandes, Gomes Rodrigues received from Antwerp large quantities of English and Flemish clothes, which he traded for leather, skins and textiles from the Balkans and the Levant. ASVat, Arm. XLI, Vol. 11, Doc. 909; *Ibid.*, Vol. 13, Doc. 475.

9. B. RAVID, *A tale of three Cities, and their Raison d'Etat: Ancona, Venice, Livorno and the Competition for Jewish Merchants in the Sixteenth Century*, «Jewish Political Studies Review», VI, 1994, pp. 83-134: 144; See the discussion in the fundamental study by B. ARBEL, *Trading Nations, Jews and Venetian in the Early Modern Eastern Mediterranean*, E.J Brill, Leiden and NewYork 1995, pp. 3-6.

10. Cfr. LEONI, *La Diplomazia Estense*, p.308.

attractive, Ercole was prepared to offer the would-be newcomers unprecedented concessions in the field of religious freedom. The Marranos who
settled in Ferrara enjoyed greater freedom than was currently available in
other Christian States. Not only could they openly return to Judaism; they
were tacitly allowed to approach their forefathers' religion at whatever
time they wanted.[11]

Among the first Portuguese who moved to Ferrara, there were important merchants such as Duarte and Bastião Pinto, Estevão Pires and
Bastião Vas: the very ones who had played an important role in developing the commercial lane between Antwerp and Ancona. They wanted to
reward the Duke for his concessions and used their experience, skills and
commercial relationships for the purpose of including Ferrara into the
new trade route.

The religious tolerance granted by the duke offered another advantage: Ferrara was the only Italian city where the Portuguese merchants
could employ their former baptismal names in their commercial dealings
while using their Jewish appellatives in their private and communal life.
The Marranos who had openly reverted to Judaism in Ancona could not
use their Jewish names in their commercial dealings with Antwerp without running the risk of having their merchandise confiscated by the imperial police, and it was not advisable for them to use their former baptismal
names in the papal city. In (or around) 1538, the Portuguese merchants of
Antwerp started to appoint Marrano factors and agents in Ferrara who
received the goods dispatched from Flanders under their Christian names,
and then forwarded them to the final destinees in Ancona in whatever way
they wanted.

Between 1538 and 1541, at least twenty Portuguese families settled
in Ferrara and joined the Spanish Community, which was officially
renamed "Università degli Ebrei Spagnoli e Portoghesi". A few years
later, owing to the continuous influx of new Portuguese elements, the
Sephardic settlement became known as the Portuguese Nation. A few
"Levantine" Jews from Venice, Ancona and Ragusa joined. The
Portuguese of Ferrara imported extra-fine clothes and precious stones
from Northern Europe, which they traded for Balkan products. They also
established (or rather maintained) direct links with the New Christian
merchants of Lisbon and Porto, from whom they received sugar and other

---

11. Emblematic is the case of Duarte Gomes who openly professed that he was Jewish
only in 1570, twenty years after his arrival in Ferrara.

colonial products, in much the same way as they had been doing previously while living in London and Antwerp. Other Portuguese opened artisan shops, often in partnership with local Jews and even with Christians.

In 1541, when the Jews were expelled from the Kingdom of Naples, Don Samuel Abravanel moved to Ferrara along with his sons and son-in-law. They were primarily engaged in banking and other financial activities, but they soon became involved in the international trade between Northern Europe and the Levant, and played a major role in the development of the Ferrarese economy. The Ducal Treasury took part in this trade and the Duke established several joint ventures with the Portuguese Jews, engaging in commerce between Western Europe and the Levant, and "in every other sort of trade for whatever purpose". At this point, Ercole's dream of transforming his city into a commercial center had come true. In the space of a few years, Ferrara became a well-established transit-entrepôt in the trade route linking London and Antwerp with Ancona and the Levant.

As Jonathan Israel has noted, it was the success of the Ferrarese policy towards the Marranos that induced the Venetian Republic to grant the famous charter allowing the Levantine Jews to settle in the "Ghetto Vecchio" in 1541. As the Senate expressly stated, the trade with Upper and Lower Romania (as the Balkans were called at the time) had been diverted from the Serenissima and had passed into the hands of the Jewish merchants of Ancona [and Ferrara].

The new Portuguese immigrants set up several commercial companies in partnership with the duke of Ferrara. In 1550 an important factory for the production of woollen *panina* was created around the Castello Nuovo, on the banks of the river Po. In 1556 the Duke of Ferrara established a new company for the production and trade of extra-fine woollen cloth together with Henrique Nunes (Abraham Benvenisti) who was described as a "magnificent, generous and noble gentleman" and a rich merchant endowed with greatest technical knowledge and entrepreneurial skills.[12] Abraham managed the factory in accordance with the modern industrial standards set by English and Flemish manufacturers. Thus the Ferrara typical scarlet, black and variously colored textiles came to occupy an important place in the range of Western products destined for the Levantine markets. The factory on the banks of the River Po employed

---

12. ASFe, not. Maurelio Taurino, Matr. 535, *pacco* 14, July 30 1556.

700 people directly, and provided work for as many artisans who carried out various technical processes in their workshops.

Another Abraham Benveniste (*alias* Agostinho Henriques), Henrique's brother in law, represented the Portuguese Nation of Ferrara in its financial dealings with the Ducal Government.[13]

In or around 1570 the Enriques-Benveniste left Italy and moved to Salonica.[14]

---

13. ASMo, Camera Ducale, *Cassa Vecchia Segreta*, folder 12, passim.
14. P. C. IOLY ZORATTINI, *Processi* III, 1570-1572, p. 263.

§ 10. The Blockade of the Road of Trent and the Boycott of Ferrara (Summer 1541)

As we have already seen, in 1539, the "commissioner" Johannes Vuysting established his headquarter in Pavia. He also set up checkpoints at the main river-ports of Lombardy. All the goods in transit were carefully inspected and the merchandise suspected of belonging to New Christians was seized. No distinction was made between the so-called "*malos Christianos*" [i.e. Judaizers] and other, "good" *conversos*. The mere fact of being Portuguese was considered an offence. Their merchandise was impounded regardless of its destination. In principle, only the goods dispatched to the Levant were liable to be seized. Nevertheless, Vuysting seized all the merchandise directed to Ferrara, as well as a great part of the goods dispatched to Ancona and Venice.

At this point the Portuguese of Antwerp took some precautions. They diverted their commercial traffic to Trent, across the Brenner-Pass. From here their goods were dispatched along the Adige River (under Venetian sovereignty) and the Po River, thus completely avoiding Spanish-controlled Lombardy. They disguised their deliveries under the trademarks of Italian merchants, such as Guicciardini and Affaitati. The traffic via this alternative route became so intense that it could not remain unnoticed.

Trent was governed by the local bishop, who was a vassal of Ferdinand of Habsburg, the "Roman King," as the Emperor elect was called.[1] In the summer of 1541, Johannes Vuysting and his men moved to Trent, where they set up roadblocks and seized all the goods dispatched to Ferrara and ports on the Adriatic Coast. The traffic through the Brenner Pass was completely blocked, thus causing serious losses to the

---

1. *Brockhaus Enziklopädie*, VI, Wiesbaden 1968, p. 144. In 1522 the administration of the Austrian *hereditary* lands of the House of Habsburg had been transferred to Ferdinand. See R.A. KANN, *A History of the Habsburg*, p. 10; J. A. VILAR SÁNCHEZ. *Dos procesos dinasticos paralelos en la decada de 1520: Carlos V y su hermano Fernando I*, «Hispania» LX, 2000, pp. 835-852.

Portuguese Nations of Ferrara and Ancona, to Duke Ercole II[2], who was variously associated with Portuguese merchants, and even to many others who had little or nothing to do with the *Marranos*.

The Burgomaster of Antwerp, pressed by the merchants of his city, sent a remonstrance[3] to the Regent, complaining that the merchandise of many of them had been blocked at Trent. He averred that these goods belonged to good Christians who had no commercial relationship, neither with Jews nor with *Marranos*. Among the petitioners was Daniel de Bomberg; the well-known publisher of Hebrew books in Venice. Towards the end of May 1541, Ercole II sent a written protest to Seigneur de Granvelle[4], asking for the release of the goods seized in Trent. In a follow up letter, the Duke outspokenly condemned the behavior of the imperial agents and branded it as contrary to good manners, diplomatic practice and the common sense of justice.

On July 25, 1541, Pope Paul III urged Christopher Madruzzo, the bishop-governor of Trent to restore to some merchants in Ancona 180 bales of western[5] clothes impounded under the pretext that they belonged to *Marranos* and infidels.[6]

Neither the Pope nor the Duke admitted in their letters that the addressees of the seized goods were Jews. On the contrary, the Duke

---

2. The Duke had established several trading ventures together with prominent Sephardic merchants. See A. di LEONE LEONI, *La Diplomazia Estense*, pp. 318-322; IDEM, *La Nation Portughesa corteggiata privilegiata, espulsa e riammessa a Ferrara (1538-1550)*, «Italia», XIII-XV, 2001, pp. 211-247.

3. AGR, PEA 560, June 4, 1541. See A. di LEONE LEONI, *Alcuni esempi di quotidiana imprenditorialità tra Ferrara Ancona e Venezia nel XVI secolo*, «Zakhor» IV, 2000, pp. 57-114: p. 108.

4. In 1541 Nicolas Perrenot, Seigneur de Granvelle, was the most influential member of Charles V's Privy Council and Secretary of State. See *Brockhaus Enziklopädie*, Vol. 7, Wiesbaden 1969, p. 562; K. de JONGE and G. JANSSENS, *Les Granvelle*, pp. 11-17.

5. Italian merchants described English and Flemish clothes as "western" .

6. S. SIMONSOHN, *The Apostolic See and the Jews, Documents 1539-1545*, The Pontifical Institute of Mediaeval Studies, Toronto 1990, pp. 2231-2232, Doc. 2047 where the Latin text is published *in extenso* and an English summary is provided. The Author (or his assistants) stated that the "western" clothes had been dispatched from Ancona to Antwerp but the contrary was true. Cf. SIMONSOHN, *Apostolic See, History*, Toronto 1991, p. 447. In realty the blockade was mainly unidirectional and affected especially the goods dispatched from Northern Europe to Italy and the Levant.

stated that they were Christian merchants belonging to noble Florentine families.[7]

When it was evident that his letters were not obtaining any result, the Duke sent a special envoy to Regensburg in order to convey a protest to the Emperor. After weeks of wearying negotiations, the envoy, together with the ambassador resident, succeeded in getting from the Emperor and the Roman King letters instructing the bishop of Trent to release the impounded goods.[8]

In a letter addressed to Nicolas de Granvelle, Queen Mary wondered why the Duke of Ferrara had intervened in favor of the New Christians. The Duke was evidently driven by the hope of gaining some hidden profit. If this had been the case, would it not be better to keep the Portuguese – and the profit – for the Emperor?[9] Until then, neither the Queen nor the Emperor had realized the usefulness of enterprising merchants.

In the meantime, Ercole II dispatched two envoys to Milan: Gerolamo Maretta and Salomon de la Ripa, an Ashkenazi Jew whom the Duke had appointed "gentleman" and a "familiar" of his court.[10] Marquis del Vasto, the Spanish governor of Milan, gave a warm welcome to the ducal envoys and granted a general safe-conduct for all the Portuguese in transit through Lombardy, on the condition that they could prove that they were en route to Ferrara in order to settle there. However, at least formally, Vuysting was not subject to the governor's authority and he continued to seize the goods belonging to the New Christians.

In 1542, Duke Ercole II sent his representatives to Milan again. They charged Vuysting with misappropriation of goods belonging to several merchants of Ferrara. The infamous commissioner was arrested by order

---

7. This was an allusion to the Guicciardini who had established in Ferrara a subsidiary branch of their company. They had also set up a commercial company together with the Ducal Chamber.

8. ASMo, CD, Estero, Ambasciatori Germania, Buste 4, 5. A. di LEONE LEONI, *Quotidiana imprenditorialità* pp. 82-84.

9. GR, PEA 204, ff. 5r-7r: October 10, 1541: Queen Mary to Lord of Granvelle. See Document 28 in Appendix.

10. On Salomon de la Ripa see A. di LEONE LEONI, *Per una storia della Nazione Tedesca di Ferrara nel Cinquecento*, «RMI» LXII, 1996, pp. 137-166: 149-150; IDEM, *Quotidiana Imprenditorialità,* p. 67.

of the Spanish governor and remained in prison for some time.[11] Salomon
della Ripa was allowed to stay in Milan as long as necessary to verify the
inventories of the goods illegally seized.[12]

As we shall see, Marquis del Vasto's favorable attitude towards the
New Christians of Antwerp was in accord with the new position provisionally adopted by the Emperor.

11. In 1544 Johannes Vuysting was appointed once again as sub-commissary *contra
malos christianos*. BM, Colmar, liasse GG 170, June 20, 1544: Jorgen von Laxon was
appointed Commissioner, Johannes Vuysting sub-commissioner. In 1547 he was involved
in the arrest and interrogations of Portuguese émigrès at Colmar. See X. MOSSMANN, *Une
épisode inédit de l'histoire des juifs de Portugal* «Archives israélites», XXVII 1866, pp.
1043-1048, 1089-1094. M. GINSBURGER *Des Marranes à Colmar*, «REJ» LXXXIII, 1927,
pp. 53-58; K. von GREYERZ, *Quelques aspects de la politique ibérique envers les
minorités religieuses: des conversos portugais en Haute Alsace en 1547*, «Revue
d'Alsace» CXVII, 1990-91, pp. 53-70; SALOMON-LEONI, *Mendes, Benveniste*, p. 173; G.
NAHON, *L'impact de l'expulsion d'Espagne sur la comunauté Juive de l'Ancienne France,
1550-1791* «Archives Juives, Revue Historique», 1980, pp. 94-105: 95-96.
12. A. di LEONE LEONI, *La Diplomazia Estense*, pp. 313-314.

§ 11. The 1537 Privilege of the Portuguese Nation of Antwerp Reconfirmed in 1542

In 1542, the Portuguese of Antwerp started negotiations with the Court and obtained a truce: they persuaded Charles V to overturn his policy and to put back in force the privileges granted to the New Christians in 1537.[1] In his *"confirmatory decree"*, he stated that many New Christians had been persecuted and their goods seized on the pretext that they were Jews, *Marranos* and heretics: therefore depriving them of all rights. These charges turned out to be groundless, so the 1537 decree was re-instated and reinforced.[2]

On March 11, 1542, Queen Mary ordered the Fiscal Receiver of Zeeland to set free all the New Christians he might have apprehended and to release all their belongings for free, without bail. In the future, he could proceed against them only on the ground of concrete evidence. A few days later, the Queen dispatched to the reluctant officer a copy of the 1537 decree in favor of the New Christians and instructed him to comply with it.[3]

The leaders of the Portuguese Nation of Antwerp took advantage of these (provisionally) favorable circumstances and asked the Queen-Regent to intervene in favor of their compatriots arrested in London on several accounts, including the secret practice of Judaism and illegal immigration.

Before we deal with these developments we shall attempt to describe the Portuguese Nation in London at the time of King Henry VIII.

---

1. LAURENT et LAMEERE, *Ordonnances des Pays-Bas*, Vol. IV, pp. 10-11, Edict of February 27 1536 [1537, Style de la Court] allowing the New Christians of Portugal to settle in Antwerp.
2. AGR, OFB, 160/1233/2, March 10, 1541 [1542]. See Document 31 in Appendix.
3. AGR, PEA reg. 129, f. 164r, March 11 1541 [1542]. The same instructions were issued a few days later in a broader form, AGR, PEA, 1627, March 22, 1541 [1542].

§ 12. The Portuguese settlement in Tudor London (1540-1543)

From a notarized deed drawn up in Ferrara, we learn about a group of Portuguese merchants living in London in the 1520's. In 1546, João Dias, the son of the late Simon, stated that, before settling in Ferrara [date unspecified], he had lived in London for many years. In 1523, he married Eleanor Nuñes and received from her mother, Messia, a dowry worth two hundred pounds ("which came to eight-hundred golden Italian ducats"). The marriage contract was registered by Master John de Verus (name unclear on deed), public notary in London.[1] Two Iberian gentlemen: one Johannes de Catia, a Spaniard, and Alvaro Pinto,[2] a *Lusitanian*, acted as witnesses.

On September 6, 1546, in Ferrara, João Dias reported that his wife Eleanor had lost her marriage contract. On his mother in-law's request, he now acknowledged that he had received, *illo tempore*, the said amount of money, as Eleanor's dowry.[3]

In his pioneering study, Lucien Wolf provided thorough information on the composition of the Portuguese settlement in Tudor London in 1540.[4] Since then, to the best of my knowledge, no substantial new contribution has come to light, with the remarkable exception of an important

---

1. Apparently the papers drawn up by this notary are no longer extant.
2. ASFe, not G. Conti, *pacco* 4, Jan. 21, 1551: Alvaro Pinto had departed from this life in Antwerp "annis elapsis": apparently before 1543 as his estate was entrusted to Diogo Mendes. He was survived by his sons: Guillermo, Roberto and Thomas (who later died in London) and by a daughter, Anna. On January 21, 1551, in Ferrara, Guillermo acknowledged that he had received the whole amount of his father's property from the Heirs of Francisco and Diogo Mendes.
3. ASFe, not G. Conti, *pacco* 2, Sept. 6, 1546.
4. L. WOLF, *Tudor England, cit.*

study by Edgar Samuel[5] who provides, *inter alia*, tacit adjustments to some of Wolf's assumptions[6]and new information on the composition of the *Marrano* settlement in London.

Like many scholars of his time, Wolf gave only vague indications of his sources. Cecil Roth expressed the hope of seeing these documents published. I am trying to accomplish, at least in part, this scholar's desire by transcribing two documents extensively that have already been perused by Wolf: copies of Gaspar Lopes' interrogations (held in Pavia on December 24 and 27, 1540).[7] The first deposition contains a long list of Portuguese New Christians living in Lisbon, Antwerp and London. The latter document[8] is specifically devoted to the Portuguese settlement in London. It provides information on the role of Luis Lopes[9], who was identified as a leader of the Nation and a member of the Rescue Organization. According to the deponent, Luis Lopes produced silk buttons and other ornaments. He housed a secret synagogue in his home that was frequented by up to twenty people every Saturday. Luis provided hospitality to the *conversos* arriving in his city and helped them to continue their journey to Antwerp and the Levant, or to remain in London if they preferred to do so.[10] As we have already seen, another Portuguese of London, António de la Ronha, performed a prominent role in the Rescue Organization. António was married to Anna Pinta[11] and, therefore, was

---

5. E. SAMUEL, *London Portuguese Jewish Community: 1540-1753*, in *From Strangers to Citizens, The Integration of Immigrant Communities in Britain, Ireland and Colonial America, 1550-1750*, edited by R. VIGNE and C. LITTLETON, Brighton and Portland 2001, pp. 239-245.

6. For instance: EDGAR SAMUEL (*locum cit.*) diplomatically avoids mentioning the "expulsion" which, according to L. WOLF (*Tudor England*, pp. 82-83) took place in 1542.

7. To the best of my knowledge, there is no mention of these documents in the folders of *Wolf's Papers*, kept at the UCL, Watson Manuscript Library.

8. AGR, *Codazzi File*, Dec. 24, 1540: Gaspar Lopes' deposition. See Document 19 in Appendix.

9. No family relationship between Luis and Gaspar Lopes is known. Lopes was a very common family name.

10. Cfr. L. WOLF, *Tudor England*, p. 81.

11. In the 16th century, Portuguese [as well as Italian] surnames were declined and had masculine/feminine, singular/plural endings.

Duarte and Bastião Rodrigues Pinto's brother-in law. [12] We do not know whether Diego de la Ronha, also living in London, was related to António.

Between the end of 1540 and the beginning of 1542, the Portuguese colony of London grew apace. In fact, in a period when the New Christians of Antwerp were persecuted and newcomers were arrested at their arrival in the ports of Zeeland, many refugees interrupted their journey in England and remained in London waiting for better times. Other émigrés chose the city as their permanent residence.

Prominent among the new arrivals was Elizabeth Rodrigues,[13] widow of Jorge Anes, who arrived in London in 1540, with her family, household, goods and merchandise.[14] Her son, Gonçalvo, married a Portuguese New Christian, Constance, the daughter of Simon Ruis. They had fourteen children and practiced Judaism in the privacy of their home.[15]

The increased size of the colony did not remain unnoticed. In January 1542, the English Privy Council ordered the apprehension of "the New Christians who came from Portugal, and the attachment of their property".[16]

By a fortunate coincidence, the persecution in London started at a time when the Portuguese colony in Antwerp was enjoying some respite. As a result of negotiations carried out at the court of Brussels, the Emperor was on the point of reinstating the privileges granted in 1537 to

---

12. Curiously enough the name of Sebastian (Bastião) Rodrigues Pinto appears three times in a list of the Portuguese of London drawn up by L. WOLF (*Tudor England*, pp. 78-79). The author enumerated: a) Rodrigo Pinto, brother-in-law of Antonio de la Rogna [Ronha]; b) Sebastian Rodrigues; c) Sebastian Rodriguo Pinto. It was always the same person. L. WOLF was probably misled by contrasting information on Sebastian's age provided by different testimonies, which did not always state his full name.

13. The Anes family is not mentioned in the witness testimony of Gaspar Lopes who had already left London at the time of Elisabeth's arrival.

14. E. SAMUEL, *London Portuguese Jewish Community*.

15. See E. SAMUEL, *locum cit.*

16. P. GAYANGOS, Ed., *Calendar of Letters and Despatches and State Papers relating to the negotiations between England and Spain preserved in the Archives in Simanca Vienna, Brussels and elsewhere under the direction of the master of the Rolls, (Henry VIII, 1542-43)*, London 1890-1895, Part I, p. 467, doc. 229, Jan. 29, 1542: Eustace Chapuys (Spanish Ambassador in London) to Seigneur de Granvelle: «this king has lately ordered the arrest and imprisonment of the New Christians who came from Portugal and that, most likely, however they may sing, they will not be able to fly away from their cages without leaving part of their feathers behind.» Cfr. E. SAMUEL, *London's Portuguese Jewish Community*.

the New Christians. Thanks to these favorable circumstances, the leaders of the Nation approached the Queen-Regent and asked her help in favor of their compatriots in London. Individual merchants asked her to intervene on their behalf in order to obtain the release of seized merchandize. This was the case of Christovão Garcia. He complained that goods in the hands of Master Diego, his factor in London, were apprehended and that Diego had been accused of heresy. Queen Mary sent a letter to this effect to the English Ambassador in Brussels.[17] In the same period, she requested the Spanish Ambassador in London[18] to intervene on behalf of Antonio Duarte, "a resident of Antwerp",[19] whose merchandise (sugar, in this case) was also confiscated.

On March 10, 1543, Eustace Chapuys informed the Queen that: «certain Portuguese, who had been arrested on the charge of Judaism, had been actually released from prison and their confiscated property restored to them». The Ambassador claimed that this had been done mainly out of respect and consideration for him. The prisoners, in fact, were the same in whose favor Queen Mary, as well as the King and the Queen of Portugal, had written to the ambassador "a few months earlier".[20] This apparently was the end of the short-lived persecutions in London.

Lucien Wolf wondered whether the 1542 arrests in London were related to the depositions of Gaspar Lopes and other prisoners in Milan [i.e. Pavia]. I would exclude this hypothesis for two reasons. The notarized copies of the interrogations of Gaspar Lopes and other Portuguese held in Pavia's jails were authenticated on January 14, 1542, by the Chancellor of the Imperial Senate of Milan and, thereafter, sent to the Emperor who later (summer 1542) forwarded a copy to the Queen-Regent.[21] By the time these documents reached the Emperor, the *Marranos* of London had already been seized. Furthermore, should Queen Mary (or the Emperor) have denounced the Portuguese of London, she then would not have been in a position to intervene in their favor.

---

17. AGR, PEA 1537, March 10, 1542: Queen Mary to the English ambassador in Brussels; L. WOLF, *Tudor England,* p. 77.

18. AGR, PEA 1627, March 28 1541 [1542]: Queen Mary to Eustace Chapuys.

19. L. WOLF (*Tudor England,* p. 77) stated that Duarte "escaped to Antwerp". I could not find any evidence that Duarte had previously lived in London.

20. P. GAYANGOS, Edit., *Calendar of Letters,* Part II, p. 270, Doc. 114, March 10, 1543: Eustace Chapuys to Queen Mary.

21. AGR, PEA 53, July 15, 1542. Charles V to Mary of Habsburg. See Document 33 in Appendix.

Diogo Pires gave a rather simplified account of this or, possibly, of another similar episode. In his letter to Paolo Giovio,[22] the poet stated that the Portuguese colony in London maintained a sumptuous and magnificent standard of living. This had aroused the jealousy of some petty officers, who accused them [of some unspecified wrongdoing]. The Portuguese could, however, prove their innocence and were set free. Diogo stated that he personally attended a public session in which the King of England addressed the Portuguese living in London, cleared them of every charge and advised them to adopt a less conspicuous way of life without attracting too much attention to themselves. From other parts of the document it can be inferred that the episode happened in, or around, 1543.[23]

England again became the destination of Portuguese immigrants in 1544, when Charles V reversed his temporarily favorable policy towards the New Christians of Antwerp.[24] Several newcomers arrested in Antwerp, in 1544, stated that they had relatives in England.[25] Others moved to London from Antwerp for business purposes.

The relationship between the Portuguese Nations in the two cities was very close and many documents are found relating to persons who subsequently lived in either place. For instance, Henrico de Tovar attended the secret synagogue in London in the fifteen-thirties. In 1544 he lived in Antwerp where he gave hospitality to Duarte de Tovar and Luis Gomes.[26] On the other hand, one Thomas Pinto moved from Antwerp to London where he later died without leaving a will.[27]

---

22. BNUE,Mo, Fondo Estense, MS Alfa 06,15, ff. 161r-162v: *Diogo Pires to Paolo Giovio;* cf. C. A. ANDRÉ, *Um judeu no desterro: Diogo Pires e a memória de Portugal,* Universidade de Coimbra 1992, pp. 158-164.

23. According to his account, Diogo Pires had read Luis Namias' [unpublished] chronicles of the Portuguese military expedition in Northern Africa. As the Arabs had kept Luis prisoner for two years after the fall of the Portuguese strongholds, he could not be in London before 1543.

24. See *infra* § 13 and § 14.

25. LUCIEN WOLF (*Tudor England*, p. 77) listed their names.

26. AGR, OFB, 160/1233/2: undated [1544] statement: «Duarte de Tovar e Luis Guomes de Porto de Portugal, vimdos na não Samto Amtonio [*sic*] capitão o Senhor Guaramatão Feles, pera fazer suas mercadorjas pera emcontinente tornar pera Portugal em companhia darmada na não Samta Maria ... alogiados nesta vila dem[ver]es na pousada de Anrjque de Tovar.»

27. ASFe. not. G. Conti, January 12, 1552. Apparently Thomas moved to England after 1543.

Sebastian Pinto informs Duke Ercole II that many Portuguese of Antwerp are willing to come to Ferrara and are devoting their energies to the Rescue Organization at great risk to their personal safety. Antwerp October 15, 1538.
Source: ASMo, *Cancelleria Ducale, Lettere Particolari*, Folder 1219.

A map of the British Channel with London and Antwerp facing each other in central position.
From Lodovico Guicciardini, *Descrittione di tutti i Paesi Bassi*, Reprint, Antwerp 1567.

§ 13. A sudden change in the Emperor's attitude towards the Portuguese of Antwerp

The Emperor's favorable disposition towards the New Christians, expressed in the 1542 safe-conduct, did not last long. In (or around) June of 1542, during a stay in the Low Countries, he ordered the Margrave of Antwerp to investigate the conduct of those Portuguese merchants who «were suspected of financing the emigration of people who pretended to go to Ferrara and Venice, but in reality went to the Levant». In fact, several Portuguese émigrés imprisoned in Pavia and Milan had confessed that they were not on their way to Ferrara and Venice, as they had alleged, but were planning to take up residence in Turkey. On July 15, 1542, Charles V addressed a complaint to the Margrave, arguing that no measure had been taken.[1]

In 1543, Diogo Mendes suddenly died. Queen Mary immediately sent her agents to seize the accounting books of the House of Mendes and ordered an inventory of his assets.[2] João Micas[3] persuaded the Regent to reverse her orders by offering her a one-year interest-free loan of 100.000 Flemish Pounds.[4] This was the first act of a long tug of war between Charles V, Queen Mary, and the heirs of Francisco and Diogo Mendes. For a long period, the Emperor and his sister spent most of their energies on no purpose other than the expropriation, by hook or by crook, of a substantial part of the Mendes' estate.[5]

---

1. AGR, PEA, reg. 53, ff. 209r-210r, July15, 1542: Charles V to Queen Mary, IDEM to the Margrave.
2. AGR, PEA 1633, July 7, 1543: Queen Mary orders to draw up the inventory of Diogo Mendes' «Maison mortuaire».
3. João was Diogo Mendes's nephew and testamentary executor. Cfr. SALOMON-LEONI, *Mendes, Benveniste*, p. 152.
4. AGR, PEA 1633, July 17, 1543, the Queen grants *"main levée et pleine jouissance des biens saisiz"*.
5. J. REZNIK, *Le Duc de Naxos*, pp. 52-72; P. GRUNEBAUM BALLIN, *Joseph Nasi Duc de Naxos*, Paris 1968, pp. 34-43; SALOMON-LEONI. *Mendes, Benveniste*, p. 155.

§ 14. New Arrests in Antwerp (1543-1544)

In August 1543, in proximity to the town of Lierre, the police inspected two wagons loaded with "some merchants of the Portuguese Nation, together with their wives and children": about twenty persons altogether. They were travelling towards Luxemburg and Strasburg where they planned to reach Basel *"par la route d'Allemagne"* (by way of German Lands). As they were not provided with the special safe-conduct necessary in wartime, they were taken to the local police station. Matthieu Strict, a high-ranking officer, was dispatched to the site to carry out an appropriate inquiry.[1] From his report to the Queen-Regent[2] we learn the prisoners' names. They were: Francisco Mennis,[3] Emanuel Alvares,[4] Garcia Martines,[5] and Emanuel Rodrigues.[6] Alvares was a physician; the

---

1. AGR, PEA 1633, August 31, 1543: file comprising the examinations of two wagon-drivers.
2. *Ibid.*
3. A native of Lisbon, 30 years old, Mennis had settled in Antwerp a few years earlier. After suffering heavy losses due to the shipwreck of a Portuguese vessel, he was now looking for better opportunities in Italy. He maintained that he was a good Christian. His children had been baptised in Saint George's Church in Antwerp.
4. Emanuel Alvares, 42 years old, a native of Evora in Portugal, a doctor, was leaving Antwerp for financial reasons, after a four years' stay.
5. Garcia Martines, sixty years old, was born in Spain. He was taken to Portugal [in 1492] when he was a small child. He left Lisbon in (or around) 1541, and broke his journey off in England, where he sold some merchandise and received a bill of exchange on Antwerp. At the moment of his arrest, he was travelling with his wife and a child whom he had fathered from a slave. AGR, OFB 160/1233/2; L. WOLF, *Tudor England,* p. 78.
6. Emanuel Rodrigues, forty-three years old, apparently unmarried, was travelling with two sisters to Venice, where he hoped to marry them off. He had left Portugal in (or around) 1537, and had lived one and half years in London before coming to Antwerp. AGR, OFB 160/1233/2; See also WOLF, *Tudor England,* p. 78. On November 2, 1551, in Ferrara (possibly the same) Manoel Rodrigues and his wife, Gracia de Lima, entrusted Simon Luisio, living in Lisbon, with the task of selling a house belonging to Gracia. ASFe, not. G. Conti, *pacco 4, sub data.*

others were modest merchants who stated that they wanted to go to Italy in the hope of finding better economic opportunities. An old woman said that she was accompanying her daughter to Venice where she was to meet her husband. Christovão Manoel was a young bachelor, in Mennis' service.[7] All the prisoners maintained that they were good Christians and stated that their departure was dictated only by economic reasons.

In June 1544, dozens of new immigrants reached the port of Veere on board vessels of the Royal Portuguese Fleet. Many of these passengers managed to reach Antwerp on carriages previously hired by the *Men of the Nation of Antwerp*, who provided the newcomers with accommodation in the city.

Local policemen arrested other refugees at Veere when it appeared that they were not provided with a Portuguese royal licence. Among these prisoners was Agnes Gomes,[8] the wife of Diego Fernandes Netto, the former agent of the New Christians at the Papal Court.[9] She was travelling with a dozen relatives: her mother (Messia Fernandes[10]), her brother Aires,[11] her sister Branca Gomes[12], and her sister-in-law Leonora Fernandes[13] who was travelling with her children. It is not clear whether a certain Hector Dias and his wife, who were also on the same ship,

---

7. After having spent a few months in London, Christovão Manoel settled in Antwerp and lived in the house of [his father] Emanuel Pinhero. (See below § 21.22). Manoel later entered Beatriz Mendes' service and became one of her most trusted agents.

8. Agnes Gomes was the daughter of the late Emanuel Gomes and Messia Fernandes. AGR, OFB, 160/1233/2, July 25, 1544: official report of examinations signed by Pierre de Fief and Jacomo de la Torre.

9. A. HERCULANO, *History of the Origin*, p. 474, 519, 522; S. SIMONSOHN, *The Apostolic See, History*, p. 398.

10. Messia Fernandes, daughter of Fernando Peres and of Anna Vas, widow of Manoel Gomes, was the mother of Agnes Gomes [and Diego Fernandes Netto' s mother-in-law]. AGR, OFB, 160/1233/2, July 25 1544: Official report of examinations by Pierre de Fief, and Jacques de la Torre.

11. AGR, *Information 1544*, f. 5r: Interrogation of Alvaro Bras, a Portuguese [apparently Old Christian] carter; AGR, OFB, 160/1233/3, Aug. 9,1544. Confession of Ruy Gomes (Aires' brother): Ruy had arrived in Antwerp from Rome, together with Diego Fernandes Netto.

12. Branca Gomes, [age not stated], unmarried. AGR, OFB, 160/1233/2, July 25, 1544: Official report of interrogations.

13. Leonora Fernandes, twenty-seven or twenty-eight years old, was the daughter of Alvarez Fernandes and Isabella Oliveri [Diego Netto's sister] and the widow of the physician Henrique de Nigro. AGR, OFB, 160/1233/3, July 25, 1544: Report of examinations by Pierre de Fief and Jacques de la Torre.

belonged to Agnes Gomes' company. Diego Netto had arrived a few days earlier from Rome to meet his wife.[14] He was provided with a papal brief granting his family protection from any form of persecution, even charges of heresy or apostasy.[15] When the Governor of Veere saw this safe-conduct,[16] he ordered Agnes Gomes and her family to be set free.

João Micas and Agostinho Henriques, who acted as representatives of the Portuguese Nation in Antwerp, interceded on behalf of their countrymen with the Governor of Veere and obtained the release of all the prisoners.[17] A ship was hired in order to transport them from Veere to Antwerp. Among the passengers were important merchants, such as the *licenciado*, Manoel Renel[18] [later known as Abraham Abendana][19] who travelled with his wife Lianor Henriques, [Doña Benveniste][20], the daughter of Nuño Henriques, and their two children. They were given hospitality in the house of Agostinho Henriques.[21] Other prominent arrivals were: Duarte Rodrigues,[22] Jorge d'Andrade, Jorge Rodrigues,

---

14. *Ibid.*, August 9, 1544: Report of examinations of Ruy Gomes (Agnes' brother and Diego Netto's brother-in-law). Ruy had arrived from Rome together with Diego Netto. *Ibid.*, August 1, 1544: report of examination of Diego Netto.

15. The papal brief was granted when Diego Netto was acting as ambassador of the Portuguese New Christians in Rome, in order to prevent the Inquisition from taking revenge on his family. The privilege had been revoked in 1542, when Diego was arrested in Rome on the charge of Judaizing. Cf. S. Simonsohn, *The Apostolic See, History*, cit. p. 398.

16. It is not clear whether the document was handed over to the governor by Diego Netto or by João Micas and Agostinho Henriques. See *infra*.

17. AGR, *Information 1544*, f. 14v: deposition of Manoel Carneyro, master of the ship San Antonio.

18. Renel: also spelled Reinel or Reiner. Manoel was the son of Bras Reinel [Isac Abendana].

19. ASFe, not. Giacomo Conti, *pacco* 16, October 16, 1579, *Absolutio pro domino Santos* [Scmtob] *de Tovar a domino Λbraam Bendana*: «Λbraam Bendana alias nuncupatus fuit Emanuel Reinellus, hebreus Nationis Portugallensis Ferrariae morantis». In 1552, Abraam (Abraham) served as Parnas of the Portuguese Nation of Ferrara. ASFe, not. Giacomo Conti, *pacco* 13S, Dec. 21 1572.

20. From a notary deed drawn up in Ferrara we learn that Lianor had been promised a 3,000 ducats dowry. On January 8, 1560 the "magnificent lady Leonora", wife of Manuel Reiner acknowledged that she had duly received this amount from her mother. ASFe, not. Andrea Coccapani, Matr. 534, *pacco* 10, *sub data*.

21. AGR, *Information 1544*, f. 28v, deposition of Pedro Fernandis, pilot of a Portuguese ship.

22. AGR, OFB, 160/1233/3, July 31, 1544, *Confession of Duarte Rodrigues*. A native of Belmonte, Duarte was the son of the late Ruy D'Andrade and of Branca Nuñes, and the husband of Beatriz Rodrigues. He had a legitimate son called Rodriguo and a small "bastard" (the son of a servant) called António. He had brought three bales of Indian cloth with him.

Emanuel Lopes[23], the licenciate Denis Nuñes[24] and Sebastião Fernandes.[25] Not all the newcomers were rich: some were modest workmen or, even, peasants. Others, who had been wealthy, had had their property seized, or stolen, or had otherwise lost them during the journey.

On June 25, 1544, the Emperor issued a decree against «those who claim to be Christians but in reality are Jews complying with Judaic law». Orders were directed to the Margrave of Antwerp to arrest all New Christians who had arrived in the city after the middle of May 1544. The inhabitants of Antwerp were summoned to expose the newcomers and their property. Those who would help the immigrants in hiding their belongings would be condemned to pay the equivalent value of the hidden goods. Those who would smuggle any New Christians out of the city were to be condemned to arbitrary corporal and financial pains.[26]

At the end of June 1544, in Antwerp, scores of Portuguese immigrants were rounded up with their families and imprisoned in local jails. Even three students, who were known to be attending courses at the University of Louvain, were arrested.[27] A special commission[28] was set up with the task of inquiring into the conduct of the newcomers, and the reasons and methods adopted to escape from Portugal. Particular attention was to be paid to the cost of their journey from Lisbon to the Low Countries, and to the activities of the Rescue Committee who planned and funded their travel. The trustees of the *Bôlsa da Esmolas* (also called *Sedaca*[29]) were to be sought out, and their property seized.

The prisoners were kept in jail indefinitely without holding regular trials or calling them to account. In September 1544, about twenty prisoners asked to be released on bail. Each of them offered varying sums of

---

23. This Emanuel Lopes is not to be confused with Manuel Lopes Bichacho, with whom we have dealt with extensively *above*.
24. *Ibid.* Confession of Denis Nuñes, July 30, 1544.
25. AGR,PEA 1177, September 10, 1544; AGR,OFB 160/1233/2, Sept. 11, 1544.
26. AGR, PEA reg. 1089, f. 230: copy on parchment with imperial seal in AGR, OFB, 160/1233/2.
27. AGR, PEA 132, July 22, 1544: Corneille Scepperus to the Queen; AGR, OFB 160/1233/3 undated supplication of Nicolas Lopez "Studens orfanus pauperissimus jn carcere publico detento morboque tertianario graviter opressus".
28. The commission was composed by Don Francisco d'Arragon "gentilhomme de la Court de l'empereur"; Charles Tisnac, a member of the Council of Brabant; Pierre de Fief, general attorney of Brabant; Jacques de la Torre, "ordinary secretary" to the Emperor.
29. ANTT, *Inquisição de Evora, Processo 11304*, f. 29, quoted by M.C.Teixera Pinto, *Manuel Dias*.

money totalling 7,500 florins.[30] They subsequently adjusted their offers
to 10,000 florins in order to also obtain the release of those prisoners who
had no money. While informing the Queen, Pierre de Fief, the general
attorney of Brabant, stated that this amount was ridiculous: it had been
discovered that merchants such as Duarte Rodrigues, Jorge de Andrade
and Jorge Rodrigues had dispatched huge quantities of merchandise to
Antwerp. The general attorney advised the Regent to request at least
25,000 florins.

In November 1544, other Portuguese were rounded up in Antwerp by
a sheriff of the Council of Brabant.[31] The prisoners were kept in jail
indefinitely. No trial date was set, under the pretext that it was necessary
to collect information on their earlier behavior in Portugal. In realty, in
October 1544, the Queen had dispatched letters to this effect to King João
III of Portugal, to *Infante* Henrique,[32] and João Mello,[33] informing them
that many New Christians had arrived in Flanders.[34] They had left
Portugal without the necessary royal licence and had entered the Low
Countries clandestinely and, therefore, had been arrested. A list of the

---

30. AGR, PEA, reg. 1177/2 ff. 86r-88v, September 10, 1544: Pierre du Fief to the Queen:
Duarte Rodrigues had offered 400 florins; Jorge Dandrade 200; Jorge Rodrigues 100;
Emmanuel Lopes 400; Vincent Lopes 400; Dennis Mennes 400; Sebastien Fernandis 400;
Diego Emmanuel 200; Emmanuel Visinho 200; Emmanuel Renel 1,500; Nuño Lopes 200;
Francisco Peris 100; Hector Pinhero 200; Francisco Mennes 200; Emmanuel Pinhero 250;
Baltasar Emmanuel 100; Henriques Jorge 250; [Pedro de] Salvaterra 100; Leonora
Rodrigues 100; Nicolas Lopes 100; Diego Fernandes Netto 2,000. Other prisoners did not
join in the initiative. Some of them declared that they were poor and unable to submit any
offer.
31. AGR, OFB, 160/1233/3. Among these prisoners were: Henriques Jorge, Emmanuel
Pinhero, Francisco Nuñes, Hector Pinhero, Pedro Fernandis, with their wives and children.
32. Henrique, the Prince *Infante* (later Cardinal), was King João' s brother. On June 22,
1539, the king appointed him as Inquisidor-Môr (Head Inquisitor or Inquisitor General).
See A. Herculano, *History of the Origin*, p. 425; A. Baião, *A Inquisição em Portugal e
no Brasil*, «AHP» IV, Lisboa 1906, p.218; F.de Almeida, *História da Igreja em Portugal*,
Portucalense Editorial, Porto 1968[2], II. p. 410; M.J.P. Ferro Tavares, *Judaísmo e
Inquisição, Estudios*, Lisbon, Editorial Presença 1987, p.153.
33. At the time Doctor João Mello was "the head of the Inquisition at Lisbon." See A.
Herculano, *History of the Origin*, 431; M.J.P. Ferro tavares, *Judaísmo e Inquisição*, pp.
153, 154, 157.
34. AGR, OFB, 160/1233/2, October 18 and 19, 1544: Original copies of Queen Mary's
letters to King João of Portugal, to Infante Henrique, and to João de Mello. See documents
56-59 in Appendix.

prisoners was attached to the dispatch.[35] The Queen asked the addressees to kindly provide all available information on the prisoners. The letters to the King and the *Infante* were drawn up in the kindest and most respectful form, according to the rules of court etiquette. The copy sent to de Melo was much more concise, unceremonious, but still polite. However, Queen Mary sent him a second, much longer and less diplomatic message wherein she brought up the first results of the inquiry held in Antwerp, as if she wanted to reproach him for not having prevented the flight of so many people. Only at the end of the lengthy message did the Queen request information on the émigrés. We do not know the reply eventually given by the King and the Inquisitors.

At a certain point, João Micas and Guilherme Fernandes approached the commissioner and proposed to pay a bail of 20,000 florins. The Queen accepted the offer and explained her decision, alluding to the difficulties of carrying out an inquiry in Portugal, such a remote country. All the prisoners were set free on the condition that they remain in Antwerp for an eventual (and improbable) trial.[36]

On May 7, 1545, Queen Mary accepted João Micas' offer to pay 10,000 florins to the Emperor. In return, the Regent allowed the former-prisoners to settle in Antwerp and carry on their trades and professions. The 20,000 florins bail was revoked.[37] Micas had to pay 559 Flemish pounds and ten pennies to the General Attorney for "legal expenses".[38]

---

35. No copy of the list is preserved in the file.
36. We do not know the date of this agreement mentioned in later documents. See next note.
37. AGR, PEA, 1631, May 7, 1545. Copy in OFB 160/1233/2. See also, *ibidem*, Pierre de Fief's statement of June 1545.
38. *Ibid.*

§ 15. The Results of the 1544 Inquiry: The Underground Route from Lisbon to Antwerp and, from there, to Italy and the Levant

Between July and August of 1544, the Commission of Inquiry examined about forty prisoners, most of them under torture or threat of torture.[1] They were interrogated on fifty points according to a detailed *questionnaire* drawn up by the Queen's councillors.[2] In a parallel investigation,[3] conducted at Veere and Antwerp, captains and masters of the Portuguese ships, cart drivers, officers of the Portuguese *Feitoria*, servants and all sorts of people who had worked for, or had had contacts with, the prisoners, were interrogated.[4] These documents provide precious information on the socio-economic background of the immigrants and their relatives in the Peninsula.[5] Among them were several *Homens de negocio* (men of business and commerce).[6] Many

---

1. According to documents kept in AGR, OFB 160/1233/2, interrogations were conducted *pede ligato* (with the prisoner's foot chained up).

2. AGR,OFB 160/1233/2, *Interrogations pour jnterroger les apprehendez en la ville danvers qui se baptisent nouveaulx xpiens venuz du Royaulme de Portugal depuis six sepmaines en ca.*

3. AGR, OFB, 160/1233/2, July 7 and 9, 1544, Louis de Schor to Pierre de Fief: A [nominally separate] commission is set up to examine the Portuguese ship captains in Zeeland. Letters of appointment to this effect are sent to Don Francisco d'Arragon, Charles Tisnac, Pierre de Fief, Jacques de la Torre. (Former appointments were only valid for the city and district of Antwerp).

4. AGR,OFB, 160/1233/2, *Information 1544.*

5. The Queen-Regent directed the Commission to interrogate the prisoners about the names of their parents, the composition of their family and the activities of their relatives. AGR,OFB,160/1233/2, *Interrogations pour jnterroger les apprehendez.*

6. For this expression see: SARAIVA, *Inquisição e Christãos Novos,* p. 185. On the "unlimited economic opportunities offered to the New Christians" in Portugal, in this period, see H.P. SALOMON, *Portrait of a New Christian, Fernão Álvares Melo, (1569-1632),* Paris, 1982, p. 20.

others were modest artisans,[7] workmen or, even, agricultural labour-
ers.[8]

In Portugal, it was generally believed that the flight of the *conversos*
was increasing because of the inquisitorial persecutions. It was reported
that at one auto-da-fé held in Lisbon, twenty people had been burnt "in
corpore".[9] Both the rich and the poor were to be found among the victims
of the Inquisition. Several people had been burnt in effigy: sculptures,
representing those sentenced by default, were symbolically given to the
flames. This was not a useless farce, as the properties of those so condemned were seized. Some of these people had been living in Antwerp.
They were: Doctor Dionisio, Emanuel Pinhero and a certain Gabriel (or
Emanuel) Fernandes.[10] Orders were given for their arrest but none of
them was found. Doctor Dionisio had left Antwerp a few years earlier.
The other two "remained in hiding" and eventually left the city.[11]

From accounts given by captains of vessels, and other "Old
Christian" witnesses, we learn about the measures put into effect in
Portugal by the police and *familiares* of the Inquisition, in order to prevent the flight of *Marranos*. We also learn that King João III re-enacted
in (or around) 1535, 1538 and again in 1541, the 1532 edict, according to
which no New Christians, or their wives, children or other relatives,
should leave Portugal without a royal licence.[12] A stern prohibition was
issued to captains and masters of vessels, forbidding the admittance on
board of any *converso* thus accompanied. Royal policemen and inquisition *familiares* patrolled the ports and inspected the vessels. The guards
arrested all New Christians found on board without a licence and seized
all goods believed to be theirs. Manoel Fernandez, master of the ship San

---

7. For instance: Pedro de Salvaterra, son of the late Mestre Thomas (a medical doctor) was
a cloth-shearer. AGR, 160/1233/3, July 26, 1544: Confession, *pede ligato et medio juramento*. See also M.C. TEIXEIRA PINTO, "Manuel Dias, um cristão-novo de Fronteira".
8. AGR,OFB, 160/1233/3, *Information 1544*, July 24, 1544: Manoel, eighteen years old,
son of the late Jorge Di[a]z, stated that his brothers were farmers. Manoel had been a shep-
herd.
9. SALOMON-LEONI, *Mendes, Benveniste*, p. 155.
10. AGR, *Information 1544*, pp. 7v-12r and *passim*.
11. In realty, Emanuel Pinhero had left Antwerp in 1539 and had moved to Ferrara.
12. *Ibid.*: interrogations of ship captains and Portuguese [old] Christian living in Antwerp.
According to LUCIO DE AZEVEDO (*História dos Christãos Novos Portugueses*, Lisboa
1921, pp. 86, 109) and other scholars, the 1532 decree was re-enacted in 1535.

Salvador, reported that, two months earlier in Lisbon, in only one of these operations, inquisition *familiares* had rounded up fifty-four people who were taken away in four boats.[13]

Fugitive *Marranos* timed their embarkation after nightfall and before sunrise, in the dark, when it was hoped that the guards had already inspected the ship for the last time.[14] The refugees set out in small boats and boarded the vessels on the side furthest from the wharf, hidden from sight. Some of these passengers managed to get their goods loaded in advance so as to be able to embark quickly without attracting unwanted attention. However, last-minute visits were always possible. Many *conversos* were arrested when they were already on board. A captain told the history about a certain *hulque*[15] that had safely set sail. When the vessel passed by the tower of Belem, it was halted by cannon shots. Guards went aboard and arrested some passengers. Other *conversos* travelling on the same ship were not detected and were able to reach Antwerp.[16]

From other sources, we learn that, in many cases, private[17] *ulcas* left the wharf before nightfall, sailed down the Tagus and waited for the passengers in the dark, at the river mouth, before entering the Ocean. The refugees reached the ship by small boats steered by Old-Christian fisher-

---

13. AGR, *Information 1544*, ff. 31v-32r: 32r: July 16 1544, deposition of Manoel Fernandiz, born in the town of Conde, in Portugal, master of the ship San Salvador: «Dict aussi avoir veu, environ deux mois en ça, mener prisoniers de par l'Inquisition, en quatre petits barques, jusques au nombre de cinquante quatre personnes tant hommes quant femmes, et que l'inquisition faict grand debvoir et diligence de prendre tous nouveaux christiens qui se veuillent retirer de par de ça...»

14. AGR, *Information 1544*, passim; AGR, OFB 160/1233/2 : *Recueil de tous ce qui se trouve substantial ... contre les nouveaux xpiens detenuz prisonies par le Procureur General de Brabant*, f. 1r: «Les dicts nouveaux xpiens sont entrez au temps de leur embarquement sur ou apres soleil couchier et depuis es [=dans les] grandes naves de nuyct».

15. *Hulque* (from the Dutch *hulch;* in Spanish and Portuguese documents the forms *urca* and/or *urque* are found): merchant ship built in the Netherlands. It was particularly employed for the grain trade.

16. AGR, *Information 1544*, ff. 30v-31r, July 16, 1544: witness testimony of Joâo Gonsales, proprietor of the ship S. Maria de Luz.

17. *Private ulcas*: see above note 15. The term "private" is used to state that these ships did not belong to the "Royal" Portuguese Fleet and were by no means associated with it.

men, boatmen and sailors,[18] or even, in a few cases, by New Christian volunteers.[19]

Not all those who wanted to leave were able to arrange their journey in advance or to have it planned by the Rescue Organization. A captain told the story of an old woman wandering on the wharf together with her daughter. After some hesitation, they approached him and asked if he could help them in finding a passage to Flanders. Before he could answer, the two women saw a couple of guards and ran away. The captain did not see them again. Two women corresponding to this description succeeded in embarking on another ship. They were arrested in Zeeland, where they arrived towards the middle of July 1544.[20]

The proceedings of the Lisbon Inquisition provide broad information on the magnitude of this migratory movement.[21] Entire communities, propelled by messianic expectations,[22] observed the "Law of Moses" and dreamed of moving to Flanders, from where they might eventually reach the "Land of Promise" and observe the Law of Moses without obstacles and impediments.[23] Scores of New Christians abandoned their

---

18. ISAIAS da ROSA PEREIRA, *Fuga de Cristãos-Novos em barcos de pescadores do Tejo*, «História e Societade», n. 8-9, Lisboa 1981, pp. 117-118; ISABEL M. R. MENDES DRUMOND BRAGA, PAULO DRUMOND BRAGA, *O embarque de Cristãos Novos para o estrangeiro, Um delito na Inquisição de Lisboa (1541-1550)* in «Gil Vicente, Revista de Cultura e Actualitades», Guimarães 1994, pp. 26-32.
19. M.C. TEIXEIRA PINTO, *Manuel Dias, um cristão-novo de Fronteira*.
20. AGR, OFGB 160/1233/3, July 16, 1544 in Zeeland, *Confession de Branca Mendes et de Leonora Mendes imprisonées par Floris van Damme, lieutenenat du Rentmeester*.
21. A. BAIÃO, *A Inquisição em Portugal e no Brasil*, «Arquivo Histórico Português»,VI, 1906, pp. 104-105; M.J.P. FERRO TAVARES, *Para o estudo dos Judeus de Tras o Monte no seculo XVI: a primera geração de cristãos-novos*, «Cultura História e Filosofia», Universidade Nova de Lisboa, IV, pp. 371-417: 388-401; M.C. TEIXEIRA PINTO, *Manuel Dias, um cristão-novo de Fronteira e as vicissitudes do seu tempo*, A.A. TAVARES, Edit., *Estudos Orientais, O Legado Cultural de Judeus e Mouros*, Lisbon 1991, pp. 267-288: pp. 274-275.
22. Y BAER, *Ha Tenua' ha-mesihit bi-Sfarad bi-Tekufat ha Gerush, Zion* V, pp. 61-67; Yosef Yerushalmi, *A Jewish Classic in the Portuguese Language*, preface to SAMUEL USQUE, *Consolaçam as Tribulações de Israel* [Reprint Fundaçâo C. Gulbenkian, Lisbon 1989] vol. I, pp. 14-123. Cf. the important study by M.J. P. FERRO TAVARES, *Caracteristicas do mes-sianesimo judaico em Portugal* in A.A. TAVARES, Edit., *Estudos Orientais, II, O Legado Cultural de Judeus e Mouros*, Lisbon 1991, pp. 245-266, based on inquisitorial documents. See also: LEONI and HERZFELD *The Orden de oraciones de mes arréo (Ferrara 1555) and a Bakasa composed by Abraham Usque*, «Sefarad» LXII, 2002, pp. 99-124.
23. M.C. TEIXEIRA PINTO, *Manuel Dias, um cristão-novo de Fronteira*, pp. 272-75 .

native regions, at risk to their lives and properties, and moved to Lisbon where they hoped to obtain the help of their co-religionists. Some of them succeeded in leaving the country; the Inquisition's agents arrested many others.[24]

New Christians paid much more than normal passengers for their fare.[25] A certain Gilbert de Cleves reported that a priest of Jewish origin was lucky to pay only 26 golden ducats while other *conversos* had to pay at least fifty.[26] Old Christian passengers usually paid three or four ducats. There were many cases where ship captains denounced to the Portuguese Inquisition those would-be passengers who were unable to pay huge fares.[27]

Captains and masters of ships frequently robbed passengers of their belongings in the knowledge that these illegal travelers would be in no position to report the theft to Flemish authorities. This was not the case of Agnes Gomes, the wife of Diego Fernandes Netto. Her husband was accustomed to difficult situations. When he learned that a coffer belonging to his wife had been forced open, and jewels worth four hundred ducats had been stolen, he denounced Manoel Carneiro, the master of the ship. Diego refused to pay the price requested for his wife's fare and accused Carneiro of extortion.[28] Carneiro was imprisoned. Diego Netto was seized a few days later, together with other Portuguese newcomers, on the charges of Judaizing and illegal immigration.[29] On July 30, 1544,

---

24. *Ibid.*, pp. 276-282.

25. AGR, OFGB 160/1233/3, undated [middle of August 1544] report to the Queen: *Recueil de tout ce qui se trouve substancial par Information contre les nouveaux xpiens detenuz prisonniers par le procureur general de Brabant.*

26. AGR, *Information 1544*, July 5, 1544, deposition of Gilbert de Cleves (Flemish passenger arrived from Portugal) «comme certain prestre natif de Castille paya en partant de la nave xxiiij ducats pour sa chambre, jl luy fut lors dict par ledict maitre marronier quil eschappoit a bon marché puis que aultres nouveaux xpiens avoient payé en aultres hulques pour une petite chambrette la somme de cinquante ducats».

27. A. Baião, *A Inquisição em Portugal e no Brasil*, pp. 104-105; M.C. Teixeira Pinto, *Manuel Dias, um cristão-novo de Fronteira*, p. 277.

28. AGR, *Information 1544*, f 16r. Carneyro claimed 50 ducats from Agnes Gomes and eight ducats each from her relatives.

29. In vain, the prisoners invoked the privilege issued in 1537 [and reconfirmed in 1542] granting all Portuguese merchants permission to settle freely and unharmed in Antwerp and perform their commercial activities in the city. AGR, OFB 160/1233/2, July 30, 1544: Queen Mary to general attorney Pierre du Fief.

when both the litigants were in prison, Diego de la Torre, the imperial secretary, settled the controversy ex officio.[30] He acquitted the ship's master
of the charge of theft, as there was only scant evidence against him. De la
Torre stated that Netto's wife and-brother-in-law had to pay only "normal" fares, in the amount of eleven ducats, for their journey.[31]

---

30. AGR,OFB, 160/1233/3 Sentence pronounced *ex officio* (in Spanish) by Diego de la
Torre in his capacity of *Commissario de su Majestad en el negocio dessos nuevos
Christianos*. See Document 52 in Appendix.
31. This amount included: eight ducats as a normal fare for two persons (Agnes Gomes
and her brother), two ducats for the special cabin used by Agnes and one ducat for food
and other expenses.

§ 16. The "Itinerary" to Ferrara

In June 1544, when the Portuguese immigrants were rounded up in Antwerp, many documents were seized together with their property. At first the inquisitors paid attention only to bills of exchange and commercial letters.[1] The other papers were mixed together and, later on, it was difficult to understand where they were originally found. Many letters sent by *conversos* living in Portugal to their relatives in Antwerp and London were also seized. They shed new light on the unprecedented violence of the inquisitorial persecutions.[2]

It was only after a second perusal that the inquisitors realized the exceptional importance of two documents taken from the house where Diego Fernandes Netto's family was temporarily accommodated along with many other immigrants. The first document was an apparently simple note, written in Portuguese, on a piece of paper folded in three. It contained the *regimento* (instructions) for the journey from Antwerp to Ferrara. It was drawn up in inelegant, difficult to decipher handwriting, full of abbreviations and diacritic symbols widely used in Portugal during the 16th century. The notoriously polyglot Queen Mary and the officers of her multi-lingual Court realized its importance but were unable to fully understand its content.[3] The second document was an unaddressed and unsigned letter (dated September 15, 1543) sent by an anonymous person who had safely reached Ferrara. It related the mishaps of the second part of his (or her) difficult journey from Basel to Ferrara.[4] An earlier letter sent from Basel was unfortunately lost.

---

1. AGR,PEA 132, July 22, 1544: Corneille Scepperus to the Queen.
2. We hope to deal with these documents in a separate study.
3. We could decipher the precious document and are publishing it in its entirety (see document 36 in Appendix). In view of its exceptional importance, we provide a complete English translation of it.
4. See Document 35 in Appendix.

On July 7, 1544, the Queen sent the two documents to the commission in Antwerp and instructed Pierre de Tisnacq to have them carefully translated by a professional. In the meantime, the inquisitors were ordered to look carefully into this matter and examine Diego Netto, who was suspected of being one of the *conductors* who smuggled the refugees out of Antwerp towards Italy. The cart-drivers who had worked for the Portuguese had to be pursued and interrogated. As a matter of fact, the commissioners did not pay much attention to this problem.

For a few weeks, Diego Netto was kept in solitary confinement. However, in the final report of his interrogations only a couple of lines are devoted to "the journey to Italy". Netto declared that the document did not belong to him or any member of his family. Apparently the inquisitors did not insist on this point, unless they had dealt with it in earlier examinations the reports of which are no longer extant.[5] Rather incongruously, the commissioners were more impressed by a "strange" piece of crystal: a sphere containing the figure of a "devil". It turned out that it was part of the furniture belonging to the landlord of the house.

The commissioners wondered why the papal brief exempted Diego's wife from any persecution on grounds of heresy or apostasy. Diego did not explain that the safe-conduct was drawn up in order to protect his family from any possible revenge from the Portuguese Inquisition when he was the "ambassador" of the *Men of the Nation* in Rome. He simply stated that the brief was worded in the most comprehensive form as to include every imaginable crime.[6]

The two documents[7] describing the journey from Antwerp to Ferrara supply precious information on the *dificil caminho*[8] (the difficult road) to Italy. We can compare them with the depositions of prisoners jailed in Vigevano and Pavia, and with accounts given in Ferrara by former prisoners who reported mistreatment and robberies suffered in the prisons of Lombardy.[9] Dramatic echoes of the risks and hardships faced by many "who have left and continue to leave Portugal" are preserved in Samuel

---

5. The only official report of Diego Netto's interrogations is dated August 1, 1544. In July, Netto had been kept in isolation for a few weeks.

6. AGR,OFB 160/1233/3, August 1,1544: Official report on the interrogations and depositions of Diego Fernandiz Netto. See Document 54 in Appendix.

7. See in Appendix documents 35 and 36

8. I am borrowing this expression from SAMUEL USQUE, *Consolaçam*, Dialogo III, § 31.

9. Cfr AGR, *Codazzi* and *Lavezzoli Files.*

Usque's *Consolaçam*.[10] All the available sources correspond to each other and describe simply, and without rhetoric, the courageous determination and spirit of sacrifice of scores of *Marranos* who ventured on this difficult and dangerous journey in order to reach a place where they could openly revert to the religion of their fathers. Through these documents, we can actually reconstruct the stages of their journey.

The émigrés left Antwerp in the dark, after sunset, on wagons that would take them as far as Basel. The Men of the Nation generally provided payment in advance, both for the wagons and the drivers. In Cologne, the émigrés were put up at the Inn Vier Escara. They were to leave their lodging early in the morning, before sunrise, so as to reach the Rhine River in the dark. A certain Pero Tonellero was to accompany them from Cologne to Mainz. When hiring the Rhine-boat that would transport them to Basel (or Mainz), they were to state that they wanted to sleep on board. This would allow them to save money and reduce the risk of being discovered. At Basel (or Mainz) they had to hire wagons, which would lead them as far as possible on the mountain slopes. The subsequent part of the journey was the most difficult as they had to avoid the main road and follow secondary, steep and deserted tracks. In some places, the route was so rugged that it was suggested that all healthy and strong individuals were to walk behind the wagons. This took weight off the wagons and placed the walkers in a position to pick up objects that fell off due to the steepness. In addition, if a wagon overturned, they would be able to help straighten it up. When the way became too steep, they had to hire horses that would carry them beyond the Alpine pass.

An anonymous letter from Ferrara[11] provided practical advice. As these refugees generally travelled in companies of twenty or more, it was impossible to find a stableman who could hire out all the necessary horses. They had to rent them from different people. Horses from the same stud farm tended to group and travel together. It was suggested that husband and wife ride on animals from the same stable; otherwise they would not see each other all day long.

Custom duties, road and bridge-tolls and the prices at the inns were not fixed. In order to avoid unpleasant discussions and surprises, it was advisable to ask in advance for the price of food and accommodations and pay immediately for what they received, without leaving outstanding

---

10. S. USQUE, *Consolaçam, locum cit.*; cfr. Y.H. YERUSHALMI, *A Jewish Classic*, p. 73.
11. See document 35 in Appendix,.

accounts. Travellers should not be ashamed to look modest; otherwise innkeepers would take advantage of them. The letter from Ferrara told the story of the daughter of Diego Netto, who wore an elegant hat one day: the officers in Magadino demanded exorbitant rates according to the old saying that "rich people can pay". Those who had only these difficulties to complain about were the luckiest ones.

For all the travellers, the crossing of the Alps was a dramatic experience that they would remember for the rest of their days. Many lost their lives in the icy cold mountains. Others were born during the journey.[12] The *Regimento* ended up with a simple but solemn call for God's help.[13] When Gasper Gomes left for Ferrara, he received Diogo Mendes' solemn blessing:[14]

«The blessing that Abraham gave to Isaac and Isaac to Jacob; so I give you my blessing. May we meet each other again in the Promised Land for many years of long life.»[15]

---

12. S. USQUE, *Consolaçam*, Dialogo III, § 31.
13. See in Appendix Document 36.
14. Gaspar Lopes' deposition of September 20, 1540.
15. « La benedicione che ha datto Abraam a Jsac et Jsac a Jacob: Così daggo la mia benedicione che se possiamo trovare l'uno et l'altro in Terra de promissione con molti anni di longa vitta».

§ 17. Nuño Henriques and Henrique Nuñes' Imprisonment

In 1545, Beatriz de Luna, her sister Brianda, their daughters and their entourage left Antwerp and settled in Venice.[1] João Micas remained in Antwerp and was engaged in negotiations with the Emperor and his sister, the Queen-Regent, to save as much as possible of the family's properties. The struggle for the Mendes' estate apparently absorbed most of Queen Mary's energies for more than two years.[2]

In 1548, Mary of Habsburg turned her attention towards two prominent merchants of Antwerp: the brothers Nuño Henriques and Henrique Nuñes.[3] Like many of the Queen's intended victims, they were partners in the pepper consortium. The attack was cut-and-dry. The unfortunate merchants were apprehended, their accounting books seized, guards stationed in their house, and their business connections broken off. The two prisoners were kept in jail for a time, long enough to drive them to despair. João Rebello, the Portuguese *Feitor* in Antwerp, and João Micas [later known as Joseph Nasi, the Duke of Naxos] led the negotiations for their release. In September 1548, an extrajudiciary settlement was agreed upon in the amount of 100,000 florins to be paid in three instalments.[4] The two merchants were allowed to leave Antwerp without any bodily

---

1. GRUNEBAUM-BALLIN, *Joseph Nasi* p. 47. For the safe-conduct granted by the Venetian Republic to Brianda de Luna, see P.C. IOLY ZORATTINI, *Processi del S. Uffizio 1548- 1560,* Firenze 1980, pp. 341-342.
2. J. REZNIK, *Le Duc de Naxos*, pp. 52-72.
3. AGR, PEA 60, f. 150, July 18, 1548: the Queen reassures the Emperor that she has been paying due attention to the problem of New Christians. When she was informed that Jewish ceremonies were performed in a Portuguese family, she had two brothers imprisoned. They were Gabriel de Negro' s brothers-in-law.
4. AGR, PEA, 821, ff. 316r-317r. See Document 62 in Appendix; ANTT, Lisboa, *Inquisição de Lisboa, Processo n. 2931*, f. 73r: witness deposition by Henrico Nuñes (Abraham Benveniste) May 29, 1579 P.C. IOLY ZORATTINI, *Processi, 1570-1572,* p. 266.

harm and to transfer themselves, along with their families and properties to any other country within two years time, with permission to leave a factor to take care of their pending business.

As in previous cases, the Queen made no provision for the salvation of their souls or for their future conduct as good Christians. As usual, the question of their alleged Jewish heresy was used as a simple pretext to extort money from them. When the two brothers were released, and the family returned to their residence, they immediately had all the rooms where the guards were stationed cleaned with hot water, and all their pots, dishes and table linen thrown away, evidently for reasons of *Kashrut* (observance of Jewish dietary laws). A servant denounced them and, for fear of new persecutions, the whole family escaped to Venice. A certain Francisco Alvares smuggled them into France. Only Jeronimo, the elder of Nuño 's sons, remained in Antwerp and took care of the family's business.

In 1548 Queen Mary issued a safe-conduct in favor of Bras Reinel,[5] allowing him to leave the Low Countries freely and without any harm.[6]

In 1549 Beatriz Mendes-de Luna [later called doña Gracia Nasi] moved to Ferrara.[7] In 1550 the Family Henriques-Benveniste and the Reinels left Venice and settled in Ferrara as well.[8] The Abravanels were already residing there since 1541.[9] Thus, in 1550, the three most wealthy and powerful Sephardic Families were simultaneously in Ferrara. Their commercial and financial activities greatly contributed to the development of the town and improved the status of the local Portuguese Nation.[10]

---

5. Bras Reinel [*alias* Isaac Abendana], was related to Violante Enriques (the wife of Nuño Henriques). See ASFe, Notary Giacomo Conte, *pacco* 8, *passim*. The family relationship became stricter when his son Manuel Reinel [*alias* Abraham Abendana] married Lianor Henriques, [later called Doña Benveniste] one of Nuño Henriques' daughters.

6. AGR,Bxl,PEA, Reg. 1635, *Passeports*, f. 54: *Laissez-passer pour Brasse Reynel, Thomas Rodrigues et Jehan Alvares*, August 30, 1548.

7. SALOMON-LEONI, *Mendes, Benveniste*, pp. 156-157.

8. P.C. Ioly Zorattini, *Processi* III, *1570-1572*, p.15.

9. A. DI LEONE LEONI, *Documenti e Notizie sulla Famiglia Abravanel a Ferrara*, «Annuario di Studi sull'Ebraismo Italiano» edited by The Italian Rabbinical College, Rome 1996, pp. 33-68: 36-38, IDEM, *Nuove notizie sugli Abravanel*, «Zakhor, Rivista di Storia degli Ebrei d'Italia», I 1997, pp. 153-206: 155-159.

10. IDEM, *Quotidiana Imprenditorialità*, pp. 72-78.

§ 18. Some Peculiar Aspects of Charles V's Policy in the Low Countries

In the preceding chapters, I have been trying to outline what was perhaps the most peculiar aspect of Charles V's approach towards the *Marranos* in the Low Countries, in contrast to the completely different policy followed in Spain.[1] Greed for money was the most important factor determining the Emperor's policy towards the Portuguese of Antwerp (and perhaps towards other minorities).[2] The wealth of many Portuguese merchants was the tool they frequently used to defend themselves and their countrymen from persecution. Unfortunately, it was also the reason for more attacks, as the Emperor and the Queen-Regent repeatedly tried to seize the property of prominent merchants.

Financial considerations were also at the basis of the imperial policy (followed between 1540 and 1548) to seize the New Christians' merchandise in transit through Lombardy. The official reason for these operations was the necessity to prevent traffic towards and trade with Turkish dominions. This was simply a pretext. The rigorous inspections of all the goods passing through the river-ports of Lombardy caused enormous delays and frequent protests from Swiss and Italian merchants.[3] The imperial governor of Milan refused to listen to reason. In 1548, the custom officers informed the Emperor that the traffic through Pavia was continuously decreasing as foreign merchants sent their goods via alternative routes. As a consequence, the customs levies were reduced. The loss was

---

1. ALVAREZ, *La España del Emperador,* pp. 106-107, 125, 874.
2. As we have seen above (§ 2) the imperial *placards* against heresy contemplated increasing pecuniary penalties.
3. ASMi, Cancelleria di Stato, Carteggio Generale, B. 36, February 9, 1542: the elders of Baden [an der Limat] to the Spanish Governor of Milan; B. 37, March 6, 1542; the governor to the Swiss ambassador in Milan; Ibid., *Registri di Cancelleria, Missive da Milano*, XV, reg. 2, March 2, 1542.

not compensated by the value of the goods seized from New Christians, which was also decreasing. Until then, Charles V had turned a deaf ear to all legal and moral arguments but he relinquished this practice when he learned that it was causing important losses of income.

Perhaps I am stressing this argument too strongly. I am doing so because many historians have erroneously assumed that Spanish laws and institutions were automatically enforced in the Low Countries which, I repeat, in the middle of the 16th century, was a separate state with its own legislation, enforced – at least formally- by its own judicial and administrative bodies. Even eminent scholars assumed that the Inquisition had been introduced into Flanders during the period that we are reviewing.[4] Their statements misled other authors.[5]

Charles V had been instrumental in obtaining Pope Paul III's approval for the institution of a "national" independent, Spanish-styled Inquisition in Portugal.[6] However, the over-zealous Emperor did not take any comparable initiative in the Low Countries. Furthermore, no churchmen ever took part in the interrogation of New Christians prisoners in Flanders. Only specially appointed imperial officers dealt with these prisoners.

At least in theory, in the early modern age, bishops could autonomously prosecute heresy according to canon law, following the procedure of the so-called Medieval or "Roman" Inquisition.[7] However, there is no evidence that ecclesiastic inquisitors ever acted against New Christians in the Low Countries or were ever associated with inquiries carried out by imperial lay-officers. As we have seen, in 1523, Charles V provisionally entrusted the repression of the Lutheran heresy in the Low Countries to bishops. He reluctantly did so in order to circumvent the

---

4. For instance: S.W. BARON, (A Social and Religious History, XIII p. 123) stated that: «in 1532 Diego was temporarily imprisoned by the Inquisition». See also S. SIMONSOHN, The Apostolic See, History, p. 447.
5. See, for instance, R. SEGRE La formazione di una Comunità Marrana, p. 782.
6. A. HERCULANO, History of the Origin, pp. 344, 386.
7. On the competence of bishops in materia fidei see the thorough study by A. PROSPERI, Tribunali della coscienza: Inquisitori, Confessori, Missionari, Torino 1996, pp. 278-289; E. BRAMBILLA, Alle Origini del S. Uffizio: Penitenze, Confessioni e Giustizia spirituale dal Medioevo al XVI secolo, Bologna 2000. See also: G. GONNET, Recent European Historiography on the Medieval Inquisition in G. HENNINGSEN and J. TEDESCHI, The Inquisition in Early Modern Europe, Studies on Sources and Methods, Dekalb, Ill., 1986.

opposition of City and Provincial Councils[8] but he managed to keep these inquiries under his direct control, and he compelled the bishops to perform them in pursuance of the imperial ordinances. We should also point out that, in Low Countries' legislation, the repression of different heresies (Lutheran, Anabaptist, Jewish) was dealt with on the basis of separate and specific provisions.[9] The prosecution was also carried out in different and separate ways.

In order to better enforce his policy against New Christians, the Emperor coined new terms such as "malos-" or "falsos-christianos" or "Jews disguised as Christians". These expressions, as far as I know, were used, especially, in Flanders and Milan; in the latter, primarily by imperial agents sent from Brussels. Even eminent scholars, unfamiliar with these particular terms did not always grasp their meaning – and the policy behind them.[10]

In the course of this book, we have frequently dealt with the Rescue Organization that planned and funded the flight of *Conversos* from the Iberian Peninsula to London and Antwerp, and, from there, to Italy and the Levant. As we have seen, the leaders of this Organization were engaged in the continuous attempt to mitigate the persecutory policy enforced by the Emperor and, in many cases, they succeeded in having his decisions temporarily overturned. In so doing, the Portuguese Nation displayed remarkable cohesiveness and a rare capacity to organize for common action.[11] In the following pages, we shall try to recapitulate the available information on the composition and the accomplishments this group.

---

8. A. Goosens, *Les Inquisitions*, p. 50.
9. *Ibid.*, pp. 50-71.
10. ASMi, Registri di Cancelleria: Missive da Milano, Serie XV, reg. 2, March 2, 1542: [unnamed] merchants of Ferrara complained that goods belonging to them were seized in Cremona by Johannes Vuysting, commissioner *contra falsos christianos*. The Governor of Milan orders the release of the impounded goods. S. Simonsohn (*The Jews in the Duchy of Milan*, Vol. I, Jerusalem 1982, Doc. 2491, p. 1085) published a summary of the document. This Author (or perhaps one of his assistants, unaware of this terminology and Charles V's policy) wrongly assumed that certain merchants were "falsely reported to be Christians".
11. I borrowed this expression from Y. H. Yerushalmi, *Prolegomenon*, p. 27.

§ 19. The Leadership of the Portuguese Nation in Antwerp

There cannot be any doubt that Diogo Mendes was the most prominent figure in the Rescue Organization. He was, however, far from being alone in this enterprise. From different sources, we know that many other *Men of the Nation* in Lisbon and Antwerp (as well as in London) devoted their energies to this organization at great risk to their personal safety. Particular mention must be made here of António Fernandes, who had already suffered many years of imprisonment on charges of Judaizing, abetting the emigration of *Marranos* and other lesser charges. In a letter of July 24, 1538, Antonio Fernandes claimed that he was performing a leading role in the Rescue Organization.[1]

In 1538 and 1539, António Fernandes negotiated with Gerolamo Maretta, determining the conditions under which the *Marranos* of Antwerp would settle in Ferrara.[2] Together with Duarte Rodrigues

---

1. ASMo,CD, Lettere Particolari, B. 837 *sub voce Maretta:* 1538 António Fernando to Gerolamo Maretta «Envers 24 de uijo ... espero que a todo se dará bom fim e asy espero [por] minha parte fazer tamto ... porque em minha mão, como sabe[i]s esta muita parte do c[uidado] que a este negocio se deve dar, asi mesmo vosa vimda ha sido muito pr[ovei]tosa e fez muito neste caso.» Renata SEGRE (*La Formazione di una Comunità Marrana*) quoted the document. She ascribed the letter to Diego Mendes, purportedly addressed to Duke Ercole II. Our perusal of the document reveals, however, that it is not signed "Diego Mendes" but "Antonio Fernandes"; it is addressed not to Duke Ercole but to Jeronimo (Gerolamo) Maretta; it is not written in a "hybrid Spanish" but in pure Portuguese; it is dated July (not October) 24, 1538 and it contains clear reference to the recent mission of Gerolamo Maretta in Antwerp.

2. Gerolamo Maretta had the task of inviting the Portuguese merchants to Ferrara. From the very moment of his ascent to power in 1534, Ercole II d'Este tried to attract Sephardic Jews, especially the Portuguese New Christians of Antwerp, to settle in his dukedom. See P.GÉNARD, *Personen te Antwerpen,* pp. 436-438; B.D. COOPERMAN, *Venetian Policy towards Levantine Jews,* p. 72; A. di LEONE LEONI, *Gli Ebrei Sefarditi a Ferrara al tempo di Ercole II'*, RMI Vol. LII, 1987, pp. 407-446: 412-414; IDEM, *La Diplomazia Estense*, pp. 309-314; B.D. COOPERMAN, *Portuguese Conversos in Ancona*: pp. 297-352.

Pinto,[3] Fernandes convinced the ducal envoy that, in order to induce many Portuguese merchants to move to Ferrara, Ercole II should allow them to openly return to Judaism. The Duke agreed to this condition and Ferrara became (for half a century) one of the most important centers in the Sephardic Diaspora.

By its very nature, the Rescue Organization was obviously secret and had no apparent structure. It lacked all the formal instruments that the Jewish Communities of the Peninsula had traditionally used to provide the financial resources necessary to their lives. The Portuguese of Antwerp were, however, able to raise the huge amounts of money indispensable to fund the emigration from the Peninsula, and to pay the *compositions* requested by the Emperor, the Queen-Regent and many officers of varying ranks. Some insights into the complex ramifications of this secret organization may be found in the files of the Fiscal Police of Brabant.[4] From the deposition of several émigrés imprisoned in Lombardy in 1540, we learn the names of several leaders of Portuguese Nation of Antwerp who were directly engaged in the management of the Organization and the indispensable accomplishment of practical tasks. Special mention must be made here of Henrique Pires, Gabriel de Negro, Manuel Serrão, Manuel Lopes, Dominico Lopes, and Lopo de Provincia. Others accomplished dangerous missions, smuggling their fellow-countrymen out of the country into France or Switzerland. They were nicknamed "the conductors" and were especially sought by the imperial police.

According to Wolf, Diogo Mendes established this "widely ramifying organization".[5] Cecil Roth went a step further and alleged that the brains behind this organization were Diogo Mendes and "his amazing sister-in-law", Beatriz.[6] Roth, basing his premise on Wolf, stated that agents of the House of Mendes, located in the other Europeans cities, helped in this

---

3. Duarte Pinto was among the first merchants prepared to accept Duke Ercole's invitation. He became one of the Nation's leaders in Ferrara.
4. Many documents relating to the Portuguese New Christians of Antwerp are gathered in AGR, OFB, 160/1233/2. Other papers are scattered in scores of different files.
5. L. WOLF, *Tudor England*, p. 81.
6. On Doña Gracia, a broad body of literature is available, scattered in dozens of reviews and journals of different countries and in different languages. A. Æ. BROOKS was able to analyze most of the existing works and add new documents to those previously found. We refer the reader to her book (*The woman who defied kings*) for an extensive treatment of the story of this great lady of the Jewish Renaissance and a complete bibliography on Doña Gracia.

process.[7] As we have seen above, this was only the result of speculative assumptions. The Portuguese who ventured on the difficult route from Antwerp to Ferrara could rely on an extremely simple but effective network of carters, boatmen, innkeepers and horse-hirers. To the best of my knowledge, in no case did ordinary émigrés meet with Diogo Mendes' commercial representatives.

I do not want to play down the exceptional importance of Diogo Mendes and Beatriz de Luna, who undoubtedly deserve unique positions in Jewish history. The greatness of their role is by no means diminished by the fact that many others took part in the undertaking, sharing risks and responsibilities.[8] I feel that it is my duty to stress that this organization was the result of the collective efforts of a large number of individuals, who assumed the leadership of the Nation and were prepared to also perform a variety of modest, but no less vital and risky functions. They were determined to save their people, their cultural and religious identity and – last but not least – their properties. The vastness of their accomplishments is impressive: first and most important, their desperate struggle against the establishment of the Inquisition in Portugal and, then, their struggle to prevent the extension of its powers.[9] The cohesiveness and efficiency of this leadership, both in Lisbon and Antwerp, is admirable, taking place decades after the 1497 forced mass conversion in Portugal.[10]

The relatively small Nation of Antwerp repeatedly succeeded in sending its representatives to the Court and obtaining – for a price – the revocation of oppressive measures, release of prisoners, and granting of privileges and safe-conducts for both those who already lived in Antwerp and other would-be immigrants. For these negotiations, the leaders of the Nation frequently employed the Portuguese Royal Factor who, in doing so, acted in contrast to the official policy of his country. The Men of the Nation also succeeded in raising the enormous amounts of money indispensable to sustain these activities – and to pay for these concessions.

---

7. C. ROTH, *Doña Gracia*, p. 31.
8. For instance, L. WOLF (*Tudor England*, p. 78) assumed that Antonio de la Ronha was «the financial agent of Diego Mendes in London». In realty he was simply described as a «merchant in London». L. WOLF stated that Gonçalo Gomes was «the agent of the Mendes firm at Milan.» This might well be possible but there is no evidence that it was so. Cfr. AGR, *Codazzi File,* Gaspar Lopes' witness depositions of September 21, and December 24 1540. See Documents 13, 14, 18 and 19 in Appendix.
9. Cfr. YERUSHALMI, *Prolegomenon,* p. 27.
10. *Ibid.*

Many Portuguese merchants left Antwerp and settled in different Italian States, where they established new "Portuguese Nations" and displayed the same diplomatic abilities and dedication to the service of their people. Perhaps, as a consequence of their past experiences in Lisbon and Antwerp, they gave life to communities where the Parnassim (lay-leaders) exerted much more power than the Rabbis.[11]

As we will see, the activities of the rescue organization did not come to an end when Diogo Mendes died, or when Beatriz de Luna and almost all the leaders of the Nation left Antwerp and moved to Italy. For a few years, João Micas and Guilherme Fernandes represented the Nation at the Court in Brussels. At various times, Agostinho Henriques joined forces with them.

In the middle of the 1540's, a new leadership emerged. Rodrigo Mendes took the place of João Micas, along with Duarte Rodrigues and Christovão Garcia. We shall discuss these important figures in the paragraph devoted to the composition of the Nation in 1549-1550. Unfortunately, at the present time, the names of many others who devoted their energies to the service of their people are not known.

---

11. G. NAHON, *Amsterdam, métropole occidentale des Sefarades*, «Cahiers Spinoza» III, 1979-80, pp. 15-50. IDEM, *Les "Nations"juives portugaises du Sud-Ouest de la France (1684-1791), Documents*, Paris 1981, IDEM "L'impact de l'expulsion", cit., Y. KAPLAN, *The Social Function of the Herem in the Portuguese Jewish Comunity of Amsterdam* in J.MICHMAN and T. LEVIE Eds., *Dutch Jewish History*, Tel Aviv 1984, 111-156.

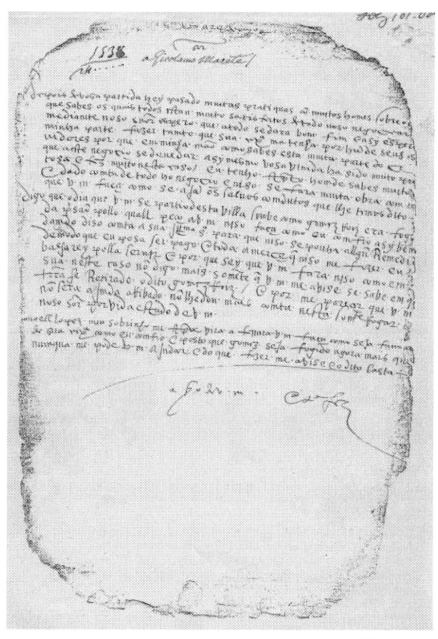

A letter of Antonio Fernandez to Gerolamo Maretta, — July 24, 1538.
Source: ASMo, CD, *Lettere Particolari*, B. 837. See Document 6 in Appendix.

§ 20. The Expulsion from Antwerp (1549)

An imperial decree issued on July 17, 1549, rescinded the privileges granted by Charles V in 1542, and forbade any further settlement of New Christians in the Netherlands. All the Portuguese émigrés who had arrived in Antwerp during the preceding six years were given one month to leave the country. The Antwerp elders raised all sorts of objections against the banishment and refused to publish the decree.[1] They stated that most of the trade between Flanders and the Iberian Peninsula was in the hands of Portuguese merchants: their departure would seriously affect the economy of their city.[2] In order to overcome these objections, the Bishop of Arras[3], acting in his capacity as secretary to the Emperor,[4] let it be known that a few Portuguese families might be allowed to remain. Charles V would examine the Margrave's recommendations to this effect, on condition that he would publish the *placard* without any further delay. The Margrave persisted in his refusal and renewed his plea in favor of the Portuguese Nation. He was later indicted on charges of insubordination.

The leaders of the Nation sent a delegation to the Court. A compromise was reached whereby twenty-five "recent arrivals" were allowed to remain. However, on March 13, 1550, Queen Mary wrote to the

---

1. AGR, PEA 1177, August 5,1549: *Advertissement au Marcgrave*
2. P. GÉNARD, *Die nieuwe Christenen the Antwerpen in de XVIe eeuw*, «Antwerpsch Archievendblad» III (s.d.), pp. 224-237; IDEM, *Personen te Antwerpen*, 2nd Part, «Antwerpsch Archievendblad» VIII, pp. 377-384. See also the new documents (63, 64, 65) that we are publishing here, in Appendix
3. Antoine Perrenot de Granvelle (son of Nicolas, the imperial State Secretary) was appointed bishop of Arras by Paul III on November 29, 1538. See K. de JONGE und G. JANSSENS, *Les Granvelles*, pp. 20-21.
4. See AGR, PEA 1652, undated [March 1549] letter of the Emperor to the bishop. See also Document 63 in Appendix.

Margrave that the concession was cancelled. All the Portuguese who had arrived in Antwerp after 1541 were to leave within five weeks. Once again the city's elders did not comply with the Emperor's orders. In fact, some of these émigrés later were found in the city. Most of those who left Antwerp in 1549 moved to Ferrara where they became the victims of another expulsion. On September 14, 1549, all the Portuguese immigrants who had arrived in the ducal city during the preceding four months were ordered to leave: they were suspected of contracting the plague during their journey through the Grisons.[5]

---

5. ASMo,CD, Gridario, Registri di Grida Manoscritte, B.1b, Vol. 1534-1559; A.di LEONI LEONI, *La Nazion Portughesa corteggiata, privilegiata, espulsa e riammessa a Ferrara (1538-1550)*, «Italia, Studi e Ricerche sulla Storia la Cultura e la Letteratura degli Ebrei d'Italia», XIII-XV, Jerusalem, The Magnes Press, 2001, pp. 211-247: 229-240. See the pathetic description in Samuel Usque's *Consolaçam*, pp. 216r-217v. On the dating of this event see the discussion in LEONI, *Manoel Lopes Bichacho*, pp. 87-88.

§ 21. Some Outstanding Figures in Antwerp in 1540

In (or around) 1540, the imperial police drew up a list with the names of twenty-six prominent New Christians living in Antwerp. A footnote states that most of these people were very rich.[1] In all likelihood, the document was drawn up with the purpose of selecting future victims from among these names. Far from providing a complete census of the New Christians in Antwerp, the document is however unique. To the best of my knowledge, this is the only list of merchants drafted in Antwerp during this period. It supplements and completes the documentation published by Révah in his fundamental study on the Portuguese Nation of Antwerp from 1571 to 1666.[2]

In the Brussels Archives, we have found lists of immigrants arrested upon their arrival in Zeeland's ports, or rounded up in Antwerp in the first half of the XVIth century. Other names of New Christians living in Antwerp, Lisbon and London are to be found in testimonies of émigrés captured in Lombardy while travelling from Antwerp towards Ferrara.[3] We have tried to assemble information on some outstanding figures provided in these different sources. We shall start with the names of the "1540 list".

---

1. AGR,Bxl, PEA B.1504. The precious document consists of one originally undated, loose, unnumbered sheet. See Document 12 in Appendix.
2. I.S. RÉVAH, *Pour l'histoire des Marranes à Anvers, recensements de la Nation Portugaise de 1571 à 1666*, «REJ» CXXII, pp. 123-147. GORIS (*Colonies marchandes*, p. 654) drew up a list of twenty Portuguese individuals supposedly living in the city in 1540. Strangely enough, it comprises, along with five prominent merchants, several recent émigrés who probably did not stay in Antwerp but continued their journey towards Italy and the Levant. In fact, the author did not mention them again.
3. AGR,B, OFB 160/1233/2: *Codazzi File*. See Documents 18 and 19 in the Appendix.

§ 21.1 Diogo Mendes: his family and entourage.

Diogo Mendes Benveniste and his sister-in-law, Beatriz de Luna, played a leading role in Jewish history. Ample literature is available on them and it is not necessary to recapitulate it here. We shall try to provide some new details.

Scholars have already stated, in part by mere guesswork, that Diogo Mendes and his family assembled for prayers in private oratories, abstained from forbidden food, ate unleavened bread on Passover and fasted on the Day of Atonement.[4] All this has been confirmed by the depositions of Gaspar Lopes,[5] a Diogo Mendes' relative kept in custody in Vigevano and Pavia.[6] He confessed that he had been in Diogo's private chapel a few times while prayers, mainly psalms in Spanish, were being said aloud by a young girl dressed in white. These *oraciones* were labeled "Tefilà in the Castilian language".[7] The testimony did not state whether they were read from a printed book or from manuscripts, so that it cannot be inferred from the document whether complete translations of the Jewish prayer book were available to the Portuguese *Marranos* in Antwerp during this period. However, in 1538, Diogo Mendes had obtained a special privilege from Pope Paul III that allowed him to choose a personal confessor, to keep a movable altar in his house and to conduct private (supposedly Catholic) services at home.[8]

A few years earlier [in 1532] some Jewish books were seized in the house of Diogo Mendes and were sent to the theologians of the Louvain University for examination. As they were unable to read Hebrew, two

---

4. C. ROTH, *Doña Gracia,* pp. 28-29.

5. On Gaspar Lopes, see below, in this same chapter.

6. AGR, *Codazzi file,* f. 27v, Dec.. 29, 1540: «in eius [Diego Mendes'] domo tenet sinagogam secretam in qua pluries fuit … quando jlla juvenis nuncupata Jsabella filia cuiusdam nuncupate *la Castigliana* … cantabat eorum officia, videlicet Psalmos Davit nuncupatos *Tefilà in lingua Castigliana* et alia faciebat et facit dictus Diegus Men[d]es prout jpse constitutus dixit».

7. On the diffusion of vulgarisations of Hebrew prayers in 16th Century Castille see I. S. Révah *Antonio Enríquez Gómez - Un écrivain marrane (v. 1600-1663), postumously edited by* Carsten L. Wilke, with a preface by Gérard Nahon, Paris 2003. This work contains an incredible wealth of information on the Marrano Ritual and is enriched by a wide documentary appendix.

8. S. SIMONSOHN, *The Apostolic See, History,* p. 447. IDEM, *The Apostolic See, Documents, 1539-1545:* Doc. 1851.

books were delivered to Andreas Baleno, professor of Hebrew at the Three-Languages-College. He stated that they were a Psalter and a prayer book according to the German rite. These prayers, he noted, were different from the ones of Spanish Jews.[9] We can infer from the deposition that Diogo had, at least, some knowledge of Hebrew. Bernardo Micas, Diogo's nephew[10], was taking Hebrew lessons from Andreas Baleno. Once he told his teacher that a Portuguese (unnamed- probably Diogo Mendes) had questioned him about his progress and had corrected one of his mistakes in the declination of a verb.[11]

Diogo Mendes had a prominent position in the Organization that promoted and planned the flight of *Marranos* from the Iberian Peninsula. He also played a direct and unique role in the establishment of the Portuguese Nation of Ferrara. On October 9, 1538, Diogo put himself at Duke Ercole's disposal. However, for some reason, Gerolamo Maretta, the Ferrara envoy in Antwerp, did not succeed in developing a good relationship with Diogo, and conducted the negotiations with António Fernandes instead.[12]

In 1541, when Bastião Rodrigues Pinto established a commercial company for trading sugar, in partnership with the Duke of Ferrara, Diogo Mendes offered a guarantee of 3,000 ducats in favor of Bastião, in the form of a bill of exchange made payable to the Duke.[13] Furthermore, Diogo saw to it that the new company was provided with regular supplies of sugar[14], a rather rare product at the time.[15] Diogo was well aware that the destiny of the newly born Portuguese Nation of Ferrara depended

---

9. AGR, OFB, 160/1233/2, *Enquete faite en 1540 ...*, October 5, 1540, witness testimony of Andreas Balenus.

10. Bernardo Micas and his brother João were the sons of Doctor Agostinho Henriques Micas (Samuel de Josef Nasi) who was married to a sister of Diogo Mendes. See SALOMON-LEONI, *Mendes, Benveniste*, pp. 169-170.

11. *Ibid.;* Cfr. SALOMON-LEONI. *Mendes, Benveniste*, pp. 189-190.

12. ASMo,CD, Lettere particolari, B. 885. A. di LEONE LEONI, *La Diplomazia Estense*, p. 302.

13. ASMo,CD, Carteggio Referendari ... Segretari, Busta 171. See Document 23 in Appendix.

14. A.di LEONE LEONI, *La Diplomazia Estense*, p. 302.

15. On the sugar market in northern Italy see LEONI, *Quotidiana imprenditorialità,* pp. 73-74.

largely on the success of these undertakings and, ultimately, on the profit accruing to the Duke and the extent of his satisfaction.

We found almost no reference to Gonçalo Mendes, Diogo's brother, in the Brussels Archives. From other sources, we learn that he settled in Antwerp around 1538.[16] He was not an associate in his brother's business but did entrust a part of his estate to Diogo. Gonçalo died in 1545, and was survived by his wife, Ana Fernandes, with whom he had no children. In his last will and testament, drawn up by notary Strict,[17] he left half of his property to his widow and the other half to his sisters-in-law and niece, Beatriz and Brianda de Luna respectively. Beatriz [later to achieve legendary fame as Doña Gracia Nasi][18] the widow of Francisco Mendes, and her sister, Brianda Mendes de Luna [later called Reina] the wife of Diogo Mendes, were the daughters of Alvaro de Luna and of Ph[ilip?]a[19] Mendes Benveniste: they were also their husbands' nieces. According to Gaspar Lopes, Brianda was even more zealous than Diogo in the observance of Jewish precepts.[20]

On Beatriz de Luna, we found in the Brussels' Archives the confirmation of an episode reported by Gerolamo Maretta, the Ferrara envoy in Antwerp. Between 1538 and 1539, Beatriz decided to leave Antwerp and settle in Ferrara, taking with her all her capital, amounting to 300,000

---

16. See S. SIMONSOHN, *The Apostolic See, Documents 1522-1538*, Doc 1851, pp. 2084-2087; Cfr. SALOMON-LEONI, p. 141, note 40.

17. Notary Strict's files relating to 1545 are no longer extant in Antwerp's Municipal Archives.

18. Cfr : A. BROOKS, *The Woman who defied Kings*. While much had been previously written on Doña Gracia Nasi, Andrée Aelion Brooks has brought attention to the legend and the deeds of this fantastic Renaissance woman.

19. The name is found in one only document [discovered and perused by Salomon] in an abridged form. "Phla" (AGR,PEA 1172/2, N.19, March 15 and 16 1541, deposition of Fernando Rodrigues, quoted in Salomon and Leoni, *Mendes, Benveniste De Luna*, p. 172, note 119. The deposition was taken by an interpreter and I am not sure about the correctness of its transcription. It may be either the shortening of a name (Philipa) or a form derived from the Judeo-Spanish word, Peloni (fem.: pelonit, pelona), which means "somebody, an un-specified person". The Hebrew (or Judeo-Spanish) word peloni or pheloni פלוני was absorbed into the Iberian languages and is still used in modern Portuguese in the form *fulano* with the same meaning of "someone, an undetermined person". In Spain the form *fuláno* is still extant but now, in the familiar jargon the word has assumed the somewhat derogatory meaning of a person whom you do not want to call by name, for instance a lover, a mistress or even a prostitute.

20. AGR, *Codazzi File*, Dec. 24, 1540. See document 18 in Appendix.

gold ducats. This decision was apparently motivated, at least in part, by delusion and jealousy, as Diogo Mendes had preferred to marry Brianda. Doctor Dionisio advised Beatriz to leave the house of Diogo and to take up separate residence while waiting for the necessary safe-conducts from the Duke of Ferrara and the King of France.[21]

The precious papers went astray and did not reach Beatriz in time for her to travel to Italy with the ducal envoy. In 1540, Gaspar Lopes, a prisoner in Pavia, confirmed some of these circumstances.[22] In May 1544, Beatriz sheltered some newcomers in her house, gave them employment and tried to keep them out of prison.[23]

Strangely enough, the documents preserved in the Royal Archives provide scant information on the entourage of Diogo Mendes, his relatives, stewards and agents. However we know that Diogo lived in a "Hostel" (palace)[24] with wide gardens.[25] He had "a very large family" of fifty to sixty people that included stewards, clerks of his trading and banking company, and domestic servants and valets.[26] Most of them were Portuguese. The "1540 list"[27] includes two young valets of Diogo Mendes: Rodrigo [no family name stated] and Gonçalo Diez. We could identify the latter as a relative of Brianda de Luna's. He was eighteen years old at the time.[28]

In his last will and testament, Diogo Mendes entrusted the administration of the "House of Mendes" to his sister-in-law Beatriz, assisted by

---

21. A. di Leone Leoni, *La Diplomazia Estense,* pp. 307-308, 323.

22. AGR, *Codazzi File,* f. 25r, Gaspar Lopes' deposition of September 22, 1540: «scit pro certo quod soror uxoris Dieg Men[d]es nomine Beatrix de Luna omnino erat ventura ...». See Document 18 in Appendix .

23. AGR, OFB, 160/1233/3 *Noms et surnoms des personnes detenuez...*See in Appendix Document 53.

24. See AGR, PEA 1177/2 ff. 15r-16r where a young woman seeking employment in Diego Mendes' *hostel* is mentioned.

25. See M. Lemos, *Amato Lusitano nos Países Baixos. Correções e Aditamentos,* «Revista da Universitade de Coimbra», X 1927, pp. 5-38: 7. The famous doctor reported that he had seen a special variety of medicinal herbs in Diogo Mendes' gardens.

26. AGR, *Codazzi file,* ff. 24r-24v, September 22, 1540, Gaspar Lopes' deposition: "Respondit quod dictus Dieg Men[d]es habet familiam numero quinquaginta vel sexaginta personarum".

27. See Document 12 in Appendix.

28. AGR, *Codazzi file,* September 22, 1540, Gaspar Lopes' deposition.

Guilherme [possibly Abraham][29] Fernandes and João Micas[30], who subsequently acted as "factores negotiorum et gestores ac gubernatores bonorum hereditatis olim Dominorum Francisci et Diegi Mendes".

From other sources, we know that Guilherme Fernandes had entered
into Francisco Mendes' service in Lisbon in 1525.[31] Guilherme was the
son of Agnes Gomes and Gonçalvo Fernandes.[32] His brothers, Duarte
Gomes [*alias* David Zaboca][33] and Thomas Gomes, were also in Doña
Beatriz's service as factors. A 1544 document describes Duarte as «gov-
erning the House of the late Diogo Mendes».[34] Five years later, in
Ferrara, the notaries used expressions of deep reverence when referring to
the three brothers. Another brother, Vicente [Iona] is mentioned in a deposition by Duarte Gomes (in 1555). At the time, he lived in Istanbul. His
profession was not stated.[35]

In his last will and testament, Diogo Mendes had stated that, in the
case of Beatriz' death, Agostinho was to replace her, both in the administration of the House of Mendes and the guardianship of Diogo's daughter. However, no particular role was assigned to him during Beatriz' life.
At a certain point, Beatriz de Luna engaged Agostinho Henriques as her
factor and agent. The appointment was reconfirmed in Ferrara, in 1549.[36]

---

29. ASVe, Santo Uffizio, Processi Busta 159, August 1, 1555: according to Duarte Gomes
his brothers Guilherme, Thomas and Vicente, now living in Istanbul, were called
Abraham, Ioseph, Iona. Cfr. P.C. IOLY ZORATTINI, *Processi 1548-1560*, p. 230.
30. See SALOMON-LEONI, *Mendes, Benveniste*, p. 152 and doc. 12, p. 195.
31. Cfr. ASVe, not. Paolo Leoncini, Busta 7818, f. 192r. Aug. 4, 1552.
32. ASFe, not. Giacomo Conti, Matr. 584, *Pacco* 3, November 12, 1549. In the notary
deeds drawn in Ferrara in 1549 Guilherme Fernandes was referred to as "Nobilis et
Magnificus Dominus Gulielmus filius quondam Nobilis et Magnifici Gondisalvi
Ferdinandi".
33. ANTT, Lisboa, Inquisição de Lisboa, Processo n. 2931, f. 73r: March 8, 1581, interrogation of Henrique Nuñes (alias Abraham Benveniste); P.C. IOLY ZORATTINI, *Processi,
1570-72*, p. 271.
34. AGR,PEA 132, July 22, 1544 Councillour Corneille Scepperus to the Queen. This
document disproves and corrects a Venetian notary deed according to which Duarte
entered Beatriz' service in 1545. Cfr. ASVe, not. Paolo Leoncini, Busta 7818, f. 194,
August 1552.
35. P.C. IOLY ZORATTINI, *Processi 1548-1560*, p. 230.
36. ASFe, not. Codegori, Matr. 582, *pacco* 9, February 1, 1549 Beatriz, now living in
Ferrara, entrusts "Agostino Enrix Venetijs habitans" with power of attorney enabling him
to manage her business and to collect all her credits. On Agostinho Enriques see P.C. Ioly
Zorattini, *Processi I, sub indice*.

Diogo Mendes also had a poor kinsman: Gaspar Lopes, the son of Baldassar Lopes, Diogo's half-brother. According to information gathered by the imperial police in Pavia,[37] Gaspar's grandmother, Mor Lopes, was either the second wife or the mistress of Diogo Mendes' father.[38] Before moving to Antwerp, Gaspar spent two and a half years in London where he lived in the house of Diego de la Ronha (probably a kinsman of the above mentioned António de la Ronha). There is no evidence that Gaspar ever worked for Diogo Mendes' company in London, as stated by Wolf.[39] During his short stay in Antwerp, Gaspar had many opportunities to spend time with his important uncle and to see, or become acquainted with, almost all the members of the Portuguese colony in the city. Gaspar was married to Agnes Fernandes. Emanuel de Provincia performed a second nuptial ceremony, according to the "Jewish rite", in Antwerp. Diogo Mendes gave to the bridegroom, as a "dowry", a 200 ducats bill of exchange drawn on Emanuel Pinhero in Ferrara. In fact, after his Jewish marriage, Gaspar left Antwerp for Ferrara, together with a "company" of about seven émigrés traveling with their families. His wife, mother-in-law, brother-in-law and sister-in-law traveled with him. They were intercepted in Lombardy (or Lucerne) and kept in custody for many months. Submitted to torture, they denounced as *falsos christianos* many Portuguese merchants of Antwerp against whom Johannes Vuysting was trying to collect incriminating evidence.[40] All the prisoners, with the exception of Gaspar Lopes, were released in either December 1540 or January 1541. Gaspar was kept in custody until July 3, 1541, when he was set free by orders of the Marquis del Vasto, governor of Milan, probably at the request of the Duke of Ferrara.[41]

From documents preserved at the Notary Archives of Ferrara, we learn that Samuel Usque, the author to-be of the *Consolaçam às Tribolações de Israel*, was at Diogo's service in Antwerp. After Diogo's death, Samuel worked for Brianda Mendes for unspecified and non-con-

---

37. AGR, *Codazzi file*, f. 23r: Dec.. 24, 1540: statement added by the public prosecutor of Pavia at the end of Gaspar's deposition: the prisoner had refrained from disclosing this information.
38. We do not know the name of Diogo's father.
39. Cfr. L. Wolf, *Tudor England*, p. 79.
40. SALOMON-LEONI, *Mendes, Benveniste*, p. 173. Gaspar's depositions of December 24, 1540, in Pavia provide wide information on Diego Mendes and many New Christians living in Lisbon, Antwerp and London. See Documents 18 and 19 in Appendix.
41. AGR, *Codazzi File,* f. 36v, July 3, 1541.

tiguous periods of time. In 1545, Samuel lived in Ancona and was described as a Portuguese Jewish merchant.[42] His commercial activities were apparently unsuccessful and, at some point, he again worked for Brianda. In 1549, a bitter quarrel erupted between Samuel and his powerful employer, who denounced him (for unstated reasons) and caused him to be detained.[43] Samuel was set free thanks to the intervention of Doña Gracia. Both he and Doña Brianda agreed to settle their dispute by means of a "compromise"[44], according to the privilege of the Portuguese Nation of Ferrara.[45] They appointed arbiters who had the task of establishing the amount of money due to Samuel in settlement of his wages for the periods he had worked for Brianda in Antwerp, Venice and Ferrara after Diogo Mendes' death.

As the baptismal name of Samuel is not known, we cannot state whether he is mentioned in the documents kept at the archives in Brussels.

Strangely enough, Samuel devoted only three words to Flanders in the chapter of the *Consolaçam* describing the hardships suffered by "those who have left and are leaving Portugal."[46]

Some of those who escaped with anguish and danger, and ultimately left the Kingdom of Portugal, fared poorly in foreign lands: they were captured in Spain, arrested in Flanders and despised and abused in England and France. Because of such difficulties many lost their fortunes and their lives .[47]

---

42. A. di LEONE LEONI, *La Diplomazia Estense*, pp. 320-21.

43. IDEM, *La Nazion Portughesa corteggiata*, p. 234.

44. ASFe, not. P.A. Franchi, matr. 495, *pacco* 3, September 24, 1549: *Compromissum inter Samuelem Usque et Briandam de Lunam*: «... a toto quod ipse Samuel habere debet vel habere dedere pretendit a dicta domina Brianda in Anversa post mortem Dieghi Mendes, Venetijs ac Ferrariæ.» This is the only known source stating that Samuel was at Diego's service. See the detailed account in M.T. GUERRINI, *New Documents on Samuel Usque,* «Sefarad» 62, 2002, pp. 99-124.

45. A. di LEONE LEONI, *Documents inédits*, pp. 147-150, 153-155 and Doc. 3 therein.

46. *Samuel Usque's Consolation for the Tribulations of Israel,* edited and translated by M. A. COHEN, Philadelphia 5737-1977, p. 208.

47. «Dos que com tanta angustia e periguo ... escaparon e ultimamente do reino portugues se sayrom, algūs em estranhos reynos pararom mal, sendo presos na Espanha, detidos em Frādes, mal vistos e recebidos em Ynglaterra e França cõ as quaēs averaçoēs muitos suas fazendas consumirom e cõ ellas as vidas e os corpos acabarom» S. Usque, *Consolaçam*, ff. 209r-209v.

As it can be seen, Antwerp is not even mentioned in his account. Another reference to Flanders is given when the author describes the generous help provided by Doña Gracia Nasi to «the refugees (who) arrived destitute, sea-sick and stuporous in Flanders».[48]

§ 21.2 Domingo Mendes

Son of the late Johannes Mendes of Lisbon, Domingo was a successful merchant, and a member of the Rescue Organization. He provided immigrants with money, moral support, carts and instructions for the journey to Ferrara.[49]

§ 21.3 Lope Mendes

All we know about him is the short mention made by Gaspar Lopes in his deposition of December 24, 1540: «Lopum Mendes in Anversia, licentiatum ettatis annorum 50 vel circa».[50]

§ 21.4 Duarte and Bastião Pinto and their brothers

Duarte was one of the leaders of the Portuguese Nation. He had influence and relations with both the Portuguese government and the Roman Curia. He was the brother of Diego (*alias* Jacob), Bastião, João, Estacio and Anna (the wife of António de la Ronha).

João had lived in the Azores Islands where he had farmed the royal customs revenues. He had also been engaged in the sugar industry and in the spice trade.[51] In 1535 Diego was in Rome where he represented the

---

48. *Ibid.* f. 239r . Cfr. MARTIN COHEN's English translation, p. 230.
49. AGR, *Codazzi file,* f. 7r, September 20 1540, deposition of Odoardo Rodrico de Castignedo: «Principalis dictæ Bursæ est Diegus Men[d]es Benvenisti et Gabriel de Nigro et prefati Manoel Saran, Dominicus Mendes, Lopes de Provincia et Manoel Lopes sunt jlli qui dant peccunias jstis qui volunt jre ad locum Salonichij in partibus Turchie pro negando fidem Xpi et jpse habuit a suprascripto Lope de Provincia scutos decem et octo prout supra dixit». See also, Michael Nuñes'deposition, *Ibid.*, f. 9r, September 20, 1540.
50. AGR, *Codazzi file,* see in appendix Document 18.
51. ASAn, not. G. Monaco, vol. 881, January 1535. Cfr. V. BONAZZOLI, *Una identità ricostruita,* p. 13. See, above, § 5, pp. 21-22.

Men of the Nation together with Duarte de Paz.[52] He died in Ancona in 1538.[53]

In (or around) 1540, João Pinto was living in Ragusa.[54] A younger brother, Estacio, about thirty years old, lived in Antwerp (until 1539-40) and traded in Indian textiles and precious stones. Duarte left Antwerp and moved to Ferrara in 1539. On the way, he was arrested by Johannes Vuysting's agents in Lombardy and subsequently was released by the Governor of Milan thanks to Duke Ercole d'Este's intervention.[55] A few months later, his brother Bastião set out on the journey to Ferrara, reportedly with Estevão Pires. Shortly after, his wife, and her father and brother [names unknown] joined him.[56] Duarte and Bastião had been among the first merchants to export large quantities of English and Flemish woolen and linen textiles from Northern Europe to Ancona.[57]

In 1541, Bastião Rodrigues Pinto established a commercial company, in partnership with the Duke of Ferrara, for the trade of sugar and "western" textiles.[58] In 1547, he obtained from Duke Cosimo de' Medici the privilege of settling in Tuscany together with six other *Men of his Nation*[59]. From the information presently available, we do not know who actually took advantage of this concession. In Ferrara, Bastião was one of the first leaders of the Portuguese Nation.[60] Amato Lusitano reported that, in Ferrara, he had cured the wife of Bastião of puerperal fever, from which she recovered, but that she subsequently died of breast cancer.[61]

---

52. A. HERCULANO, *History of the Origin*, pp. 359, 383-84.
53. See S. SIMONSOHN, *The Apostolic See, Documents 1539-1545*: Doc. 1913.
54. ASMo, Cancelleria Estero, *Ambasciatori Milano,* October 10, 1540: Gerolamo Maretta to the Duke. See A. di LEONE LEONI, *La Diplomazia Estense,* p. 311.
55. A. di Leone Leoni, *La Diplomazia Estense,* pp. 309-310. See Document 10 in Appendix.
56. AGR, OFB 1601233/2, *Enquete faite à Anvers en 1540 au sujet des Nouveaux Christiens,* October 19 1540: interrogation and deposition of Diego de Redondo. See Document 15 in Appendix.
57. See A. di LEONE LEONI, *Ancona e Pesaro*, pp. 31-32.
58. A. di LEONE LEONI, *La Diplomazia Estense*, pp. 319, IDEM, *La Nazion Portughesa corteggiata,* p. 217.
59. See L. FRATTARELLI FISCHER, *Cristiani Nuovi e Nuovi Ebrei in Toscana fra Cinque e Seicento,* in P.C. IOLY ZORATTINI, Edit., *L'identità dissimulata,* pp. 99-150: p. 101.
60. See LEONI, *La Nazion Portughesa corteggiata,* p. 235.
61. Amato Lusitano, *In Dioscoridis Anarzabei de medica materia, Curatio XXXI*, p. 55. Amato did not give her name but stated that she was thirty years old. «Uxor Sebastiani Pinti etate triginta annorum puellam optime peperit ...».

In (or around) 1540, Estacio left Antwerp and moved to Italy. He was intercepted by Vuysting's agents and kept prisoner in Cremona. He was released thanks to the intervention of Don Lopez de Soria.[62]

§ 21.5 Luis Peres

Luis Peres (or Pires) was among the first members of the pepper consortium, and took part in its organization. In 1527, he contributed 30,000 Flemish pounds for a loan to the Emperor.[63] He did not limit his activities to spices, but also dispatched ships fully loaded with wheat to Portugal.[64] He was engaged in the sugar industry and imported huge amounts of this precious merchandise from the Portuguese "African" Islands.[65] He imported dry fruits (especially figs) and wines to Antwerp. Luis Pires died in or around 1550.[66]

§ 21.6 Luis de Sevilla

In 1540, he was described as a sixty-year-old merchant. According to rumors, his wife was in Salonica.[67] On April 10, 1540, he hired the Breton ship *Saint Paul de Léon* and dispatched it to the Algarve to load dry fruits.[68]

§ 21.7 Gabriel de Negro

As we have seen, Gabriel was an important merchant and prominent partner in the pepper consortium. He imported full shiploads of sugar from

---

62. AGR, Bx, PEA 1631.

63. J.A. GORIS, *Colonies marchandes*, p. 563.

64. *Ibid.*, pp. 162-167, Tableaux "A" (1535) and "B" (1540).

65. DENUCÉ, Jean, *L'Afrique au XVIe siècle et le commerce anversois, cit.,* pp. 93-96 : Appendix I, *Départs et arrivées de navires d'Afrique, aux annés 1549-1555, d'après le fragment d'un livre d'assurances maritimes anversoises.*

66. *Ibid.*, pp. 93-96 : between 1550 and 1556, five ships were loaded in the Atlantic Island of São Tomé on account of the "heirs of Luis Pires."

67. AGR, *Codazzi file*, f. 30r, Dec.. 24, 1540, witness testimony of Gaspar Lopes: «Aluisium de Scivilia, in Anversia, cuius uxor manebat in Salonico prout jpse jntellexit, annorum 60 vel circa». See Document 18 in Appendix.

68. J. DENUCÉ, *L'Afrique au XVIe siècle et le commerce anversois,* Appendix I, *cit.*; J.A. GORIS, *Colonies marchandes*, p. 164-165, Tableau "A". Curiously enough, Goris described Luys de Sevilla as Spanish, probably on the basis of his name.

the Atlantic Islands, and dispatched wheat and extra-fine clothes to Portugal.[69] Gabriel was one of the leaders of the Nation and a member of the Rescue Organization. One of his daughters was said to have married Ignacio Lopes Coronel,[70] and to have fled to the Levant. Another daughter was married to Fernando Peres Coronel,[71] a former officer of the House of Mendes.[72]After his famous escape from Antwerp in 1540, Gabriel settled in the Venetian Ghetto where he was known as Moshe Yaḥia de Negro.[73] We do not know whether he was related to Gedalia Yaḥia, who was reported to be living in Venice at the same time. Some time after 1543, Moshe moved to the Levant.[74] In the 1560's, his sons "Don" David and "Don" Abraham, returned to Italy and settled in Ferrara, where they were highly respected and usually referred to as "nobiles et magnifici domini". They served as Massari (Parnassim) of the Portuguese Nation for many terms.[75] They later returned to Salonica and were primarily engaged in trade with Venice.[76] The Family Yaḥia is still extant in Italy.

§ 21.8 Henrique Pires [*alias* Iacob Cohen] and his Family.

A prominent merchant, partner of the pepper consortium and member of the Rescue Organization in Antwerp, he was one of the twenty-five martyrs burned on the stake in Ancona in 1556 (see below). Henrique had, at

---

69. *Ibid*. pp. 162-167, Tableaux "A" (1535) and "B" (1540).
70. AGR, *Lavezzoli File*, f. 61.
71. Fernando (Jewish name unknown) settled in Ancona in or around 1539. See V. BONAZZOLI, *Una identità ricostruita, I Portoghesi ad Ancona* , pp. 22, 24, 25.
72. AGR, OFCB, B. 160/1233/2: *Enquete sur les nouveaux Christiens*, witness testimonies of Andreas de Salamanca, Guillaume van Raet, Nicolas Fernandes, Jacob Raet (?), "vieux chrètiens".
73. A. di LEONE LEONI, *La presenza sefardita*, pp. 63-64.
74. ASFE, not. Andrea Coccapani, Matr. 534, *pacco* 10, October 8 1558 The "Magnifici Domini" Davit and Abraam Jaḥia, sons of the late Gabriel de Nigro *alias* Moyses Jaḥia, state that in 1543, in Venice, their father had received a bill of exchange on behalf of Ezra Vezinho [*alias* Mendes Francesco, ASFE, not. Andrea Coccapani, *pacco* 9, January 5 and 15 1558]. On December 15, 1543, in Venice, Gabriel de Negro signed a statement to this effect.
75. ASFe, not. G. Conti, matr. 584, *pacco* 7S, Dec. 14, 1557.
76. Cfr. A. di LEONE LEONI, *Una Teshuba del Ma"haRaShdaM di Salonicco su una vertenza tra due Consoli dei mercanti ebrei nella Venezia del Cinquecento*, «Zakhor» VII/2004 pp. 143–192: 188 and document 19 therein.

least, four sons and one daughter: Diogo Pires [Isaia Cohen],[77] Emanuel
Henriques [David Cohen], Duarte Henriques [Abraham Cohen], Simão
Anriques [Ḥayim Cohen] and Anna Henriques married to Estevão
Pires.[78]

In (or about) 1541, Henrique moved to Ferrara. His son, Emanuel
Henriques[79], was already living there. Diego Pires reached Ferrara in the
same period. Duarte Henriques remained in Antwerp and took care of the
family business.[80] He later went to Ferrara where he was known as
Abraham Cohen. In 1545, Henrique was involved in a financial dispute
between his nephew (and associate) Estevão and the Ducal Chamber (see
below). Towards 1552, he moved to Ancona.

In 1555, the fanatical Pope Paul IV (formerly Cardinal Carafa) succeeded Julius III to the throne of St. Peter. In the beginning, he formally
approved the privileges granted to the Portuguese Nation by his prede-
cessors, but a few months later he abruptly changed his mind and adopted an infamous policy towards the Jews, in general, and the former
Portuguese conversos in particular. On July 14, 1555, he enacted the infamous Papal Bull *Cum nimis absurdum*[81], imposing severe hardships on
the Jews. Two months later, he unilaterally revoked all the concessions
granted to (and negotiated with) the former conversos of Ancona, and
unleashed cruel persecutions against them.[82] The papal police rounded up
all the Portuguese they could find and carefully seized all their goods and
credits.[83] Iacob Cohen was among the prisoners. Together with twenty-
four other former Marranos, he endured tortures and refused any propos-

---

77. The famous poet known by his *nom-de-plume* as Pyrrhus Lusitanus.

78. See below, § 22.9

79. AGR, *Lavezzoli file*: on February 26, 1541 "Nobilis vir" Emanuel described himself
as "filius et coniuncta persona Domini Anrici Pires".

80. ASFe, not. Lavezzoli, *pacco* 5, f. 57, May 17, 1541: Enrico Piris, Portuguese merchant living in Ferrara, entrusts his son "Oduardus Enricus" living in Antwerp with power
of attorney.

81. C. Roth, *The History of the Jews of Italy*, Philadelphia 1946, pp. 294-309; A. Milano,
Storia degli Ebrei in Italia, cit., pp. 244-253. R. BONFIL, *the Spanish and Portuguese Jews
in Italy, cit.*, pp. 224-227.

82. S. W. BARON, *A Social and Religious History of the Jews*, Vol. XIV, pp. 37-49;

83. See the inventories published by R. SEGRE, *Nuovi documenti sui Marrani di
Ancona,(1555-1559)* in «Michael» IX Tel Aviv 1985; V. BONAZZOLI, *Ebrei Italiani,
Portoghesi, Levantini sulla piazza commerciale di Ancona intorno alla metà del
Cinquecento* in G. COZZI, Edit.., *Gli Ebrei a Venezia*, Milano 1987, pp. 727-770: 755-757.

als to be reconciliated to the Church and have his life spared.[84] He died in one of the autos da fé celebrated in Ancona between May and June 1556.[85] Several *Marranos* succeeded in fleeing from Ancona and found shelter in Pesaro.[86] Among these fugitives there were two of Iacob's sons: Emanuel[87], and Diogo[88] who later moved to Ragusa.

In 1562, Duarte Henriques was living in London: his sister, Anna, the widow of Estevão Pires, entrusted him and Henrique Nuñes, a medical doctor, with power of attorney, enabling them to deal with the business and to collect all the credits of her late husband.[89] We do not know exactly when Duarte settled in the Venetian Ghetto where he was called Abraham Cohen. In 1572, he was denounced, apparently anonymously, to the Venetian Inquisition; accused of trading in Rialto dressed in Christian garb [i.e. without the red or yellow hat of the Jews]. The Santo Uffizio did not proceed against him[90], probably because Abraham, together with the other merchants of the Portuguese Nation of Ferrara, enjoyed extensive privileges.[91]

In 1575 Abraham was in Ferrara where he served as Parnas of the Portuguese Nation.[92] He lived in the center of town on *Sarraceno* Street, in front of the house of Isaac Benefray. Lopo Luis, a prisoner in Lisbon,

---

84. I am deeply indebted to Dr. António Manuel Lopes Andrade of the University of Aveiro for his precious bibliographical advice and for helping me in identifying Enrique Pires with the martyr Iacob Cohen. António Andrade is preparing an important study on *O Cato Minor de Diogo Pires e a poesia didáctica do século XVI.*

85. See BENIAMIN NEHEMIAH ben ELNATAN's Cronicle: *Divrè ha-Yamim* published *in extenso* by I. SONNE, *Mi Paulo ha-Revi'ì 'ad Pius ha-Hamishì*, Jerusalem 1964, pp. 79 ff.; A. TOAFF, *Nuova luce sui Marrani di Ancona*, in E. TOAFF, Edit., *Studi sull'Ebraismo Italiano in memoria di C. Roth*, Roma 1974, pp. 261-80. Cf. P.C. IOLY-ZORATTINI, *Ancora sui Giudaizzanti Portoghesi di Ancona, (1556): Condanna e Riconciliazione*, «Zakhor» V, 2001-2002, pp. 39-51: 49.

86. See A. di Leone Leoni, *Manuel Lopes Bichacho*, cit.; Id. *Ancona e Pesaro*, pp. 72-86.

87. In Ancona, Emanuel (*alias* Davit Cohen) had married Ester Bruda, the daughter of the late Doctor Dionisio (see below).

88. See A.di LEONE LEONI, *Manoel Lopez Bichacho*, p. 91.

89. ASFE, not. Giacomo Ferrarini, matr 593, June 18, 1562. By the same deed Anna revoked a similar appointment previously granted to Simão Henriques who was also living in London.

90. Ioly Zorattini, *Processi*, XIII, *Appendici*, Firenze 1997, p. 193.

91. A. di LEONE LEONI, *La presenza Sefardita*, pp. 69-77.

92. ASFe, not. Giacomo Conti, *Pacco* 14S, May 1st and May 31st, 1575.

described him as "a real gentleman," about sixty years old, tall, white bearded, unmarried, and very rich with wide interests in Lyon.[93]

Simão Anriques [later known as Ḥayim Cohen] lived in London for many years.[94] In 1578 he was in Venice.[95]

Isaia Cohen [Diogo Pires] died in Ragusa [Dubrovnik] in 1599. By his last wills and testament, registered on November 6, 1597, he appointed as universal heir Ḥayim Cohen [Simão Anriques] who apparently lived in Ragusa as well.[96]

§ 21.9 Estevão Pires [alias David Cohen][97]

A prominent merchant in Antwerp, Estevão was the son of Diogo Pires[98] [Jewish name unknown] and the nephew of Henrique Pires' (see above).[99] They were among the first Portuguese who accepted Duke Ercole II's invitation and settled in Ferrara. In 1541, Estevão established a trading company in partnership with the Ducal Treasury[100], the purpose of which

93. ANTT, Inquisição de Lisboa, N. 5817, *Reconciliação de Lopo Luis que veio de Italia natural desta Citade de Lixboa*, ff. 18v-19r: «Aos seis dias do mes de Marco de milquin-hentos e oitenta e hum annos na citade de Lixboa nos estãos na casa do despacho … Lopo Luis … perguntado» … stated «que em Ferrara vio um Judeu portugues que la se chama Abraam Coen o qual e hum homen alto de corpo gentilhomen egresso de idade de sessenta annos pouco mais ou menos e a barba raa toda branca E he homen rico e nunqua casou nem tem filhos e mora junto [da rua] do Serrazim de fronte de Jsac Benefray e la he Judeu publico e em nome portugues se chama Duarte Anrriques secundo ele test.º vio em Lião de França per cartas suas onde elle traz dinheiro seu a ganho e ele test.º falou com elle em Ferrara e não sabe de que lugar deste Reino …».

94. ASFEe, not. Agostino del Vecchio, April 1st,1562: Anna Enriques, widow of Estevão Pires and mother of Diogo and Enrique Pires entrusts Simão Anriques, residing in London, with power of attorney enabling him to manage her business and to collect her credits.

95. ASFe, not. G. Conti, Pacco 15S, March 3, 1578: Abraam de Iacob Cohen entrusts his brother Ḥim Cohen living in Venice with the task of collecting his credits from the banker Angelo Sanudo.

96. Historical Archives of Dubrovnik, Testamenta Not. 51, ff. 27v-28v. Cf. J. TADIC, *Didak Pir* in «Zbornik Jevrejski Istorijski Muzei» 1 (1971) pp. 239-251: 245.

97. AGR, OFB,160/1233/2, undated [1549-1550] report on the New Christians of Antwerp.

98. ASAn, not. A. Pilestri, reg. 991, Dec. 17 1539.

99. ASFe, not. Maurelio Taurino, Matr. 535 *pacco* 7, Sept. 10, 1546: "Stephanus nepos …solertissimi mercatoris Domini Henrici Piris eius patrui".

100. ASFe, not. Battista Saracco, Matr. 493, *pacco* 27S, November 3, 1541.

was to deal with "western and oriental" goods and other merchandise. This enterprise was not successful. In 1545, its initial capital (in the amount of 30,000 ducats)[101] was almost completely lost. The reasons for this huge setback are not mentioned in the documents preserved in either the Archives of Ferrara or Modena. At least in part, the losses were probably due to the continuous confiscations and pillages perpetrated by the imperial agents in Lombardy.

The Duke refused to assume liability for his share of the losses, and forced Estevão and Henrique Pires to reimburse his investments in the company, and even the *lucrum mancatum* (missed profit). The Abravanels, and other prominent Sephardic merchants, provided financial support to the unfortunate merchants. They knew that, in so doing, they were safeguarding the continuity of the Portuguese Nation in Ferrara.[102]

In or around 1552 Estevão moved to Ancona where he was known as David Cohen. From a document dated December 17, 1558 we learn that his wife, Anna Enriques, was administering his estate on account of their sons Diogo and Henrique.[103]

§ 21.10 Manoel Lopes (*alias* Manoel Bichacho)

Manoel Lopes was already settled in Antwerp in 1535, and enjoyed a remarkable economic position: he rented the ship S. Maria da Consolacion and dispatched it to the Barbary Coast with a freight of *ultra-fine* clothing[104]. We have already dealt in this book with his activities as a leader of the Nation in Antwerp. Around 1546, Manoel settled in Ancona where he traded fine English and Flemish clothing in exchange for products from the Levant.[105] In 1548, he obtained the *condotta* (license) for a bank in Pesaro from Guidobaldo, Duke of Urbino,

According to Samuel Usque, in 1549, when the Duke of Ferrara expelled all the Portuguese who had entered Ferrara during the previous

---

101. ASFe, not. Maurelio Taurino, Matr. 535, *pacco* 6: April 20, 21 and 26 1545; pacco 7: May 5,1546; Spet. 10 and 29, 1546, Oct. 4, 1546; July 30, 1547.

102. A. di Leone Leoni, *Nuove Notizie sugli Abravanel*, «Zakhor» I, 1997, pp. 153-206: 158-159.

103. ASFe, Not. Giacomo Ferrarini, matr. 593, December 17, 1558.

104. J. A Goris, *Colonies marchandes,* pp. 162-163: Tables des navires affrétés en 1535.

105. ASAn, not. A. Pilestri, reg. 1000, On January 25, 1546 Ysac Moysis "Hyspanus" acknowledges that he had received 31 carpets from Emanuel Lopes. Cf. V. Bonazzoli, *Una identità ricostruita*, p. 28.

four months,[106] Manoel Bichacho persuaded Duke Guidobaldo II della Rovere to allow some of the refugees to settle in his lands.[107] Manoel was later allowed to include up to thirty-five Portuguese merchants in his *condotta*. This was the rather unusual beginning of the Portuguese Nation in Pesaro.[108]

In July 1556, after the death of the twenty-six Martyrs of Ancona, Gracia Nasi conceived her famous but unsuccessful plan to engage in open commercial war against the Church, to boycott the Ancona *entrepôt* and to develop the port of Pesaro as a new centre for maritime trade between Italy and the Levant.[109] As stated before, this daring and ambitious program did not succeed.

The Duke of Urbino was embittered and disappointed by the unsuccessful attempts to develop the port of his city.[110] Overwhelmed by diplomatic pressure from the Church, in March 1558, he yielded to the wishes of the Pope and decreed the expulsion of all the *Marranos*, including those who had already been living there before the Ancona affair.[111]

Several historians have stated that Guidobaldo d'Urbino granted those expelled with the necessary time to settle their business, but it was not so. At least in the case of Manoel Bichacho, the departure from Pesaro

---

106. S. USQUE, *Consolaçam, Dialogo Tercero*, § 36, *Ytalia Año 5311*, ff. 216r-217v. On the dating of this episode see LEONI, *Manoel Lopes Bichacho*.
107. *Ibid*.
108. A. di LEONE LEONI, *Manoel Lopes Bichacho*, pp. 87-90.
109. Extensive information on the whole history, and a detailed account of many of the *Responsa* of contemporary Rabbis are provided by C. ROTH in *The House of Nasi: Doña Gracia*, Philadelphia 1948 [Reprint 1977], pp. 134-75 and by I. SONNE *Mi Paulus ha-Revi'ì 'ad Pius ha-Hamishì* (= *From Paul IV to Pius V*), Jerusalem 1964, pp. 149-157 with the full edition of BENJAMIN NEHEMIAH BEN ELNATHAN 's chronicle *Dibrè ha-Yamim* (*appendix*, pp.79 ff.); Cfr. S.W. BARON, *A Social and Religious History*, XIV, pp. 35-43 and 320, note 39, where a list of the main rabbinical responsa is provided; Cfr. H.H. BEN SASSON *A History of the Jewish* People, Cambridge, Mass., 1976, pp. 667-669; A. TOAFF, *L' Universitas Hebraeorum Portugalensium nel Cinquecento, interesssi economici ed ambiguità religiosa,* in, *Mercati, mercanti, denaro nelle Marche (secoli XIV-XIX)* published by the DEPUTAZIONE DI STORIA PATRIA PER LE MARCHE, 1982, pp. 115-145: 125-26, 131; V. BONAZZOLI, *Ebrei Italiani, portoghesi, levantini sulla piazza commerciale di Ancona intorno alla metà del Cinquecento* in G. COZZI, Edit., *Gli Ebrei a Venezia*, Milano 1987, pp. 727-770 ; A. di LEONE LEONI, *Ancona e Pesaro*, pp. 79-86; P.C. IOLY-ZORATTINI, *Ancora sui Giudaizzanti Portoghesi di Ancona, (1556)*.
110. LEONI, *Manoel Lopez Bicacho*, pp. 92-93.
111. Cfr. A. MILANO, *Storia degli Ebrei in Italia*, Torino 1963, pp. 251-52.

was not painless. From a number of 1558 notary deeds, we learn that the Duke ordered the confiscation of all properties and goods belonging to Manoel and his son-in-law, Samuel Catelan. This punitive provision was carefully enforced. Furthermore, all the debtors of the two Portuguese bankers were exempted from paying back whatever amount of money they had borrowed.

We know that Manoel Bichacho succeeded in escaping from Pesaro. The fate of Samuel Catelan is unknown. Samuel's wife, Ora Bichacho, was kept prisoner for a long time and moved from place to place. On December 17, 1558, Duke Guidobaldo ordered that she be set free.[112] We do not know where Manoel Bichacho and his family settled immediately afterwards. In 1562 Manoel was in Ferrara.[113] In 1564, together with Salomon Dardero, he was appointed arbiter and "friendly judge", settling a conflict between Violante Henriques and Hyia Barochas,[114] according to the privilege accorded the Portuguese Nation of Ferrara.[115]

At some point, Ora Bichacho, the widow of Samuel Catelan[116], married Abraham, the son of Rabbi Lazarino da Pisa, a member of the renowned family of bankers and scholars. On June 4, 1565, Manoel Bichacho entrusted his son-in-law with power of attorney, enabling him to collect from one Antonio Bergamasco of Pesaro a delinquent credit of 120 gold scudi. This amount was to be calculated as an installment to the account of Ora's dowry.

In 1568, Manoel settled in Venice as a professing Jew.[117] In August 1568, he undersigned, as a witness, a *compromissum* [קומפרומיסו] i.e. a declaration by which Samuel Dardero (acting for his uncle, Salomon Dardero, living in Ferrara) and Hayim Cohen (living in the Ghetto Vecchio) stated their readiness to settle their dispute by means of arbitra-

---

112. ASPs, Notary Francesco Fattori, Reg. 1554-1558, December 12, 1558. Cf. LEONI, *Manoel Lopez Bicacho*, pp. 92.93, 97-98.
113. ASMO, Consiglio di Segnatura,Reg.15, Mention of an undated explanatory statement presented by Manoel Bichacho and his "nipoti" [Italian meaning either "nephews" or "grandchildren"], registered in September 1562.
114. ASFe, not. G. Conti, *pacco* 10, September 18, 1964.
115. A. di LEONE LEONI, *Documents inédits*, pp. 147-150, 153-155 and Doc. 3 therein.
116. We do not know when and in which circumstances Samuel Catelan died.
117. On June 14, 1568 he entrusted Yoseph and Samuel Boyno with the task of collecting from one Lorenzo de Granarola, living in Pesaro, an old credit which went back to 1551. ASVe, not. G.B. Monti, reg. 8256, *sub data*.

tion[118] according to the Law and the custom of Israel. The document was drawn up in Hebrew. An Italian translation was registered by a Venetian notary.[119] The presence in the Ghetto of a well-known figure of *Marrano* origins constitutes additional proof that, by the middle of the 16th century, Portuguese Jews could freely establish themselves in the Ghetto Vecchio without posing as Levantine Jews. In the case of Bichacho, we do not know whether he enjoyed a personal safe-conduct, or if he availed himself of the privilege granted to the Portuguese Nation of Ferrara. In 1570, Manoel was living in Ferrara.[120]

§ 21.11 Denis Rodrigues, [*alias* Asher Brudo] and his family

Better known as Doctor Dionisio, formerly a physician to Donha Catharina, the Queen of Portugal,[121] Denis Rodrigues was considered the spiritual leader of the Nation in Antwerp.[122] Doña Beatriz de Luna turned to him for advice in (or around) 1537, after a disagreement with Diogo Mendes (see above). In 1539, Cardinal Ippolito d'Este, the brother of Duke Ercole of Ferrara, succeeded in providing Denis Rodrigues with a safe-conduct issued by the King of France.[123] However, he apparently reached England and later moved to Ferrara.[124] In Italy, Doctor Dionisio assumed his Jewish name, Asher Brudo, as it may be inferred from various circumstances. In 1541, Denis was burnt in effigy in an auto da fé celebrated in Lisbon.[125] The fact was known in Antwerp in 1544, after the doctor's death in Ferrara. The widow, Doña Clara, and several sons and daughters survived him. At least two of them, Fabiano [Fabião] and

---

118. On the *compromissum* see R. Bonfil, *Rabbis and Jewish Communities* pp. 221-230.
119. ASVe, not. G.B. Monti, reg. 8256, August 30, 1568.
120. ASFe, not. G. Conti, *pacco* 12S, April 11, 1570, *Mandatum domine Hester Calaravone*: «cum presentia ... Emanuelis Bichachij hebrei Ferrariæ morantis ... eius proximioris attinentis».
121. Sousa Viterbo, *Noticias sobre alguns medicos portugueses,* Lisboa 1893, p. 15; Amato Lusitano, Centuria I, Curatio 2.
122. ASMo,CD, Estero, May 24, 1539: Gerolamo Maretta's report to the Duke of Ferrara; A. di Leone Leoni, *La Diplomazia Estense*, pp. 307-308, 323.
123. *Ibid.*
124. AGR, *Information 1544, passim*
125. *Ibid.* Cfr. I.S. Révah, *Les marranes portugais et l'Inquisition au XVIe siécle, in* R. Barnett, Editor, *The Sephardi Heritage,* London 1972, Vol. I, pp. 479-526: 505. I did not succeed in finding Denis Rodrigues' process at the ANTT in Lisboa.

Manoel Rodrigues, remained in (or returned to) Antwerp after a long sojourn in London.[126] They were regarded as rich merchants, engaging in trade with the Levant. Fabio married Beatriz, the daughter of Antonio Gomes, a wealthy businessman.[127]

Manoel Rodrigues was a physician,[128] author of an important medical tract[129], published in Venice in 1544 under the name of Manuel Brudo and subsequently reprinted several times. Some chapters deal with his patients in London, where he practiced between 1541 and 1542.[130] In his book, Manoel professed to be Doctor Dionisio's son.[131]

According to inquiries carried out in Antwerp in (or around) 1549, Fabio and Manoel Rodrigues had started a commercial relationship with their brother, possibly named Bernardo Rodrigues, who was then living in Ancona where he was called Josef Brudo.[132] From other sources, we learn that Josef's baptismal name was Fernando Lopes.[133] In any case, Josef Brudo, whatever his Christian name might have been, was the brother of Fabiano and Manuel Rodrigues.[134]

One Fernando Lopes [probably the same Josef Brudo] and Agostinho Lopes, who in some documents is described as his brother, left Antwerp in 1539. Together with Luis Alvares, they were arrested in Cremona by Johannes Vuysting. They were set free thanks to the diplomatic intervention of Ercole II, the Duke of Ferrara.[135]

---

126. On June 22 1543 Emanuel Fernandes, an *Hispanic* merchant living in Ancona, entrusted doctor Diego Fernandes [*alias* David Charavon, brother in law of Cristovão Garcia], with the charge of collecting 107 ducats from the merchant Fabiano Rodigues in London, or from his agents in Antwerp. ASAn, not. G. Senili, reg. 1138. V. BONAZZOLI, *Una identità ricostruita,* p. 35.

127. Both Antonio and Anselmo Gomes [possibly his son] were in Ancona in July 1554. Their Jewish names are unknown. ASAn, not. Manfredi, reg.754, ff. 265v -266r.

128. Amato Lusitano, *Dioscorides,* Liber II, *enarratio* 101.

129. *Liber de ratione victus in singulis febribus secundum Hippocratem, Brudo Lusitano auctore ad Anglos,* Venice 1544.

130. BARON, *Social and Religious*, Vol. XIII, p. 126.

131. *Liber de ratione victus in singulis febribus,* f. A12: "Brudi lusitani Dionysii medici filii."

132. Bernardo might have been the name of yet another brother living in Ancona. See *infra*.

133. According to Goris, *Colonies Marchandes*, p. 654, one Fernando Lopes was present in Antwerp in 1540.

134. ASAN, not. Manfredi, reg. 754, ff. 392v-394r, October 26 1554, *Donatio Joseph cum Emanuellis aliter Brudo, hebrei lusitani.*

135. AGR, PEA 1631, undated [1540] statement by Johannes Vuysting.

We do not know where Josef first settled in Italy. In 1542, Fernando Lopes was occasionally found in Ancona, where he sold 250 Cordova-styled skins to a local merchant.[136] Towards 1548, he lived in the Adriatic town and enjoyed a remarkable financial position. Many documents provide evidence of his activities. He lent large sums of money to artisans, farmers, bankers, merchants, and businessmen,[137] generally in the form of "chirographary" deposits.[138] Through his brothers in Antwerp, he imported huge quantities of English and Flemish woolen and linen clothes, which he then traded for leather, skins and textiles from the Balkans and the Levant. He soon became one of the leaders of the Portuguese Nation, and served for several terms as Massaro (Parnas). He was treated for intermittent fevers by Amato Lusitano, who referred to him as *Brudus* and described him as an auburn-haired, sanguine thirty-four year old gentleman.[139]

One of Josef's brothers, Asher (baptismal name unknown) also lived in Ancona and was an important merchant-banker.[140] Their sister Luna was a dynamic and independent businesswoman. On December 18, 1548, she sold to the Italian bankers, Leo (Yehuda) Menini and Isac Trabot de Bari, six pieces of woolen cloth and one piece of Flemish cloth for the

---

136. V. Bonazzoli, *Una identità ricostruita*, p. 29.

137. Wide evidence on the extension of his commercial activities is provided by the deeds registered on March 12, 1554 by notary Manfredi, ASAN, reg. 754, ff. 85r-87r.

138. *Chirographary* = handwritten, registered. This expression was used to designate unsecured credits, granted without pledge, generally (but not always) registered by a notary.

Deposit (from Latin *diu positum* = placed for a long time). In the 16th century, this term was used to designate a loan without payment of interests. However, in many cases, the amount of the interests was already agreed on and included in the sum to be paid back at the end of a stated length of time.

139. Amato Lusitano, *Enarrationes*, En. XLVI, pp. 77-78: "Brudus [first name unstated] vir trigintaquatuor ruffus, sanguineus plerumque ephimera febri corripit solebat." We assume that the person in question was Josef, who in Ancona was better known than his brother Asher.

140. ASAn, not. Manfredi, reg. 735, f. 202v, October 27, 1553: The Portuguese Jew Abraham Josef [Nahmias, called] *Francese* acknowledges that he had received the amount of 352 golden *scudi* from the brothers Josef and Asher Brudo (i.e. 209 *scudi* from Asher and 143 *scudi* from Josef) to be returned before February 1554. On that same day Josef Brudo together with his associate, the Portuguese banker Abraham Cohen, lent Abraham Josef *Francese* 109 additional golden *scudi*.

total amount 143 ducats.[141] She was apparently unmarried and lived in a house of her own[142]. On the same day, Doña Clara, "the widow of the late Asher Brudo de Portugalia," another businesswoman, lent the above mentioned Italian bankers 318 golden ducats.[143] In 1552, Doña Clara and Doña Luna Brudæ [144] were registered in the list of creditors of the Italian banker, "Simuel" Bonaventura, who was on the verge of bankruptcy.[145] Josef Brudo was among the six commissaries entrusted with the task of working out a fair apportionment. Another sister, Ester Bruda, was married to Manuel Henriques (David Cohen), son of Henrique Pires and brother of the poet Diogo.[146]

From several notary deeds drawn up in Ancona, we learn that Clara was the mother of Josef Brudo.[147] It may therefore be inferred that she was the widow of the famous Doctor Dionisio whose Jewish name was Asher Brudo. After the doctor's death, one of his sons assumed the same name.

We do not know when Fabião Rodrigues left Antwerp. In 1553, he died, apparently during a journey, in Cremona in Lombardy, probably while he was trying to reach Ferrara. He managed to dictate his last will. As he had no sons, in accordance with Jewish law,[148] he left all his property to his brother Fernando Lopes [Josef Brudo]. The widow was to receive only her dowry and a 200 ducats bequest. At first, Antonio Gomes, the widow's father, refused to accept Fabião's disposal of his property, but later agreed to settle the dispute under arbitration. The Jews

---

141. ASAn, reg. 223, not. G.B. AGLI, f. 332r, Dec. 18, 1548.: Domina Luna, *hebrea de Portugalia*, habitratix Anconae, soror Aserris et Yoseph Brudi.

142. ASAn, reg. 754, not. Manfredi, f. 208v, June 11 1554: «Domina Luna, *soror Ascer Brudi, hebrea lusitana*», lends Samuel Caro, a Portuguese Jew, 106 *scudi*. Luna is constantly described as the sister of either Asher or Josef Brudo, never as a wife or a widow.

143. Cfr. ASAn, not. Agli Vol. 221. 104r-104v. Cfr. V. BONAZZOLI, *Ebrei italiani, portoghesi*, p. 751.

Ibid. ff. 331v-332r.

144. Brudæ = feminine plural. Notaries used to decline family names.

145. ASAn, not. Agli, reg. 221. 104r-104v. Cfr. V. BONAZZOLI, *Ebrei italiani*, p. 751. Doña Clara claimed 213 *scudi*, doña Luna 166. For more information on the two ladies' financial activities see: ASAn, not. G. B. Agli, Reg. 223 (1548), 224 (1549), 205 (1550, *Alphabetical Repertorium*).

146. ASAn, not. G.B. Agli, reg. 205 (*Alphabetical Repertorium*), Sept. 17, 1550.

147. *Ibid*, reg. 221, February 1552, ff. 101r-115v: *Jnstrumenta concordiæ inter Simuellem Bonaventuram et deputatos* ...; f. 110v: *Ratificatio Joseph Brudi nomine dominæ Claræ Brudæ eius matris*.

148. Num. 27, 8-11; Deut. 21, 16-17.

living in the Papal States did not enjoy any juridical autonomy[149]. However, Portuguese merchants availed themselves of the privileges accorded to local merchants, and settled their disputes using those guidelines. The parties would privately agree, in advance, that the arbiters were to rule according to Jewish law.[150] Josef Brudo and Antonio Gomes appointed two of the Nation's Parnassim: doctor Davit del Porto, who also went under the name Charavon, and Josef Reuben. They ruled in favor of Josef Brudo. Beatrice Gomes, the widow of Fabio Rodrigues, accepted the judgment.[151]

Josef was faced with other legal problems. Cremona, in Lombardy, was under Spanish rule and the right of a Jew to inherit from a Christian (as his brother Fabio had presented himself) could be questioned. Josef was consequently obliged to use his baptismal name (Fernando Lopes). Since he was known only by his Jewish name in Ancona, Josef had to state before a notary that Fernando was the same person known as Brudo.[152] For some reason, Josef had this particular deed drawn up by a notary with whom he did not do regular business.

We do not know what happened to the Brudo family during the persecutions waged by Pope Paul IV against the Portuguese Jews of Ancona in 1555 and 1556.

In 1580, Manuel Brudo was in Istanbul, where he held the influential position of personal physician and protégé of Nūr Bānū, the "Most Serene Queen Mother of the Grand Sultan." He was also engaged in international trade, and claimed that the Levantine merchant, Ḥayym Saruq, living in Venice, owed him 2,593 ducats for a large supply of "extra-fine" red cloth.[153]

---

149. R. BONFIL, *Rabbis and Jewish Communities,* pp. 209-211.

150. Cfr. A. di LEONE LEONI, *Ancona e Pesaro,* pp. 52-53. R. BONFIL, *Rabbis and Jewish Communities*, pp. 211-212.

151. ASAN. not. A. Manfredi, reg. 754, ff. 264r-267r, July1554: *transactio inter Joseph Brudun hebreum lusitanum et Antonium Gomes pariter Lusitanum*; ASFe, not. G. Conti, Matr. 584, *pacco* 6, May 30, 1554 (Beatrice Gomes entrusts her father with powers of attorney); *Ibid. pacco* 6, January 24, 1555 and March 28, 1555: *Approbatio et ratificatio D. Beatricis Gomes pro Josef Brudo).*

152. ASAn, not. Scalamonti, reg 1152, ff. 62v-67r, August 25, 1554. Fernando Lopes *aliter* Brudo entrusts to Antonio Gomes (living in Cremona) the care of collecting the estate of his brother Fabio Rodrigues.

153. ARBEL, *Trading Nations, Jews and Venetians in the Early Modern Eastern Mediterranean,* Leiden , 1995, pp. 165-166.

§ 21.12 António and Gabriel Fernandes

They were Manoel Lopes' brothers[154]. In 1540, Gabriel was about 23 years old.[155] Another brother, Odoardo Lopes lived in Ancona.[156]

§ 21.13 Luis Fernandes

Luis Fernandes was a partner in the pepper consortium.[157] He is probably the same Luis Fernandes who, in 1546, together with other Portuguese merchants of Ferrara, provided the Ducal Chamber with guarantees in favor of Estevão and Henrique Pires.[158]

§ 21.14 Manoel da Provincia

Manoel da Provincia was a prominent merchant in Antwerp and the father of Lopo. In 1539 (or 1540), he reportedly acted as a "priest" and officiated at the wedding of Gaspar Lopes and Agnes Fernandes, who were married according to the Jewish rite.[159]

§ 21.15 Lopo de Provincia

In 1540, some refugees detained in Pavia confessed under torture that they had received money from merchants of Antwerp and, among others,

---

154. In the 1540 list, António Fernandes is described as her[man]o de Manoel Lopes See Doc. 2 in Appendix.

155. AGR, *Codazzi file*, f. 32: "Gabriellem Fernandum fratrem suprascripti Antonij, in Anversia, annorum 23 vel circa". See in Appendix Document 18.

156. In 1539, in Ancona, Odoardo Lopes entrusted his brother Emanuel Lopes with the charge of collecting 22 golden ducats from Duarte Pinto. ASAn, not. Antonio Pavesi, reg. 957, ff. 120r-120v. See also ASAn, not. G.B. Agli, reg. 489, January 7, 1539.

157. AGR, GRM, reg. 145: Queen Mary's explanatory statement.

158. ASFe, not. M. Taurini, Matr. 535, *pacco* 7, April 5, 1546. About Estevão Pires see *above* § 21.9.

159. AGR, *Codazzi file*, f. 25v, September 22 1540: witness testimony of Gaspar Lopes, «Jnterrogatus dicit quod Emmanuel de Provincia pater Lopi de Provincia desponsavit jpsum testem cum eius uxore uti sacerdos, presentibus Vigelanta Nones et Agnese matre jpsius sponse et fratre nec non et Maria Georgia eius sorrore, Alvisio Ferrera et eorum matre, et multis alijs novis et falsis xpianis». It cannot be inferred from this deposition whether Manoel de Provincia served as a rabbi or simply gave his blessing to bride and groom.

denounced Lopo de Provincia whom they identified as one of the heads of the Rescue Committee.[160] At the beginning of 1550, Lopo lived in Ferrara and stayed in Beatriz de Luna's palace. He later moved to Venice.[161]

§ 21.16 Diego Nuñes

Only scant information is available about Diego Nuñes. In 1540, a Portuguese detained in Lombardy described him as a merchant of approximately 35 years of age, of average height and overweight.[162] According to the deposition of another prisoner, Diego gave hospitality to several New Christians in Antwerp.[163]

§ 21.17 Ruy Lopes

In 1540 Gaspar Lopes, a prisoner in Pavia, described him as "mercatorem jn Anversa, annorum 25 vel circa".[164]

§ 21.18 Lorenço Alvares

In 1540, Gaspar Lopes described him as approximately sixty years old and a merchant dealing in woolen cloth.[165]

§ 21.19 The *Licenciado* Luis Alvares

Together with Duarte Pinto, Luis Alvares, a college graduate, was one of the first Portuguese merchants who moved from Antwerp to Ferrara under

---

160. AGR, *Codazzi file*, f. 7r, 11v, *et passim*: Dec. 20, 1540, witness testimonies of Duarte Rodrigues, Michael Nunes.
161. ASFe, not. G. Conti, Matr. 584, *pacco* 3, Ferrara, Janunary 26, 1550: Lopo de Provincia entrusts Cristovão Garcia and Gomes de Lião with the task of collecting his credits in Antwerp; April 11,1550: one Petro Dias entrusts Lopo de Provincia, living in Venice, with power of attorney. *Ibid*, August 22, 1550: Luys Henriques living in Ferrara appoints Lopo with the task of recovering a credit from two Venetian merchants.
162. AGR, *Codazzi file*, f. 8r, Dec.. 20 1540: witness testimony of Duarte Rodrigues.
163. AGR, OFB, 160/1233/2, July 16, 1540: interrogation and deposition of Simon Fernandes detained in Milan.
164. AGR, *Codazzi file*, f. 32v. See, in Appendix, Document 18.
165. AGR, *Ibid*.

a safe-conduct issued by Duke Ercole II. He is probably the Luis Alvares Victoria who, in (or around) 1539, was detained in Cremona in the Duchy of Milan with other Portuguese who had been traveling with him. He was released by order of the Marquis del Vasto, governor of Milan, on the request of the Duke of Ferrara.[166] In 1540, in Ferrara, for some unstated reasons[167], the Ducal Treasury claimed from Luis Alvares 1,000 golden scudi that he was unable to pay. On November 2, 1540, four merchants of the Portuguese Nation of Ferrara: Bastião Vas [168], Emanuel Pinhero,[169] Emanuel Butiglio (or possibly, Botilho)[170] and Statio Pinto intervened in his favor and promised to pay on his behalf.[171]

§ 21.20 Manoel Serrão

Manoel Serrão was one of the prominent leaders of the Nation and has been extensively discussed in previous passages in this book. In December 1546, he was in Ancona, where he imported extra-fine English and Flemish clothes.[172]

§ 21.21 Joan Duardo

Joan Duardo was one of the first of Antwerp's merchants to accept Duke Ercole II's invitation to settle in Ferrara.

---

166. AGR, PEA 1631, undated [1540] statement by Johannes Vuysting. Among the prisoners there were Augustinho Lopes and Fernando Lopes. The report, filled with recriminations and complaints, provides an account of "irregularities" committed by the Marquis del Vasto: forty-two bales of goods were restored to the proprietor(s).

167. The episode is probably related to merchandise impounded in the Duchy of Milan by the commissioner *contra falsos christianos*. The ducal secretary Gerolamo Magnanini and Gerolamo Maretta (who had recently been employed as ducal envoy in Milano) acted as witnesses to a notary deed registered by Battista Saracco, on November 2, 1540. See *infra*.

168. AGR, *Codazzi File*, f. 8r. On December. 20, 1540 Duarte Rodrigues, prisoner in Pavia, described him as "Sebastianum Vas annorum 35 usque in 45 comunalis stature, mercatorem".

169. See *infra, sub voce*.

170. On February 11, 1540 Duke Ercole II issued a safe-conduct in his favor. ASMo,CD, Decreti e chirografi sciolti 1B, 1540.

171. ASFe, not. Battista Saracco, Matr. 493, *pacco 16*, *Protocollo 1540*, November 2, 1540.

172. ASAn, not. G. Monaco, Dec. 24 1546; not. A. Pilestri, reg. 1000, Dec. 16, 1546; V. BONAZZOLI, *Una identità ricostruita*, p. 27.

§ 21.22 Emanuel Pinhero[173]

Little is known about his activities in Antwerp before 1540, apart from the fact that he was on particularly good terms with the Portuguese Royal *Feitor*. He was generally considered a Judaizer. In (or around) 1540, he was burned in effigy in Lisbon.[174]

In 1539, Emanuel settled in Ferrara, together with two of his sons: Pero Pinhero [Josef Navarro] and Salomon Navarro. They also carried out their commercial activities in Ancona.[175] In 1540, Emanuel, together with three merchants of the Portuguese Nation in Ferrara, paid the Ducal Chamber 1,000 golden scudi on behalf of Luis Alvares.[176] Josef was to become an outstanding personality of the Portuguese Nation of Ferrara and served for many terms as Parnas.[177] He was one of the first Portuguese merchants of Ferrara to establish trading and banking activities in Ancona, where he spent long periods. Imprisoned in 1555 by the papal police, he managed to escape to Pesaro and later reached Ferrara. Duke Ercole II provided him with a liberal safe-conduct and granted him immunity against prosecution on charges of heresy.[178] In his old age, Josef was saddened by a long dispute with the Mahamad (Board of Directors) of the Portuguese Nation of Ferrara. In 1585, when he refused to comply with a decision reached through arbitration, he was excommunicated. [179]

---

173. So far we have dealt with persons whose names are comprised in the "1540 list" (see Document 12 in Appendix). When this list was drawn up Emanuel Pinhero, whose name does not appear in it, had already left Antwerp for Ferrara.
174. AGR, *Information 1544*, ff. 9,r, 9v, 10r, 11v, 12v, 19r *et passim*.
175. See Leoni, *Ancona e Pesaro*, pp. 52, 59, 70; V. Bonazzoli, *Una identità ricostruita*, pp. 31, 33.
176. ASFe, not. Battista Saracco, Matr. 493, *pacco* 16, *Protocollo 1540*, November 2, 1540.
177. ASFe, not. Maurelio Taurini, Matr. 535, *pacco* 7: September 10, 1546; July 30,1547; cfr. A. di Leone Leoni *La Nazion Portughesa corteggiata*, pp. 218, 222.
178. A. di Leone Leoni, *Manoel Lopes Bichacho*, pp. 89-90; Idem, *Per una storia della Nazione Portoghese ad Ancona ed a Pesaro*, pp. 70-71.
179. A. di Leone Leoni, Documents inédits sur la Nation Portugaise de Ferrare", *REJ* 1993, pp. 137-176: 153-155.

§ 21.23 Christovão Manoel

Christovão was the son of Emanuel Pinhero,[180] and lived in London for several years. In (or around) 1542, he moved to Antwerp. In August 1543, Christovão was arrested while traveling by carriage near Strasbourg on his way to Italy. He was freed on bail. In 1548, Christovão was in Doña Beatriz de Luna's service[181] and accomplished delicate missions in Lyons and Spain, where he succeeded in collecting important debts for the House of Mendes.[182]

§ 21.24 Amato Lusitano

He was, without doubt, the most illustrious member of the Portuguese Nation of Antwerp. Our research did not provide any new information on his seven-year stay (1534-1541) in the northern city.[183] In exchange we found in his works an incredible wealth of information on several outstanding personalities whom he cured in Antwerp and later in Ferrara and Ancona.

---

180. ASFe, not. G.B. Codegori, Matr. 582, *pacco* 20S, March 20, 1549. "Christoforum Emanuelem filium quondam Emanuelis Pignerij".
181. SALOMON-LEONI *Mendes, Benveniste* p. 156, note 57.
182. A. di LEONE LEONI, *Quotidiana imprenditorialità*, pp. 85-86.
183. M. LEMOS, *Amato Lusitano, a sua vida e a sua obra*, pp. 68; IDEM, *Amato Lusitano, Novas Investigações*, «Arquivos de História da Medicina Portuguesa», VI, 1915, pp. 1-12, 33-43, 89-96, 97-106, 129-145: 4-6.

§ 22. Some figures of the Portuguese Nation of Antwerp, 1549-1550

The papers related to the Portuguese of Antwerp between 1548 and 1550 (i.e. immediately before and after the 1549 expulsion) are intermingled with documents concerning one Manoel Lopes, nephew of António Fernandes.[1] According to rumours, Manoel had lived in Italy for a few months; when he returned to Antwerp (in or around 1547) his uncle refused to employ him. Thereafter, Manoel lived by hook and crook, became a police informer and denounced four Portuguese merchants. Manoel did not keep his stealthy profession a secret, but let it be known in order to squeeze money out of his countrymen, even to the extent of blackmailing them. Some of his victims denounced him to the Margrave, who ordered Manoel seized on charges of extortion and fraud.[2] It is not our intent to deal here with his trial, but rather use some of the lengthy papers involved in order to provide information on the Portuguese settlement.[3]

Two lists of names drawn up by Manoel Lopes are preserved in the Brussels Archives. The first one begins with the name of this same Manoel, described as the «author of these [unstated] negotiations»,[4] and followed by the names of nineteen Old-Christians whose part in this history is unclear. The second list[5] provides the names of twenty-five New

---

1. This Manoel Lopes is not to be confused with Manoel Lopes Bichacho or with the merchant arrested upon his arrival in Flanders in 1544.
2. AGR,OFB,115/1, where are preserved several (mostly undated) official reports to the Queen-Regent and a number of statements by the same Lopes. Manoel denounced Christovão Garcia, Duarte Rodrigues, Lionel Pardo, Jeronimo Lindo and Ruy Lopes on account of Judaism. They counter-denounced him on account of fraud and blackmailing.
3. The papers related to Manoel's process are scattered in different files. I could locate a part of them in OFB, 115/1; OFB,160/1233/2; PEA 1656; PEA 1177/2.
4. AGR, OFB, 160/1233/2: "Manoel Lopes autor destos negocios".
5. See Document 66 in Appendix.

Christians. Manoel Lopes, in his capacity as police confident, had most likely proposed to exempt them from the order to leave the city, obviously for a price.

Most of the names on Manoel's list are mentioned in an undated (circa 1550) official report to the Queen listing the usual grievances held against the New Christians.[6] All the twenty-five persons mentioned in this report were routinely accused of abetting the immigration from Portugal and Castile to Antwerp and, from there, to Italy, of practicing Jewish rites, observing strange dietary laws, keeping secret synagogues, and using their trade relationships to ship merchandise and transfer capital out of Christendom. All the names listed in this report[7] can be found in the appendix. Only those below shall be discussed in further detail.

§ 22.1 Jeronimo Henriques [Senior Benveniste]

Jeronimo Henriques was the eldest of Nuño Henriques' sons and remained in Antwerp to take care of the family business. Between 1550 and 1551, he reached his family in Ferrara where he died in 1552.[8] After his death, his uncle and brother-in-law Henriques Nuñes [Mayer Benveniste] assumed the management of the family company. Henrique died in 1555. In the same year, Violante Henriques [Vellida Benveniste][9] and Marquesa Henriques [Reina Benveniste][10] obtained a generous privilege from the Duke of Ferrara, allowing them to officially return to Judaism, and keep private synagogues in their homes, even if they had been previously using Christian names. They were also allowed to keep Christian servants and slaves in their homes.[11] A few months later, these concessions were extended to the Spanish and Portuguese Nation of Ferrara.[12]

---

6. AGR, OFB, 160/1233/2.
7. See Document 67 in Appendix.
8. See P.C. Ioly Zorattini, *Processi* III, *sub indice*.
9. Vellida was the widow of Nuño Henriques and the mother of Hyeronimo and Marquesa.
10. Marquesa was the daughter of Nuño and Violante Henriques and the widow of (her uncle) Henriques Nuñes [*alias* Mayer Benveniste].
11. The safe-conduct was published *in extenso* by A.di LEONE LEONI, *Documenti e Notizie sulle Famiglie Nassì e Benevenisti,*. pp. 126-127.
12. On the privilege of the Spanish and Portuguese Nation of Ferrara see A.di LEONI LEONI *La Nazione Ebraica Spagnola e Portogese negli Stati Estensi*, Rimini 1992, pp. 194-197; 213-218.

§ 22.2 Francisco Alvares

Francisco Alvares was believed to be one of the *conductors* «who led the New Christians out of the Country». He smuggled Nuño Henriques and Henriques Nuñes, along with their families, to France.

§ 22.3 Rodrigo Mendes

Rodrigo Mendes was one of the Nation's new leaders. He purportedly organized the clandestine "journey" of many émigrés to Ferrara. If their carriages were stopped on the way, he went to rescue them.

§ 22.4 Jorge Lopes

Jorge Lopes was a member of the delegation sent to the Court to negotiate a partial rescinding of the 1549 decree of expulsion.

§ 22.5 Duarte Rodrigues

Duarte Rodrigues was also a member of the above-mentioned delegation.[13] When he arrived in the Low Countries in 1544, he was seized in the roundup carried out at the end of June (or the beginning of July) of that year.

§ 22.6 António de Noronha

It is very possible that this was the same person previously mentioned as António de la Ronha,[14] one of the Nation's leaders in Antwerp and London, and who was also mentioned as "Antoine de Loroingne" in a 1541 document.[15] In 1554, António de Noronha lived in Lyons: he was entrusted with powers of attorney by Felipa Rodrigues, the widow of

---

13. See above, § 22.4.
14. Regarding de la Ronha, see § 5, §12.
15. AGR, PEA 1177/2, ff. 63r-68v: *Enquete faite en la ville de Middelbourg le 15e et le 16e jour de mars 1540 [=1541] pardevant le rentmaister assisté de l'advocat fiscal du Grand Conseil,* deposition of Fernando Rodrigues.

Thomas Gomes da India[16], living in Ferrara.[17] At some point, he apparently moved to Ferrara where, rather incongruously, his daughter Isabel re-converted to Catholicism in order to marry a Christian.[18]

§ 22.7 Luis Alvares

He was suspected of keeping a secret synagogue in his home. He is not to be confused with two other persons bearing the same name with whom we have already dealt.

§ 22.8 Gabriel Jacome (*alias* Isac Aben Hini)[19]

Gabriel managed the family business on behalf of his mother Maria Jacome [formerly the widow of Francisco Lopes[20]] and his brother António Lopes.[21] He exported "extra-fine" textiles from Antwerp to Portugal.
Although Gabriel was apparently included among the twenty-five heads-of-house allowed to remain in Antwerp, he left the city.

In June 1550, Gabriel was in Ferrara where he found the "magnifico domino licentiato", Luis Alvares,[22] one of his former customers in

---

16. This is not to be confused with the other Thomas Gomes, brother of Guilherme Fernandes and Duarte Gomes.

17. ASFe, not. G. Conti, *pacco* 6, Dec.. 5, 1554: «Antonio de Norogna Lugduni residente» was entrusted with the task of collecting 1,248 ducats from the Italian merchant Barolomeo Panciatichi.

18. P.C. Yoli Zorattini, *Processi 1571-1580*, Firenze 1985, p. 144.

19. We learn Gabriel's Jewish name from an official statement made by his daughter Letizia formerly called Dina], the widow of di Meir Alcala'i, in front of a Sephardic Bet Din in Safed, on the twentieth day of the month of Av 5334 (July 28, 1574). The lady made it known that she was the daughter of the late Isac Abenhini who was formerly called Gabriel Jacome. She gave her agreement to the sale of a house, located in a central street of Ferrara, which was part of her father's estate. The statement, in Hebrew, is kept among the papers of notary Giacomo Conti, in the State Archives of Ferrara.

20. ASFe, not. A. Coccapani, "Informationes sumptæ die vigesimo octavo augusti 1555 in domo habitationis Domini Gabrielis Jacomi f.q. D. Francisci Lopes, Ferrariæ in contrata Sanctæ Agnesis", attached to a deed drawn up on August 28, 1555.

21. ASFe, not. G. Conti, Dec.. 15, 1551: Maria Jacome entrusts her son António Lopes with the task of collecting from Graziano Levi a letter of exchange of 1.386 golden ducats issued by Don Jacob Abravanel in Ferrara.

22. ASFe, not. Romano Calcetta, Matr 451, August 28, 1553.

Lisbon. They had a difference of opinion on the sharing of expenses and profits related to some lots of goods (including clothes interwoven with gold) that Gabriel had dispatched to Lisbon. The litigants agreed to settle the dispute by means of arbitration. They appointed as sole arbiter Thomas Gomes and pledged to comply with his decisions without right of appeal. Thomas passed his judgement one year later, after a complete examination of all papers and accounts.[23]

Gabriel lived in the S. Romano Quarter, close to the Portuguese Synagogue. He had two sons: Josef and Moshe Abenini and a daughter, Benvenida, married to an important merchant, Moshe Namias. In the 1560's, Gabriel represented Marquesa Henriques (Reina Beneniste) in a bitter quarrel with the Mahamad (Boards of Directors) of the Portuguese Nation.[24] His brother, Moshe Abenini, was among the first Portuguese merchants who settled in the Venetian Ghetto. Besides being a merchant, Moshe was also involved in maritime insurances in Venice.[25]

§ 22.9 Christovão Garcia

Christovão Garcia was a prominent merchant active both in Antwerp and London, well received at the court in Brussels. In 1542, the Queen Regent intervened with the English government on behalf of Garcia for the release of his impounded merchandise. On this occasion, Christovão acted in a rather selfish and arrogant way: he claimed to be an *hidalgo*, familiar to Queen Catalina of Portugal, and pretended that he should not be confused with other New Christians. He later behaved with a greater sense of responsibility and eventually became a leader of the Nation. In 1544, Garcia sheltered some refugees in his house in an attempt to prevent their arrest.[26]

In 1549, Christovão was a member of the Portuguese delegation at the Court of Brussels and succeeded in getting the decree of banishment partially rescinded. He was a brother-in-law of David Haravon (also called Doctor del Porto, or Diego Fernandes), one of the leaders of the Portuguese Nation of Ancona, with whom he traded English and Flemish

---

23. ASFe, not. G. Conti, *Protocollo* 1551, ff. 51r-52v, July 30 and 31, 1551.
24. Aron di Leone Leoni, *Documents inédits,* p. 149.
25. IDEM, *Quotidiana imprenditorialità,* pp. 101-102.
26. AGR, OFB 160/1233/2, *Noms et surnoms des personnes detenueéz ... en 1544.* See Document 53 in Appendix.

textiles for "oriental" products, mainly leather. Garcia was suspected of using his banking and trading company to hide his undercover activities: the transporting of the properties of the immigrants who continued to reach Antwerp in spite of all imperial ordinances. Garcia was also responsible for planning, together with other volunteers, the itinerary of those who "undertook the journey" to Italy and the Levant.

From a notary deed drawn up in Ferrara, we learn that Christovão Garcia was still in Antwerp in 1555, when Francisco Nuñes, a Portuguese merchant living in Ferrara, acknowledged that he had received 140 Italian ducats from Pedro Fernando, Garcia's representative. This was the last installment of an unstated sum of money that, a few years earlier, Francisco Nuñes had entrusted to Garcia in Antwerp.[27]

On January 22, 1555, Constança Gomes, widow of Alvares Vas, together with their sons Henriques and Salvador Vas, aquitted Christovão of all debts due to her late husband: money, merchandise, goods and jewellery.[28] On the same day, Constança aquitted a certain Emanuel Fregosio, from whom she received 250 golden ducats that Emanuel, now living in Ferrara, had been holding in Antwerp on Alvares' behalf.

§ 22.10 Gaspar Rodrigues

Gaspar Rodriguez was in Antwerp in 1554 when Emanuel Caldera, living in Ferrara, entrusted him with the task of collecting his credits in the northern city.[29]

§ 22.11 Henrique de Tovar

According to Gaspar Lopes, in 1540, Henrique, a merchant, was living in London with his wife Anna and a sister.[30] We do not know whether Henrique was among the Portuguese seized in London in 1542.[31] In

---

27. ASFe, not. G. Conti, March 22, 1555: Xpoforum Garciam mercatorem lusitanum Antuerpie residentem.
28. *Ibid.*, January 22, 1555.
29. ASFe, not. G. Conti, *pacco* 6, July 19, 1544.
30. «Rodricum de Tuar [Tovar] et Annam de Tuar eius uxorem in Londres mercatorem, videlicet Rodricus annorum 28 vel circa, Anna vero 20 vel circa.» See document 19 in Appendix.
31. See *above* § 12.

1544, in Antwerp, he hosted Duarte de Tovar and Luis Gomes.[32] He was in Antwerp in 1554, when Hyeronimo Rodrigues, who was living in Ferrara, stated that he approved all that Henrique had done on his behalf in Antwerp.[33]

§ 22.12 Duarte Pinel [*alias* Abraham Usque]

In the Royal Archives of Brussels, I could find the name of Duarte Pinel mentioned in one only document, drawn up in or around 1549. Together with Lionel Pardo,[34] he was included in a list of Portuguese émigrés[35] who tried to remain in Antwerp after the 1549 expulsion.[36] As his name does not appear in the report on the twenty-five families allowed to remain in Antwerp after the 1549 decree of expulsion,[37] it may be inferred that he left the city.

A few years later he was in Ferrara where he achieved fame as the printer, co-editor and co-translator[38] of the Biblia Española (Ferrara 1553), and as the publisher of many books, both in the vernacular and Hebrew.[39]

We do not know where he lived before 1552, when he started his activity in Ferrara; nor we know how, and where, he acquired his noteworthy knowledge of the Hebrew language and Jewish sacred texts. It is difficult to imagine that he could develop his many skills in only three years (between 1550 and 1552) and we are tempted to assume that he might have cultivated his studies in Portugal (before the mass conversion in 1497) or in Antwerp.

---

32. AGR, OFB, 160/1233/2: undated [1544] statement.

33. ASFe, not. G. Conti, *pacco* 6, April 16, 1554.

34. Probably the Moshe Pardo who later became Abraham Usque's partner in the Ferrara printing press. ASFe, not. G. Conti, March 18 1555: *Creditum Domini Hieronimi Vargas in Abraam Usque [et] Moisem Pardum*. See R. SEGRE, *La Tipografia Ebraica a Ferrara e la stampa della Biblia (1551-59)* in «Italia Medioevale e Umanistica», XXXV, 1992, pp. 305-332: 325-326.

35. See document 66 in Appendix

36. See above, § 20.

37. See document 67 in Appendix.

38. On Abraham Usque's role as co-editor of the Biblia see E. ROMERO, *La creación literaria en lengua sefardí*, Madrid, Collección Sefarad, 1992, p. 46. Romero was probably the first scholar to state that Abraham was not only a printer but also one of the editors of the Biblía de Ferrara. See also Y. H. YERUSHALMI, *A Jewish Classic in the Portuguese Language,* p. 93. Cfr. A. di LEONE LEONI, *A hitherto unknown edition of the Spanish Psalter by Abraham Usque (Ferrara 1554)*, «Sefarad» 2001, pp. 127-136.

39. See Y.H. YERUSHALMI, *A Jewish Classic,* p. 93.

Conclusion

Contrary to what many eminent scholars have assumed, a Spanish-styled Inquisition was not introduced into the Low Countries in the first half of the 16th Century. Charles V, and his sister Mary, directed high-ranking officers of the Court to carry out inquiries, arrests and other forms of persecutions against the Portuguese merchants of Antwerp and the new immigrants. A special corps of police was set up with the task of dealing with the New Christians. These agents were specifically employed for the sole purpose of pursuing, capturing, imprisoning and interrogating the émigrés who tried to leave Antwerp and move to Ferrara and Venice.

Contrary to what has been widely stated, in 1532 Diogo Mendes was not imprisoned by the Inquisition. He was apprehended and kept in custody by imperial agents who acted under specific orders of the Emperor and the Queen-Regent.[1] The secular authorities in Antwerp did not exert any pressure on the New Christians, but repeatedly defended them. The magistrates of the city frequently opposed and refused to implement the imperial *placards* against the Portuguese New Christians.

Extensive information has been gathered on several figures of the Portuguese Nation in Antwerp and London and, in some cases, it was possible to follow their trail in Italy. In many cases, it was possible to find the correspondences of the Portuguese baptismal names used by several prominent figures in the northern cities, along with the Jewish names they assumed in different Italian States.

A surprisingly large number of New Christians devoted themselves to the service of their people, and worked towards the rescue of the *Men of the Nation* and the preservation of their religious and cultural traditions.

After the death of Diogo Mendes, and the emigration of many leaders who left Antwerp and moved to places where they could openly

---

1. See above §§ 2, 3.

123

observe their ancient faith, João Micas and Guilherme Fernandes took up the leadership of the Nation, obviously with the consent and, perhaps, under the guidance of Beatriz Mendes. When they also left the city, a new generation of leaders emerged.

Many of these figures combined their faithfulness to the Jewish religion with their interest in scholarship (or, at least, with the patronage of scholars), and coupled their technical knowledge and entrepreneurial skills with generosity. They displayed noteworthy diplomatic capabilities in their relations with emperors, kings, princes and popes, and represented with dignity the interests of their Nation in countries where its existence was hardly recognized. Many of these leaders embodied the social and cultural values (and, also, some of the defects) that were typical of Sephardic Jewry.[2] Some of them founded new "Portuguese Nations" in Italian lands, where they displayed abilities and skills similar to those previously displayed in Flanders. As a consequence of the experience developed in Antwerp, and in other towns where they were not allowed to officially have rabbis, the leaders of the new Nations tended to concentrate all communal powers (including the right to dispense the Ḥerem in their own hands, to the detriment of accredited rabbis, whose powers were somewhat limited.

They also developed the activities of the Rescue Organization, which continued to be called "Sedakah", from the name given in Lisbon[3] and Antwerp to the fund dedicated to the rescue and assistance of refugees. For a long time, this was the most important – and the most expensive – communal activity of the "Western" Sephardic Communities. The funds collected for the Sedakah were used to support many, if not all, sectors of Jewish life. The leadership of the Rescue Organization was composed of the same individuals who directed the new "Nations". In many places, the term Sedakah was frequently used to designate the Nation itself.[4] In 1573, in Ferrara, when Agostinho Henriques was requested to prove that

2. See R.BONFIL *The Legacy of Sephardic Jewry in Historical Writing* in H. BEINART, Editor, *Moreshet Sepharad, the Sephardi Legacy*, Jerusalem, The Magnes Press, 1992, pp. 461-478: 464, 468.

3. ANNT, *Inquisição de Evora, Processo* 11304, f. 29, quoted by M.C. TEIXERA PINTO, "Manuel Dias".

4. S. SCHWARZFUCHS, *Le Registre de Deliberations de la Nation Juive Portugaise de Bordeaux*, Paris 1981, pp. 9-10.

Abraham Allalvo and Abraham Abensussan belonged to the Portuguese
Nation of that city (and thereafter were entitled to frequent the Rialto
emporium in Venice[5]), he simply stated that the two merchants were regular contributors to the "Charities" of the Nation.[6]

---

5. On the privilege granted by the Serenissima Repubblica to the Spanish and Portuguese
Nation of Ferrara see A. di LEONE LEONI: *La presenza Sefardita a Venezia*, pp. 69-77.
6. ASMo, CD, EBREI, Busta 1, Processi, N. 74, ff. 20-21, February 4, 1573, witness testimony of Agostinho Henriques: «So che Abraam Allalvo et Abraam Ambensussan sono
hebrei portughesi compresi nel salvocondotto di S.E. et che pagano le sue tasse a li poveri
con li hebrei della Scola de portughesi». See A.di LEONE LEONI, *La presenza sefardita a
Venezia,* Doc. 13, p 89.

Abbreviations

Archivistic Abbreviations

AGR	=	Archives Générales du Royame, Brussels;
AGR, GRM	=	AGR, Grote Raad van Mechelen (= Grand Conseil de Malines);
AGR, PEA	=	AGR, Papiers de l'Etat en Audience;
AGR, OFB	=	AGR, Office Fiscal du Conseil de Brabant;
ANTT, Lisbon	=	Instituto dos Arquivos Nacionais da Torre do Tombo, Lisbon.
ASAn	=	Archivio di Stato di Ancona;
ASFe	=	Archivio di Stato di Ferrara;
ASMi	=	Archivio di Stato di Milano;
ASMo	=	Archivio di Stato di Modena;
ASMo,CD	=	ASMo, Cancelleria Ducale;
ASPs	=	Archivio di Stato di Pesaro;
ASPv	=	Archivio di Stato di Pavia;
ASVat	=	Archivio Segreto Vaticano, Vatican City;
ASVe	=	Archivio di Stato di Venezia;
BL, London	=	British Library, London;
BM,Colmar	=	Bibliothèque Municipale, Colmar;
BNM,Ve	=	Biblioteca Nazionale Marciana, Venice;
BNUE,Mo	=	Biblioteca Nazionale ed Universitaria Estense, Modena;
LJTS,Ny	=	Library of the Jewish Theological Seminary, New York;
SAA,Antwerp	=	Stadsarchief, Antwerpen;
UCL,WML, London	=	University College of London, Watson Manuscript Library, London.

Codazzi File = AGR, OFB, 160/1233/2, gathering of 38 unnumbered leaves comprising selected records of interrogations of Portuguese prisoners held in Pavia between September and December 1540, drawn up by notary G.B. Codazzi and authenticated by the Chancellor of the Imperial Senate of Milan on January 14, 1542.

Lavezzoli File, AGR, OFB160/1233/3, gathering of 67 leaves, comprising the depositions of several Portuguese immigrants formerly imprisoned in Lombardy, registered in January-February 1541 by Notary Nicola Lavezzoli in Ferrara

Information 1544 = AGR, OFB, 160/1233/3, gathering of 40 unnumbered leaves, entitled *Jnformation commenchée à prendre en la ville d'anvers le premier jour de juillet lan 1544 ... au faict des nouveaulx Christiens venuz de Portugal avec la derniere flote et armee.*

Bibliographic Abbreviations

AHP	=	Archivo Histórico Portuguez,
BCP	=	Bulletin de la Casa de Portugal, Anvers ;
ARG	=	Archiv für Reformationsgeschicte, Berlin.
Italia	=	Italia, Studi e Ricerche sulla Storia la Cultura e la Letteratura degli Ebrei d'Italia, The Hebrew University, Jerusalem,
JQR	=	Jewish Quarterly Review
MÖS	=	Mitteilungen des Österreichen Staatsarchivs, Wien;
Processi	=	P.C. IOLY ZORATTINI, Edit., *Processi del S. Uffizio di Venezia contro Ebrei e Giudaizzanti*, 14 Volumes, *1548-1734*, Firenze Leo S. Olschki Editore, 1980-2000;
RMI	=	Rassegna Mensile di Israel, Rome,
REJ	=	Revues des Études Juives. Paris;
Sefarad	=	Sefarad, Revista de Estudios Hebraicos, Sefardíes y de Oriente Proximo;
TRE	=	Theologische Realenzyklopädie, G. Müller Ed., Berlin New York, 1977 ;
Zakhor	=	Zakhor, Rivista di Storia degli Ebrei d'Italia, Roma.

DIACRITIC SYMBOLS

<words>	=	words written above the line;
{words}	=	words added in the margin of the sheet;
***	=	illegible words, due to deterioration of MS;
~~words~~	=	barred words
xyxyxy	=	illegible, undeciphered word;
~~xyxyxy~~	=	barred illegible words;
[words]	=	words inserted or reconstructed by the editor

A list with the names of twenty-six prominent New Christians living in Antwerp, drawn up by the police of Brabant in or around 1540. A footnote states that most of these people were very rich.
AGR,Bxl, PEA B.1504. See Document 12 in Appendix.

Charles V's decree reinstating the privileges granted in 1537 to the Portuguese
New Christians of Antwerp, March 10, 1542.
AGR,Bx, OFB, folder 160/1233/2. See Document 31 in Appendix.

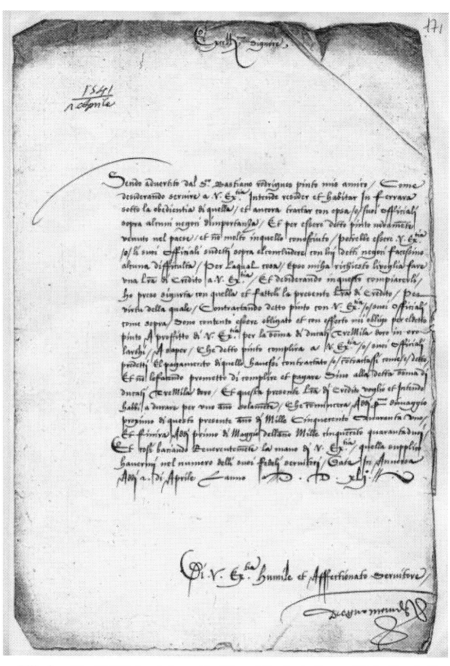

Bill of credit of 3,000 ducats issued by Diogo Mendes in favor of Duke Ercole II
d'Este, April 2, 1541.
ASMo, Camera Ducale, *Carteggio Referendari*, folder 171.

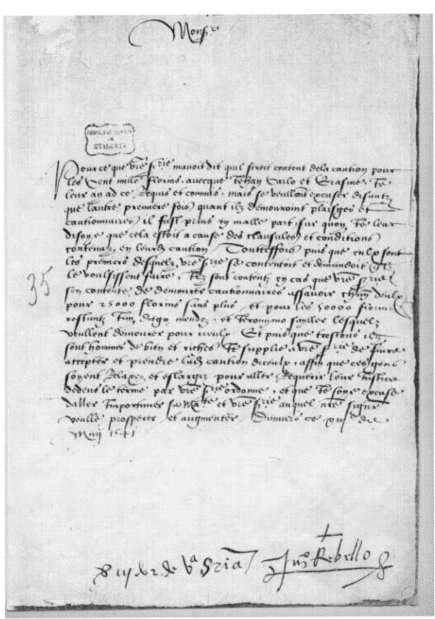

Juan Rebello, the Portuguese Royal *Feitor* informs Loys de Schorr, President of the Privy Council, that four merchants are prepared to provide a 100.000 ducats guarantee in favor of Agostinho Henriques and Fernando Pires, May 13, 1541. Source: AGR,Bx, PEA 1560, f. 52r. See Document 24 in Appendix.

I. A. Cattaneo, Secretary of the Imperial Senate of Milan, certifies that the transcription of the witness depositions registered in Pavia by notary Codazzi are authentical.

Source: AGR, Bx, OFB 160/1233/2, *Codazzi File,* unnumbered folio 36, January 14, 1542.

Regimento para o caminho: undated (circa 1544) instructions for the journey from Antwerp to Ferrara. See Document 36 in Appendix (with English translation).

Brudo Lusitano's medical tract, *Liber de Ratione victus in singulis Febribus,*
Venice 1544, Title page.
Courtesy of Biblioteca Nazionale Braidense, Milan.

Queen Mary, the governor of the Low Countries, informs King Ioão III of Portugal that many New Christians have entered Flanders clandestinely and, therefore, have been arrested.

AGR,Bx, OFB 160/1233/2. See Document 56 in Appendix.

On the twentieth day of the month of Av 5334 (July 28, 1574), in front of a Sephardic Bet Din in Safed, Letizia (formerly called Dina), the daughter of the late Isac Abenhini (formerly called Gabriel Jacome) gave her agreement to the sale of a house, located in a central street of Ferrara, which was part of her father's estate.

The document is preserved among the papers of notary Giacomo Conti, in the State Archives of Ferrara.

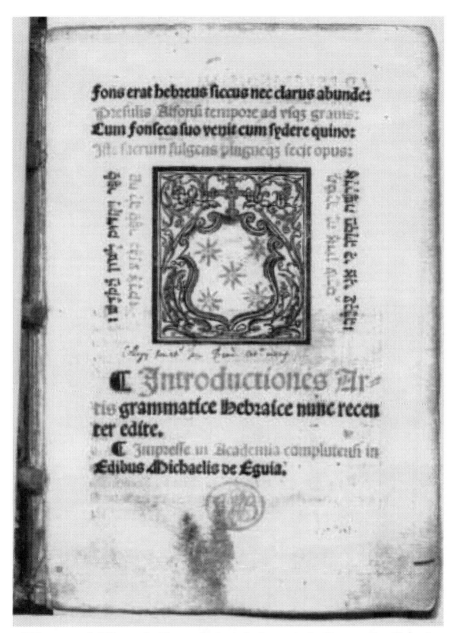

Title page of Alfonso de Zamora's *Introduciones Artis Grammatice Hebraice nunc recenter edite* (second edition, circa 1526). A Hebrew grammer book drawn up by a *Converso* according to Sephardic pronunciation rules.
Courtesy of the Biblioteca Nazionale Marciana, Milan.

Documentary Appendix

[Document 1]
[The Ferrara envoys to the Conference of Bologna report to
Duke Alfonso I on their meeting with Monseigneur de Granvelle –
December 30, 1529]

... et partendoci d[a lui]^1 ne chiamò indietro et disse ritrovarsi in
Ferrara un Judeo el qual, ostendendo in f[uori] et fingendo essere
christiano et buon mercante havea havuto assaj mercan[tie da] varij et
assaj mercantj fiandreschi, de li quali moltj parenti stanno qui alla [Corte]
de lo Imperatore, et poi era fugito et sotto salvo condutto di V. Excellentia
si era [con]dutto a Ferrara et perche li predetti ~~mercantj~~ parenti de essi
mercanti si doleano *** con la Maestà Cesarea, esso Monsignore di
Gravella havea prohibito che li predetti non si *** doluti et tolto lo
assunto di parlar con noj et operare che il predetto Judeo fusse
re[consegna]to non ostante il sopradetto salvo condutto, qual non si
extendea a simil ladroneria, V.Excellentia, sapendo tal mancamento, lo
avrebbe concesso. Noj li rispondessimo che era vero che V.Ex.^{tia} per non
mancar de la fede sua solea volere che li salvicondotti si osservassero in
ogni caso, ma che sapeamo anchor tanta e[ssere] la osservantia che porta
V. Excellentia verso S.Maestà et tuttj li suoi et in specie che havea a S.
Excellentia et desiderio di farle piacere, che pur che si possa trovare ***
che si possa dire ch'ella non manca de la fede sua, che sarà per fare
retenere detto Judeo che scrivessimo a V.Excellentia...

Source: ASMo,Cancelleria Ducale, Estero, Ambasciatori Roma, Busta
33.
1) lui = Nicolas Perrenot de Granvelle, Imperial State Secretary (*in
pectore*).

[Document 2]
[The Ferrara delegates to the Conference of Bologna to Duke Alfonso I
– January 4, 1530]

Monsignor de Granvella questa sera ne ha parlato un'altra volta sopra
quel che scrissemo a questi dì a Vostra Excellentia in quella cosa di quello
hebreo, et ne ha mostrata una lettera che le scrive lo Imperatore a favore
de quellj mercanti che alhor intese Vostra Excellentia essere stati
ingannati dal sudetto giudeo, et molto caldamente ce ha raccomandata
questa cosa pregandocj a scriverle ch'esso desydera che li sia fatta iustitia
favorevole. Per il che, sapendo quanto Vostra Excellentia desideri far cosa
grata in questo et in maggior cosa al predetto monsignor, non diremo altro
se non che più per sattisfattione di Sua Signoria che per bisogno, la
supplichiamo ch'ella sia contenta fare con effetto ch'el presente <latore>
ritorni ben contento et sattisfatto ... Vostra Excellentia sa, senza che le
dicemo a quanto importi haver favorevole questo Signor et maximamente
al presente, per questo da far ogni cosa per conservarlo amico ... Di
Bologna alli iiij di gennaro M.D.XXX.

Source: ASMo,CE, Amb. Roma, B 33.

[Document 3]
[Charles V appoints Corneil Scepperus to the rank of General
Commissioner "against false and bad Christians" April 4, 1530]

CAROLUS QUINTUS, Augustus, Divina favente clemencia
Romanorum Imperator, ac Germaniae, Hispaniarum, utriusque Sicilliæ,
Hierusalem, insularum Balearium Fortunatarumque et novi orbis
Indiarum, etc. Rex, Archidux Austriæ, Dux Burgundiæ et Galliæ Belgicæ
Dominus. etc. Cum audiamus quamplures Cristianam religionem
similantes Cristianosque sub cristiana specie atque habitu decipientes,
partim, collectis rebus suis omnibus atque etiam alienis, fugam in
Orientem et ad Turcarum aliorumque hostium Cristianæ fidei dominia et
terras parare, partim, occasionem commodiorem temporis expectantes, in
dominiis terrisque tam Imperii quam Galliæ Belgicæ Germaniæque
hereditariis Nostris degere, alios etiam ad frequentanda commercia et
coëmenda quæ eis ex usu videntur, quæque postea transmittant vel secum
ferant, ad eadem dominia Nostra frequenter commigrare, subditos

Nostros decipientes, facultatibus spoliare hisque hostes fidei Nostræ et
Nostros clandestine et aperte etiam iuvare, quo sic melius ipsi tandem ad
dictas terras hostium Cristianæ fidei et Nostros commigrare et se cum suis
omnibus conferre possint, prout multi eorum iam fecerunt mercatores,
etiam quosdam arma offensiva ad eosdem Turcas secreto mittere,
Nostraque intersit in hujusmodi mentitos Christianos mercatoresque, qui
arma offensiva transmittunt, animadvertere eosque meritis poenis afficere
et punire, prohibereque ne Nostram ditionem ac subditos facultatibus
spolient hisque hostes Nostros iuvent, de fide, industria atque dexteritate
spectabilis, fidelis Nobis dilecti CORNELII DUPLICII SCEPPERI,
Consiliarii et Secretarii Nostri plurimum confisi, eumdem Commissarium
Nostrum ad eam rem elegimus, creavimus ac deputavimus, ac tenore
praesentium eligimus, creamus ac deputamus, cum facultate ac potestate
unum vel plures Commisriarium vel Commissarios idoneos, tamen ubi
ipse personaliter his exequendis interesse nequiverit, loco sui
substituendi, subrogandi ac subdelegandi, qui similem aut alias limitatam
habeant potestatem ut, vi ac nomine Nostro, et tanquam Noster in hac
parte Commissarius aut Commissarii in quascumque nostræ ac Romani
Imperii ditionis ac dominiorum, Nostrarum Galliæ Belgicæ et Germaniæ
partes se conferant, atque hujusinodi mentitos ac simulatos Christianos,
alios etiam mercatores arma offensiva ad Turcas mittentes eorumque
merces ac bona mobilia et immobilia, si quæ illos habere contigerit et
quæcumque ea fuerint, ubivis gentium repertos et reperta capiant seu capi
ac carceribus detineri faciant, et officialibus ac iudicibus ordinariis
locorum in quibus capti fuerint, tradant, ut, in eos summarie procedendo,
processus forment, instruant, decidant, et expeditam iusticiam, et, si casus
id exigere videatur, causa cognita et iusticia prævia etiam usque ad
ultimum supplicium et hujusmodi bonorum confiscationem procedant et
procedi faciant, atque alia omnia et singula exequantur quæ in præmissis
et circa prææmissa necessaria visa fuerint; mandantes et serio
praecipientes quibuscumque locum tenentibus, Gubernatoribus et
Officiariis Nostris, tam mediatis quam immediatis, seu eorum locum
tenentibus, in Romano Imperio et aliis dominiis ac provinciis Nostris
hereditariis, tam in Italia scilicet quam in Gallia Belgica et Germania,
institutis vel instituendis, quocumque nomine nuncupatis et quavis
fungantur dignitate, officio vel auctoritate, atque universis et singulis
Principibus, tam ecclesiasticis quam secularibus, Ducibus, Marcionibus,
Comitibus, Baronibus, Militibus, Capitaneis, Tribunalibus quoque

generalibus et particularibus, Consiliariis, Regentibus, Potestatibus, Burgimagistris, Consulibus ceterisque Magistratibus quarumcumque provinciarum, civitatum, oppidorum, locorum et terrarum atque aliis quibuscumque Nostris et Romani Imperii subditis, quocumque nomine nuncupatis et cujuscumque status, dignitatis aut conditionis fuerint, ut quotiescumque ab ipso Cornelio, Commissario Nostro, aut a Commissariis ab eo subdelegandis aut deputandis, admoniti, et his litteris Nostris aut earum auctentico exemplari requisiti fuerint, hujusmodi reos capiant, detineant et arrestent seu capi, detineri, et arrestari faciant; videlicet tam personas et corpora præfatorum ementitorum Christianorum et ad Turcas iter parantium, ac eorum qui meliorem occasionem eo conferendi se expectantes, inter Christianos et subditos Nostros, sub habitu et specie christiana, in dominiis Imperii et Galliæ Belgicæ Germaniæque, hereditariis Nostris, degunt vel degere comperti fuerint, aut ad ea dominia, specie ut supra, coëmpturi res necessarias occulte se conferunt mercatores, etiam eos qui arma offensiva ad dictos Turcas transmittere comperti fuerint, quam bona, tam mobilia quam immobilia, si quæ illos habere contigerit et quæcumque ea fuerint, et merces taliter delinquentium subditosque Nostros fraudantium; quas quidem merces et bona, Nobis expositum est illos sub falsis insigniis extrahere solitos, sarcinas etiam mercatorum quorumcumque signis signatas, de quibus legitima informatio erit, quod in eis præfatorum ementitorum Christianorum bona contineantur, quæ tam diu teneantur, donec constiterit certo ad quos pertineant et quorum sint, utque etiam illi mercatores qui talia bona aliquando sub suis marcis et signis foras misere aut mittere comperti sunt, desuper via iuris requirantur, coganturque deponere et testificari veritatem, quid et quantum sciant, et bona, apud se deposita vel commissa, pandere et in manus iudicum assignare, ubicumque inveniantur et capi poterunt, et nullo pacto relaxent, donec de hujusmodi delictis atque excessibus constito debite ministretur iusticia, declareturque quid de hujusmodi personis et bonis sic detentis iure prævio sit statuendum et alias ab eis qui, ut præmittitur, capientur, omnibus mediis legitimis et a iure permissis veritas eruatur et passim ab eis intelligatnr, etiam per questionem, si iusticiæ et indiciorum qualitates id exigere videautur, quid inter se designaverint, quosque hujusmodi conspirationis socios habuerint, qui ejus rei fuerint conscii, et, his habitis, in alios quoque meritis poenis animadverti possit, bona autem ita adjudicata serventur et custodiantur fideliter et integre, eodem in loco ubi

sentencia contra illos prolata erit, neque ad cujusque arbitrium aut voluntatem dimoveantur aut distrahantur, donec et quousque, alio Nostro mandato, quid de illis fieri mandaverimus apparuerit. Et cum hoc, per universum Romanum Imperium ac dominia Nostra hereditaria Galliæ Belgicæ et Germaniæ et Italiæ, ut præmittitur, exequi debeant, volumus, decernimus et iubemus ut his litteris, vel earum auctentico esemplari, ab omnibus et ubique pareatur et obediatur, non obstantibus salvis conductibus, indultis, litteris passagii et quibuscumque aliis permissionibus, per ipsos falsos et mentitos Cristianos, sub Christianitatis colore, aut alios praedictos fraudulenter, subrepticie et obreptive impetratis et quovis prætextu ab eisdem allegato concessis, ac omnibus aliis in contrarium facientibus, cessantibus quibuscumque, quibus omnibus et singulis, pro hac vice tantum, derogamus et derogatum esse volumus, harum testimonio litterarum manu Nostra subscriptarum et sigilli Nostri Cæsarei appensione munitarum. Datum Mantuae, die XV1L mensis Aprilis, anno Domini millesimo quingentesimo tricesimo, Imperii Nostri decimo, aliorumque Regnorum decimo quinto.
Carolus

Source: AGR,Bx, PEA 1541.
Publications: Génard, Personen te Antwerpen, pp. 191–194, from a copy conserved at the Stadsarchief Antwerpen.

[Document 4]
[Queen Mary's official statement on the proceedings against Diogo Mendes and instructions for the imperial Commissioners in Antwerp – August 24, 1532]

Comme puis naguere Lempereur nostre seigneur estant adverty que depuis certaines annees ença plusieurs personnes quon dit nouveaulx cristiens ayant receu le baptisme et nostre saincte foy catholique et eulx faignans disans et simulans vrays cristiens sont secretement partiz du royaulme de Portugal venuz et arrivez avec leurs femmes et famile <et enffans> es pays de pardeça, et mesmement en la ville danvers et dela aucuns deulx sont allez par les allemaignes et aucuns par France vers Venise et de la en Salonique et autres villes, terres et seignories estans soubz le turcq, ennemy de nostre saincte foy catholique, au moyen de quoy grand nombre et quantite dor et dargent y est transferee et par ce ledit Turcq a este et est grandement fortiffie et multipliee tant de personnes que en biens or et chevanse et la saincte foy catholicque grandement diminuee, commettans ainsi lesdites personnes eulx transportans comme dessus apostasie publicque. Et pour ce que Lempereur nostredit seigneur en apres a este adverty et deuement informe que des longtemps et mesmement plus aucuns annes ensa, ung nomme Diego Mendis marchand portugaloys demourant en la dite ville danvers a este aydant et favorisant ausdites personnes et nouveaulx christiens et quilz ont eu devers icelluy Diego leur refuge, comme a leur patron et fauteur, lequel Diego est aussi fort suspect dentretenir et observer en ses adoracions ceremonies estranges selon la secte Judaicque, A ceste cause et apres information precedente sur ce sommairement prinse, Lempereur nostre seigneur par certains ses officiers a au mois de juillet dernier passe fait arrester saisir et inventorier tous lesdits nouveaux christiens avec leurs femmes famile et bien quelzconques trouvez tant en ladite ville danvers que ailleurs au pays et duche de Brabant, et aussi fait constituer prisonnier la personne dudit Diego Mendis et prendre et mettre en ses mains tous et quelzquonques biens, denrees, marchandises, livres, papiers et registres appartenans a icelluy Diego trouvez en ladite ville danvers, / f. 1v/ comme le tout appert par les lettres patentes inventoire et autres pieces de ce faisans mention. Et apres ce que ledit Diego Mendis a este par aucun temps destenu en prison, et sesdits biens en arrest, icelluy Diego a requis ou fait requerir devers la royne douaigiere de hongrie regente et gouvernante es pays de pardeça estre traicte par voye de justice et sur tout bon et brief droit, actendu le grand interest quil pretendoit par son emprisonnement et inventorisation de ses biens luy estre administre. Et considere que le cas cy dessus mentionne, pour austant que touche ledit Diego Mendis est cas privilegie et exempt, dont a Lempereur nostre Seigneur ou a messeigneures les chancellier et autre de son conseil en Brabant, par seclusion de tous autres juges la congnoissance doibt appartenir, et que ledit Diego <Mendis> comme lon doubte, soubz umbre quil est marchand, demourant et fouant domicile en ladite ville danvers, vouldroit soubstenir ou pretendre quil ne pourrait estre meme prisonnier hors ladite ville danvers soubz umbre des privileges dicelle ville et que, touchant dedit cas et de tous autres cas dont on le vouldroit charger, on le debvroit poursuyr et estre a droit par devant le bourgmaistre et eschevins dicelle ville danvers. A ceste cause et pour eviter question et debat en matiere de jurisdition, la Royne au nom dudit seigneur Empereur a commis et especialement autorizez maistres Loys de Heilwygen, Jehan van der Beken et Josse van der Dusschen tous conseilleurs dudit seigneur empereur en son conseil de Brabant pour eulx transporter en ladite ville danvers et pardevant eulx faire et instruire le proces dudit Diego Mendis. Comme aussi en ensuyvant lesdits seigneurs et commis se sont trouvez en ladite ville danvers et au mercredi le septieme jour daoust dernier passe /f. 2r/ le procureur general de lempereur nostre seigneur en son pays et duchee de Brabant, comparant pardevant lesdits commis en personne et aussi ledit Diego Mendis prisonnier avec Jehan van den Dycke son procureur, apres certaines protestations par ledit procureur general faicte, que procedant en ceste matiere contre ledit Diego, prisonnier en ladite ville danvers pardevant lesdits commis comme juges deleguez, il nentende par ce faire aucun preiudice pour les temps advenir a la majeste imperiale, ne a son haulter ne a la jurisdiction de son conseil en Brabant en autres et semblables causes privilegiees que cy apres pourroient advenir ou de part sa majeste estre intentez [sic !] contre autres personnes ou prisonniers et dont a sa majeste ou a sondit conseil de Brabant la congnoissance pourroit competer. Icelluy procurer general soubz ceste protestation par les raisons et les moyens cy dessus et plus au long par ladvocat fiscal dicelluy seigneur emperateur aussi y comparant en personnes verbalement alleguez, a contendu affin que par sentence de mesdits seigneurs les chancellier et autres de sondit conseil en Brabant sera dit et declaire pour droit ledit Diego Mendis prisonnier avoir forfait et confisque son corps et tous ses biens au prouffit de la Majeste Imperiale. Et ou cas que pour aucunes considerations la court a ce mouvans, ceste conclusion ne luy pourroit servyr, que ledit prisonnier sera dumoings puny et corrige arbitrairement, ainsi que selon ses delictz et demerites ou autrement selon lexigence du cas lon trouvera appartenir par raison, cum expensis, en cas de ce derriere membre. Et apres plusieurs specifications desdits faitz et ceremonies Judaicques, viscin et copie des plusiers lettres pieces et munimens, par ledit procureur general faisant sa demande alleguez et par ledit Diego ou son procureur audit procureur general requises /f. 2v/ et a luy en partie accordees en suyvant lappointement desdits commis, ledit Diego avec sondit procureur a le xii^e dudit mois daoust respondu a la demande et conclusion dudit procureur general declinatoire et autrement contendu a la fin, comme il a donne devers lesdits commis par escrit et dont la teneur sen suit de mot a autre : ledit deffenseur proteste soubz toutes reverence que par ce que desia en ceste cause par luy a este fait et se fera na este et nest dintention de proroguer ou consentir en la juridiction du Conseil de Brabant, ne de vous messieurs les commissaires par ledit Conseil de Brabant commis autrement ne plus avant que de droit appartient, mais actendu que le demandeur icelluy deffendeur cristien, inculpe et accuse par ses ii^e et iii^e article de heresie, quil auroit judaise et a present seroit juif, lequel crime dheresie est totalment ecclesiastique subjet a la congnoissance du juge ecclesiastique et en tous autre article entant le demandeur icelles pose et par icelles entend accuser afin dheresie.

En ce cas respond le deffendeur declinatoirement et conclu quil sera declaire de droit que audit Conseil de Brabant et par consequance ne a vous messieurs le commissaires dudit pretendu delict dheresie nappartient aucune congnoissance et que pourtant ledit demandeur ayant pardevant vous messieurs accuse procede et contendu contre icelluy deffendeur en la maniere comme par luy fait a este pardevant vous Messieurs les commissaires ne fait a recevoir, ainsi sera la cause renvoye aux Juges ecclesiastiques et en ce cas le demandeur, ledit iii^e et tout les autres subsequantes articles de sa demande dicelles articles a autre fin dexces et mesus /f. 3r/ que a la fin du delict de heresie susdite de ce nappartiendroit la congnoissance en la premiere instance au Conseil de Brabant ne pardevant vous Messeigneurs les commissaires, ains pardevant ceulx danvers, pour ce quil est leur inhabitant et ensuyvant leurs privileges. Conclud aussi pourtant afin de declinatoire que le demandeur pour ce pardevant vous Messeigneurs avoit fait ~~fait~~ demande et procedure pardevant vous Messeigneurs nest a recevoir ains sera la cause renvoyee pardevant ceulx danvers. Sera pour ce declaire que lapprehension et detention de sa personne et larrest et occupation de ses biens comme par juges incompetents faiz, nullement et a tort sont faictes, seront ostez et mis a neant, luy et ses biens diceulx franchement deschargez et relaxez et faisant aussi demande de despens, dommaiges et interestz.

A quoy de la part dudit procureur general, ayant en vision et copie de la conclusion dudit Diego Mendis, a este le xiii^e jour dudit mois daoust en ladite matiere declinatoire respondu et soubstenu par les raisons et moyens par luy ou ledit advocat fiscal verbalement alleguez, que reiectant lexception declinatoire par ledit prisonnier ou son procureur proposee, icelluy prisonnier sera tenu de respondre plus amplement au principal, pardevant lesdits commis sur la conclusion par icelluy procureur general faisant sa demande prinse. Surquoy a este par iceluy prisonier ou son procureur au xiiii^e jour dicelluy mois daoust replique et par les raisons et moyens par luy par cy devant et audit xiii^e jour daoust verbalement au long alleguez persiste en ladite declinatoire et /f. 3v/ ledit procureur general pour les raisons et moyens par luy autreffois respondant en ladite matiere declinatoire et audit jour de rechief alleguez a aussi persiste par duplicque en ses fins et conclusions cy devant prinses. Et le plaidoie des dites parties ouy par les dits commis et juges deleguez, actendu et considere limportance et qualite de ceste cause, ont ordonne et appoincte que lesdites partie escripront en ladite matiere declinatoire par advertissement et y prindront toutes telles lettres titres et muniments dont ilz se vouldront ayder dun couste et dautre et en se serviront es mains du greffier endedans lundi xix^e jour dudit mois daoust. Auquel appoinctement lesdites parties ont depuiz fourny et requis instamment droit et justice touchant ladite matiere declinatoire leur estre faicte. Et combien que lesdits commis et juges deleguez en vertu de la commission et povoir a eulx donne depar la majeste jmperiale, avoient auctorite de juger, decider et determiner ladite matiere declinatoire estant ainsi instruicte et en estat de juger, neantmoins iceulx commis pour aucunes considerations a ce les mouvans ont differe ce faire, ains se sont parctiz de ladite ville danvers et se sont trouvez vers la Royne a Bruxelles. A la majeste de laquelle lesdits commis ont, en presence des messieurs de conseil destat, remonstree aucune difficultez sur ladite exception declinatoire, ou fut finablement conclud que mesdits seigneurs les chancellier et autres dudit conseil en Brabant pour limportance dicelle matiere la decideroient en plein conseil. Et apres ce que mesdits seigneurs les chancellier et conseil en ont veut et visite le playdoye /f. 4r/ desdites parties sur ladite exception declinatoire de la part du dit prisonnier deffendeur proposee ensemble les advertissements pieces et munimens serviz par devant lesdits commis, et sur tout eu bon et meur advis, mesdits seigneurs de la chancellerie et autres dudit conseil en Brabant disent et declarent pour droit que, non obstant les raisons et moyens depar ledit Diego deffendeur affin de renvoy proposees, il sera tenu de respondre par devant lesdits du conseil au premier jour plaidoiable par procureur souffisamment constitue.

A quoy la court lauctorize tenant sa personne prison en la ville danvers. Et ce sur tous le faiz par ledit procureur alleguez, saulf et reserve le fait et le poinct concernant quil auroit tenu ou observe en ses orasions au adoracions les ceremonies des Juifz accoustumees duser en leurs sinagogues, sur lequel ne sera encoires tenu plusavant litem contestez. Pour sadite response sur lesdiz autres faiz ouye, este procede et appoincte comme de raison condempnant icelluy deffenseur en ce que dessus ensemble aussi es trois pars des despens en ceste cause faiz, lautre quarte diceulx pour cause compense. Fait en la ville de Bruxelles le xxiiii^e jour dudit mois daoust mil cinq cens trente deux. Soubzescript moy present et signe Boudeewins

Source: AGR,Bx,PEA, Reg. 1504, August 24 1532.

[Document 5]
[Queen Mary's instructions for the release of Diogo Mendes upon payment of bail – September 10, 1532]

Jnstruction pour Maistres Loys de Heylwygen et Pierrre de Walhem conseilleurs de lempereur pour leslargissement et relaxation de la personne de Diego Mendis et la man levee de larrest fait sur ses byens, le tous en esuyvant lappointement signe de la Royne en date de vij^e de septembre xv^cxxxij

Que lesdits commissaires prendreront dudict Diego Mendis caution de cincquante mil ducats, suyvant ledit appointement, dez marchanz telz dont Wolfganch Haller tresorier de la Royne et Lazarus Turcher se contentent et lesquelz ilz declareront ausdits commissaires estre souffisans pour telles sommes quilz vouldront obliger. Bien entendu que ledit Diego Mendis pourra bailler tant de marchans quil luy plaira qui se pourront obliger pour telles sommes et ladite caution baillee jusques a ladite somme de cincquante mil ducats suyvant ledit appointement et acte que en est faitte, lesdits commissaires relaxeront ledit Diego Mendis de la prison en que il est presentement detenu et se levera larrest fait sur ses byens selon le contenu dudit appointement.

Semblement lesdits commissaires prendront dudit Diego telles promesses pour la seurte de lempereur comme ilz selon ledit appointement trouveront appartenir. Et ne pourront lesdits commissaires fer ladite relaxacion de corps ou des byens dudit Diego Mendis nestoit que ledit tresoriers Haller et Lazarus declaireront estre contens. Et ainsi fait par la Royne en conseil a Bruxelles le xe jour de septembre lan xv^cxxxij, soubzsigne Marie.

Source: AGR,Bx,PEA 1504.

[Document 6]
[Antonio Fernandez to Gerolamo Maretta – July 24, 1538]

1538 Envers 24 de uijo a Girolamo Marete

Despois de vosa partida hey pasado muitas pratiquas com muitos home[n]s sobre o a[ssunto] que sabe[i]s, os quais todos estan muito satisfeitos de todo noso negociar. Mediante Noso Senhor, espero que a todo se dará bom fim e asy espero [por] minha parte fazer tamto que sua Ex.tia me tenha por hum de seus servidores porque em minha mâo, como sabe[i]s esta muita parte do c[uidado] que a este negocio se deve dar, asi mesmo vosa vimda ha sido muito pr[ovei]tosa e fez muito neste caso.

Eu tenho escrito homde sabe[i]s muit[as] v[ezes] e dado comta de todo ho negocio e niso se fará muita obra, com t[ant]o que V[ossa] M[ercê] faça como se aja os salvos comdutos que lhe temos ditos.

Digo que, o dia que V[ossa] M[ercê] se partio desta villa, soube como Gomez Rodriguez era fog[ido] da prisão pollo qual praça a V[ossa] M[ercê] niso fará como eu comfio asy bem [?] damdo diso comta a Sua Ill.ma Senhoria para que niso se ponha allgum remedio de modo que eu possa ser pago. E toda a mercê que niso me fizer eu baixarej polla servir e por que sey que fará niso como em sua. Neste caso non digo mais, somente que V[ossa] M[ercê] me avise se sabe em que terra he retirado o dito Gomes Rodriguez.

E por me parecer que V[ossa] M[ercê] non sera ajmda aribado non lhe dou mais comta nesta, somente rogar a noso Senhor por vida e estado de V[ossa] M[ercê].

Manoell Lopez meu sobrinho me escrive virá a Ferrara. V[ossa] M[ercê] fará como seja fa[vorecido] de Sua Ex.cia como eu comfio e posto que Gomez seja fogido, agora mais que numqua me pode V[ossa] M[ercê] ajudar. E do que fizer me avise e o ditto basta.

O Servidor de V[ossa] M[ercê]
Antonio Fernandez

Source: ASMo,CD, *Lettere Particolari*, B. 837.

[Document 7]
[Duke Ercole II to some (unnamed) Portuguese merchants living in
Antwerp – July 29, 1538.]

Amici charissimi,
    Jo ho inteso da M. Hieronymo Maretta tutto quello che per nome
vostro mi ha exposto, et quello ancho che per nome vostro mi ha richiesto.
<Jl tutto son stato contento>, et è tale l'affetione che per le buone offerte
vostre vi porto, et per la buona relatione fattami de voi per esso Maretta,
che summamente desydero che voi veniate accioche vi possi mostrare con
li effetti quanto mi sia grata <il conversare vostro> nella città et terre mie.
Et perche il predetto Maretta anderà al viaggio di Fiandra jnanzi la venuta
vostra, occorrendovi cosa alcuna farete capo a Bondi Carri hebreo il quale
habita in questa terra, che non se ne mancherà, come sel Maretta ci fosse
presente, in conto alcuno, et ad esso Bondi medesemamente prastarete
fede che così è di mia jntentione. Anzi se non fosse stata la jndispositione
sua, già per ordine mio sarebbe venuto a voi per conoscerlo, [è] persona
del quale me ne posso servire e fidare. State sani.
Di Ferrara jl di xxviiij luio 1538.
                Alex[ander Guarinus]

Source: ASMo,CD, *Minutario Generale Cronologico*, Folder 9.

[Document 8]
[Diogo Mendes to Duke Ercole II d'Este – October 9, 1538]

Molto Ill.mo et Ex.mo S.or S.or mio Oss.mo,
    Per una [lettera] di Vostra Excellentia che ho recevuto per mano di
messer Hieronimo Maretta, consulo delli portughesi in Ancona [*sic*!], ho
inteso quanto bisogna et come dal ditto consulo Vostra Excellentia
Illustrissima jntenderà, jo sono tanto desideroso di servirla, come le opere
inanzi mostrarano la mia voluntade, et per tanto non sarò prolisso a Vostra
Excellentia perche luj con parole, io con le opere suppliremo a tutto
quello che Vostra Excellentia commanda, alla quale molto humilmente
[...] basso la mano: et se in cosa alcuna lo posso servir, mi comandi Vostra
Excellentia che mi trovarà tanto promto come quale de maggiori suoj
servitori.

Molto Excellentissimo Signor, Nostro Signore lo Stato di Vostra Signoria Excellentissima augumenti.

Di Anversa VIIII octobre 1538
Di Vostra Signoria Jllustrissima et Excellentissima
S[ervit]or Diego Mendez

Source: ASMo,CD, *Lettere particolari*, B. 885.

[Document 9]
[Gerolamo Maretta to Duke Ercole II of Ferrara – undated fragment of a lost dispatch – 1539]

Four Portuguese merchants are prepared to move to Ferrara with their families. Maretta suggests to issue safe-conducts and patent-letters in favour of the would-be immigrants.

Messer Giovanni Duarte ⎫
                       ⎬ et loro famiglie
Messer Aduarto Pinto   ⎭

Messer Francesco Chaldere ⎫
                           ⎬ et loro famiglie
Messer Luix Alvere dottore ⎭

Una lettera al Reverendissimo [Cardinale Ippolito d'Este] di Milano chomo chostoro si partono di qui et hanno qui loro famiglie per tornare qui al servitio di Sua Reverendissima Signoria e che tutti i favori che si può li presti

Una patente chome sono familiari di Sua Ex.tia. e che per tutto loro et loro famiglie siano lasciati [passare] perche vengono qui ad abitare et a servitij di Sua Ex.tia. Questa è la sustantia.

Source: ASMo,CD, *Carteggio Referendari*, Busta 171: loose undated [August 1539] leaf originally attached to a (lost) mesage.

[Document 10]
[Duke Ercole II instructs his ambassador in Milan to request the
immediate release of Duarte Pinto –
(undated, August 1539)]

Jnstruttioni a voj che havete andare allo Ill.mo et Ex.mo Signor
marchese del Guasto per eseguire lo jnfrascritto negotio:

Gionto che voi sarete in Cremona, ove di presente si trova Sua Ex.,
farete opera di presentarvj a luj et, dopo che haverete fat[to] le mie
raccomandationi, li presentarete le lettere nostre di credenza in v[irtù]
delle quali ~~li farete intendere come Noj facessimo uno salvo~~ li direte che
havemo inteso come messer Aduardo Pinto gentilhomo portug[ese] ad
jnstanza d'uno Gioannes dalla Foglia fiamengo e stato per commis[sione]
di Sua Ex. distenuto con volerli dare imputatione che essendo che andava
in Turchia per spia: et perche noj sapiamo questo ess[ere] alieno dalla
veritade, perche havendoci luj fatto intendere il desiderio che teniva di
venir habitare in questa terra con sua famiglia, sino dell'anno passato del
mese di agosto non solo li facessimo salvocondotto in ampla forma ma
per essere ancho persona di molte buone qualitade e meritevole d'ogni
grata dimostratione, ci movessimo a perseguirlo di alcune favorevoli
gratie per fare a ciascuno noto quanto ci fosse grato la venuta e
conversatione sua. Et di tale maniera che ancho fui contento accettare
nella casa mia uno suo figliolo di quello modo e forma et con lj medesimj
ordinj et provisioni che siamo soliti tenere in casa nostra lj altri figliolj de
gentilhomini. Però vi abbiamo mandato acciò che in nome nostro pregate
Sua Ex., et così la pregarete ben strettamente, che voglia essere contenta
farlo rilassare acciò che se ne possi venire al suo destinato viaggio et non
siano intertenuto con false calunnie di persone malevole che cercano con
tale meggio fare danno e vergogna, che de ciò Sua Ex. ce ne farà piacere
grandissimo et jl maggiore che da luj potessimo expettare di questo tempo
et del quale noi li restaremo con molto obligo: et così vederete fare ogni
opera a voi possibile per la liberazione sua usando tutti quelle parole e
tenendo tutti quej modi che conoscerete esser necessarij e convenientj
perche tutto seguiti lo effetto lo quale noi oltramodo desideramo.

[Hercole Secondo]

Source: ASMo,CD, Estero, *Ambasciatori Milano*, B.30, undated [1539].

[Document 11]
[Official report on Loys Garces' accusations against Manuel Serrano,
Gabriel Negro, Manuel Manriques, Diogo Mendes and Enrique Pires –
July 5 and 6, 1540]

En bruxas a ~~quatro~~ cinco de jullio de mjll y quinjentos y quarenta los
muy reverendos señores el maestro fray Diego de S. Pedro confessor de
su magestad y el doctor vaguer regente de aragon por comission de su
magestad vive vocis oraculo a ellos hecha pera lo ynfrascripto y a ello
tocante + escribien con juramento en forma a luys garçes natural de
lisbona hijo del doctor maestre airas medico y de margarida enrriquez
naturales de lisbona, so cargo del qual dixo lo sigujente.

dixo que el vino delante de suplicante con zelo de discargar su
conçiençia de çiertas cosas que le paresçian mal, y dixo que no conosceria
suplicante a este declarante pero que el era hijo del dicho doctor arias el
qual era medico del rey de portogal y privado e favorido suyo, y que
estando en conpañya del dicho suplicante le enseño todo lo que deve
saber vn buen cristiano, y que en aquel tienpo su madre puso a este
declarante com otros tress hijos suyos dios gracias y avn viven y con
astuçia siendo ellos muy mochachos porque a honze años que ~~pa~~ los puso
en vn batel y se vinjeron a flandres. y quedo el dicho suplicante en
Portugal, y estuvjeron la dicha su madre y hijos obra de vn mes en
flandres. y que vn Diego Mendez mercader de Envers les dio a este
declarante y madre y hijos casa en que estoviesen y les visitava cada dia
y finalmente les persuadio que se fuesen a turquia y les dio la memoria
del camjno y les dio mucha presa pera que se partiesen luego y segun
piensa este declarante era porque como su padre era favorido del rey de
Portugal temya oviese cartas pera bolvellos alla, y asy se fueron tan breve.
y esta la dicha su madre con los dichos sus hijos en vna civdad que se
llama Saloniquez que es en la provincia de tesalia. y que es vna çivdad
muy principal donde ay moros y turcos y Judios y que la major parte es
de Judios y que estano en aquella terra cinco o seys años y el menos
tienpo desto con su madre y hijos y que en este tienpo el foie inçenoso y
vivio como vivjan los Judios haziendo sus cerimonyas y yendo a la
syn[ag]oga porque no podia hazer otra cosa y que lo mas presto que jndo
este declarante se ~~sup~~ vino de aquella terra a Roma y confeso a nuestro
muy Santo padre sus culpas delo que avya hecho contra nuestra fee
catholica syendo batizado a nuestro y su Santidad le absolvjo de todo lo

que hasta entonçes avya ofendido a dios en aquel caso, y despois se
entretuvo en Ytalia per espacio de quatro años. acordo de yr a buscare a
su padre y vino Envers y ay le dixo el dicho Diego Mendez como su padre
era ydo a la dicha Çivdad de Saloniquez donde estava la dicha su madre
y hijos. y que el dicho Diego Mendez y vn Gabriel de Nebro y vn
Enryquez /f. 1v/ Perez todos tress le ynduzian que se volviese a
Saloniquez donde estava su padre y madre y aun que estos mas
particularmente le convencyan pera que hiziese esto. todos casi los otros
le corriam y persuadian que se fuese. Y que el dicho Graviel de Enebro le
dezia que se fuese con su padre madre que aca no estava como le
convencya que estava como vn perdido y que su madre por averse ydo
como se fue a turquia. meresia <corona de> p̶ reyna y avya hecho vna
cosa grande y muy bien hecha. y que el Enrriquez le hablo muchas vezes
mas que los otros dandole a entender que fuese a vivjr com sus padres
pera vivjr como ellos viven. y que praticando este declarante con el dicho
Enrriquez Perez de como el avya venydo por Roma y demandado
absolucion a nuestro muy Santo padre de sus culpas pues venya a vivjr a
ca a estos Reynos. y que entonçes le dixo el dicho Enriquez Perez anda
que byen sabe <os> aca lo que aveys hecho en Roma diziendose lo por
menos presion. y que aquello no era conforme a lo que del se esperaua y
de donde venya. de manera que en sustançia le persuadia que fuese a
vivyr con sus padres como ellos viven aunque se las palavras se recatavan,
y que platicando con vn Manuel Serrano f̶a̶t̶t̶o̶r̶ a quien nos el dicho djego
mendez se descubre le puso crecidos temores a este declarante […] que
les podia acusar e descubrir algo trayendo a consequencia un duarte de
paz que estava en Roma por negociador dellos porque pidio doss mjll
ducados que dixo que avya gastado en solicitar los negocios dellos. le
hizieron yr por la posta mas que de passo y sy esperara no liberara byen
todo esto me dezia pera meterme miedo mostrandome quaez poderosos
estavan y quanto ellos podian tambyen me dixo que tenyan patentes del
Regente con que non temyan a nadie. y que el dicho Diego Mendez en la
primera vista suya le puso algunos temores diziendo que quien soys vos
y como venys asy y que no darian pedido a suplicante dando a entender
que si hablase le echarja en vn pozo y esto dezia syn causa alguna mas de
querer mostrar su poder y pera que no dicese nada delo que sabya y avya
visto.

+ Item dixo que lo que le movyo a este de lo venyr a hablar al padre
confessor fue el zelo que tenya de merescer con dios en dezirlle el daño

que se hazia a las anymas y religion christiana por medio de los susodichos y es que por yndustria y persuasion vienen muchos de los christianos nuevos de Portugal a Envers y des que estan ay con la mysma yndustria y persuasyon los an hjr a turquia donde van hobrar rias item yndustriosos y por esta vya dan avyso de todas las cosas que aqui passan que ny se ay por pequena que sea do que ellos non avysan a sus respondientes y ellos lo pueden dezir al turco especialmente por vn Judio medico que tiene /f. 2r/ el turco el qual tiene parientes en Envers uno de los quales es uno que se dize Coronel y que tienen ynteligencia los unos con los otros. En tratos y otras cosas.

+ Item dixo este declarante que ahora en Envers del tienpo que ay a estado a entendido que los susodichos tress y todos los demas cristianos nuevos que ay estan guardan todas las çerimonyas dela ley Judayca ny mas ni menos que lo hazian antes que se tornasen cristianos. preguntado como lo sabya dixo que avn que el pera verse apartado dellos y de su conversaçion no a visto cosa alguna destas claramente pero por la experiencia que el tiene del tienpo que este declarante hazia las çerimonyas y por conocia claramente como guardavan las dichas çerimonyas mosaycas porque los dias de ayuno segun la ley que no comen hasta la noche yendose los otros dela bolsa a comer ellos se yvan por el campo. por otras partes hasta la noche lo qual no hazian los otros dias y que en el tiempo que se come el pan çençeño los que no tenjan casas por si yvan a comer com los que eran casados pera donde podia comer de los manjares de la ley syn que fuesen senydos y asy acreseo algunas vezes que aun que solian comer con el factor del rey de Portugal allgunos dellos en tales dias como estes nunca podia acabar con ellos que fuese sus convydados el porque yo de que el factor non lo sabja pero yo que tenya la experiençia que tengo dicho luego caya en la mente que hazia esto por yr a las casas donde seguramente podia comer de sus <los> manjares dela ley. tanbyen sy hablan a algunos mançebos cristianos nuevos que dezian ahora que viene la pascoa donde comeremos pan çençeño uno dezia yr comere en casa de Gabriel de Negro porque tiene casa por sy, destes mançebos no se quien son ny acyos hijos son.

+ fue le dicho so el del juramento que tiene hecho que diga sy sabe alguna cosa mas deles que asy a dicho pera descargo de consciencia o que otras personas sepan algo acerca desto porque no parese en que se prueba bjen e lo que el absolutamente dixo que sabya que estos vivyan ala manera de los Judios por solamente tener unos yndicios de tan poca ynportancia como dixo por eso le preguntarom que dixese otras causas mas ynportantes y mas clara y abyertamente que esto probase mejor que nelas cosas que hasta ahora a dicho todavya torno a afirmar y dezir que el tenya por cierto que ellos aujan dela manera que el tiene dicho avn que no tyene otras /f. 2v/ razones mas de las dichas. y que sy el fuese a Envers podria mostrarlo palpablemente esto que tiene dicho :

+ en seys de Jullio. Paresçeo el dicho luys garçes por mandado de sus mayestades y estando presente le fue leydo todo lo que ayer avya dicho y asy leydo le fue dicho que ya sabe que ayer le encargaron que recurriese bien su memoria pera si alguna cosa se le acordase mas delo que dicho tiene. Lo dixese y si se afirmava en lo que avia dicho.

+ item luego dixo el dicho declarante que todo lo que ayer dixo esta aqui escripto es verdad y que se afirmava en ello. y que no se acuerda mas delo que dicho tiene mas que <le> tene por cierto que ellos se estan en la ley que antes estavam de moysen. y que el se prefiere demostralo palpablemente quando fuere mostrado.

+ despois de todo <esto> dixo este declarante que estando en Envers avya reçebydo vna carta de su padre hecha en regusa la qual vino en el enboelto del dicho Enrriquez Perez. item firmo lo de su nombre

> es verdad que todo lo sobredicho segundo esta
> esprito [sic!] y portanto
> afirme de my propia mano
>   luis garces

[Document 12]
[A list of prominent New Christians living in Antwerp in (or around) 1540]

[posthumous note:]
1541/1542

Diego Mendez Bienveniste,
Brianda de Luna su muger,
Beatriz de Luna her[man]a dela Bria[n]da,
    Dos criados de Diego Mendes: el uno se dize

    Rodrigo y el otro Gonçalo Dies
Dominico Mendez,
el licenciado Lope Mendez,
Odoardo Pinto,
Estacio Pinto,
Luys Perez,
Luys de Sevilla,
Gabriel del Negro,
Enrique Perez,
Estevan Perez,
Manoel Lopez,
El doctor dionisio medico,
António Fernandez her[man]o de Manoel Lopez,
Gabriel Fernandez,
Luys Fernandez,
Manoel de Provincia,
Lope de Provincia su hijo,
Diego Nuñes,
Ruy Lopez,
Lorenço Alvarez,
Luys Alvarez el mercador no el medico,
Manoel Serrão
Joan Duarte].

Todos estos son christianos nuevos de nacion portogueses, habita' en Anveres, Son mercadores los mas y muchos dellos muy ricos

Source: AGR,Bx,PEA 1504, loose, unnumbered and originally undated sheet.

[Document 13]
[Johannes Vuysting accuses Diogo Mendes and other Portuguese merchants of Antwerp, London and Milan of plotting to have him assassinated – September 21, 1540]

1540 Die septembris 21
    (/f. 19v/ Conquestus est Magnificus Dominus Johannes Vuistingh alias de la Foglia de civitate Trutensi[1] Flandrie, Cesareus Comissarius

super falsos et novos christianos, mediantibus litteris patentibus predicte
Majestatis Cesaree sibi concesse datis Mantue 17 mensis aprilis 1530
subsignatis "Carolus" et sigilatis sigillo Cesareo solito, [dixit] quomodo
esse possunt menses decem et octo vel circa preteritj quod ipse D.nus
querellans residet super Statu Mediolani pro dicta eius comissione
exequenda et providendo fraudibus dictorum falsorum et novorum
christianorum juxta comissionem suam et, sic stando, Diego Menes
Benvenistis habitator Anversie una cum Antonio della Rogna monoculo
habitatore Alundre, partibus Jnghilterre, tractatum fecerunt jnvicem ad
mensam in domo suprascripti Dieg Menes de interfici faciendo dictum
presentem querellantem, quo tractatu factu, participaverunt dictum eorum
votum cum: /f. 20r/

    Emanuelle Lopes,
    Emanuelle Sarrano et
    Lopo de Provincia

et unanimiter concordes exbursaverunt peccunias ad summam
scutorum plusquam duomille et inter cetera dictus Antonius della Rogna
exbursavit scutos centum et predicti alij residuum et direxerunt litteras in
civitatem Mediolani in manibus Gonsales Gomes, portugalensis et in jpsa
civitate Mediolani residentis, pro ipsis scutis duobus mille recipiendis ut
homicidium in personam dictj querellantis committeretur adeo quod ipse
peccunie erant destinate pro talea et literis ut vulgo dicitur de cambio pro
interfici faciendo jpsum Dominum querellantem ut supra. Qui Gonsales
Gomes est agens et respondens in civitate Mediolani pro falsis et novis
christianis et gerit negocia eorum et quod de dicto tractatu potest esse
informatus Gaspar Lopes et est nepos dictj Dieghi Menes.

Et etiam querellat quod anno presentj et mense iunij seu iulij vel circa
preteritis, dum in civitate Mediolani vulneratus fuisset Ill.^{mus} Marchio
Saluciorum, ipse D. querellans /f. 20v/ obviam habuit in dicta civitate et
in ecclesia majori suprascriptum Gonsales Gomes, quodam die de quo
certo non recordatur sed erat post prandium et esse poterant tres dies (ex)
quo dictus Marchio vulneratus fuerat, ipsi querellantj dixit quod habebat
informationes qualiter ipse querellans dederat signa nonnullarum
ballarum novorum christianorum ut retinerentur, qui querellans ej
respondidit nihil scire et tunc dictus Gonsalves Gomes respondidit hec
verba vel similia: «jo so che si» et ipse querellans ej ostendidit quamdam
cartam super qua aderant nonnulle marche, qui Gonsalves Gomes dixit:
«questa è la mia» tangendo unam ex dictis marchis cum digito et ipse

querellans dixit: «jo voglio fare intertenire quelle balle delli christiani novi», qui Gonsalves Gomes dixit: «Jo sono christiano novo, donque volete far intertenire le mie robe et de altri christiani novi, se pur volete fare intertenire le robe de christiani novi, fate donque intertenire le robe del'jmperator et del Duca d'Alva. /f. 21r/ Et se volete andar dreto a queste cose, a voj ve sarà fatto quello ch'è sta fatto al Marchese de Salucio» et tandem, multis inter eos dictis, dictus Gonsalves Gomes jpso querellante se conquerente et dicente: «voletj farmi voj questo» qui respondit quod non, sed dixit «se voletj andar dreto a questo, ve sarà fatto da le altre persone» et tenet firmiter quod dictus Gonsalves Gomes sit particeps dicti tractatus et quod habuerit dictas litteras cambij pro jpsum querellantem interfici faciendo et etiam quia semper comparet et fidembet ac intercedit pro dictis falsis christianis et solvit pro eis rellaxandis et gerit eorum negocia et etiam pro detentis comitendo predicta —

Source: AGR,Bx,OFB, 160/1233/2, *Codazzi File,* ff. 19v–21r.
1) *de civitate Trutensi* = from Uthect.

[Document 14]

[Gaspar Lopes (prisoner in Pavia) states under torture that Diogo Mendes and other Portuguese merchants of Antwerp and London planned to have Johannes Vuysting murdered – September 21, 1540]

1540 die 21 septembris

Gaspar Lopes filius quondam D.ni Baldassaris Lopes de Minentis de Terra Alegrete, diocesis Castigliensis veteris, testis productus per suprascriptum qurerellantem, monitus, iuratus, /f. 21v/ interrogatus receptus et examinatus super suprascripta querela sibi lecta, interrogatus suo juramento prestito etc, respondit et dixit quod veritas fuit et est quod de anno presenti et mense marcij seu aprilis dum ipse testis esset in civitate Anversie post prandium in domo Dieg Menes de Benvenistis et ibi etiam esset cum prefato Dieg Menes, Antonius de la Rogna monoculus qui venebat de Anglia seu ex civitate Londra, insimul venerunt loqui quod in civitate Mediolani vel alibj in Italia manebat dictus Johannes della Foglia, querellans, qui habebat comissionem a Ser.^{mo} Imperatore capiendo novos christianos et suas robas et peccunias et qualiter hoc agebat, et ipse Rogna respondit quod bene eum cognoscebat et qui erat unus latro derobator strate et quod fuerat captivatus ab eo et quod tunc

dictus Dieg Menes dixit quod esset bonum eum facere occidere et evellere
tam malum hominem ex mondo et dare eum /f. 22r/ diabolo et tunc ipse
Dieg Menes dixit quod deberent facere consilia et ponere peccunias
insimul pro mittendo Mediolanum in manibus cuiusdam affinis
Emanuellis Sarrani portugalensis, qui Emanuel manet in Anversia et qui
affinis eiusdem manet Mediolani et nominatur Gonsales Gomes et
mitteretur ej pecunias ut faceret interficere Dominum Joannem della
Foglia et tunc misserunt vocatum tres videlicet: Emmanuellem Lopes,
Emmanuellem Sarranum, Lopem de Provincia cum quibus predicta
comuni convenerunt et omnes dixerunt quod erat bene factum et bene
ordinatum et tunc dictus Rogna exbursavit scutos centum actualiter, inter
quos aderant alique corone anglerie [sic], et alij invenerunt ad domum ad
accipiendum peccunias et postea reversi fuerunt circa horam unam et
portaverunt omnes peccunias quas non vidit numerare sed fuit presens
pratice et tractatui facto et etiam /f. 22v/ jpsos omnes vidit exbursare
Emanuellj Lopes qui portavit ad eius domum, quasvis ponctualiter
numerare non viderit, et etiam vidit super tabula massam peccuniarum
quam dicebant insimul quod erant de scutis duobus mille prout ad
jnvicem ibi insimul, videlicet ipse testi et alij astantes, dicebant et
judicabant et

interrogatus dicit quod erant scuti et ducatj portugalenses et corone
d'Inghilterra et

interrogatus dicit quod dicte peccunie tote fuerunt consignate
Emanuellj Lopes habitatori Anversie et Emanuelli Sarrano pro mittendo
dicto Gonsales Gomes pro faciendo homicidium predictum et interfici
dictum dominum Johannem della Foglia et

interrogatus dicit quod vidit scribere tunc per Manuellem Lopem
quasdam litteras que tunc fuerunt subscripte a Manuello Sarrano quas
tenet pro certo quod jlle fuerunt littere cambij directive Gonsales Gomes
pro commitere faciendo dictum homicidium et

interrogatus dicit quod predictis aderat presens quidam /f. 23r/
Gonsales Dies affinis uxoris Dieg Menes et etiam affinis matris ipsius
Rogne et predicta dicit scire rationibus et causis suprascriptis et quia
predicta vidit, audivit et presens fuit modis et formis quibus dicit, singula
singulis refferendo.

Super generalibus, factis debitis interrogatorijs, recte respondit salvo
quod avia materna ipsius testis se matrimonio copulaverat cum patre

suprascripti Dieg Mens Benvenisti, quis avia nominabatur Mor Lopes.

Signatum: Franciscus Stremerius et Franciscus Maria advocatus fiscalis.

AGR,Bx,OFB, 160/1233/2, *Codazzi File*, ff. 21r–23r.

[Document 15]
[Interrogation and deposition of Diego de Redondo, an *Old Christian* merchant living in Antwerp – October 19, 1540]

A Anvers le xix^e d'octobre 1540, Diego de Redondo, eage de xlvi ans peu plus ou moings, marchant resident en Anvers, adjure par foy et serment de tenyr secret la matiere subscripte et de dire verite sur ce que sera interrogue, dict et depose par son dict serment que touchant le faict des nouveaulx christiens estans en cestedicte ville ne scauroit dire aultre chose sinon que voit et cognoist journellement plusieurs desdicts nouveaulx christiens arriver en cestedicte ville, lesquelz on dict estre fugitifs de Portugal pour peur de linquisition, ce que le faict presumer que iceulx fugitifs ne doibvent gueres estre bons christiens. Dict aussi que ne voit gueres desdicts nouveaulx christiens hanter leglise. Et aulcune fois luy deposant et aultres ont rencontre en beau temps alans promener hors la ville aulcuns desdicts nouveaulx christiens.Et disoit ledict deposant et aultres de son compaignie par maniere de risee que lesdicts nouveaulx christiens venoient de feryr leur feste sainct.

Dict davantaige il a ouy dire que plusieurs desdicts nouveaulx christiens, quon pensoit estre bons catholiques, se sont partiz de cestedicte ville et alle en Salonique; desquelz ne scauroit le deposant personne nommer hors ung Bastien Roderigues lequel aleuns et Estevan Peres lesquelz se sont partiz d ici ensemble peust avoir ung an peu plus ou moings. Et apres eulx lon dict estre aussi partyz la femme dudict Bastien Roderigues et le pere et frere de ladicte femme, Et peult avoir quattre ou cinq mois, et est le commung bruyt que sont tous alez a Salonique, combien que aulcuns veulent dire que lesdicts Roderigues et Estevan Peres sont ale en Italie pour recouvrer leur debts.

Interrogue si na point veu ou cogneu quelque signes exterieurs, conversation ou maniere de vivre esdicts nouveaulx christiens par lesquelz il at peu conjecturer quilz tenoient de leur ancienne loy comme de garder et solemniser le jour du samedy, non mangier char de porc et

aultres semblables, ou sil a ouy deulx quelque propos contredisant a
nostre saincte foy, dict que non, car lesdicts nouveaulx christiens se
maintiennent exterieurement si cautement quon ne sen peult donner garde
et serchent voluntiers les maisons es lieux abstraiz et remotz ou ne
demeurent gens qui sont de consideration ou jugement qui se pouroient
apercevoir de leur facon de faire.

Dict aussi que lesdicts nouveaulx christiens puis leur venue pardeça
ont fort corrumpu la contractation de la bourse, par ce quilz ont donne
leur argent a manifeste usure, faisant ordinairement les changes a deux
ou trois festes ou le marchant estoit desestime qui donnoit argent a
change plus longuement que dune feste a lautre. Et maintenant par
lintroduction desdicts nouveaulx christiens la chose est venue si avant
que non seulement aulcuns marchans ne se hontissent de donner argent
a change a deux ou trois festes mais lont donne sans mention desdictes
festes comme pour demy ou ung an a x et xx pour cent, quest la
destruction du bien commung. Et semble audict deposant que ce fut este
tresgrant bien pour les paiz de pardeça que ny fussent onques entrez.
Interrogue si ne scauroit enseigner ou nommer quelcung par cuy ceste
affaire se puist enfoncer et quon puist avoir entiere et vraie
congnoissance de leur vye et conduicte, dist que non.

Interrogue ce que scet de la venue pardeça de la veufve, belle seur de
Diego Mendis, et de sen aler aux baings, dict quil a ouy dirc que ladicte
veufve apres le trespas de son mary pour ce que le roy de Portugal avoit
ordonne que la fille de ladicte veufve seroit prinse et ~~mariee a quelque
grant.... du royaulme que navoit grans bains~~ pour la marier a ung grant
seigneur de parentaige du comte de Castanneda, se seroit avec sadicte
fille refugiee pardeça, apres touteffois quelle avoit quelque temps
seiourne en Angleterre. Et ~~peut avoir~~ au mois de juillet dernier icelle
veufve sen alla aux baings pres au paiz de Liege dont sourdist ung bruyt
entre les marchans quelle estoit alle en la Salonique ce que le deposant ne
volut croire par ce que il avoit ouy dire quelle nestoit du sang des Juifz
mais de bonne et ancienne lignee; et est depuis revenue, aiant este absente
environ deux mois.

Interrogue si la femme de Diego Menis est parente a iceluy Diego
Menis et si elle est fille de son frere ou sa seur, dict que ne pense quilz
soient si prochains lung a laultre, mais a ouy dire quilz estoient au
troisiesme degre assavoir issuz de germains ou cousins germains, sans le
scavoir au vray.

Interrogue si cognoist ung jeune filz qui a demeure aultreffois a

Louvain, quon dict estre parent dudict Diego Mendis, dict que il pense que sest ung nomme Jehan Menis, quon dict estre filz du cousin dudict Diego Mendis, et le cognoist par ce quil a eu affaire a luy et scet que na garde sa parole luy deposant en ung contract qui sestoit passe entre eulx deux et est tout ce que scet en ceste matiere, sur tout bien et diligemment examine et a signe ceste sa deposition.

Diego de Redondo

Source: AGR,Bx,OFB 160/1233/2, *Enquete faite en 1540 au sujet des nouveaux christiens.*
1) *de civitate trutensi* = from Utrecht.

[Document 16]
[Charles Boisot's report to the Emperor on the difficult beginning of his mission in Antwerp –November 1540]

Suyvant lordonnance de lempereur et le contenu en certaine instructions faicte a Lille le viii^e jour de novembre xv^{c}xl [=1540] signe Charles, ... par moi recevue le xiii^e dudict mois, je me suis le xiiii^e du dicte mois transporte en la ville danvers ou suis arrive sur le tard, entre le cincq et six heures et, apres avoir communique ma charge au procureur general du Brabant, qui estoit aussi venu audict Anvers, jay envoie maistre Marcelin secretaire en Brabant devers le marcgrave et messieurs lancelot van vosche et françois van der dilst bourgmaistres affin que le lendemain xv^e dudict mois ilz se trouvassent devers moy en mon logis a VI heures du matin, lequel ma rapporte avoir trouve ledict marcgrave malade des febvres et neantmoins si povoit se trouveroit a ladicte heure, et quant aux bourgmaistres luy auroient respondu que combien ce nestoit la saisson de faire departir si matin du logis touteffois quilz si trouverount.

Le xv^e jour avant six heures du matin se trouva devers moy l'escoutette dudict Anvers qui me feit les excuses dudict marcgrave estant quil estoit si malade quil ne luy estoit possible de venir et tantost apres vint le pensionnaire de ladite ville qui me dit que messieurs le bourgmaistres me priouent dattendre jusques au jour et que l'aller par nuict et hors heure donneroit quelque mauvaise suspicion au peuple, surquoy luy respondiz que lheure de six heures du matin nestoit si temprueuse quelle deubt donner ceste impression au peuple, et pour

lindisposition dudict marcgrave me deliberay aller au logis dudict
marcgrave dont advertiz ledict pensionnaire affin quil le deist ausdicts
bourgmaistres et que incontinent se trouvassent la, a six heures et demye,
m'en alay vers le logis dudict marcgrave lequel se trouvay couche en son
lict encoires comme il disoit et sembloit feble a cause dung grand exces
de febvre qui lavoit tenu le jour precedent. /f. 1v/ Ou jattendiz jusque
apres sept heures la venue desdicts bourgmaistres lesquelz estre venuz,
leur delivray une lettre de lempereur adressante a eulx portant evidence
sur moy et donnay une autre semblable lettre audit marcgrave, lequelles
estre lecte, je leur declaray la cause de ma venue, et la charge que javoye
selon le contenu de madicte jnstruction et nommement audict marcgrave
qui feit debuoir de prendre et apprehender les personnes de Gabriel de
Negro, Manuel Serano et Manuel Manriques et quant et quant [*sic* !]
saisir leurs biens, lettres, livres et carthulaires et mectre gardes en leur
maisons affin que rien ne se perdist ou recelast.

Surquoy lesdicts marcgrave et bourgmaistres ont faict plusieurs
grandes difficulteez mesmes que ledict Gabriel de Negro et Manuel
Serano avoient este en ladicte ville longuement avant le previlege octroie
aux nouveaux chrestiens et que ledit Gabriel estoit homme riche et
puissant et ayant plusieurs amiz en la ville. Aussi que desia lon avoit
murmure par les compagnies des marchans a table et partout que lon
sestoit informc sur lesdicts nouveaux chrestiens et que apres on
sinformeroit sur les luthereins Et pour eviter ce dangier parloient lesdicts
marchans de se trasporter eulx et leurs biens en autres pays. Et que sa
majeste, peult estre, auroit este mal informee et que lon savoit par la ville
communement les tesmoings qui avoient este ouyz et ce quilz avoient
depose et que aucuns deulx auroient deposez par haine quilz avoient
contre les delatez par ce que iceulx delatez ne leur auroient volu faire la
finance ou prester les deniers quilz demandoient et quilz veoient grant
dangier a ladicte prinse, et que celuy qui avoit ouvert le chemin de
linformation estoit un homme arragonnois frere cordelier tres mal
condicionne. / f. 2r/

Enfin le marcgrave dict que quant ausdicts Gabriel de Negro et
Manuel Serano pensoit bien sasseurer de leur personnes et quilz navoient
garde deulx fuyr veu les biens quilz avoient et que ledict de Negro
trouveroit en cestedicte ville caution de sa personne pour centmille ducaz,
mais quant aux biens ne veoit comment il y puist toucher veu quil navoit
aucune information contre eulx, Je luy repondiz que linformation

precedente que avoit este tenue contre eulx avoit este veue par ceulx que
sa majeste avoit commis et que depuis le rapport fait du contenu et toutes
choses bien pesees avoit este ordonne ladicte prinse tant des personnes
que des biens.

Ledict marcgrave replica que lapprehension desdicts biens feroit
murmurer tous marchans estrangiers que la presente poursuyte se fait plus
pour les biens que pour chastier les personnes, je luy respondiz que
lesbiens saisiz nestoient perduz et qui nestoit question fore de le garder
por la seurte dun chacun mesmes que par les livres et charthulaires lon
pourroit trouver plus ample preuve contre eulx et autres et tout ce faisoit
pour scavoir la verite de la vie et conduicte desdicts nouveaux chrestiens
et que sa majeste y procedoit par ung vray zele de la foy et affin que
lesdicts nouveaux christiens subz umbre qui se faindent telz nattentassent
es pays de pardeça cose preiudiciable a iceulx pays comme ilz avoient feit
ailleurs et qui ne semblast que sadicte majeste les voulsist porter a
soustenir en leurs erreurs.

En fin ledict marcgrave a ordonne a son escoutette daller au logis de
Gabriel de Negro et luy dire quil vuis parler a luy et qui feit le semblable
dudict Serano et, quant a Manuel de Menriques dit quil ne le cognoissoit
aussi ne saisoient lesdicts Bourgmaistres et escoutette neantmoings qui
sen seroit enquerir et satisferoit entant que luy estoit au bon vouloir de
ladicte majeste.

Aussi se condescendist ledict marcgrave quon enviast une paire de
gens de bien es maisons desdicts Gabriel et Serano pour avoir loeve
partout et garder que rien ne se transportast et fut assez advise quon
envoyeront ledict Marcelin secretaire en l'hostel dudict <de> Negro apres
touteffois quon seroit asseure de sa personne et quelque autre bon
pesonnaige en la maison dudict Serano.

Jadvisay ledict marcgrave de proceder ausdictes prinses avec toute
diligence et a la plus grande discretion que faire pouroit et que sur tout il
sasseurast des personnes.

A dix heures du matin audict jour est venu vers moy lescoutette
dudict Anvers qui ma dit que Manuel Serano estoit au logis dudict
marcgrave et que je le feisse interroguer, je lui respondiz que ne le ferois
interroguer jusque a ce que ledict Negro fut aussi prisonnier, il me dit que
lavoit cherche en son logis mais qui ne lavoit trouve et avoit donne charge
de luy dire que se trouvasst devers devers [sic !] le marcgrave devant
disner. Je respondiz audict escoutette qui regardast devant luy et meist si

bon ordre a la prinse dudict de Negro quil en sceust respondre autrement que sadicte majeste nauroit cause de se contenter de luy ne dudict marcgrave, surquoy il me dist quil en feroit tout le debvoir a luy possible.

Le prevost des marischaulx ma dit ce mesme matin avoir mis ses gens hors la ville sur les passaiges tant ordonnaires /f. 3r/ que autres chemins forains et avoit ses espions sur le vberf et ou lieu des chariots pour se donner garde sur la fuyte ou emport des personnes et biens des nouveaulx chrestiens.

Ledict jour environ deux heures apres midy set trouve vers moy ledict escoutette qui ma dit avoir fait espier sur la boursse le dict Gabriel de Negro y seroit mais que il ny auroit este et par ce suspicionnoit quil sestoit cache quelque part, et a ceste cause avoit le marcgrave faite renforcer les gardes en la maison et mesme y fait aller ledict Marcelin qui ma depuis dit avoir ~~b~~ tout serre et seelle et quil y avait bonne garde, au semblable ma relate de la maison dudict Manuel Serano.

Vuyant que ledict de Negro se faisot celer et sestoit muche en quelque maison de maniere que pour ce jour il estoit mal recouvrable, affin de tant plustost pourveoir a la publication du placcart contre les fugitifz, je me suis avec ledict procureur general trouve sur la maison de la ville ung peu avant les trois heures mais les bourgmaistres et eschevins ne sont este rassemblez que ne soit este pres de quatre heures, et eulx estans tous rassemblcz, lcur ay, en vertu de ma credence, rafreschy la cause de ma venue, selon quil est contenu en madite jnstruction, et leur ay delivre les lettres patentes de lempereur contenant commission sur eulx pour cognoistre de la matiere presente et si leur ay encoires delivre lesdictes lettres en forme de placcart contre lesdicts fugitifz quilz ont promis faire publier au lendemain xvi^e dudict mois, et au surplus on declaire quilz vouloient obeir et en tout et partout au bon vouloir / f. 3v/ de sa majeste combien que la maniere leur semblast estrange.

et <si> lon asseure que ilz fermeroient ce jour et autres nuytz cy apres leurs portes plus tempre que les autres foiz et si les tiendroient lendemain et autres jours plus longuement fermees, et de fait me suis bien apercu quilz avoient ferme cedict soir lesdictes portes une demie heure plus tost que les autres fois.

Quant a Manuel Menriques il est desloge du lieu ou il souloit demeurer, lescoutette madit ce soir qui pense latraper demain le matin. Ainsi signe C[harles] Boisot.

Source: AGR,Bx,OFB 160/1233/2.

[Document 17]
[Ordinance directing the authorities and the inhabitants of Antwerp to
denounce all persons infected by the Judaic fallacy –
December 12, 1540]

Ordonnance de declarer ceulx qui sont infectez de l' heresie judaique
Sur ce que de la part de Lempereur a este dit et declaire aux depputez
de la ville d'Anvers touchant les procedures par eulx tenues contre aucuns
suspectz de la secte /f. 31v/ Judaique et larrest faict sur la personne du
prevost de lhostel de sa majeste et oy ce que lesdits depputez ont
remonstrez au contraire ensemble sur la requeste desdits d' Anvers et
considere limportance de laffaire, sa Majeste desirant sur tout que les
Juifs ne soient favorisez ne soustenuz audit Anvers ny ailleurs, a ordonne
et ordonne que lesdits d'Anvers feront publier tel placcart que leur sera
envoye, tendant a fin que chacun soit tenu de declairer et anoncer tous
ceulx quilz scauront ou cognoisseront estre infectez de lerreur judaique
ou vivre selon la loi de Moyse ou tenir cerimonies ou sollempnites des
Juifs reprouvez par nostre mere saincte eglise, a peine destre tenuz et
reputez fauteurs er receptateurs des Juifz, et comme telz punis et corrigez.
Et avec ce que lesdits d'Anvers se feront bien et deuement informer des
hostes, voisins et autres hantans et frequentans les nouveaulx christiens
qui seroint venuz pardeça en vertu de certain privilege a eulx octroye, de
la vie et conversation desdits nouveaulx christiens et silz vivent comme
christiens doibment et sont accoustumez de faire, et silz trouvent aucuns
vivans comme Juifs ou vehementement de ce suspectez, seroint tenuz les
apprehendre et contre eulx procedder par ladvis de tel commissaire que
sadite Majeste ou la royne douaigiere de hongrie sa seur regente es pays
de pardeça ordonnera et seront aussi tenuz de monstrer lesdites
informations quand requiz en seront et quilz se conduisent de sorte que sa
majeste /f. 32r/ imperialle ait cause de se contenter et n'ayt occasion de y
autrement pourvoyr. Et pour ce que lesdits depputez on remonstrez que
plusiers marchans a cause du dernier placcart publye en Anvers different
de aller a leurs negoces, craignans estre prins par les sergens du prevost
de lhostel surattendans les Juifz, sadite Majeste a ordonne que lung des
Bourgmaistres porra consentir a tous marchans non supectz de ladite
secte ou de fuyte, ou qui bailleront souffisante caution de retourner, quilz
et chacun deulx pourront aller a leur dites negociations en deffendant
audit prevost de lhostel et se sergens de non apprehender detenyr, arrester

ny molester ceulx qui monstreront avoir consentement de lung desdits bourgmaistres. En oultre pour mettre ordre a ladministration des biens de Gabriel de Nigro, Sadite majeste commectra Commissaires pour faire vray estat desdits biens et des debtes actives et passives et payement aux vrais crediteurs dicelluy Gabriel, voullant et ordonnant que les livres et marchandises dudit gavriel soyent delivrez es mains desdits Commissaires, sans avoir regard a la caution bayllee a la requeste de beau filz diceluy Gabriel pour en user comme par sa majeste sera ordonne. Et quant a larrest fait par lesdits d'Anvers sur la personne dudit prevost de lhostel, sa majeste ordonne ausdits d'Anvers envoyer a la dite dame Roine endedans la fin du mois de janvier prochainement venant coppie autentique des privileges ou daultres enseignemens paour lesquels ilz vouledroyent maintenir ledit /f. 32v/ arrest, pour aprez par icelle dame Roine ~~endedans la fin du mois de janvier~~ ordonner ce que de raison. Ainsi fait a Valenciennes le xvijᵉ jour de decembre xvᶜxl [1540].

Source: AGR,Bx,PEA 820, ff. 31r–32v.

[Document 18]
[Deposition of Gaspar Lopes, prisoner in Pavia – December 24, 1540]

The prisoner discloses the names of prominent Portuguese
New Christians living in Lisbon, Antwerp and London and accuses them
of Judaizing, of helping and abetting the emigration of
New Christians from the Iberian Peninsula to Antwerp and
thence to Italy and the Levant]

1540 die 24 decembris

(f. 27r) Constitutus Gaspar Lopes filius quondam Baldassaris de Castiglia Hispanie coram Magnifico Domino Johanne Vujstingh Comissario ut supra ac M.ᶜᵒ D. Francisco Stremenio potestate civitatis et comitatus Papie, in sala residentie predicti pretoris.

Et interrogatus si ipse constitutus retroacto tempore dum fuit tam in Lusitania in partibus Hispanie, in Anglia, quam etiam in partibus Flandrie et in Italia cognoverit et cognoscat aliquas personas qui extrinsece appareant esse boni et verj christiani et tamen secrete et in abscondito sunt hebrej et vivunt secondum legem hebraicam et quod eos exprimat per nomina, cognomina, patriam et alias qualitates si eas memorie tenet, suo

juramento mediante respondit et dicit cognovisse et cognoscere
jnfradictos omnes videlicet:

Diegum Men[d]es Benvenisti, quem cognovit in Flandriam et nunc
habitat in civitate Anversie, qui est ettatis annorum 60 vel circa, homo
dittissimus et qui est ipsius constituti in affinitate, constitutus [dixit] hoc
modo videlicet: quia avia materna ipsius constitutj se copulavit in
matrimonium /f. 27v/ cum patre ipsius Dieg Men[d]es Benvenisti qui
tenet maximam familiam et se ostendit in publicum esse verum
christianum tamen in eius domo tenet sinagogam secretam in qua pluries
fuit et fuit per binas veces, prout recordatur, quando jlla juvenis
nuncupata Jsabella filia cuiusdam nuncupate la Castigliana erat jnducta
vestibus albis more sacerdotali hebreorum, cantabat eorum officia,
videlicet Psalmos Davit nuncupatos *Tefilà in lingua Castigliana* et allia
faciebat et facit dictus Diegus Men[d]es prout ipse constitutus dixit in
quodam suo examine rogato per me Johannem BaptIstan Codacium
notarium.

Item cognovit Briandam de Luna eius uxorem que similem vitam
~~hebr facit~~ hebraicam facit et plus facit in tali lege quam faciat eius
maritus.

Item cognovit Beatricem de Luna sorrorem ipsius Briandæ, que
Beatrix est relicta /f. 28r/ quondam Francisci Mendes Benvenisti qui
mortuus est in Lisbona et que de Lisbona anffugit in Anversia propter
timorem Regis Portugallj.

Item cognovit et cognoscit Franciscum Vas Berram [= Beirão]
habitatorem in Lisbona qui habet in uxorem unam sorrorem dicte
Beatricis et Briande nuncupatam G[u]iomar de Luna qui, una cum eius
uxore, apparenter videntur esse boni christiani sed secrete habent
quamdam mulierem nuncupatam Franciscam Mendes que habet curam
ipsius sinagoge secrete et curam occidendi animalia more hebraico et
curam faciendi panes azimos et festa pascalia prout faciunt verj hebrej.

Item cognovit et cognoscit Dominicum Mendes habitatorem Anversie
ettatis annorum trentagintaquinque vel circa, mercatorem divitem qui dat
ellemosinam ex bursa caritatis omnibus christianis novis /f. 28v/
portugalensibus venientibus ex Lisbona in Anversiam et tam jllis qui
vadunt ad Salonicum quam ibidem morantibus vel euntibus ad alias partes
et tam diu quam diu ipse constitutus stetit et moratus fuit in dicta civitate
Anversie, omni die veneris in sero [dedit] eidem constituto pro
sustentacione sua et eius uxoris ac fratris et alterius sorroris ipsius uxoris

et matris eorum, scutum unum cum dimidio pro elemosina, quas peccunias habebat ex manu Dominici Mendes de comissione Dieg Men[d]es Benvenistis ex bursa caritatis.

Item cognovit Jam Mendes Pincto quem vidit in Anversia pluries tam in domo Manuellis Lopes quam alibj, mercatorem ettatis annorum 30 vel circa, quem jntellexit esse in civitate Venetiarum et vendit /f. 29r/ telas Jndie.

Item cognovit et cognoscit Lopum Mendes in Anversia, licentiatum ettatis annorum 50 vel circa.

Item cognovit et cognoscit Georgium Vas in Lisbona ettatis annorum 40 vel circa, mercatorem pannorum lane.

Item cognovit et cognoscit Alverum Vas et Diegum Vas fratres, habitatores in Lisbona, mercatores pannorum lane, christianos novos et quos jntellexit secrete vivere more hebraico prout est fama publica inter jpsos christianos novos.

Item cognovit et cognoscit Annam Calderam in Lisbona uxorem relictam Doardi Fernandj aromatarij et que semel capta fuit per Inquisitionem heretice pravitatis.

Item cognovit et cognoscit Sebastianum Rodricum Pinctum, habitatorem Anversie et prius eum viderat in civitate Londre in Anglia et quia fecit bancum ruttum, videlecit decoxit, jntellexit anffugisse et nescit ubi sit et est bonus judeus, secrete vivens secondum legem hebraicam, prout vivere vidit ipse constitutus in civitate Londre et est ettatis annorum 45 vel circa, magne stature.

Item cognovit et cognoscit Odoardum Pinctum /f. 29v/ in Anversia, fratrem suprascripti Sebastianj mercatorem diversarum rerum, ettatis annorum 36 vel circa.

Item cognovit et cognoscit Stacium Pinctum in Anversia, mercatorem pannorum Jndie et lapidum preciosorum, annorum 30 vel circa.

Item cognovit et cognoscit Antonium Pinctum ~~in Lisbona~~ mercatorem in Anversia diversarum rerum, annorum 40 vel circa.

Item cognovit et cognoscit Lopem Pinctum in Lisbona mercatorem ut supra, ettatis annorum 35 vel circa.

Item cognovit et cognoscit Antonium de la Rogna magnum Judeum monoculum, magistrum in Tehologia hebrea, mercatorem ut supra in Londres Anglie annorum 40 vel circa.

Item cognovit et cognoscit Annam Pintam, uxorem suprascripti Antonij della Rogna annorum 28 vel circa.

Item cognoscit Aluisium Piris in Anversia, mercatorem diversarum rerum, annorum 40 vel circa.

Item cognoscit ut supra Alonsium della Barera in Lisbona, mercatorem mercium, annorum 40 vel circa. /f. 30r/

Item cognovit et cognoscit Aluisium de Scivilia, in Anversia, cuius uxor manet in Salonico prout ipse jntellexit, annorum 60 vel circa.

Item cognoscit ut supra Antonium Dies in Lisbona, mercatorem aromatarie, annorum 35 vel circa.

Item cognovit et cognoscit ut supra Diegum Dies in Lisbona, mercatorem lapidorum preciosorum, annorum 28 vel circa.

Item cognovit et cognoscit Manuelem Dies in Lisbona, annorum 40 vel circa, mercatorem pannorum lane.

Item cognovit et cognoscit doctorem Antonium Dies in Lisbona, annorum 60.

Item cognovit et cognoscit Giorgium Dies in Londra Anglie, mercatorem rerum diversarum annorum 48 vel circa.

Item cognovit et cognoscit Gabriellem de Negro in Anversia, annorum 40 vel circa, mercatorem divitem, parve persone.

Item cognovit et cognoscit Enricum Pirris /f. 30v/ in Anversia, mercatorem rerum diversarum, annorum 45 vel 50.

Item cognovit et cognoscit Stefanum Pirris in Anversia, mercatorem diversarum rerum, annorum 55 vel circa.

Item cognovit et cognoscit Manuellem Lopem in Anversia, negociorum gestorem burse falsorum christianorum, annorum 30 vel circa a quo ipse constitutus cum eius familia habuit scutos 46 pro eundo ad Salonichum ad renegandam fidem christi. Et insuper predictus Manoel dedit ex bursa dicte caritatis scutos decem pro quolibet 25 alijs personis inter masculos et feminas qui similiter jbant ad Salonicum ad effectum ut supra, pueris autem dedit et dabat scuta quinque auri pro eodem effectu et

Interrogatus ut exprimat nomina et cognomina eorum qui habuerunt supradictas peccunias a suprascripto Manuelle, Respondit quod ~~erant~~

Odoardus Fernandus et eius uxor cum tribus filijs

Simon Fernandus et eius uxor cum tribus filijs

Manoel Rodricus

Franciscus de Valle Dolvia.

De alijs non recordatur

Et qui Manoel Lopes providit ipsi constituto et socijs plaustrum pro conducendo eos et dedit jtinerarium in scriptis ad Salonicum.

Item cognovit et cognoscit Simonem Lopes in Lisbona et alterum Simonem Lopes in Anversia, ambos mercatores lane quorum alter qui remanet in Anversia est ettatis annorum 35 vel circa, alter vero est ettatis annorum 40 vel circa.

Item cognoscit ut supra Rodricum Scieres [sic!], mercatorem annorum 50 vel circa in Anversia.

Item cognovit et cognoscit Martinum Rebellum in Lisbona, annorum 60 vel circa, mercatorem sete.

Item cognovit et cognoscit in Anversia doctorem Dionisium fisicum, annorum 60 vel circa.

Item cognovit et cognoscit doctorem magistrum Enricum fisicum, in Anversia, annorum 55 vel circa.

Item doctorem Aluisium Alveres soresanum /f. 31v/ in Anversia, fisicum, negociorum gestorem Regis Portugalie annorum 55 vel circa.

Item magistrum Aluisium de Cusana in Malinas partibus Flandrie annorum 55 vel circa et Elisabet Mendes eius uxorem, sororem Dieghi Nones.

Item Fernandum Alveres, scribam domus Jndie in Lisbona, annorum 55 vel circa.

Item Thomas Sarranum in Lisbona annorum 70 vel circa et

Manuellem Saranum eius filium in Anversia, annorum 30 vel circa, ambo mercatores et qui Manoel est pariter unus ex negociorum gestoribus burse caritatis suprascripte.

Item per vocem et famam cognovit Manuelem Pignerum, affinem eius constituti uxoris, commorantem in civitate Ferrarie, prout jntellexit est pariter unus ex jllis qui faciunt vitam hebream et eodem modo cognovit per famam Petrum Pignerum et Antonium Pignerum, fratres et filios eius Manuellis susprascripti habitatores in civitate Ferrarie prout /f. 32r/ jntellexit nec non etiam Lopem Pignerum eorum fratrem in Lisbona.

Item cognovit Antonium Fernandum fratrem Emmanuelis Lopes in Anversia, mercatorem pannorum lane, annorum 25 vel circa.

Item cognovit Gabriellem Fernandum fratrem suprascripti Antonij, in Anversia, annorum 23 vel circa.

Item Aluisium Fernandum in Anversia, mercatorem annorum 30 vel circa.

Item Manuellem de Provincia, in Anversia, qui secondum legem hebraicam interficit animalia comedenda, annorum 60 vel circa.

Item Lopem de Provincia filium dicti Manuellis, annorum 28 vel circa, in Anversia et qui similiter est unus ex gubernatoribus burse caritatis de qua supra.

Item Diegum Nones in Anversia mercatorem divitem annorum 45 vel circa.

Item Enricum Nunes et Nones Anricum fratres in Lisbona, mercatores, annorum videlicet: Nones Anricus 45 vel circa et Enricus 40 vel circa. /f. 32v/

Item Alonsum Lopes in Lisbona mercatorem annorum 40 vel circa.

Item Petrum Alveres,mercatorem lane in Lisbona annorum 45 vel circa.

Item Antonium de Aghiar [Aguillar] equitem in Lisbona annorum 30 vel circa.

Item Manuellem Fernandum in Londra annorum 26 vel circa mercatorem sete.

Item Ronchiglium, mercatorem in Anversa, annorum 30 vel circa.

Item Rui Lopes, mercatorem in Anversa, annorum 25 vel circa.

Item unum hominem cuius nomen jgnorat, magne stature, cum barba nigra, colloris in facie albi et rubej manentem apud ecclesiam Virginis Marie, qui tenet sinagogam in domo et habet puellam unam nomine Beatricem, sorrorem Emanuellis Fererij que loquitur hebraice et cantat in sinagoga et habet unum alium famullum etiopem in /f. 33r/ domo, hebraice loquentem.

Item Diegum della Rogia, in Londres, profumerium annorum 40 vel circa et Jsabellam Nunes eius uxorem et quatuor eorum filias feminas et duos masculos in quorum domo stetit ipse constitutus per annorum duos cum dimidio et vidit eos vivere more hebraico.

Item Simon Rui mercatorem in Londres et Annam eius uxorem, qui Simon est annorum 35 vel circa et habet tres filias feminas et duos masculos et habet eius matrem vivam.

Item Rodricum de Tuar [Tovar] et Annam de Tuar eius uxorem in Londres mercatorem, videlicet Rodricus annorum 28 vel circa Anna vero 20 vel circa.

Item Mariam Dies viduam pauperem in Londres annorum 70 vel circa et etiam cognoscit Manuellum Lopes, eius filium viventem, habitatorem in domo Aluisij Lopes. /f. 33v/

Item Sebastianum Rodricum annorum 35 vel circa, habitacionem eius nescit sed eum vidit et conversatus est cum eo tam in Londra quam in Anversa, et est circoncisus, et qui est mercator.

Item Petrum de Palma in Lisbona scribam ad dacium Lisbone, annorum 70 vel circa et qui est circoncisus prout jntellexit.

Item Diegum de Palma, fratrem dicti Petrj, in Lisbona, similiter scribam ad dictum dacium.

Item Gasparem Dragum, annorum 40 vel circa. in Lisbona, licentiatum jure.

Item Diegum Mendes Bisciordum in Lisbona, annorum 55 vel circa, mercatorem divitem.

Item Franciscum Berram [= Beirão] et duos eius fratres in Lisbona, mercatores.

Item Ferrandum Lopem della Nave in Lisbona, annorum 45 vel circa.
/f. 34r/

Item Fernandum Lopem scribam ad domum Jndie in Lisbona, annorum 25 vel circa.

Item Georgium Lopem platerium in Lisbona aurificem annorum 25 vel circa.

Item Georgium Lopem della Nave, annorum 50 vel circa in Lisbona, mercatorem.

Item Alonsum Lopem platerium, annorum 45 vel circa in Lisbona.

Item Doardum Tristanum della Nave in Lisbona, annorum 75 vel circa.

Item Abraam Bensamim, respondentem Dieg Mencs in Salonico, sacerdotem in lege hebraica prout jntellexit, ad cuis domum et ad eum reperendum ipse constitutus et eius familia jturi erant ut vitam ebraicam ducerent et hoc de jmpositione sibi constituto facta per dictum Dieg Menes Benvenisti.

Item Antonium Fernandum barbam longam in Anversia, confeterium apud Sainctam Claram, annorum 40 vel circa. /f. 34v/

Item Laurentium Alveres in Anversia, mercatorem pannorum lane, annorum 60 vel circa.

Item Aluisium Alveres Victoria annorum 65, mercatorem.

Item Johannem Rodricum in Lisbona, scribam a los contos, annorum 35 vel circa.

Item Mariam Annam et Marchesam sorrores de Oliverijs que Marchesa est uxor Stacij Pincti in Anversia.

Item, prout jntellexit et dicj audivit, cognovit per famam Aris fisicum Judeum qui anfugit ex Lusitania ad Salonicum, qui solebat circoncidere alios novos christianos et habet filium parve stature cum barba rubia qui manet in Anversia cum negociorum gestore Regis Portugalensis et qui filius dicitur esse explorator Regis Turcorum prout intellexit publice et palam.

Item Manuellem Barbosum mercatorem divitem in Anversia annorum 40 vel circa.

quos omnes suprascriptos cognovit prout supra dixit et qui, licet videantur esse apparenter et extrinsece fideles et boni et veri christiani, /f. 35r/ tamen intrinsece et occulte ac secrete vivunt more hebraico servando legem hebraicam, tam circa festa solemnia, quam circa victum eorum et jta etiam inter jpsos novos christianos est publica vox et fama quod sint boni et veri hebrej, occulte tamen, propter metum christianorum bonorum et principum et jta ipse constitutus eos tenet et reputat pro talibus et ut supra dixit singulariter refferendo.

Quo examine facto, prout nunc fuit consignatus custodi carcerorum et jnde etc.

Signatum: Johannes Vuisting, Franciscus Stremerius, et Franciscus Maria advocatus fiscalis

Source: AGR,Bx,OFB, 160/1233/2, *Codazzi File*, ff. 27r–35r.

[Document 19]
[Gaspar Gomes, detained in Pavia, discloses under torture the names of several Portuguese Judaizing in London – December 27, 1540]

1540 die 27 decembris

Suprascriptus Gaspar Lopes constitutus in Camera studij M.ci D.ni Pretoris Papie coram predicto D.Comissario nec non et ipso domino Pretore pro tribunalibus sedentibus etc....

...interrogatus dicit quod etiam recordatur cognovisse Aluisium Lopem habitatorem in Londres in cuius domo ipse constitutus stetit per quatuor seu quinque dies ad laborandum de eius constituti servicio, videlicet in conficiendo bottones et alia ornamenta de sirico, et qui in eius domo facit sinagogam et vitam more judeorum, secrete tamen, prout ipse constitutus predicta fieri vidit et in qua sinagoga singulo die sabatj se conveniunt et uniuntur in dicta domo Aluisij alij falsi christiani aliquando numero viginti inter quos vidit suprascriptos: /f. 36r/

Diegum della Rogia [= Ronha] et eius uxorem
Enricum de Tuar et eius uxorem
Gio Dies
Gonsalos de Capra,

Petrum eius filium et eorum uxores
Antonium della Rogna
Annam Pinctam et
[Bastião] Rodricum Pinctum eius fratrem
et alios de dicta civitate Londres quorum nomina in presentiarum
nescit et verum esse quod quando aliquis discedit de partibus
portugalensibus ex falsis christianis pro eundo in Angliam et Flandriam et
successive in Turchiam vel alibi ad ducendum vitam hebreorum, veniunt
ad domum dictj Aluisij qui eis auxilium prestat ut vadant quo voluerint ad
tale effectum.

Source: AGR,Bx,OFB 160/1233/2, *Codazzi file*, ff. 35r–36r.

[Document 20]
[Queen Mary's instructions to Jerome Sandelin (rough draft) –
February 21, 1541]

De par l'Empereur.
   Chier et feal, Ayant fait veoir en nostre prive conseil lexamen par
vous fait sur aucuns nouveaulx christiens par vous detenuz prisonniers
ensemble leurs confessions a diverses fois faictes et reiteree et les
presumptions, suspicions et autres abus resultants desdites confessions,
nous avons rendu telles sentences allencontre deulx comme verrez par
trois dicemus que vous envoyons avec cestes, vous ordonnant selon ce
vous regler et conduire.
   Et quant aux ~~biens desdites prisonnier~~ ausdits assavoir Alvaro
Gonsales <Margareta Dyas>, Duarte Redriges, Ysabelle Noenges et
Emanuel leur fils et Maior leur fille, Fernando Dyas, Agnes Fernandes et
Francisco Fernandes, nous les avons absoulz a condition quilz instruiront
mieulx leurs enffants au fait de la foy. Et leur restituerez tels biens que
trouverez a eulx appartenir, comme aussi ferez a ceulx qui seront banniz
sans adiudication et confiscation. /f. 1v/
   Au surplus nous vous ordonnons proceder a la vendition des biens et
marchandises appartenans, ausdicts prisonniers declarez confisquez a
nostre prouffict ~~aussi de marchandise perissable et aussy~~ {et aussy de
toutes autres marchandises par vous arrestes non appartenans a ceulx que
avons absoulz, si avant quelles sont perissables ou que} la saison requiert
quelles soient vendues <promptement> au plus offrant <et plus grant
prouffit que faire se [peut]> gardant largent au proffit de celuy quil

appartiendra sans permettre que arrest y puist estre mis par nul que ce soit, sans notre expresse ordonnance ou de nostre tres chere et tres amee soeur la royne douaigiere de Hongrie, regente en nos pays de pardeça, sans differir fer les venditions soubz umbre ou a loccasion des arrestz que on pourroit fer sur lesdits biens, et non obstant opposition ou appellation faite ou a fer et quil ny ait faulte, car de ce fer vous donnons povoir et auctorite par cestes.

Escript a Bruxelles, le xxi^e jour de fevrier anno xv^cxl. /f. 2r/

A nostre ame et feal conseiller et recepveur de Zelande et Bewesterschelt, Jerome Sandelin.

Veu au prive conseil de l'Empereur les confessions de Martin Alphonso <et Eleonora Fernandes sa femme>, et Alphonso Rubero {et de Helena Mendes} detenuz prisonnniers, par le Rentmaistre de Bewesterschelt en Zelande, a diverses foiz faites et reiterees, ensemble les presumptions, suspicions et autres abuz resultans desdites confessions, Sa Majeste bannis lesdits Martin ~~et~~ Alphonso, Eleonora <et Helena> hors de tous les pays de pardeça a tousiours et <a> perpetuel, sur paine de la hart, a en partir trois jours apres quilz seront relaxez de prison et declairons tous leurs biens confisquez a son prouffit.

Fait a Bruxelles le xxi^e de fevrier xv^cxl.

Veu au prive conseil de l'Empereur les confesssions de Fernando Dayras et G[ui]omar Dyas sa femme, Petro Fernandis, Maria Fernandis, Sperancia et Gracia Fernandis ~~Helena Mendis~~ <et> Katherine Alvares, ~~Eleonora Fernandis~~ detenuz prisonniers, comme dessus, Sa Majeste bannyt les dessusnommez prisonniers hors de tous les pays de pardeça <a perpetuite>, sur paine de la hart a en partir trois jours apres quilz seront relaxez de prison. /f. 2v/

Veues au prive conseil de l'Empereur les confessions de Loys ~~Fernandes~~ et Marco Fernandis {Juifz}, detenuz prisonniers par le rentmaistre de Zellande, Bewesterschelt, a diverses foiz faictes et reiterees. Sa Majeste {pour les mesuz, delictz et crismes par eulx perpetrez et dont il est apparu par leurs confessions,} les condempne destre mis au dernier supplice par le feu et declaire tous et quelzconques leurs biens confisquez au proffit de Sa Majete. Fait comme dessus.

[Attached list]

Marco Fernandis, passera le pas.
Helena Mendis sa femme, bannye et ses biens confisquez

Katarina Alvares, bannye.
Alvaro Gonsales, absoulz.
Martin Alphonso, banny et ses biens confisquez.
Elenora Fernandis, sa femme, bannye aussi comme dessus

Duarte Rodrigues, Ysabelle Noenges, Emmamuel leur fils, Maior leur fille absoulz a condition quilz instruiront mieulx leurs enffans.

Margareta Diaz, absoulz.
Fernando Dayras et Gomar Dyas sa femme, bannis sans confiscation.
Petro Fernandez, Maria Fernandis, Sperança et
Gracia Fernandis, bannis sans confiscation.

Fernando Dyas, Agnes Fernandis, Francisco Fernandis, absoulz.

Loys Fernandiz passera le pas.

Alphonso Rubero, banny et ses biens confisquez.

Source: AGR,Bx,PEA 1504.

[Document 21]
[Queen Mary to Corneille Sceperus, *imperial commissioner against the false Christians* – February 22, 1541]

Marie par la grace de dieu Royne douaiere de Hongrie, de Boheme etc., Regente [des Pays Bas]

Tres chier er bien ame, Nous escripvons presentement au president du prive conseil ad ce quil vous communique les affaires des nouveaulx chrestiens, et l'estat diceulx, pour conioinctement y adviser. Sy vous requerons, que suivant le propoz que en avons tenuz avant votre partement, vous declairez audict president tout ouvertement et sans aulcun scrupule, ce que scavez concernant lesdits nouveaulx chrestiens avec les moyens que estimez convenables a ladvainchement desdites affaires estans desia en train et pour enfonser daultres, tant pour le service de dieu que de lempereur mon seigneur et frere. Et nous ferez plaisir bien agreable ...le xxij jour de febvrier 1540 [= 1541, *style de la court*].

Source: AGR,Bx, PEA, Reg. 1540, *sub data*.

[Document 22]
[Queen Mary's explanatory statement to the General Procurator of Brabant and denunciation against the authorities of Antwerp – March 12, 1541]

Lempereur estant derrenierement en ses pays de pardeça adverty que aucuns marchans et autres residens en la ville danvers observoyent la loy moisaicque et vivoient comme juifz, ordonna a Seigneur Charles Boisot, docteur et conseillier destat de sa Majeste, soy jnformer et la dite information faicte et veue au Conseil de Sadite Majeste pour ce que ung Gabriel de Negro fust trouve fort suspect de ladite secte et aussi jnfame dautres crismes, renvoya ledit conseillier en la dite ville danvers, avec trois lettres de credence au marcgrave et bourgmaistres danvers contenant commandement bien expres audit marcgrave et bourgmaistres de faire et accomplir tout ce que par le ledit conseillier seroit ordonne et commande.

Suyvant lesquelles lettres ledit conseillier commanda bien expressement audit marcgrave en presence des bourgmaistres de apprehender ledit Gabriel de Negro. Surquoy ledit marcgrave et bourgmaistres feirent plusieurs difficultez, et finablement ne sceut ledit conseillier obtenir autre chose sinon que le marcgrave dist que manderoit ledit Gabriel venir vers luy, ce quil charga a lescoutette ainsi de faire. Comme appert par le verbal dudit conseiller, cy joinct marque par "A".

Et combien que ledit marcgrave disoit quil se tenoit asseure de la personne dudit de Negro, touteffois nen a sceu rendre bon compte avis sest ledit Negro rendu fugitif de sorte que le procureur general a este coustraint de proceder contre luy par adjournement personnel et deffaultz.

Et pour ce que lempereur avoit ordonne au prevost de son hostel se tenir autour danvers pour apprehender tous ceulx qui aucunement estoient suspecte de ladite secte judaique, ledit prevost, apres avoir leve aucuns compaignons et les mis sur les passaiges, a trouve ung bourgois danvers accuse daucuns crismes surannez. Lequel jl auroit constitue prisonnier et fait mener a Canterroy.

(f. 1v) Dont adverti lesdicts danvers auroient fait constituer prisonnier ledit prevost en son logis audit Anvers, le faisant garder jour et nuyt bien estroictement. Et quelque remoustrance que le conseillier Boisot leur faisoit et non obstant l'offre dudit prevost qui presentoit caution de poinct toucher a leur bourgois et le rendre ou jl seroit ordonne par l'empereur, ne voulurent oncques eslargir ledit prevost jusques a ce quil eust reallement delivre ledit bourgois en leur mains comme de ce appert tant par le rapport dudit prevost que par extrait dune lettre dudit Boisot.

ledit rapport cotte par "B" et ledit extrait par "C".

Tellement que ledit prevost par ladite constrainte a delivre ledit bourgois. Et combien que il ait depuis presente a lescoutette les informations quil avoit tenu contre icelluy bourgois, touttefois ledit escouttette ne la voulu accepter ne calenger, dont les causes et suspicions se pourront veoir par ledit rapport du prevost.

Que lempereur adverti de ladite apprehension et dicelle tresmal content, manda jncontinent ausdicts danvers denvoyer vers sa Majeste leurs deputez pour declairer par quelle auctorite et occasion ilz avoient constitue prisonnier ledit prevost.

Et apres que sa Majeste avoit fait ouyr tout ce que par lesdites deputez fust dit et propose, fist certaine ordonnance en date du xvij jour de decembre md^{c}xl, cy joincte, marcque "D".

Par laquelle, entre autres choses, sa Majeste ordonna ausdits danvers de mettre es mains de telz commis que ordonneroit tous le livres de Gabriel de Negro pour faire estat de debtes diceluy /f. 2r / Gabriel, tant actives que passives, et que endedens la fin du mois de Janvier, lors prochain, ils envoyeroient vers la Royne copie des previleges ou autres eneseignemens par lesquelz ilz vouloient maintenir larrest fait sur la personne dudit prevost.

Et combien que lesdits danvers ne debuoient faire difficulte de sattisfaire a ladite ordonnance et suyvant icelle avoir delivre les livres trouvez en la maison dudit Gabriel a Pierre Boisot et Jeromme van Hamme, maistres de la chambre des comptes en Brabant, a ce commis par sadite Majeste, touttefois ny ont voulu sattisfaire pour remonstrance que lesdits commis ont sceu faire, mais en sont demourez reffusans comme appert par le rapport desdits commis cy joinct marque par "E".

Mais ont envoye vers la Royne leur pensionnaire qui a presente requeste afin quil pleut a sa Majeste permettre que deulx dentre eulx feussent presens a faire le dit estat, sur laquelle requeste a este appostille du xx^e de janvier quils debuoient absoluctement obeyr a lordonnance de lempereur. Laquelle la Royne ne vouloit ne poivoit changer comme par le double de ladite requeste et apostille cy joinct appert marcque par "F".

La Royne, esperant que lesdits danvers satisferroient a la seconde jussion, a ordonne ausdits commissaires de eulx trouver de rechief en Anvers et accomplir leur premiere commission, lesquels y ont autant fait que a la premiere foiz par ce que lesdits danvers nont voulu delivrer lesdits livres, comme appert par le rapport desdits commissaires marque au doz par "G".

Et sur ce que lesdits danvers ont renvoye vers sa Majeste pour obtenir que aucuns dentre eulx pourroient estre presens a visiter les /f. 2v/ livres dudit Gabriel, Sadite Majeste leur a tres estroictement commande de livrer lesdits livres es mains desdits commis comme appert par ladite ordonnance en date du ix^e jour de fevrier xv^{c}xl marque par "H".

Et apres que lesdits commis ont requiz avoir lesdits livres, ceulx de la loy danvers ayant traisne deux jours iceulx commis, ont declaire quilz ne povoient delivrer lesdits livres sans premiers communiquer avec les marchans. Et apres avoir communique avec les marchans ont delivre lesdits livres soubz certaine protestation comme appert par le rapport desdits commis marque par "J".

Et pour ce que durant ses interfaites le procureur general de Brabant a si avant procede que apres avoir obtenu tous ses deffaulz, sentence diffinitive a este rendue, par laquel ledit Gabriel pour sa contumace a este banny et tous ses biens declairez confisquez, la Royne a ordonne ~~a ordonne~~ a maistre Loys de Heylewege conseillier et recepteur des eploitz en Brabant, de faire mettre a execution ladite sentence et, en vertu dicelle, prendre en ses mains tous les biens trouvez en la possession dudit Gabriel pour en user selon linstruction sur ce luy baillee.

Lequel avec ung hussier sest transporte pardevers ceulx de la loy danvers ou il a aussi fait venir lescoutette et amman dudit Anvers et, apres aucune remonstrances, leur seist faite commandement de delivrer tous les biens et marchandises trouvez en la possession dudit Gabriel. Et pour ce que lesdits danvers ont differe de furnir ausdits commandemens, apres plusieurs remonstrances et offres faites, ledit conseillier considerant /f. 3r/ que lesdits danvers ne vouloient obtemperer ausdits commandemens, ordonna audit huissier de proceder plus avant a ladite execution. Ce que l'huissier a fait et de nouveau fait commandement ausdits amman, escoutette et bourgmaistres, eschevins et pensionnaire jllecq presens, declairez par nom et surnom es verbal dudit Heylewege, de jncontinent livrer les biens et marchandises selon linventoire sur ce fait es mains dudit conseillier. Sur paine de fourfaire, assavoir: lesdits amman et escoutette et bourgmaistres chacun deulx mil carolus en leur propre prive nom et aux eschevins et pensionnaire chacun deulx cincq cens carolus. Non obstant ce ilz ont persiste en leur refuz comme de tout ce appert par ledit verbal marquee par "L".

Et pour ce que telles manieres de faire tomberent finablement en manifeste rebellion, la Royne du tout advertie pour son acquit en gardant les droitz haulteurs et auctoritez de lempereur ne les peult passer soubz dissimulation.

A ceste cause y vuellant proceder par voye de Justice a advise par meure deliberation de conseil de envoyer toutes lesdites pieces a ladvocat et procureur general du Brabant afin de les visiter et hors dicelles faire une requeste narrative des desobeissances commises par lesdits danvers et obtenir adjournement contre tous ceulx qui sont denommez au verbal dudit Heylewege, assavoir: personnel contre l'amman et escoutette et contre les autres simple, veu que lesdits amman et escoutette qui sont officiers de lempereur et ne debuoyent non seullement obeyr aux commandemens dudit huissier mais le assister suyvant leur serment. Et partant ont plus delinque que les autres pour /f. 3v/ respondre a telz fins et conclusions que ledit procureur general voudra prendre en estime.

Et que au tour servant on doibt conclure contre lesdits amman et escoutette afin destre privez de leurs offices et declairez jnhabiles et condempnez es paines jndictes par lhuissier ou autrement arbitrairement corrigez a larbitraige de la court; et contre tous les autres, afin quilz soient condempnez es paines jndites par lhuyssier ou autrement arbitrairement.

Et pardessus ce, que tous ensemble soyent condempnez de promptement delivrer lesdits biens es mains dudit receveur ou autre commis de sa Majeste, et ce par provision sans figure de proces, veu quil concerne sentence rendue par lesdits du conseil en Brabant. Ainsi fait a Byns le xij^e jour de mars xv^{c}xl.

        Marie
        Moy present Verreyhzen.

Source: AGR,Bx,OFB,160/1233/2, (Copy) We did not succeed in finding the original document and the attached pieces.

[Document 23]
[Bill of credit of 3,000 ducats issued by Diogo Mendes in favour of
Duke Ercole II – April 2, 1541]

Excellentissimo Signore

Sendo advertito dal Signor Bastiano Rodrigues Pinto mio amico come, desiderando servire a Vostra Excellentia jntende resider et habitar in Ferrara sotto la obedientia di quella, et ancora tractar con epsa, o suoi officialj, sopra alcuni negoci d'importanza, et per essere detto Pinto novamente venuto nel paese, et non molto in quello conosciuto, potrebbe essere Vostra Excellentia, o li suoi officiali sudettj sopra el concludere con luj detti negoci facessino alcuna difficultà, per la qual cosa epso mi ha richiesto li voglia fare una Lettera di Credito a Vostra Excellentia, et desiderando in questo compiacerli, ho preso sigurtà con quella et fattoli la presente Lettera di Credito, per virtù della quale contractando detto Pinto con Vostra Excellentia, o suoi offitialj come sopra. sono contento essere obligato et con effetto mi obligo per el detto Pinto, a proffitto di Vostra Excellentia per la somma di ducati tremila d'oro in oro larghi, A saper che detto Pinto compirà a Vostra Excellentia, o suoi offitialj, predettj el pagamento de quello havesse contractato, o contractasse come è detto, Et non lo facendo prometto di complire et pagare sino alla detta somma dj ducatj tremilla d'oro .

Et questa presente lettera di credito voglio et intendo habbi a durare per uno anno solamente, che comincerà addì primo di maggio proximo mille cinquecento quaranta uno, et finirà addì primo di Maggio mille cinquecento quarantaduoj.

Et cossì, baciando reverentemente la mano di Vostra Excellentia, quella supplico havermi nel numero delli suoi fedeli servitorj. Data in Anversa addj 2 di Aprile Anno M.D.XLJ.

Di Vostra Excellentia
humile et Affetionato S[ervit]or

Diegho Mendes

Source: ASMo,CD, *Carteggio Referendari*, B. 171.

[Document 24]
[Juan Rebello to Loys de Schorr, President of the Privy Council –
May 13, 1541]

Pour ce que votre Seigneurie mavoit dit quil seroit content de la
caution pour les cent mille florins avecque Jehan Carlo [Affaitati] et
Erasme [Schetz], je leur ay ad ce requis et commis, mais se veulloint
excuser disants que laultre premier fois, quant ilz demouroint plaisges et
cautionnaires il fust prins en malle part, sur quoy je leur disoye que cela
estoit a cause des clausules et conditions contenuz en leurs caution.
Toutteffois puis que eulx sont les premiers desquelz votre Seigneurie se
contentoit et demandoit quilz le voulsissent faire, ilz sont contentz en cas
que votre Seigneurie sen contente de demourer cautionnaires assavoir
chacun deulx pour 25000 florins sans plus et pour les 50000 florins
restantz jay Diego Mendez et Jeronymo Suyller lesquelz veullent
demeurer pour iceulx. Et puisque trestous ilz sont hommes de bien et
riches, je supplie votre Seigneurie de faire accepter et prendre ladite
caution diceulx, affin que se gens soient relaxe et eslargez pour aller
requerir leur justice dedens le terme par votre Seigneurie ordonne, et que
je soye excuse daller emportuner sa Majeste et votre Seigneurie auquel
notre Seigneur veulle prosperer et augmenter. Danvers ce xiij^e de may
1541
                        Servidor de Vossa Senhoria Juan Rebello

Source: AGR,Bx, PEA 1560, f. 52r.

[Document 25]
[Daniel Bomberg and other merchants in Antwerp to Queen Mary –
June 4, 1541]

Tres Illustre, tres haulte et tres puissante Princesse, tres redoubtee
Dame, nous nous recommandons en toute obeissance à Vostre Royale
Majeste, laquelle plaise scavoir comment plusieurs marchans bourgeois
manans et residans en ceste Ville d'Anvers tractans et negocians à Rome,
Venise, Naples et aultres places d'Italie et des pays de la les mons
mesmement Anthoine et Daniel de Bomberges, Baltazar Charles,
Matheus Pomerecaulx, Jilles de Greve leurs consors et aultres nous ont
remonstre comment tous leurs biens, denrees et marchandises allans
d'ichy vers Jtalie et venans de là jchy sont, depuis troys mois encha en la

ville de Trente et aultres passaiges d'Alemaigne arrestez et detenuz et les arrestoy encores journellement ainsy quilz perdent leurs foires festes et credence et tous les cours et trains de marchandise cesse et est par ce moyen empeschie. Ce que redunde à leurs tres grandz foulles pertez, interests et dommaiges jrrecuperables et aussy a tres grande preiudice de notre Seigneur Lempereur, ses droicts, tolles et proffytz, et destruction de tous ses pays de par de cha, lesquelz arrestz et empesschements se font (ainsy qu'ilz disent) à cause de quon veult dire que aulcuns conducteurs (à lencontre des mandements de notre Seigneur Lempereur) auroient aultresffois fait mener par les voicturiers aulcuns biens appartenains aux Juifs, maranes, ou aultres noveaulx christiaens Judaisans, des quels conducteurs lesdictes nos bourgeois et marchans nont riens à faire.

Aussy nont ilz (ne nul d'eulx) aulcune societe ne compaignie en marchandise ne aultrement avecq lesdites personnes deffendues ou leurs alies.

Ilz sont contents se purger se besoing et par leur serrements ayant pour ce a nous requis tres instamment (en leur faiveur) de ce vouloir advertir Vostre Majeste affin que sur ce peut estre pourveu. Si est que escripvons presentement devers Vostre Royale Majeste, prians et humblement requerrans quil plaise à icelle vostre Majeste, en ce que dit est pourveoir et faire mectre telle remede comme Vostre Illustre Majeste (au bien et au mieux de la Majeste imperiale ses bons subjectz et pays de par de cha ensemble pour la conservation du cours de marchandise et bien publicq) verra appartenir Tres Illustre, tres puissante et tres redubtee dame, sil pluist aulcune chose à Vostre Royal Majeste de ce serons trouves vos bons et loyaulx subiects à l'ayde de Dieu qui a Icelle Vostre Majeste donne prosperite et bonne sante.

Escript en Anvers la quatriesme jour de juing XV^c quarante ung.

Source: AGR,Bx,PEA, Reg. 560.

[Document 26]
[Duke Ercole II to Nicolas Perrenot de Granvelle (rough draft)
June 20, 1541]

Reverendissimo et Jllustrissimo Monsignore,

Havendo alli dj passati mandato a V.Signoria Reverendissima Cassio da Narnj mio familiare per ottenere da lej che fossero levati li jmpedimenti che jo havea inteso <che erano> ~~esser~~ stati interposti da uno certo Gio[vanni] dalla Foglia sopra alcune balle de Mercantj fiorentini che habitano in questa Città ~~et li qualj assicurati da me~~ <et> traficano et fanno faccende per Fiandra sotto pretexto che siano robbe de maranj over falsi christiani ~~et lassatj liberamente venire al suo viaggio~~ et per pregarla che ~~siano lassati~~ fossero lassati liberamemte venire al suo viaggio, non mi parendo che Ella dovesse tolerare che nella Terra sua fossero usati tcrmini così poco convenienti a buoni et leali mercanti <et nobili fiorentini e conseguentemente> christianissimi. Et expettando jo de intender che per V.S. fosse fatto per justitia conveniente provisione al caso loro, mj sono pervenute le lettere sue de x con le qualj in loco di havermi fatto restituir le balle come ~~comportava~~ <mi pareva che comportasse> la Justitia, mi ha dato racordo et proposto modo col quale le pare ch'io possj provedere alla perdita loro con dire che habbia regresso lj ledere ~~la qual cosa parendomi fuori di proposito et aliena d'ogni dovere~~ <del quale ricordo io ben ne ringratio V. Signoria ma perché mi pare male sattisfare al bisogno et ancho fuori del dovere> ho deliberato mandare a far querela con la Maestà Cesarea, la qual mi rendo certissimo che non vorà tolerare, per la sua infinita buontade, che sia fatto un tanto torto a mercantj christianj huomini da bene et gentilhuomini habitanti in questa ~~terra~~ <mia citade> con tanto mio scorno et sanza alcuno suo servitio essendolj io quel buon vasalo et fidele servitore che le son ~~anzi vorà che sia dato castigo conveniente a tal demerito del che mi~~ <Ma mi> ha parso dare un aviso a Vostra Signoria Reverendissima acciò se le paresse fare quella provisione che merita in caso tale et fare restituire le robbe intertenute, lo possi far senza ch'io habbia per questa causa mandarne a fare querela con Sua Maestà certificandola che io non son per manchare per quanto si estenderano le forze mie in maniera alcuna di soccorrere alla indennità di detti mercanti et di fare ogni opera perché non li sia fatta così manifesta iniustitia ma che le sia restituita la robba loro come confidamo che sarà di mente de Sua Maestà et a Vostra Signoria Reverendissima molto mi raccomando. Ferrara XX junij 1541.

Source: ASMo,CD, Minutario Generale Cronologico, Busta 9.

[Document 27]

[Jeromme Sandelin, *rentmeester* at Bewesterschelt to Loys de Schorr, president of the Privy Council – October 8, 1541]

… estant adverty de la venue des aultres nouveaulx christiaens ay songe pour fair mon debvoir et garder le droict de lempereur, mais la fortune a este contraire comme les personnes, asscavoir Pedro Loupez avecq ungue femme et deux enfans biens charges dor et argent sont descendus en dengleterre [*sic!*] au port de Hampton. Neants moins ay trouve ung couffre par eulx assigne a Diego Mendiz mais devant que le sceu avoir es mains a este overt par force de marteaulx non par la closure mais par le coste derrier et mest impossible de poveoir scavoir de marroniers qui ou comment cela soit avvenu et y ay trouve choses de nulle importance non vallans deux florins except ungue seconde lettre de cambio de quattre cens crusades la quelle vous envoye priant men vouloir ordonner ce que doresdavant y abvurais besoingne.

Source: AGR,Bx,PEA 1177/2, october 8, 1541.

[Document 28]

[Queen Mary to Monseigneur de Granvelle – October 15, 1541]

… Je escripts au conseiller Boisot de vous communiquer ce que je luj respondz sur l'instance faite par le duc de Ferrare pour le passage de nouveaux cristiens par le pays de pardassa et me samble puis que la poursuyte duceste duc se fait pour en tirer proufft, quil serait mieulx fait de rexcuser et prendre ce proufft pour sa majeste a quoy veulliez preindre regart et me adviser de vos advis.

Source: AGR,Bx, PEA 204, ff. 5r–7r: 7r.

[Document 29]

[Christovão Garcia' s undated letter to Queen Mary of Habsburg – (February/March 1542)]

Christoforus Garcia, æques lusitanus venit Antuerpiam conficiendi sua negotia et, reginæ gratia, is habebat in Anglia suum factorem cui nomen magistro Didaco qui nuper fuit hæreseos postulatus et ejque bona s[aber] duæ cistæ panni olandici et 40 untiæ ambræ et 5 balæ grani squarlatini sunt intercepta, ad quæ asserenda misit suum procuratorem. Petit, cum ipse sit æques et alumnus reginæ, et habeat penes se comineatus regis, quo se muniret ne forte aliquando haberetur ex grege novorum christianorum, ut eum commendet regina legato et regi et dicat ac referat quas causas cur huic favere fuerit mota.

Source: AGR, Bx, PEA 1537, *Correspondance avec l'Angleterre,* s.d. (February/March 1542).

[Document 30]
[Queen Mary to Eustace Chapuys, the Spanish Ambassador in London, March 3, 1542.]

Monseigneur l'ambassadeur,
    Messire Christofre Garcia de Portugale nous a remonstre quil a eu en Angleterre ung sien facteur nomme maistre Diego lequel naguere a este accuse d'heresie, et les biens dudit messire Christofle ~~confisquez~~ a scavoir deux coffres de toille de Hollande, quarante onces d'ambre et cinq bales de grans descarlate, draps por estre trovez soubz ledict maistre Diego et pour ce que le dict messire Christofle est serviteur domestique de la Royne notre bonne sœur du Portugal, dont il nous a fait apparoir par lettre dicelle Royne et aultres preuves […] suffisantes, nous vous requirons voulloir tant faire vers ledit roi d'Angleterre et aultres que trouverez convenir que lesdits biens soient renduz et restituez audit messire Christofle ou son facteur porteur de ceste, lequel a ceste fin il anvoye presentement [a] celle part, lassistant en ce favorablement.
    Et ce me sera plaisir agreable. Sur ce priant Dieu, monseigneur lambassadeur vous avoir en sa sainte garde. De Bruxelles le Xe de mars 1541 [=1542].

Source: AGR,Bx, PEA 1627.

[Document 31]
[The Emperor reinstates the privileges granted in 1537 to the Portuguese New Christians – March 10, 1542]

    Charles V … empereur des Romains… A tous ceulx qui ces presentes verrons, salut!

Comme de la part de ceulx quon dit les nouveaulx christiens nous ait este remonstre que en l'an xv^c et trente six [= 1537, *Style de la Court*] le xxvij^e jour de febvrier, ilz ayent de nous obtenu certaines lettres d'octroy contenans, entre aultres, que deslors en avant ilz pourroyent librement et franchement avecq leurs femmes, enffans, serviteurs, familles, biens, denrees, marchandises, joyaulx et meubles quelzconcques, ainsy que bon leur sembleroit, venir, demourer, hanter et frequenter nostre ville danvers et aultres villes de nos pays de pardeça et y user de telz droitz, libertez et franchises dont usent aultres marchans estranguiers parmy payant le thonlieuz et aultres droitz telz que lesdits marchands estranguiers sont accoustumez de payer. Ainssy quilz porroyent toutes les foys que bon leur sembleroit avecq leursdites femmes, enffans, familles, biens, denrees et marchandises, bagues et joyaulx, retourner au Royaulme de Portugal ou en aultres pays, royaulmes et provinces de la chestiennete que bon leur sembleroit, librement et franchement sans mesprendre et tout ainsi que peulvent et que est permis a tous aultres marchans estranguiers sans que lesdits remonstrans aprez quils seroyent venuz et arrivez en nostredite ville danvers ou en aultre [ville]^1 comme dessus pourroyent estre traveillez, molestez, pris, arrestez ou detenuz en corps ne en biens pour quelcque crisme ou delict quilz ou aulcun deulx pourroyent avoir commis et perpetrez audit royaulme de Portugal ou aultres pays non estans de nostre obeyssance avant la date dudit octroy.

Et que, si le cas advenoit que aulcuns desdits remonstrans ou aulcuns de leurs familles a ladvenir commectoyent quelque delict ou cas de crisme en nostredite ville danvers ou aultres villes et lieux de nostre pays de pardeça, leur ayons consenty et accorde que a celle cause ilz ne seroyent tirez ou attraictz ne amenez prisonniers ou aultrement traveillez en corps ne en biens hors dicelle ville danvers ne aultres [villes et]^1 lieux de nostre pays de pardeça.

Eulx voulans que combien ce considere ne fuist permis ne loysible a aulcun de traveiller ou molester lesdits remostrans, au contraire de ce que dit est, ce touteffois non obstant depuys naguerres plusieurs nos officiers et mesmement nostre Recepveur de Zellande Bewesterschelt se seroyent advanchez dinferer plusieurs grosses foulles a aulcuns desdits remonstrans, ayans leur personnes, femmes, enfans, familles, biens, denyers et denrees prins et arrestez soubz umbre que ledit recepveur et aultres nosdits officiers ont voulu imposer a iceulx ainsi foullez destre Juyfs, marans, heretiques, apostates et de semblables /f. 2r/ reprouves

conditions et sectes, soustenans que pour estre telz, ces previlegies en
iceulx ne debuoit nuliter lesdits previlege sans que touteffoys a nosdites
recepveur et officiers soit preallablement apparu par information
precedente souffisante et devement prinse que lesdits foullez fuissent de
tells sortes ou conditions, leurs rendans par telz et semblables manieres
de faire nostredit privilege et octroy jllusoir et sans effect, comme ilz
disent, nous supplians tres humblement y voulloir remedier et pourveoir
a lobservation de nostres lettres doctroy et a leur asseurance pour
l'advenir, scavoir faisons que nous ces choses considerees jnclinans
favorablement a la supplication desdits nouveaulx chrestiens supplians,
avons declaire et declairons par cestes que nostre voulunte et jntention est
que lesdits supplians avec leurs femmes, enffans, familles, biens, deniers
et denrees quelzconcques puissent et pourront hanter et frequenter nostre
pays de pardeça et y user de telz droictz, libertes et franchises dont usent
et peuvent user aultres marchans estranguiers parmy payans thonlieuz,
droictz et debtes que lesdits [marchands] estranguiers sont accoustumez
de payer selon le contenu dudict previlege du xxvij^e de febvrier en lan xv^c
trente six [= 1537, *style de la Court*] lequel a cest effect avons approuve
et conferme, approuvons et confermons par ceste et le voulons avoyr pour
icy repete ci donnons en mandement a nos amez et feaulx les chief,
president et gens de notre prive et grant consaulx …de notre conseil en
Flandres [et coetera] … et generallement tous aultres nos justiciers
officiers et subyectz cui ce regardera et chacuns deulx endroyct soy … et
a luy appartiendra que dudict previlege ensembe de ceste nostre
declaration approbation et confirmation en la maniere dicte seuffrent et
laissent plainement et paisiblement joyr et user sans leur faire mectre ou
donner ne souffrir leur estre faict, mis ou donne aulcun trouble ou
empeschement en corps ou en biens au contraire en maniere quelconcque,
si nest que par information precedentement prinse jl leur appere
preallablement tant que pour souffire daulcun cas meritant pugnition
criminelle et pour lequel de droit, stil, usance de nostre pays lon peult e
doibt proceder par apprehension de corps et des biens, car ainsi nous
plaist il, en tesmoing de ce nous [avons] faict mectre notre seel a ces
presentes.
　　Donne en nostre ville de Bruxelles le xme jour de mars lan de grace
milcincqcent quarante et ung de nostre empire le xxij^{me} …

Source: AGR,Bx,OFB, 160/1233/2.

1) The words in square brackets are gathered from the text of the 1537 privilege, AGR, PEA 117, ff 23r–25r, February 2, 1536 [= 1537, *Style de la Court*].

[Document 32]
[Queen Mary To Jerome Sandelin – March 11, 1542]

Marie per la grace de Dieu Royne douaigere
De hongrie, de Boheme et Regente [des Pays Bas]

Tres chier et bien ame,

Pour aulcunes bonnes considerations Nous vous ordonnons relaxer tous les christiens nouveaulx que pouvez avoir apprehendez {ou arrestez a cause de suspicions contre eulx} ensembles ~~leurs~~ <les> biens quelzconcques confisques <appartenans a eulx> ~~et ceulx~~ ou a marchans estans a Anvers <arrestez pour les susdictes raisons> {et non pour altre cause}, sans por ce leur demander caution, et notamment les deux couffres de plumaiges et aultres choses de Henrique Fernandes demourant a Lyssebonne envoyes et adressees a Christofre Garcia Ch[evali]er et serviteur du Roy de Portugal. Et que de cy en avant vous deportez de plus arrester ou detenir aulcuns nouveaulx christiens ou leurs bien si ne soit que, par information precedente deuemente prinse, il vous appere preallablement cant que pour suffir, daulcuns cas par eulx commis meritant pugnition criminelle et pour lequel de droit, stil et usance du pays lon peult e doibt proceder par apprehension de corps et des biens {suyvant la teneur ~~de leur~~ des lettres patentes et privilege a eulx ~~concede~~ octroyez dont vous envoyons copie avec cestes}, sans y faire faulte car ainsi nous plaist il.

A tant tres chier et bien ame, nostre Seigneur Dieu soit garde de vous. De Bruxelles le xj^e jour de Mars 1541 [=1542].

[on the reverse of the sheet:]
Au recepteur de Zeelande-Bewesterschelt afin de relaxer tous les nouveaulx chrispiens par lui apprehendez et leurs biens.

Source: AGR, Bx,PEA reg. 129, f. 164r, March 11 1541 [= 1542].

[Document 33]
[Charles V to Queen Mary of Hungary (rough draft) – July 15, 1542]

Madame ma bonne sœur,

Je vous ai naguere faict en bons les ~~bons~~ doubles des extraitz authentiques des examens <et responses> ~~et depositions et responses~~ daulcuns nouveaulx christiens qui estoient venus d' Anvers en Italia avec intention, comme ils ont confesse, de passer en Turquie et ont ete ~~interroguez~~ detenuz xyxyxy a Milan, Pavie et Viglievano et interrogues par ~~celuy qui~~ Jehan Wuystinck, substitut de Messieur Corneille Sceperus, commissaire principal et les officiers des dicts lieux. parlesquelles confessions, <ilz chargent aulcuns nouveaux christiens> ~~auleuns des xyxyxy~~ qui resident a Anvers, dinduire les aultres de aller a Salonique et a ce leur donner les moiens et assistent dargent et combien que je ne doubte vous les avoir faite veoir a viste … conforme a la raison et mon intention de laquelle ultre la demontration que je fez estans pardela vous ay souvent adverty par lettres, touttefois estant la chose de telle qualite et tant importante a notre saincte foy et le bien de mes pays je vous en ai bien voulu escripvre ~~encore ceste fois~~ <de neuf> et vous prier tres affectuesement que ~~selon le foundament que trouvez par lesdit extraits~~ / f. 209v/ vous faiste proceder contre les ~~coulpables~~ <suspects>.et que vous trouverez par les vestres et ~~les chastier exemplerement~~ {la chose estant de ceste qualite et tant emportance} ~~pour le bien de la republique crestien et de nostre paiz~~.

Source:AGR,Bx, PEA, 53, ff. 209r–209v.

[Document 34]
[Charles V to the Marcgrave of Antwerp (rough draft) – July 15, 1542]

Au Marcgrave danvers
{ung aultre semblable aux bourgmaistres et escevins danvers}

Cher et feal, avant notre partement de pardela vous avons fait advertir de notre intention touchant les procedures qui avons ordonne estre faicte contre les nouveaux crestiens residens en notre ville danvers observans les ceremonies de la loy Judaique et pour que depuis notredit partement elles ne se sont continuees comme lavions ordonne, Pour que entendons journellement et prestement que plusieurs soubz umbre daler a Ferrare ou

Venise <et aultre costes> passent en turquie induicts a ceste par aultres de
la mesme secte faissans residence audit Anvers, queste chose tres p*** a
nostre saincte foiz et repubblique crestienne et tres dommageable ... A
quoy vous ordonnons tres expressement que ...tous coulpables et
delinquantz soient prins et chasties ... xij^e de juillet 1542.

Source:AGR,Bx, PEA, 53, ff. 209r–209v.

[Document 35]
[An unsigned and unadressed letter found in the house of Diego Netto
in 1544 – September 15, 1543].
*An anonimous Portuguese who had succeeded in safely reaching
Ferrara describes the difficulties of his (or her) journey. –*

De Ferara 15 de setembro 1543
De Basylea escrevy a Vossa Merce as cousas que ate ly tyneamos
pasados sim embarguo que todavya me remety a carta de neto de Senhor
Dioguo F[ernande]z. E de Basylea devems de dyantar algum da
companhya que ouber de ver a jgualar a pousada por que não façam como
fizeram a nos outros que nos levaram por tres comydas de vynte pesoas
sete escudos. Diguo ysto porque não he lugar Basylea que eys da ter medo
de dizer que não quereys comer a taboa somente que lhes quereys conprar
seus mantimentos a boms preço e com seu [dineyro] e pagarlhes loguo
porque seys jente povre porque neste caminho não quer fantasya
nenhuma nem trajo se não como jente povre. Em Basylea tomamos tres
caros para toda a jente e fato que nos custarão xxj escudos ate Lucerne e
foy con condição que abyamos nos outros de pagar os direytos e trabalhos
de manera que no partido que fizerdes ajnda que saybays dar dous
escudos mais em cada tres caros que eles paguem os dyreytos e todos
porque se ouberdes de pagar custarnos ha[lem] de tres escudos para cyma
de Basylea ate Lucerne porque os mesmos careyros os fazem levar
demasyado. De Basilea ate Lucerne estyvemos tres dyas e meio posto que
não sam mays de diz [*sic!*] leguas. Em Lucerne alugamos barcas por
quatro escudos e hum quarto ate o Tufo que he honde alugam as bestas
ate Magadino. Fomos enganados na barca porque se aproveçaramos mays
achacamos por dous escudos ho que ouber dever de fazer com os careyros
que vam pousar a ostarya que esta antes que paseys o ponte. Porque en
Lucer[ne] nos levaram dous escudos de direytos [traba]lhos. En Lucerne

vos abers de guardar de Jaques por que o trouxemos com nos y vendyanos polo caminho que nos fazya levar e pagar por as cousas mays de que valya. Guardayvos que se vos requerir que quer ir en vosa companhia, que dizays que ho não habeis myster que seys jente povre. No Tufo honde abeys de alugar bestas esta hum homes que se chama Escrivel Anrique y he latino e coxo de hua perna e ten cinco bestas e he bon homen por pouca cousa que lhe deys pasara com vos outros os Alpes. Quando alugardes almocreves mostraylhe primeyro ho que a de levar porque hay muitos deleteryo e trabalhay se puderdes que com duas bestas venha hum homo lesto que va aborda das mulheres polos ryios pasos por que a nos otros nos custarão de XVII bestas XXVIII escudos e ainda que vos custem mays do que a nos custarão por que venhan com cada duas besta hum homen por ser ho caminho trabalhoso e cada hum tome bestas que ouber myster que seian de hum dono o de doys por que van sempre a par de hums [otros] por que se não as bestas trastocadas as vezes va vosa mulher com hum almocreves e vos com outro, afastado hum de outro que não hay rezon que vos valha com eles e por isto diguo que cada hum tome almocreve para sua companhya para que va junta. E todavya trabalhay por trazer passaporto que venha meter em huma caxa por que o selo de cera não venha desmanchado por que por o noso selo ver desfeito nos levaran que he como Justeça de Magadin treze cruzados. Roubados que não oube remedyo e esto foy tamben por fantasia de mulheres que vyran hum barete na cabeça a filha de Dioguo Fernandez e perguntarão que que seia aquela senhora como que diz he jente rica paguem, e quando se fez por trezes escu dos credamos que tinhamos feyto muyto por que demandavan cynquanta escudos e por ysto diguo que quer este caminho ver antes en abito de povres que de ricas. Todavya se ben se puder vyr algun homo latyno in vosa companhya guarday vos em Magadin de hum homo que da barcas hasta Sesto que he ruyvo e tem huma casa e que da de comer, que não façais nada com ele por que vos defaltar da verdad que ele nos tinha fretada a barca por dous escudos e despoys dise por des e meie de que nos teve na barca demandaba cinco e quando ho acabamos por tres escudos foy muyto caro. Abysayvos que não alugueys de Magadino barca mays que ate Sesto. Não deys palabra a nynguns. Em Sesta preguntareys por Bernardino e por seus jrmão e parecenos que por poco mas de vynte ducados vyra e abisayvos que se Bernaldino no vynha com vos otros não venhays com seus jrmãos porque me dyzen que não san boms homens e por eso diguo que va Bernaldino com vos otros e todavya vos alysa que não trayais mas que vos comportais e mantenimeto e aynda que trayais hum baryll com azeyte e vynagre não vos pesara com ele para ho camynho porque os dyreytos san tantos de fato que he mylhor e mays barato mandalo en bala que trazerlo con vos e tamben por não lhes parecer se não que he jente povra e isto todo seja avyso para aquem ouber de vyr este caminho outra se contenha que nos caros fose pocas pesoas e poco fato por rezan do camihno fragoso e que os homens que o puderen fazer apar dos caros e tanben van homens nos caros para se for neçesario em allgum caminho fragoso [..] fazer o carro mays leve: ho façam por que, não ho fazendo, muytas vezes se torcem hos carros he caen e se malltrata a jente. E que van bastecedo de pan e queyjo para ho camynho e confeitado e outras cousas, E que trabalhe por não jr ter[se] em dya santo nem domyngo en nenhum lugar por que se chegua jente a velo como a negros. E que leven outro callçado afora ho que levarem por que polo camynho não se acharam a conprar se não ruis e muyto caro. A moeda que levarem escudos de sole e que sejam de peso e allguas patacas por que valen a trezzentos cadahumo e tragua quem puder allguas tigelas de pão e colhares para comer leyte. Em alguas partes comen a taboa, em outras partes cadahum demande ho que queser e pague o loguo ho yguall por que não tenha a pagua deferencia. E asy como forem tomando van pagando e as camas antes que se deitem nelas fação o preço, por que volas daran a dez ho a quinze m[aravedis] cada huma e de outra maneyra pedyrvos como XXX.

Source: AGR,Bx,OFB, B.160/1233/2.

[Document 36]
[Undated (circa 1544) instructions for the journey from Antwerp to Ferrara]
(Given the exceptional importance of this document, we provide both the original Portuguese text and a complete English translation)
**Regimento para o caminho que aveys de llevar
com aiuda de Dio desta villa de Jmvers para fferara**

Primeramente da quy parteis em hum carro que vous lleva ate Collonja, que custa 12 # pouco mais ou menos, o quall carro e seus omens de guisa fica paguo e vos outros não lhe aveis de dar nada. O carreteyro vos metera na pouzada em Colonya que se chama Vi[e]r Escara e tambem vos buscara ahy a barqua que vos lheve ate Magamça, a quall barca custara 6 # pouquo mays ou menos e ay em Collonya esta hum omen que se chama P[er]o Tonelleyro que falla bem espanholl: este yra com vos a sua custa. Este omen he nesesario que o lheveys por caso que pello ryo arriba ay guardas que vem ver os navyos. Não ajais medo de elles por que he custume de vysitar as barcas a ver se llevão mercadorias e não lhe aveis de dar cousa nihuma e quando sayrdes de Collonya para entrar no navyo, sera de madrugada e o mais secreto que puderdes porque as cousas mansas e onestas em toda parte são boas, e quando fretardes o navyo tyrareis por condyção que de noyte aveis de dormir nelle por que vos sera menos despeza e quando fordes pelo ryo ariba os que forem de vos mylhor tratados sairão em tera com o P[ero] Tonellero a comprar de comer e o que vos for nesesario e fazey todos como omens de bem vosas cousas, não avemdo desavemça nehuma hums com os outros como say de aver emtre as gentes.

As despezas que fyzerdes juntamente tales assaber em carros, em barcas, em pouzadas que forem despezas em caminhos, estas repartyda [a] solldos [e] a llivra ygualmente: dous mosos de jdade de 11 ou 12 anos a baixo por hum omen e day para ariba para omen e porem as cryamças de mama não pagarão nada asy nos caminhos e barcas e caretas como en todas las despezas porque estas criamças são foras e não pagarão nada.

E despois que em boa ora partyrdes de Collonja aonde aveis de yr ate a sydad aomde aveis de pouzar na emxenha de bade[io] dally mandareis com o P[ero] Tonellero chamar a Comrate que he hum omen que falla bom espanholl e e omen muito de bem Elle vos emcamjnhara aos caros que aveis myster dizeylhe que quereys yr para Ferara pello camynho velho assaber o caminho d'alltorfe [Altdorf] e dellago a Pavja, emvesso que some de mais, e porem ay em Magamça tomareis carro que vous lleve bem 50 ou 60 lleguas. Custa cada carro 16 ou 17 escudos. Em os carros aveis de jr ate o llago e pasado este llago aveis de alugar cavallos para pasar os Alpes d'Allemanha e os que forem bem despostos poderão yr a pe por fazer menos despeza e farão bem de aprouveytar quall quer cousa por que ys por reynos estranhos e não tem dos que volla de avyzarvos que não sunga. Em estes cavallos que aqui tomardes aveys de yr ate omde aveis de allugar huma barca que vos lleve ata Ferara e fretareis a barca para todos porque doutra maneyra não ay pasagem e Dio vos lleve em pas. Como dezeyais fazer sempre como boms e Dio vos ajudara. Despois que fordes em Ferara vos emcamynharão para dyante, os que vos quyzerdes yr vyver em Ancona. Nestes portos que aquy vous tenho dytos tomay sempre emformação de caminho adyante e as menos pallabras que puderdes fallareis. Dio vos emcompanhe a todos. Amen.

Source: AGR,Bx,OFB, B. 160/1233/2.

Translation
Instructions for those who set out, with God's help, on the journey from Antwerp to Ferrara

In the first place, you will leave from here in a carriage, which will take you to Cologne. The carriage costs around twelve ducats. Carriage and carter are pre-paid and you must not pay anything. The carter will take you to the inn called Vier Escara in Cologne. He will also hire on your behalf a boat that will take you to Mainz. The boat will cost six ducats (more or less). In Cologne there is a man called Pero Tonnellero who speaks good Spanish. He will accompany you at his own expense. You need to take him along in case there might be guards inspecting the boats along the river. Do not be afraid of them. It is normal that they come to inspect the ships to see if they carry merchandise. Do not give them anything. When you leave Cologne and board the boat (early in the morning), it shall be in a secret manner as discretion and honesty are appropriate everywhere. You will rent the boat on condition that you may sleep on board overnight, so you will have fewer expenses. During the journey along the river, the stronger ones among you will go with Pedro Tonellero to buy food and other provisions that you might need. And, under any circumstance you will behave as decent people avoiding all quarrels and arguments that may occur among people. And you will share all expenses: for carriages and boats and the inns during the journey; the expenses shall be divided in equal shares. Two eleven- or twelve-years old boys will pay as one adult. Older boys will be counted as one man. Babies will not pay anything: neither along the journey nor in the inns, boats or wagons, or anything else, as these creatures are not counted and do not pay anything.

After you leave Cologne (early in the morning) you will proceed to the city [of Mainz] where you will stay at the inn with the sign of a fish; you will send [one of your company] with Pedro Tonellero to look for Comrade. He is a very decent person who speaks good Spanish. He will lead you to [the place where you will hire] wagons. You must state that you want to go to Ferrara along the old route, i.e. the route of Altdorf and along the lake, as far as Pavia. So, in Mainz you are to rent wagons that will take you for fifty or sixty miles. The cost of every wagon is sixteen or seventeen ducats. By these wagons, you will travel as far as the lake and, after the lake; you will hire horses in order to cross the German Alps. Those who are in better shape can go on foot in order to save some money. It shall be wise to buy some food as you will be traveling through foreign countries and you will not find anybody who will help you. By horseback, you will go until the place where you will rent the boat that will take you to Ferrara. You will hire the boat for all of you, as there is no other way of reaching Ferrara. As we stated before, always behave as decent people and God will help you. Once in Ferrara those who wish to live in Ancona will be told how to proceed further. In each of the above-mentioned ports you will get information about the way ahead. The less you talk, the better.

May God lead you. Amen.

[Document 37]
Questionnaire to be used for the interrogation of Portuguese clandestine immigrants rounded up in Antwerp in 1544

Interrogatoires pour interroger les apprehendez en la ville danvers qui se baptisent nouveaux christiens venuz du Royaulme de Portugal d'apres six sepmaines en ça

1) Premier de se bien enquester de leurs noms et surnoms parce quilz les changent. Aussi des noms et surnoms de leurs peres et meres.

2) Dont ilz et leurs parens sont natifz, si leurs parens sont vyfz et ou ilz demeurent et tousiours ont demeure, sil[z] sont mortz ou non et depuis quel temps.

3) Silz ont freres ou soeurs et comment ilz se nomment, silz sont maryez du nom de leurs femmes ou marys, dont jls sont et ou jls demeurent.

4) Si aulcuns deulx se sont retirez de Portugal, demander ou ilz se sont retirez, porquoy, en quelle sorte, de combien de temps et de quoy ilz se meslent.

5) De scavoir le temps que le prisonnier est party de Portugal, comment, a quelle occasion, a quelle compagnie et navire, le nom du patron dicelle et si elle estoit du Roy ou navire de marchant.

6) Sil est marie et ayt des enffans, ou sa femme et enffans sont demeurez, ou sil les a amene avec luy.

7) Quant ilz se sont embarquez et quel lieu ou port, a quelle heure, si de jour ou de nuyct et si tous ensemble ou separement, publicquement ou secretement.

8) Quelz biens ou marchandises ilz ont amene avec eulx, si en leur navire ou aultres et comment elles se nomment et le patron dicelles.

9) A quelle occasion le Roy du Portugal ayt faict deffense que nul nouveau christiens ne viendra sans son congie du son Royaulme et de semblable [congie] de l'jnquisiteur.

10) Combien de temps y a que lesdites ~~sentences~~ deffenses ont este faictes.

11) Silz nont veu ~~plusieurs~~ <nuls> executer en Portugal par ce quilz sont estes trouvez Judaissant et faillant en la loy christienne, tant par le feu que en statue et aultres condampnez a porter enseignement et faire penitence.

12) Quelles personnes desdicts executez ou comdampnez ilz ont cogneu, comment ilz ont nom et surnom dou ilz sont estez, quelle leur correction a este ou faicte ou advenue et se ilz ou aulcuns diceulx ne sont este de la parente du prisonnier ou d'aulcuns des presentement arrivez et partiz de Portugal.

13) Si linquisteur de la foy est celluy qui en faict fer les poursuytes et corrections et depuis quant linquisition cest encommenchee. Et sil ny a nuls partiz de Portugal et jci arrive <qui> attainctz, ou craindant destre attaintz se soit enfuy jcy. /f. 1v/

14) Si le prisonnier partant de Portugal en a obtenu le congie du Roy ou de linquisiteur, et ou ledict congie est.

15) Quant ilz sont arrivez par de ça et ou premierement.

16) Sil n'a este arreste en Zeelande ou detenu, porquoy et comment jl sest appoincte pour estre delivre et venir en la ville danvers.

17) Quelles gens de cognoissance il et aultres ont trouve audicte Zeelande et quelle faveur et adresse. Idem interrogandum de la ville danvers.

18) Quant ilz y sont arrivez, a quelle heure et combien de temps apres ilz sont sortiz des bateaux, si de jour ou de nuyct.

19) Ou ilz ont eu premierement et de temps en temps leur logis.

20) Qui les a assiste a vuyder lesdicts bateaux, dentrer en ladicte ville meme et dresse en leur logis et silz y sont menez de pieds ou de chariot.

21) Aquelle jntention ilz viennent par de ça. Et silz entendent tirer plus avant ou non. De quoy ilz entendent jcy gaigner leur vye.

22) Et silz sont pouvres et entendent voiaiger plus avant, ou ilz ont eu largent pour payer le frait de leur navigation, combien de frait ilz ont paye. Et ou ilz trouveront largent pour la reste de leur voyage et leur entretenement.

23) Silz sont richez et nont amene avec eulx marchandises ne les actendent. Ou leur bien et argent est demoure, si mis sur change a c[ombien?] pour ou recouvrer, quant et ou les lettres de change sont, si elles sont accepteez ou non.

24) Si marchandises, ou elle sont et si elles sont en asseurance ou conduicte de qui et quelles marchandises se sont.

25) Lesquelz dentre eulx sont assistez de la bourche de la charite que ilz ont. Qui est la personne qui en a la garde et administration dicelle et sa demeure.

26) Comment jl se regle et doibt conduire en ladicte administration et surquoy se collectent les deniers de ladicte charite.

27) Si ledict gardien et administrateur a tous les deniers dicelle en ses mains et si iceulx son grans.

28) Sil est baptize en enfance, ou apres estre venu en eaige et fut circonsis.

29) Que nom on luy a donne au baptesme, commment il se nommoit auparavant et en quel lieu il a este baptize.

30) Sil scet sa [priere du] p[ate]r n[oste]r et le credo.

31) Sil scet pourqoy Jesu crist est venu en ce monde et qui jl fut et sil est ne d'une vierge.

32) Sil scet que les Juifz lont crucifie et pourquoy. /f. 2r/

33) Comment et pourquoy apres sa mort jl est descendu aux jnfers et par quel moyen resuscite.

34) Comment et par quel moyen il est monte es cieulx et sil a envoie le sainct esprit et pourquoy.

35) Quant le sainct esprit a este envoie, apres la mort de Jesu crist ou ~~apres~~ devant.

36) Quelle femme a este la vierge marie si elle est mere de dieu et ou elle est.

37) Que sont devenuz les apostres et aultres sainctz et sainctes.

38) Si dieu le pere, Jesu crist et le sainct esprit sont tous trois ung dieu ou lung dieu et laultre point.

39) Quant lon dict que viendra celluy qui nous est promis en la loy qui nous delivrera de la captivite et nous remectra en franchise.

40) Et combien jl sera plus grand que Jesu crist.

41) Depuis quel temps jl s'est commence a confesser et de recepvoir le sainct sacrament de lautel.

42) A qui et comment jl a este a confesse[r] et quant jl feit la derniere confession et receupt son sacrament.

43) Combien souvent jl sest confesse en sa vye et quant et combien jl se doibt confesser suyvant la loy, ordonnances et commandemens dicelle.

44) Que chose se veult estre la confession et le sainct sacrament et sil y a au pain consacre aultre chose que pain.

45) Sil y a prestres en leur compaignie et se leur prestres ne leur ont expose et dict quel homme estait Jesu crist, la vierge Marie, les apostres.

46) Comment lon se doibt confesser et recepvoir le sainct sacrament.

47) Se lon est tenu de uyr messe sur les dimenches ou jl la est accoustume de uyr, et sa femme et enffans.

48) Quel jour se doibt plus garder la dimenche ou le sabat.

49) Si lon doibt juner et sil y a jeusnez commandez et si en tous jours lon ne peult menger chair et poisson.

50) Si la Loy ne deffend lusaige daulcunes viandes et quelles.

[on the reverse of the last sheet:]
Interrogatoire pour examiner les prisonniers pede ligato, 1544.

Source: AGR, Bx,OFB, B. 160/1233/2.

[Document 38]
[Deposition of Garamatão Telis, captain of the ship S. Antonio – July 2, 1544]

Le ij de juillet
Le capitaine de la navire du Roy de Portugal nommee Sainct Anthoine ayant nom Garamatantelis [= Garamatão Telis], portugalois eaige de quarante deux ans ou environs <tesmoing> jure ~~dict~~ <et sermente> interrogue (quel edict ledict Seigneur Roy a faict contre les nouveaux christiens, qui se pouroient absenter du dict royaulme) <dict> que passe cincq /f. 1v/ ou six ans (sans reprehension du temps preciz) ledict Seigneur Roy a faict publier par tout son royaulme mesmement par

tous ses portz de mer par forme de placcart que nulz nouveaux christiens ne presume de ce absenter ou partir dudict royaulme avec femme ou enffans sans expresse license et congie de sa Majeste, soubz paine dapprehension de leurs personnes, et confiscation de leurs biens et que ce que dessus est tous notoire a ung chascun dudict royaulme.

Interrogue quelz nouveaux christiens jl deposant scet estre venus par de ça par congie et permission dudict Seigneur Roy pour devienre par de ça avec ceste derniere armee et quelz non, dict quil ne scet aulcuns qui soient venuz avec la permission dudict Seigneur Roy, dont jl presume certainement que tous ceulx qui sont venuz avec ladicte armee, estre venuz sans licence dudict Roy nestoit quilz facent apparoir expressement leurdict conge.

Interrogue aussi sil ne cognoissoit ung nomme Francisco Gomez {Francisco Gomez} venu en sadicte nave de Sainct Anthoine, dict que oy, mais que jl deposant sestoit au prime apperceu de la presence dudict Francisco a son arrivee en Zeelande ou il le auroit detenu trois ou quatre jours, sans luy vouloir donner congie de sortir sadicte nave, jusques a ce quil fut jnforme que ledict Francisco nestoit marye mais venu par de ça avec jntention dachapter certaine marchandise et apres sen retourner en son pays et que lors luy auroit permis de sortir de sadicte navire.

Interrogue sil ne scet ou cognoit alcuns desdicts nouveaux christiens venuz avec femmes ou enffans ny en quelles naves jls soient venuz, dict que non et quil na sceu de la venue des susdicts jusques apres estre arrivez en ce pays dont /f. 2r/ adverty et de la multitude desdicts arrivez, se seroit trouve comme es[pouv]ante et plus que esbahy, considere ladicte publication et que avant le partement de ladicte Armee avoit este de nouveau de la part de la Saincte Inquisition commande a chacun capitaine de estroictement se regler selon icelle et de non embarquer aulcuns diceulx nouveaux christiens soubz payne dexcommunication.

Et dict davaintaige que avant son partement jl fut requis du maistre marronier de sa nave de pourpovoir recepvoir et amener certaine compagnie, laquelle jl ne declairoit, mai quen ce jl ne luy auroit voulu consentir, craindant ladicte contrevention parquoy dict jl qui nest venu aultre que ledict Francisco Gomez et deux aultres nommez Duarte Toar et Loyz Gomez, marchands ayant eu congie du Roy, dont lung estoit marye et laultre non, retournans, comme il a entendu presentement, avec la flote mais en aultre navire que la sienne.

Interrogue de la cause du partement de tous dessudicts, dict quil presume, sans avoir aultre cause de science, quilz soient tous partiz pour craincte de linquisition et quil a entendu en ceste ville de certains portugalois (desquelz il ne scet les noms) quil y a trois ou quatre par de ça desquelz les figures ou statues ont este bruslees en Portugal et que lung diceulx sappelle Pignero, vieil homme mais (comme il entend) ne sont venuz avec ceste derniere flote mais ont este residens en ceste ville passe deux ou trois ans.

Dict aussi que cest une fame commune en Portugal desque ung homme avec sa femme ou enffans estant nouveau christien, se retire dudict Portugal et se absente, quil le faict se sentant jnfecte et craindant linquisition et que ceste / f. 2v/ opinion est tout commune entre tous les gens de bien dudict Royaulme et est telle la presumption dudict deposant, non scachant de ou ladicte fame ayt prims commencement, sinon que lon dict jllec publicquement que plusieurs desdicts retirez se sont renduz en ce pays et, apres y avoir sejournez ou residez quelques temps, se seroient retires tousiours dillec a ceste fin et que sadicte presumption doibt estre bien reputeee et tenue pour vray semblable, considere la grande multitude que lon dict estre partye dudict Royaulme et le petit nombre demeurans en residence par de ça.

Source: AGR,Bx,OFB, 160/1233/3, *Information 1544*, ff. 1r–2v.

[Document 39]
[Deposition of Simon de Vega, Captain general of the Portuguese Royal Fleet – July 2, 1544]

Le capitaine general de larmee du Roy du Portugal dernierement arrivee au pays de par deça, nomme Simon de Vega, eaige environ de quarante sept ans, tesmoing jure, dict que a son partement avec ladicte armee luy fuit mande de la part de linfant du Portugal Inquisiteur major de la Saincte foy, non laisser embarquer aulcuns nouveuax christiens avec leurs femmes ou enffans sans les advertir pour scavoir les coulpables et iceulx chastier. Mais que ne luy fut deffendu laisser embarquer nouveaux christiens mariez ou non mariez allans et venans a cause de leur train de marchandise.

Et quant a la publication que seroit faicte, passe cincq ou six ans, alencontre lesdicts nouveaux christiens, dict quil nen scet a parler par ce quil ne sest guaires tenu audict Portugal mais ayant la plus part du temps este aux Jndes pour capitaine, non obstant quil presume bien que telle publication doibt avoir este faicte.

Interrogue sil ne scet ou cognoit aulcuns telz christiens venuz par de ça /f. 3r/ sans congie du Roy et si ne luy est apparu de quelque congie, dict que non, mais bien estre vray que aulcuns soient venuz devers luy avec lettres patentes des villes tesmoignans iceulx estre vieulx christiens. Et si aulcuns soient venuz par de ça avec femme au enffans, que iceulx doibvent estre venuz secretement et a son desceu en ulques des marchans et non en naves dudict Seigneur Roy.

Interrogue de la cause de leur fuyte ou partement, dict quil ne scauroit a la verite depposer a quelle jntention ilz se partent, sinon que lon dict publicquement audict Royaulme quant telz christiens sont partiz, quilz se retirent par de ça pour aller vers Ferrare ou en Turquye.

Interrogue aussi, dict quil cognoit ung des apprehendez nomme Bastian Fernandez lequel jl a veu publicquement converser et hanter train de marchandises en Portugal, ayant aussi cogneu ses parens nouveaulx christiens. Non scachant touteffois sil est venu avec congie du Roy, non ayant aussi sceu de son embarquement avec ses femme et enffans, car si jl depposant en fut este adverty, jl ne lu y eust permis le passaige, sans congie et licence, ne fut quil fut seul venu laissant audict Royaulme sesdicts femmes et enffans.

Source: AGR,Bx,OFB, B.160/1233/3, *Information 1544*, ff. 2v–3r.

[Document 40]
[Deposition of Jsabeau Alaert, housemaid of Sebastian Fernandiz –
July 4, 1544]
le iiij^e de juillet [1544]

Jsabeau fille de Jehan Alaert de Frasne, demeurant en la ville danvers eaigee de xxiij ans ou environ, adjournee et sermentee, dict quelle est venue a servir en la sepmaine apres la pentecouste dernier certains portugalois qui ont leur maison empres de […] en la dicte ville, qui de present sont apprehendez et detenuz ou gardez comme prisonniers en ladicte maison, dict que au temps quelle depposante a este en son service, qui a este /f. 6r/ jusques au jour de ladicte apprehension excluz comme cy apres elle dira, ne scet avoir veu que son maistre et maistresse avec leur famille, qui sont {Sebastian Fernandiz} Sebastian Fernandiz et sa femme tenans leur mesnaige en la chambre dembas, se soient aultrement conduyctz en boire et manger sur vendredy et samedy que ne font aultres

natifz par de ça. Ains ont use de poison, delaissant la chair sur le
vendrediz et samediz pour autant quelle depposante a peu veoir. Mais
aussi que en ladicte maison y a diverse mesnaige tenant chacun sa
chambre et lieu a part, a elle deposante bien veu que une longue femme
qui se dict veufue, sans scavoir le nom, a faict sur les vendrediz et
samediz plusieur poullez et poissons, sans scavoir si sur telz jours les ayt
menge. Par ce quelle depposante na converse le lieu ou chambre ou
ladicte femme tenoit son mesnaige.

  Dict interrogue[e] que lesdictes personnes sont accoustumeez de
jncontinent apres avoir tue quelque poullaige, de le quant et quant ~~de~~
plumer et le manger sans le reserver plus longuement.

  Dict quelle scet que lesdictes prisonniers tiennent plus dextime ou
cessent plus de ouvrer les samediz que en aultres jours et quelle sest
donnee garde que sa maistresse et aultres femmes detenuez [*sic*!] audict
logis se sont accoustrez [*sic*!] et parees plus sur le samedy que en aultres
jours et que elles usoient de leur paremens et habillemens le samediz,
dont elles deussent user le dimenche, se reglant sur les dimenches et
festes ~~dont~~ <soit> de nostre dame ou aultre comme en tous aultres jours
ferialz, faisant leurs affaires sicomme laver, buer et semblables par leurs
servantes comme sur aultres jours, sans jamais oyr messe ou aller a
leglise, ne faire semblant de y vouloir aller, mais quant elle depposante
sur festes et dimenchez a este oyr la messe et service de Dieu a leglise et
que lesdicts prisonniers luy ont demande dont elle venoit ou avoit este et
quelle leur a respondu de la misse ou de leglise, ilz ne disoient ne
faisoient semblant de riens. Et combien que durant la demeure delle
deposante jl y a eu diverses jours de jeusnes a observer suyvant
lordonnance de Saincte Eglise, comme le quatre temps, le veille de Sainct
Jehan, de Sainct Pierre, et Sainct Pol, si nen ont lesdicts /f. 6v/ prisonniers
faict aulcuns mention ne semblant de jeusner, sinon quelle scet et a bien
retenu que esdicts jours de jeusne ses maistre et maistresse ne mengarent
que poisson sans scavoir de quelles viandes les aultres lors usarent. Disant
ladicte deposante que combien sadicte maistresse et aultres prisonniers ne
sceuvent sur festes et dimenches trouver le chemin daller a leglise et que
au temps du service divin elles garderent leurs chambres, quelles scavent
bien vuyder et se pourmener dehors a leur plaisirs ou elles veullent,
mesmement et communement sur le soir.

  Dict que sur le samedy au soir, devant le jour de leur apprehension,
qui se fut lundy dernier, survient au logis de sondict maistre, environ le x

ou xj heurs de nuyct, un espaignart ou portugalois, quelle deposante ne
cogneut, auquel ledict son maistre, qui desia estoit au lict, alla parler et
veut elle depposante que apres avoir en certaines conferences euste, et
que ledict homme fut party, que sondict maistre appella tous les aultres
dudict logis qui se rassemblarent, lesquels ayant oy le rapport dudict
Bastian, maistre delle depposante, commencerent tous a se lamenter et
demener grand dueil estans tous fort esp[auv]antez. Et veyt elle deposante
que ledict Bastian et sa femme qui plouroit, rassemblerent en ung coffret
leur argent qui estoit de bonne somme et leur chaines et joyaulx et comme
ilz lenfermerent en ung grand coffre, sans avoir veu que lors ne le
demenche apres ledict coffret fut transporte et si de present jl soit hors de
ladicte maison, ce est advenu lundy, par ce que la dicte maistresse avoit
un frere en la dicte maison qui nestoit trouve en faisant ladicte
apprehension ains estoit caschie entre les gourdines du lict sur lequel leur
seur est gisante en couche en ladicte maison, mais ayda sondict frere
secretement oultre une muraille au desceu de gardes et luy donna ou rua
quelque chose pour lemporter avec luy, ayant elle deposante la fantasie
que se sera este ledict argent avec lesdicts joyaulx.

   Dict en oultre que jl convient que lesdicts prisonniers estoient ledict
samedy et dimenche dintention de se partir de ladicte ville ou de se
caschier en aultre logis car ledicte dimenche vint ledict Bastian son
maistre a elle deposante et demanda combien quelle avoit demeure avec
luy et combien montoit ce quelle avoit deservy, disant quelle luy estoit /f.
7r/ trop chiere servante par ce quelle gaignoit par an huyct carolus et que
jl nen vouloit donner que six, quelle chose comme elle deposante lors
bien se doubta, ledict son maistre mist en avant pour estre quicte delle, car
le louaige delle estait faict pour ung an et pour le pris de huyct carolus,
parquoy elle luy dict quelle ne vouloit moings gaigner et que, en ayant
son louaige a rate du temps quelle y avoit demoure, quelle estoit contente
sen aller; quoy dict luy donna ledict son maistre son argent et se debvoit
partir le lendemain, que fut le jour de ladicte apprehension, disant elle
deposante sur ce expressement interroguee, quelle na veu au logis de son
maistre faire sur samediy ou aultres jours aulcunes assemblees, aultres
que celle dont devant elle a depose et na veu faire aultres aprestes de
leurdict partement.

Source: AGR,Bx,OFB, B.160/1233/3, *Information 1544*, ff. 5v–7r.

[Document 41]
[Deposition of Gilbert de Cleves – July 5, 1544
Le ve de Juillet

(f. 9v) Gilbert de Cleves natif de Vuijt pres de Drecht, eaigé environ de xvij ans, adjourné et sermenté, dict avoir demeuré /f. 9v/ trois ans et demy en Portugal et estre venu avec la derniere flote en certaine hulque de maistre Claye Dunsch natif de Edam, aupres de Amsterdam, et que en la dicte hulque ne sont venuz aulcuns nouveaux christiens. Mais, comme il a entendu, plusieurs diceulx sont venuz en aultres hulques marchandes, ce quil scet aussi parce que, comme certain prestre natif de Castille paya en partant de la nave xxiiij ducats pour sa chambre, jl luy fut lors dict par ledict maistre marronier quil eschappoit a bon marche puis que aultres nouveaux christiens avoient payé es aultres hulques pour une petite chambrette la somme de cinquante ducats.

Ne cognoit touteffois il deposant nulz desdict nouveaux christiens ne les a veu en Postugal.

A aussi il deposant veu breusler ceste caresme passee viii nouveaux christiens en leurs personnes, mais nulz en figure ayant plusieurs este comdampnez a aultres penitences.

Interrogue sil ne cognoit ung nomme Pignero {Pignero} frequentant sur le facteur de Portugal, dict que si et ce depuis son retour de par de ça et non auparavant mai quil a bien oy dire icy dalcuns, dont il nest recors des noms, que ledict Pignero auroit este brusle en Lisbonne en figure, combien quil a aussi oy que ledict Pignero sexcuse Envers ceux qui le chargent de ce, disant que ce navoit este luy, mais ung aultre fugitif en Italye et ne scet il deposant avoir veu brusler en Portugal ledict Pignero par figure, comme aussi il na jamais declare a personne lavoir veu ainsi brusler.

Dict aussi ne scavoir aultrement a parler des deffences faictes aux maistres marroniers de ne mener aulcuns nouveaux christiens ou Juyfz en leurs naves, sinon par ce quil a esté present avec le maistre de sadicte hulque, qui ne scavoit le langaige portugalois, au port de Bellem ou que ledict maistre juroit au chastellain de chasteau dillec quil navoit aulcuns telz [nouveaux] christiens ou Juyfz en sadicte hulque, dont jl presume que tous les aultres maistres marroniers des aultres hulques auront faict le semblable serment, et que il deposant scaschant le languaige portugalois fut au temps dudict serment aupres ledict maistre pour lassister pour ce quil scavoit le deux langaiges.

Source: AGR,Bx,OFB, B.160/1233, Informations 1544, ff.9r–9v.

[Document 42]
[Deposition of Manuel Carneyro, pilote of the ship S. Antonio imprisoned in Antwerp – July 6, 1544]

(f. 14r) Manuel Carneyro natif de la Ville de Conde maistre pilotte de sa navire nommee Sainct Anthoine eaige de xxxiij ans, adjourne et sermente, dict estre venu avec la derniere armee du Portugal et que en sadicte navire (sienne pour ung tiers) et que avant le partement dicelle armee, ung des officiers de linquisition seroit venu enquerir en sadicte nave sil ny avoit aulcun nouveau christien et quil nen trova nulz. Mais que apres le partement dudict officier, seroient venuez plusieures femmes (au desceu touttefois de luy deposant estant malade et absent de la dicte navire jusques à son partement), assavoir {La femme de Diego Fernandiz et sa compaignie} la femme de Diego Fernandiz comme elle mesmes se descouvrit audict deposant, les meres dedicts Diego e de sa femme, semblablement le beau frere et seur dudict Diego, une nourrice et deux cnffans de la seur dicelluy Diego avec une petite garse et non ledict Diego qui, passe quatre ans, comme sa femme dict audict deposant, avoit este en Italye. Dict davantaige estre venuz en sadicte nave quatre aultres femmes et ung homme nomme ~~Estendiz~~ <hector Diz> {Hector Diz} sans scavoir les noms des femmes. Et dict interrogue navoir cogneu nulz des susdicts en Portugal, ne scavoir la cause de leur parternement ne le logis diceulx en ceste ville, sinon que lune desdictes femmes dict a luy deposant en la navire quelle venoit pour se loger en ceste ville au logis de Diego Fernandiz de la Piedra. Dict aussi que en sadicte navire sont venuez encoires trois aultres femmes et ung homme vieux christien, comme il pense, ayant lettres de congie du Roy de Portugal. Et dict, interrogue, que comme jl deposant sapperceust de la presence desdicts nouveaux christiens, dont il estoit esbahy et quil les vouloit faire sortir de sa nave, la femme dudict Diego Fernandiz luy promist cinquante ducats pour sa personne seulle, disant quelle venoit pardeça pour visiter son mary et les aultres de sa compaignie jusques au nombre de dix ou xij personnes, promisrent pour leur passaige la somme de iiijxx

[=quatrevingt] viij ducats dont luy fut donne certaine cedule et obbligation. Et que ledict Estendiz et sa femme d promirent viij ducats et une aultre vieille femme avec une fille seize ducats. Et quant aux vieux christiens venuz en la mesme navire, n'a este entre luy deposant et eulx convention daulcun certain pris, sinon quilz promirent de payer a discretion deulx et de luy deposant, desquelz il n'a encoires riens receu et sera beaucoup si payent trois ou quatre ducats pour teste, selon la coustume.

Dict aussi que apres le desembarquement la {femme dudict Diego} la femme dudict Diego et sa compaignie par le moyen dudict Diego ne luy ont voulu payer ce questoit convenu mais le remist jusques en Anvers, ou estant venu à reffuse le payement et nen est encoires paye pour le jourdhuy pour ce que Diego maintenoit que lon avoit desrobe a sa femme hors dung coffre (en la nave dudict deposant) certains /f. 14v/ bages jusques e la valeur de quatrecens ducats, dont est jl deposant a proces contre ledict Diego et a cause dicelluy est arreste en ceste ville, mais que des aultres que lon dict estre nouveaux christiens il a este paye et contente.

Dict aussi que, a l'arrivement de ladicte flote à la Vere, la femme dudict Diego avec toute la compaignie a este arrestee et constituee prisonniere du bailly dillec, maintenant que elle avec sadicte compaignie estoit Juifue ou nouvelle christienne et que, estant ladicte compaignie ainsi arrestee environ deux jours, seroient venuz audicte Vere Jehan Micus {Micus} demeurant jcy au logis de Diego Mendis et Augustinn Henriques {Augustinn Henriques} apres la venue desquelz lesdictes femmes auroint bien tost este delivrees sans quil deposant sache par moyen ou a l'intercession de qui.

Dict interroge ne scavoir si aulcuns dessusdicts ayent este en Portugal ou ailleurs bruslez par figure ou aultrement condampnez à penitence ny de la vye deulx. Mais, comme il semble audict deposant, ont vescu en la navire comme bons christiens. Et ne scet semblablement de la vye de nulz aultres estans venuz en aultres navires de ladicte flote.

Source: AGR,Bx,OFB, *Informations 1544*, ff. 14r–14v.

[Document 43]
[Queen Mary to Don Fernando d'Arragon, Charles Tisnacq, Pierre de
Fief – July 9, 1544]

Marie par la grace de Dieu Royne douaigiere d' Hongroi,
de Boheme et Regente

Tres chiers et bien ames, conforme aux lettres a nous escriptes poer
vouz, don Francisco d'Arragon, nous avonz fait despescher nouvelles
lettres de commission cy joinctes pour, en vertu dicelles, faire
informations en Zeelande, que desirons estre faictes a toute diligence,
pour apres adviser de la pugnition condigne de ceulx qui seront trouvez
coulpables, vous renvoiant les deux lettres trouvees au logis de Diego de
Roma. Et ordonnons a vous Pierre de Fief, procureur general, les
seurement garder et bien faire translater pour en apres sur le contenu bien
et estroictement interroguer ledict Diego, mesmes sur toutes les
circonstances et jndices que lon peult prendre de la substance desdictes
lettres, et pourquoy jl veult ainsi celerement faire conduire les nouveaux
christiens venans de Portugal, et ça quilz font quant ils sont en Ferrare,
aussi faire cherrer le charton qui les a conduit jusques a Coloigne et le
bien interroguer combien jl en a mene audicte Coloigne et qui luy respond
de son argent avec autres circonstances qui en dependent. Et en ce faire
tout bon debuoir comme esperons que ferez et nous advertirez de votre
besoingne sur ce tout a la meilleure dilligence que pouvez sans en faire
faulte. Tres chers et bien aimez, notre Seigneur vous ait en garde.
    Escript a Bruxelles le IX de juillet 1544.
    Marie

Depuis estres escriptes avons receu voz lettres du jour d'huy et vous
scavons bon gre de voz advertissemens.

[on the reverse of the sheet:]
Noz tres cherez et bien amez don Francisco Darragon,
Charles Tusnacq consellier, Pierre du Fief procureur
general et Jacques de la Tour estans presentement en Anvers

Source: AGR,Bx,OFB, B.160/1233/2.

[Document 44]
[Deposition of Paulo Araez – July 13, 1544]

Le XIIJ de Juillet

(f. 23r) Paulo Araez natif de Almadiz en Portugal varlet de chambre du roy eaige de xxiiij ans, adjourne et sermente, dict avoir veu venir es naves de larmee certains officiers de linquisition pour veoir sil y avoit aulcuns nouveaux christiens qui vouloient partir sans license. et quil avoit ung en la nave du capitaine general, qui, adverty de leurs venue, se seroit salve en delaissant jllec ung sien serviteur et coffre, lequel coffre fut prins et emporte par ladicte Inquisition et fut lors deffence publiquement faicte que nulz capitaine ou marroniers receussent en leurs navires aulcuns telz christiens soubs payne dexcommunication.

Dict ne cognoistre aulcuns desdicts nouveaux christiens venuz par de ça avec ceste derniere armeee <ou> auparavant. Si non ung nomme {Fernande Galindo} Fernande Galindo natif de Evora et de son mestier orfevre demeurant en Anverse derriere la nouvelle bourse en la rue des crucifix et que certain maistre de navire, dont il ne scet le nom, a dict a lui depposant que ledict Galindo seroit venu en sa navire passe an et demy et ce secretement et quil auroit este bien eureux considere que plusieurs aultres caschiez comme luy avoient este trouvez et apprehendez par linquisition et le dict Galindo seroit eschappe et a il depposant hier jci oy dire a Diego Lopez varlet de chambre du Roy que le pere dudict Galindo avoit este brusle en Evora. /f. 23v/

Dict aussi ne scavoir a parler de contenu es x, xj, xij, xiij et xiiij^e articles des interoogatoires

Dict davantaige que le frere dung nomme Denys Gomez {Denys Gomez et son freres} ayant demeure quelques annees en Anverse, seroit venu par de ça avec ceste derniere armee a jntention, comme il mesmes a dict a luy depposant, de demeurer jcy avec ledict Gomez son frere et que a ceste fin avoient les deux freres loue une maison audict Anvers, non scachant aultrement a parler de leurs qualitez ou maniere de vivre, ou cause de leur partement dudict Portugal.

Source: AGR,Bx,OFB, *Information 1544*, ff. 23r–23v.

[Document 45]

[Deposition of Cristoval de Maya boatswain of the ship S. Clara –
July 15, 1544]

(f. 27r) Christoval de Maya natif de la ville del Conde, maistre de la
navire nommeee Santa Clara, sienne pour ung quart, eaige de xxxvij ans
adjourne et sermente dict, interrogue sur le huyct premiers articles des
interrogatoires, avoir amene en sadicte navire ung nouveau christien
nomme Henrrique Jorge avec son mesnaige, scavoir sa femme, belle
mere, avec trois petitz enffans dont il ne scet leurs noms. Encoires ung
nomme Francisco Nugnes beau frere dudict Henrrique Jorge, avec sa
femme et une petite fille non scachant leurs noms. Item ung aultre appelle
Manuel Pignero, jeusne homme marye depuis deux ans en ça, venu avec
sa femme tant seullement. Tous les susdicts natifz de certain lieu voisin
de Covillan, parens et alliez les ung aux aultres, venuz depuis naguaire en
Lisbone. Item Manuel Lopes avec sa femme et deux petitz enffans
residens audict Lisbone devant leur partement et ung jeusne garson dudict
Pignero servant a toute la compaignie.

Non scachant a parler de la richesse de nulz de susdicts sinon que luy
semble que ledict Hennrique Jorge doibt estre riche, considere quil a ung
sien frere nomme Manuel Jorge traictant pour luy au pays de Hoolst et
Denemarche et venant coustumierement deux fois par an de Portugal par
de ça avec bonnne marchandise. Et a il deposant oy et entendu desdicts
deux freres quilz avoient quatorze ou quinze fardeax des fynes toilles de
Jnde es navires du Roy asscavoir de Jehan Alfonso Villamarin et de
Bastian Andree maistre de Montdragon mais que lesdicts freres navoient
nulles marchandises en sadicte nave sinon quelque peu de mesnaige pour
leur entretenement. Et quant audict Manuel Lopez, dict avoir entendu de
luy quil avoit charge de la navire capitaine la marchandise jusques a la
valeur de cincq cens ducats. Et que tous les susdicts se sont embarquez
sur le soir apres le soleil couchie. Et ont les susdicts Henrrique Jorge et
Manuel Pignero a leur embarquement dict a luy deposant quilz estoient
tous dung lignaige et voulaient aller vivre en Flandres pour les
persecutions que lon faisoit audict Portugal contre les nouveaux
christiens, prians a luy deposant /f. 27v/ tenir la main quilz ne feussent
molestez ne mocquez de ses marroniers puis quilz estoient bons
christiens. Et ne scet il que aulcuns des susdicts ayent estes bruslez en
figures ou condampnez ou aultrement suspectez dheresie mais dict quilz

se sont tenuz en Portugal tractant publicquement jusques a leur partement et que les susdicts ont vescuz en la navire comme bons christiens, et a il deposant eu deulx cent et xx ducats et dict que aultres passagiers vieulx christiens sont accoustumez de payer parfois deux, trois ou cincq ducats selon les temps, aulcunes fois plus et aultresffois moins.

Non scachant <si> lesdicts venuz en sa navire ayent eu licence, laquelle il pense quilz la <nous> monstreront en cas quilz soient venuz avec icelle.

Sur le xv^e [article de l'interrogatoire] dict avoir oy dir jcy, non scachant de qui, que ung nomme Licentiado Renel, ne si de son nom sapelloit Manuel, seroit venu pardeça avec sa femme en ceste derniere flote et que ledict Licentiado est homme de reputation, frequentant publiquement en Lisbone, marye avec la fille de Nugnes Henrricques, homme riche et qui, passe environs deux annes, a paye au Roy du Portugal quarante mille ducats non pour cas dheresye mais a cause de la grande hantise et faveur, aussi contractation quil avoit contre le commandements dudict roy avec le cardinal don Michel de Viseo. Et ne scet jl deposant que ledict Renel soit oncques este coulpe ou accuse de Linquisition.

Dict aussi avoir veu avant son partement de Lisbone et depuis sur la bourse Danvers ung nomme Bastian Fernandiz, non scachant touteffois a parler de la qualite dicelluy aultrement que ledict Bastian auroit preste a ceulx qui sont venuz en la navire, comme eulx mesmes lont dict audict deposant, cent et vingt ducats pour payer leur voiture.

Dict davantaige avoir cogneu, passe environs six ans en Lisbone ung nomme Diego Fernandiz qui avoit este chanoine devant son mariage, traictant en Lisle de Madere comme fermier du droit de quint des sucres venant au Roy du Portugal et, comme il deposant a uy dire, ledict Diego sest retire du dict Portugal a loccasion dung homicide quil avoit commis en ladicte j͟s͟l͟ jsle et de la seroit enfuy en Italye, non scachant comment il se soit despuis gouverne. Et / f. 28r/ a il deposant a l'arrivee de la derniere flotte en ceste ville, estant sa femme avec sa compaignie arreste icy par le bailly, veu venir ung serviteur (venu avec ladicte femme de Diego) au logis dudict bally, disant que la susdicte compaignie nestoit de prinse ne arrestable, actendu certain breve apostolique que ledict Diego avoit obtenu du pape contenant en effect que ledict Diego avec sa compaignie et famille pourroient partout librement aller par mer et par terre ou bon luy sembleroit et veyt lors il deposant tirer hors dune garde faicte de letton

certaines lettres, non scachant sil l'estoit ung breve au aultres lettres
apostoliques.

Sur le x, xj, xij, xiij, xiiij^e articles dict ne scavoir a parler du contenu
en iceulx, plus avant quil na declaire cy dessus, sinon quil a bien oy dire
pardeça, depuis deux ou trois jours, non ayant retenu leurs noms, quil
avoit en Anvers ung homme vieux frequentant la maison du facteur de
Portugal qui auroit este brusle par figure en Lisbon, non scachant sil
sappelle Pignero ne aultrement sa qualite.

Source: AGR,Bx,OFB, *Information 1544*, ff. 27r–28r.

[Document 46]
[Deposition of Yenes Gomes, boatswain of the ship S. Antonio –
July 15, 1544]

(f. 28r) Gomes Yenes natif de la Ville del Conde maistre pilotte de la
navire de Sainct Anthoine, sienne por ung tiers, eaige environ de xl ans,
adjourne et sermente, dict sur le huyct premiers articles quil est party de
Lisbone dix ou xij jours après le partement de la dernière armee du Roy
du Portugal et arrive en ceste ville huyct ou dix jour après icelle et quil a
receu en sa dicte navire Anthoine Rodriguez et son frere aisne, non
scachant ~~leurs~~ <son> nom, avec leurs femmes desquelles aussi il ne scet
le noms. Aussi George d'Andrade, beau filz dedict frere aisne, aussi avec
sa femme et ung quatriesme [homme] marye et allye avec une parente des
susdicts, tous ensemble avec leurs varlets et enffans jusques au nombre de
seize personnes non scachant du lieu /f. 28v/ ny comment ilz se sont
conduictz par de la, pour ce quil ne les avait jamais veu auparavant et en
la navire se sont conduitz comme aultres bons christiens et luy ont paye
pour leur passaige tous ensemble cent et dix ducatz contre la coustume
des aultres christiens nouveaux. Dict aussi que les susdicts nont apporte
aultres bagaiges, sinon quelques mesnaige pour leur service, combien que
il deposant a receu en Lisbone certains petit coffre que lui a este delivre
par ung quidam dont il ne scet le nom, pour le porter en Anvers en la
maison de Augustin Henrriques et comme il ne vouloit entreprendre la
charge ~~et~~ <ne> se obliguer de le delivrer audicte Anvers, pour non estre
asseure sil y arriveront, que lors luy fut dict que, en cas de non aborder
audict Anvers, tiendroit ledict deposant pour descharge en delivrant ledict
coffres a ung de susdicts comme il a faict, le donnant a Nicolao Lopes
susdict duquel estoient selon que alcuns de la susdicte compagnie on dict

a luy deposant certains joyaulx et bages. Sur le ix^e interrogue dict ne scavoir nulz sinon ung surnomme Renel avec sa compaignie, lequel il deposant a veu en Anvers devant lhuys de la maison de Augustin Henrriques. Non scachant de la qualite dicelluy, sinon quil la veu hanter publicquement en Lisbone jusques environs a lheure de son embarquement. Dict aussi riens scavoir a parler de contenu es X, XJ, XIJ, XIIJ, XIIJ et XIIIJ^e articles, sur tout deuement et bien au long interroge.

Source: AGR,Bx,OFB, *Information* 1544, ff. 29r–29v.

[Document 47]
[Deposition of João Perez boatswain of the ship S. Cruz –
July 16, 1544]

(f. 29v) Jehan Perez natif de la Ville del Conde, maistre de la navire nommee Saincte Croix, eaige de xxxij ans, sermente, dict quil est arrive en ceste ville le xiiij^e de ce mois en compaignie de quarante deux voiles et party de Portugal. Et que a son partement, estant au port de Setubal, avoit receu en sadicte navire treze ou quatorze personnes, non scachant silz estoient /f. 30r/ nouveaux christiens et que la justice de par linquisition survient et les amena tous prisoniers, parquoy na amene nulz nouveaux chritiens et ne scet quil y soit venu aulcun avec ceste flote, sinon quil a u dire que en certaine hulque de par de ça soient venuz trois ou quatre, desquelz il en a veu jcy deux. Mais ne scauroit a la verite dire silz sont de la dicte compaignie. A aussi bien oy dire que certaine navire portugaloise venue avec ceste flote, dont estoit maistre pilotte Jehan Gonçales, natif de la ville del Conde, auroit prins dicy leur chemin droit vers Anvers sans avaller voile et que en icelle avoit beaucoup de gens, non ayant oy dire silz estoient nouveaux christiens, et ne scet nulz nouveaux christiens par de ça.

Dict aussi avoir oy dire que ung nomme Manuel Fernandiz, natif de Ville del Conde, venu avec cestedicte flote, auroit amene en sa navire sept ou huyct personnes, et entre icelles deux femmes, lesquelles jl deposant a veu, non scachant touteffois silz sont nouveaux christiens ou non. Et dict que avant ledict partement ladicte jnquisition auroit emmene ung nouveau christien et mis en la prison, trouve en la navire de Pedro Lopez de la Ville del Conde, estant ledict maistre presente en ce port.

Source: AGR,Bx,OFB, 160/1333/3, *Information* 1544, 29v–30r.

[Document 48]
[Deposition of João Gonsales boatswain of the ship S. Maria de Luz –
July 16, 1544]

(f. 30v) Jehan Gonsales natif de Porto, maistre de sa navire nommee
Sainte Marie de Luz alias dict La Verzeira, eaige de xliij ans, sermente
dict: est arrive en ce port devant hier, xiiij^e de ce mois en compaignie de
quarante deux voiles dont les huyct estoient portugaloises et que avant
son partement comme certaine compaignie de nouveaux christiens
jusques au nombre de xv ou xx personne estans en certaine barque pour
se mectre es navire et venir par ça, jl deposant a oy dung sien marronier
que de la part de linquisition /f. 31r/ icelle compaignie avec le marronier
fut mene prisonniere combien que icel marronier fut despuis delivre.
Disant aussi que en sadicte navire nest venu nul nouveau christiens mais
que en certaine hulque de pardeça seroient venuz aulcuns, ayant veu deux
ou trois dyceulx que avant son partement de Portugal, comme icelle ou
semblable hulque devant certaine tour au port de Bellem, la garde dicelle
estant advertie quelle amenoit tout plain desdicts nouveaux christiens,
pour non les laisser passer oultre auroit tire plusieurs coups dartillerye
apres ycelle. De laquelle estant arrestee, <combien que plusieurs> furent
tires ~~plusieurs~~ dehors, ce non obstant [cette hulque] auroit amene aulcuns
mais ne scet si les personnes venuez pour ladicte hulque soient encoires
jcy. Dict aussi que certaine navire portugaloise venue avec la dicte
compaignie est allee en Anvers ayant plusieurs personnes, femmes et
enffans, lesquelz voyant que ceux de la nave dudict deposant faisant
grand semblant de regarder sur eulx, se casseront et estonpperent le
fenestres de la nave. Et ne cognoit et ne scet aulcuns nouveaux christiens
pardeça aultrement que dict est, ne de la cause de leur partement.

Source: AGR,Bx,OFB, 160/1333/3, *Information 1544*, ff. 30v–31r.

[Document 49]
[Deposition of Manuel Fernandiz boatswain of the Ship San Salvador –
July 16, 1544

(f. 31v) Manuel Fernandiz natif de la ville del Conde maistre de la
navire de San Salvador sienne pour ung quart, eaige de quarante ans
sermente, dict … estre arrive en ce port le lundy passe en compagnie de

quarantedeux voiles entre lesquelles il avoit dix portugaloiseis et amene
de Lisbone deux hommes nommez Manuel Lopez de Alvas et Francisco
Rodriguez, et trois femmes scavoir: Anna Pays, Agnes Fernandiz de
Doveras et une vieille mere de ladicte Anna Pays avec trois enffans et luy
semble quilz son tous nouveaulx christiens desia partiz pour Anvers et ne
scet il deposant a parler de la qualite diceulx, ne de la cause de leur
partement, sinon quil presume que sest de poeur de linquisition, considere
que pour ce temps nulluy se retire avec femme et enffans sinon de crainte
dicelle. Et que ladicte Agnes est femme dung demeurant au logis de feu
Diego Mendiz, nomme comme luy semble Francisco Fernandiz et sert
illec de clercq ou escripvano, venu par de ça depuis deux ans en ça
comme il deposant a entendu delle. Et na il veu que les susdicts ayent
vefcuz en sa navire aultremet /f. 32r/ que le bons christiens, mesmement
que ladite Agnes est femme bien devote comme luy semble et sont les
sudicts embarquez de nuyct et ont paye ensemble trente deux ducats et
demy a cincq ducats pour teste et quilz nont amene avec eulx sinon quatre
coffres plains de abillemens et aultre petit mesnaige et ne sont appareus
destre gens riches et dict ne les avoir jamais cogneu ne veu pardela sinon
apres leur embarquement. Dict aussi que Jehan Gonsalves boitteux et
Gonçalo Alvares maistre et pilotte ont amene dedict Portugal en leur
navire certains nouveaulx christiens lesquelz seroient alle vers Anvers et
ne les cognoit aultrement que pour les avoir veu en passant en mer et luy
semble selon la presumption que telz gens se sont retirez de Portugal de
poeur du feu ou de linquisition. A il aussi veu en certaine hulque aultres
nouveaulx christiens mais na nulle cognoissance deulx. Et dit ne scavoir
a parler de ceulx qui ont este bruslez en figure ou aultrement condampnez
par ladicte Inquisition. Dict aussi avoir oy dire en Lisbonne de plusieurs
que pour le mois daoust se doibvent embarquer certaines personnes de
pris que desia ont loue secretement la navire de Manuel Diz de la ville de
Conde pour eulx tant ~~secretement~~ seullement et combien quilz hantent
pour le present publicquement en Lisbone font neantmoins desia leurs
apprestes pour partir pour ledict mois daoust. Dict aussi avoir veu depuis
environs deux mois en ça mener prisonniers de par linquisition en quatre
petites barques jusques au nombre de cincquante quatre personnes que
hommes que femmes et que linquisition faict grand debvoir et dilegence
de prendre tous nouveaux christiens qui se veuillent retirer par de ça en
punissant les coulpables et delivrant les bons.

Source: AGR,Bx,OFB, 160/1333/3, *Information 1544*, ff. 31v– 32r.

[Document 50]
[Corneille Sceperus' secret report to Queen Mary on the inquiry against
the Portuguese imprisoned in Antwerp, – July 22, 1544]

(f. 157r) Madame,

Aiant le jour dhier longuement communique avec don Francisco
daragon sur le fait de ces nouvelz christiens, et redige le tout par escript
je me suis apres trouve, avec ledit Don Francisco et le procureur general
de Brabant devers monsieur le president, par advis duquel ledit don
Francisco sest transporte a Louvain affin dillecq examiner trois estudiants
portugalois qui on dit avoir veu en Anvers aulcuns de leur nation dont les
ymages avoient este bruslees en Portugal. Et ledit procureur general sen
est alle en Anvers pour entendre aussi bien a laffaire des anababtistes que
desdits nouvelz christiens. Et affin que votre majeste soit sommerement
advertie de ce que jay peu comprendre dudit don Francisco, plaise a icelle
scavoir que le foundament dudit don Francisco est avoir suffisamment fait
apparoir que lesdits nouvclz christiens venans de Portugal viennent
fuyants et par crainte quilz ont destre bruslez audit Portugal. Que ne
procede poinct de leur bonne vie ains fault que le roy de Portugal ayt juste
et legitime occasion de les persecuter.

Secondement: jl a fait assez apparoir que lesdits nouvelz christiens se
vont rendre Juifz en Turquie et y amenent tous les biens que leur est
possible. En oultre que il na tenu a luy que ung appelle le Pignero et ung
aultre nomme Gabriel nayant este pris, du moings ledit Gabriel aiant ledit
don Francisco eu espie certaine dedans la maison ou estoit cache ledit
Gabriel et fait monstrer a lescoutette danvers ladite maison, lequel
escoutette par deux fois a failly de prendre ledit Gabriel, l'une fois
prenant une maison pour lautre, lautre fois sadressant a lhoste et le
prenant prisonnier audit lieu dudit Gabriel qui estoit a la chambre dehhaut
de ladite maison (et que ledit don Francisco en ma presence et du
procureur general susdit a dit audit escoutette lequel ny a point contredit.
Et est ce que dessus que ledit don Francisco allegue pour son escouse
soubstenant que on naurait jamais pu amener les marins /f. 157v/ et
aultres capitaines portugallois a descouvrir le secret desdits nouvelz
christiens et quilz venoient fuyantz et au deçou du roy, que aussi entre
iceulx nouvelz christiens estoient plusieurs dont les ymages avoient este
bruslees (et aussi il dit avoir verifie par tesmoings de veue et ouye,

Mais touchant son advis, puis que a votre majeste jl a pleu le luy
demander, cest que lon doibt examiner les prisonniers a part, quon doibt

interroger le facteur de Portugal et ses domesticques de ce quil scait desdits nouvelz christiens. Quon doibt questionner ung Diego de Roma venu de Rome pour querir sa femme et enfans puis quil y a indices bien vehemens et grands contre ledit Diego. Lequel samble estre un conducteur et guyde de tous aultres. Et oultre ce lon a trouve au comptoir dudit Diego une piere de christal en forme dune boitie dedans de lequel y a ung diable noir et jaulne chose hydeuse a veoir ne scay ce quil signifie. Quant au premier point, le president et procureur general furent bien de ceste advis que lexamination se fist a part. Quant a interroger le facteur, jlz sont aussi bien dopinion que le facteur soit interrogue, et a ceste fin votre majeste a signee une lettre adressant audit facteur. Mais quant a questionner ledit Diego, le procureur general veullant garder le train de la justice ne y veult encoires entendre. Mais dit voloir prendre advis avec aulcuns de conseil de Brabant estant en Anvers et selon ce proceder ou non proceder a la torture. De quoy ledit don Francisco ne se contente point tres bien. Ains proteste que le doibt torturer et que sans torture lon naura riens de luy. Il persiste aussi quon doibt fer des rechief publier que ung chacung sera tenu reveler sil scait ou sont devenuz ledit Pignero et Gabriel. A quoy le president a condescendu et pareillement que les biens dudit Gabriel soient mis en arrest. Parquoy madame ne reste que faire ladite examinations de prisoniers et du facteur pour une fois avoir la fin decest affaire.

/f. 158r/ Touchant la lettre de change que votre majeste me bailla, elle nest vallable car le licenciado Eduarte Gomez qui a soubsigne ladite lettre na point receu les deuxmille trois cens ducats mentionnez a ladite lettre mais ladite lettre a este faicte pour une cautelle. Touteffois largent principal est arreste es mains dung Jehan de Lerma. Et est le cas tel. Ung portugallois est puis naguere venu en Anvers apportant cinq mil ducat en jntention de louher quelque chambre affin de fer jllec venir sa mere et trois seurs estans en Portugal. Et quant adverty de cest nouvelle information quon prenoit contre les nouvelz christiens mit ij^m iij^c [= 2.300] ducats es mains dung Jehan de Lerma, castillian, et prit une lettre de change du licentie Emmanuel Gomez gouvernant la maison de feu Diego Mendiz pour recouvrer ledit argent a Medina de Riosero en cas que ledit Gomez eust primiers sceu recouvrer hors des mains dudit Lerma lesdits ij^m iij^c ducats, despuis ledit portugalois achapta dung homme de bien danvers aultant des fustaines que mountoient lesdits ij^m iij^c ducats, en luy baillant en payement ladite lettre de change. Touteffois ledit homme danveres volut avoir respondant pour ladite lettre de change, sans laisser emporter de son logis lesdites festaines [*sic !*]. Et comme ledit portugois craindoit perdre le tout il sescappa avec les iij^m ducats delaissant les ij^m iij^c es mains dudit Lerma lesquelz ont illecq este arrestez car ledit homme de bien pour son interest et apres la publication faicte que chacung seroit tenu reveler ce quel scavoit des biens des nouvelz cristiens, il le vint dire audit don Francisco, lequel fit arrester lesdits ij^m iij^c ducats au nom de lempereur de sorte que cest argent segur et ne demande ledit homme de bien senon son interesse seullement qui pourra monter environs trois cens florins. Comme il ma dit. Et par ainsi jay par conseil de monseigneur le president delivre ladite lettre de change audit procureur general pour le prouffit de lempereur. Qu'est toute histoire de ce qu'est icy passe. A lendroit dudit Seigneur don Francisco jay entendu par monseigneur le duc darschot lopinion que votre majeste a de luy. A quoy ne scauroit que dire, sinon que de tant que jay parle avec luy, questoy hier seullement, je nay sceu apercevoir aultre chose en luy, fors quil va a bonne / f. 158v/ foy. Et sil fait aultrement il mabuse. Touteffois votre majeste le cognoist mieux que je ne fay. A quoy me remectz. Madame, je prie le Createur avoir votre majeste en sa saincte protection et garde. de Bruxelles ce xxij^e de juillet 1544.

Tres humble et tres obeisant serviteur
Corneille Scepperus

Source: AGR,Bx,PEA 132 ff 157r–158v.

[Document 51]
[Deposition of Manuel Bernaldis, cashier of the Portuguese Royal Feitor in Antwerp July 30, 1544]

(f. 36r) Manuel Bernaldis cassier du facteur [du Roy] de Portugal eaige de XXXJ ans, sermente et interroge sil ne scet la cause de la retraicte de pardeça des nouveaux christiens, dict quil luy semble, et selon la commune opinion, quilz senfuyent dudict Portugal de poeur destre bruslez ou aultrement tomber es mains de linquisition et que entre eulx aulcuns viennent aussi a cause de leurs marchandises et aultres pour avoir pardeça plus grande liberte de vivre.

Dict ne cognoistre par de ça aulcuns bruslez [en figure] a Portugal ou aultrement condampnez sinon quil a jcy aultreffois veu ung nomme le docteur Dionisio brusle en Lisbonne en statue, lequel dicy senfuyt en

Angleterre et de la vers Ferrare ou il est trespasse depuis deux ou trois ans en ça, delaissant en ceste ville deux de ses enffans tractans en gros.

Aussi dict quil a oy dire que Manuel Pignero, qui souloit hanter la maison dudict facteur et a present se tient absent et caschie, seroit este brusle en figure audict Lisbone non scachant ou il se tient pour le present.

Dict davantaige avoir oy jcy de plusieurs portugalois que la femme de Denis Gomes a present en ceste ville, a este bruslee audict Lisbone avec plusieurs aultres enfuyz, en statue, et a il deposant veu la femme dudict Denys Gomes enterrer en ceste ville au Carmes en terre vierge quest terre, comme il deposant declare, en laquelle na jamais este interre aultre, *sicut mos est Judeis sepelire* et dont les Juyfz selon leurs ceremonyes sont accoustumez den user.

Dict aussi avoir oy dire que avec ceste derniere armee ung ou deux personnes seroient venues pardeça, bruslees en statue audict Lisbone.

Dict et afferme avoir oy dire commment, passe six ou sept ans, quil y a entre les nouveaux christiens une bourse [de] charite mais ne scet quil l'a entre mains ny l'administration dicelle, samblement /f. 36v/ quilz ont jcy une Synagogue empres de Jehan de Haro derriere les carmes sans scavoir aultre chose a deposer.

Dict que plusieurs nouveaux christiens se sont retirez de ceste ville vers Ferrare depuis trois ou quatre ans en ça, mais ne scet leurs noms sinon de Gabriel de Negro qui se tient a Venise et Loys Fernandis à present à Ferrare et Fernand Perez, cassier de feu Diego Mendis ayant espouse la fille dudict Gabriel, tous les susdicts retirez dicy avec leurs femmes et enffans. Et ne scet pour le present que aultres ayent volunte de partire dicy.

Dict ne scavoir a parler de nulz deniers ou lettres de change appertenans ausdicts nouveaux christiens venuz par ceste derniere flote sinon dung nouveau christien venu depuis naguerres mais il deposant ne le peult manifester a cause du serment quil a faict a son maistre de tenir secret combien quil le cognoit et la qualite dicelluy.

Dict que Gilles de Solbrecht qui fut cassier de feu Diego de Mendis est accoustume de traicter pour les nouveaux christiens comme facteur et luy semble quil en debvroit rendre bon compte, considere que jl deposant a receu depuis trois mois en ça de certains marchans portugalois lettres pour scavoir si ledict Gilles navoit en ses mains nulz deniers de certains nouveaux christiens mentionne esdictes lettres estant a present en Portugal pour ce que ledict marchand que icelluy nouveau christien pourroit devenir non solment et pour estre asseure de luy et comme luy deposant demandoit audict Gilles que cestoit cest affere, icelluy Gilles luy demandoit le nom dicelluy nouveau christien et depuis non a tenu propos plus avant.

Et dict depuis que le Seigneur don Francisco [d'Arragon] est en ceste ville, que jl deposant ayant af[faire] avec Manuel Pignero pour avoir de luy une lettre de quarante livres de gros plus ou moins que ledict Gilles a la requeste dudict Pignero a donne a luy deposant ses lettres dobligation, non se fiant dedict Pignero pour ce quil est nouveau christien et journellement semblables gens se rendent fugitifz comme il a faict de present.

Dict navoir receu aulcunes lettres de Portugal depuis l'arrivee de ceste derniere flote, faisans mention du faict des nouveaux christiens et ne scet que aulcuns en ayent.

Dict avoir oy dire en ceste ville depuis deux mois en ça /f. 37r/ de plusieurs que Diego Fernadis se mesloit a Rome des affaires de nouveaux christiens et quil y auroit este prisonier.

Source: AGR,Bx, OFB, 160/1233/3, *Information 1544* ff. 36r–37r.

[Document 52]
[Judgement issued by Diego de la Torre on the dispute between Diego Fernandiz Netto and Manuel Carneiro, July 30, 1544]

Visto por los Commissarios de su Magestad enel negocio dessos nuevos cristianos sommariamente la pendencia entre Manuel Carneiro maestre de la nao de Sant Antonio de una parte y Diego Fernandiz Netto de otra, con los medios y razones de cada uno dellos por justificaçion de su demandas. Vistos tambien los dichos de algunos testigos que se examinaron *ex officio* en essa pendencia y todo muy bien considerado. Ha les parecido que los dichos Manuel Carneiro y Diego Fernandiz se han de reglar por forma de concierto en la maniera que se sigue. Es a saber quanto a la demanda de dicho Manuel sobre el frete de nao que pretiende le ser devido por aver trahido aca la muger del sobredicho e Diego Fernandiz y otros gastos quel dize haver echo por mandado del mismo Diego Fernandiz, pues Manuel declaro en presencia de los suso dichos commissarios no tener otra prueva a veriguar sa demanda, quel dicho Diego sera libre pagando al dicho Manuel por rata a soldo y libra como pagaron los otros que venieron en la misma nao, ~~solo~~ y mas quanto por respecto de la comodidad que tuvo su muger en aquella nao davantaije que los otros. Y quanto a lo quel dicho Diego Fernandiz pide contra el dicho maestre sobre la perdida de las jojas de su muger en la dicha nao, considerando la flaca prueva y evitar demandas y gastos, el dicho Diego Fernandiz desistera de tal demanda alchando las fianzas de modo quel dicho Manuel pueda hazer de si lo que por bien tuviere. Sin ser por esta dicha causa al presete detenido. Quedando al dicho Diego Fernandiz su derecho resguardado para quando por bien tuviere y liquidando lo que ha de pagar el dicho Diego Fernandiz del frete y ventaje y gastos, han declarado a plazimiento de las partes hasta la suma de onze ducados por la dicha su muger y cognado. Comvene a saber: ocho por el frete, dos por la ventaja de la camera que su muger uvo y uno por los gastos della y del dicho su cognado.el qual concierto los sobredicho Manuel Carneiro y Diego Fernandiz han aprobado en todos sus puntos y han firmado de sus proprias manos. En la ciudad de Emberes a treynta de Julio 1544.

[Original signatures of]: Diego Fernandiz Manuel Carneiro

Yo Diego de la Torre Secretario de su magestad y uno de los commissarios sobredichos, en testimonio de la verdad he firmado la presente de mi propria mano el ano, mez y dia sobredichos De la Torre.

Source: AGR,Bx,OFB, 160/1233/3.

[Document 53]
[A list of Portuguese immigrants arrested in Antwerp in 1544]

Noms et surnoms des personnes detenuez, venans avec la derniere armee ou flote de Portugal qui se baptisent nouveaulx christiens, faict le dict arrest par le procurateur general dc Brabant en la Ville d'Anvers <depuis> le dernier et de Jung 1544.

Empres le Feu de parfums(?)

Sebastien Fernandiz
Gracia Linda sa femme
Diego et Francisco leur filz
Agnes et Clara leur filles
Hector leur negre

En la mesmes maison
Pierre Loys
Leonora Linda sa femme

En la mesmes [maison]
O   Diego Manuel
Ysabella Roderigo sa femme
O   Alvaro leur filz
Major Lagnes et Branca leur
filles

Aultre mesnaige Ibidem
Diego Fernandiz Netto qui
se faisoit nommer
messieur Diego de
Roma, chevalier
au present en la
prison publicque
Agnes Gomes sa femme
Maria sa negre

Altre Mesnaige Ibidem

Ruy Gomez Jeusne homme
Messia Fernandiz sa mere
Branca Gomez sa soeur
Esperance Fernante

Aultre Mesnaige en ladicte Maison

Branca Fernandiz vevfve de feu Henrico
de Negro
Elizabet Oliverj
Andreu et Alvaro ses filz

En la Rue dict de
Grunendale Straethen

Francisco Gomez sur ung peltrier   +
marchant non marie relaxe par ce quil
retournoit en Portugal et nestoit
du nombre des fugitifz

En la Mesmes rue
Denis Nuñes   *examiné*
Dyonis Violenta Sola et trois petis   *idem*
enffans, sur ung nectoyer despez

En la mesmes rue
au tamburin dor

Augustin Henrique Dias   O *examine*
Violente Lopez sa femme avec cincq O *idem*
petitz enffans
sa mere nommee Violente Dias   O *idem*
Jl ya en ceste maison une esclave
et la mere
Maria Dias Veufue

Examine Baltazar Emanuel son filz   In den Bock empres le Poiz aux fers
Idem br. Anna et Branca Emanuel
    ses filles
    Geomar Roderiguez   ung nomme Borrazo
                                  Leonora Gonsalez avec trois ses enffans

        En la mesme maison

                                  Sur Jehan de Calstero en
    Petro de Salva Terra   la Paille d'or
    Lucretia Nugnes
    Thomas Nugnes   Ysabella de Fariga veufue de Fernando Gomez
    Leonora, Gracia et Thamar   examinee
    ses filles
                                  Ysabella Gomez sa fille femme
                                  de Jeronimo   ○
        Sur Louvre sur la veufve   Lopez qui est encores en Portugal
        de Martin de Vuyfe   Ysabella leur servante
                                  Nicolas ~~Gomes~~ <Lopez> frere dudict
                                  Jerosnimo
    Tristram [*sic*!] dagoste   examine
    Françoise Perera sa femme
    Biolenta Perera sa mere
    Emanuel, Eduart, Francisco,   En la Mesme Maison
    leurs filz
    Phylippa Gracia filles dudict   <u>Nugnes Lopes</u>   examine
    Tristram
    Caterina leur esclave   Anna sa femme   idem
                                  Beatrix leur fille et François leur filz   idem

        En la Rue de
        Saint Anthoine
                                  Sur [la maison d'] ung verroier nomme
                                  Pieter Goos

<u>Francisco Nugnes</u>
Gracia Fernandis et Anna
ses filles
                                François Peras
        En la mesme Maison   Jmagen sa femme
                                Emanuel, ~~fr.~~ Branca et Marques, leurs enffans
Emanuel Pignero jeusne homme
Beatrix Antunis sa femme   Le premier de Juillet apprehendez
Caterina Gomez sa mere   ceulx qui senfuyrent
George frere dudict Emanuel
        En la Mesme [Maison]   Emanuel Pinto
            <u>Henry Jorge</u>   Ygnes de France sa femme et cincq enffans
Leonora Piera sa femme et trois   laissez en leurs maison sans garde por
Leurs enffan**s**   quilz sont de ceulx qui sont venuz
                                depuis ung an en ça

Sur la Veufue de Nicolas
Nuyts sur la Lombarde   Sur le grenier
Veste

Jsabella Olivery, Anna Vas et   Jorge Rodrigues, Gracia Rodriguez
Leonora
ses filles et nyece   avec trois enffans, Jsabella Fernandiz   ○
Simon Vas son filz   mere de Gracia

Au mesmes Logis   En la chambre en bas
Anna Ferrera veufue de
Bras Alvares
Thomas et Diego ses filz   Jeorge dandrade, Branca Nugnes sa
                                  femme et leur deux enffans

Sur Poeter Bordinck   Sur Jejan Wylant
Emanuel Dies non marie   Maria Lopes avec deux enffans et
comme il dict
Lancellotto son serviteur   une jeusne fille nommee Messia soeur
                                  a George Diaz mary deladicte Maria
Sur Ulrich Orfevre   qui nest trouve a lhostel et dit ladicte
Ylbain Martin et sa femme et   Marye quelle ne scet sison dict mary reviendra
une aultre nommee Damiana
Lobata

Sur Roches le Voirrier   A l'opposite
                                  Anthoine Rodriguez Beatriz de Luzenne
Gracia Carzoros est icy passe   sa femme et quatre leurs enffans
deux ans
                                  arrivez environ depuis iiij moys
Sur damoiselle Ysabeau   Francisco Rodriguez et Violante sa femme
de Rosendale   et ung leur enffant

Vincent Lopez, Gracia Coree   En la mesmes Maison en hault
sa femme
Brigitta Lopez et Ysabella   Anthonio Rodrigues Andrade
ses seurs
                                  Blanca Rodrigues sa femme avec
En la chambre hault   deux leurs enffans. Ledict Anthoine
Fernande Coree et Leonora   nest trouve a lhostel
Coree sa seur

En la mesme chambre
○   Emmanuel Lopez,
Beatrix Fernandiz
et leurs deux enffans

Sur la chambre derriere

Examine Douart Rodriguez et Beatrix
        sa femme
        Roderigo leur filz et <encores>
        ung jeusne b[astar]d
        [appelle Antonio]

En la maison de la veufve   Registre du Procureur General
de feu
Francisco Mendes

Alberto eaige de 14 ans
Diego eaige de 12 ans
Beatrix Vas cuisiniere
Elena et Violenta jeusnes filles
Tous pour la service de sa
maison
Giomar Pintiaga,
femme de Bras Fernandiz,
Eleonora Gracia et Violenta ses
trois filles

En la maison de Augustin
Enriques

Emanuel Renel
Eleonora Henriques sa femme
Ung enffant eaige de deux ans
avec la nourrice

En la maison de Christofle
Garcia

George Fernandez
Anna Laynes sa femme
Jeronimo leur filz

Venuz pardeça depuis
le xv^e
de ce mois de juillet

examine   Pedro Fernandiz
Idem   Manoel son serviteur
Idem   Jsabel Rodriguez
Idem   Hector Pignero
Idem   Jsabel Nunes
Idem   Jsabel Beraldis

Et a Middelburg en Zeelande le
Lieutenant a pris
une femme avec la fille
et deux jeusnes compaignons

Source: AGR,Bx, OFB 160/1233/2.

[Document 54]

[Official report on the interrogations and depositions of Diego
Fernandiz Netto – August 1 1544]

Confession de Diego Fernandez Netto qui se fest auparavant faict
nommer Diego de Roma, faicte en la ville danvers le premier jour daust,
pede ligato et medio iuramento, pardevant nous don Francisco darragon,
Tisnac, du Fief et de la Torre

Diego Fernandiz Netto eaige de XL ans ou environ, sermente, dict
estre natif de Lolle en Portugal, et avoir eu pour pere Alvaro Fernandiz,
trespasse ~~apr~~ environ xxiiij ou xxv ans, natif de Lisbone, et pour mere
Isabelle Oliveri, natifue dudict Lolle, a present en ceste ville, ayans
sesdicts pere et mere du passe tenu leur residence et domicille en lisle de
Saint Michel et Madera.

Dict avoir eu deux freres, Christophe et Garcia trespassez des leur
jeusnesse, et une ~~une~~ seulle seur, Branca Fernandiz, a present veufve de
feu Henrico de Negro, licencie es droix, trespasse audicte Lisbone.

Dict estre marye passe cincq ou six ans avec Agnes Gomez, fille de
Manuel Gomez trespasse depuis trois ou iiij ans, et de Missia Fernandiz,
de present en ceste ville avec ladicte Agnes sa fille. Et avoir tenu sa
residence avant se maryer esdictes isles de Madera et Saint Michel et
depuis en Libonne ou il a reside avec sa femme environ lespace dung an,
et avoir este chanoine esdictes isles en l'eglise cathedrale de Sonchal
environ dix ou xii ans, et delaisse ladicte prebende librement sans prouffit
et en avoir dispose dicelle le Roy de Portugal comme patron, mais navoir
jamais receu aucun ordres ecclesiastique et avoir renonce a ladicte
prebende, pour poursuyr les affaires et proces que son pere avoit delaisses
avant son trespas, ayant icelluy son pere este esdictes isles facteur du Roy.
Et que il qui parle na jamais eu aulcune offre audict lieu ne ailleurs au
Royaulme de Portugal et que les susdicts affaires et proces estoient contre
gens particulier et non contre ledict Roy.

Dict estre parti dudict Lisbone passe iiij ou v ans vers Rome et ce a
la requeste de certains marchans portugais, assavoir: Jorge Lopez, Nuño
Henriquez et Thomas Saran, nouveaux christiens, lesquelz avoient este
excommuniez a Rome, a linstance de Diego /f. 1v/ Antonio, demandans
aux susdicts la somme de trois mille deux cens ducats (avec les changes
et rechanges) pour les mises faictes par luy a cause de certaine bulles que

ledict Antonio substenoit avoir obtenu en ladicte court Rome en faveur desdicts marchands, laquelle bulle iceulx marchans soustenoient daultre couste nestre impetre par leur commandement.

Icelle bulle venue premierement es mains de lambassadeur du Roy de Portugal et depuis dudict Roy. ~~Mais~~ ne scet il qui parle en façon quil soit du contenu en icelle, sinon que ledict Diego Antonio soustenoit en son proces quelle estoit en faveur deulx, non scachant il qui parle a quelle fin tendoit ladict faveur, considere quil na jamais veu ladicte bulle, ne copie dicelle, combien que luy semble assez quelle debuoit moderer aulcuns articles de Linstitution de la nouvelle inquisition ordonnee en Portugal.

Dict estre alle *libere et sponte sua* en ladicte court pour solliciter seulement laffere susdict, et quil najamais commis aulcune crisme ne homicide audict Portugal ou lisle de Madere, parquoy il deubt abandonner le pays.

Dict aussi avoir accepte ladicte sollicitation pour remedier a sa pouvrete et pour myeulx maintenir ses mere, femme et soeur et quil a este tousiours audict Portugal et ailleurs *boni nominis et fame.*

Dict quil ne sest jamais mesle audict Rome daultre affaire touchant les nouveaux christiens, sinon le susdict particulier. Lequel il a tellement poursuy que [les] parties se sont appoinctees a Deuxmill iiij^c [= 2,400] ducats.

Et combien que laffaire que il qui parle poursuivoit tant fellicement a la charge des susdicts, que touteffois la bulle dont est esme*** le proces concernoit en general a tous les nouveaux christiens.

Dict que les susdicts luy avoient promis pour son salaire durant la sollicitation dudict proces trois cens ducats par an et luy faire ~~aultre~~ beaucoup de bien en cas quil gagnasst icelluy et quil y a deux ans passes quil a faict ledict appoienctement et que ledict Diego Antonio a este paye de la susdicte somme mectant la excommunication a neant par les mains propres de luy qui parle, ayant a cest effect receu lettres de change a luy envoiees dudict Lisbon par Lucas Girardi marchant. /f. 2r/

Dict que les susdicts marchans luy doibvent encorres deux ans de son salaire, lequel il est delibere demander par justice audict Rome, avec ce quils luy ont promis sil gaignait ledict proces.

Et na il qui parle, depuis ledict appoinctement, sollicite en ladicte court nulz aultres affaires, sinon une dispensation pour ledict Thomas Saron pour ung mariaige ~~de~~ <en> *secundo et tertio consanguinitatis grado.*

Dict navoir cogneu Duarte Pais, ne scavoir sil a este solliciteur en la dicte court des affairs des nouveaux christiens, mais quil a bien oy dire, que ledict Pays, ayant certain proces alencontre deulx, non sachant a quelle occasion, sinon selon quil a oy dire ausdicts nouveaux christiens, quilz se delaingnoient de luy, et ne scet ou icellui duarte est trespasse, si non par oy dire, au camp de l'empereur en Hongrie. Ne scet aussi si le susdict Diego Antonio a este successeur aux affairs dudicte Duarte, mais dict que il qui parle na jamais este successeur des susdicts es semblables affairs et que ledict Diego est nouveau crestien, layant laisse a son partement a Rome, non scachant si les deux susdicts ayent traictez aultres affairs desdicts nouveaux christiens.

Dict avoir este detenu prisonnier au chasteu de St. Ange a Rome et este delivre au mois de septembre dernier, et quil a este prisonnier pour avoir envoie certaines lettres par ung pieton aux susdicts trois marchans, contenans quil avoit donne pour servire aux faveurs deulx a certain Nonce apostolique venesien, allans lors audict Portugal, non scachant son nom, deux ~~mille~~ ducats, lesquelles lettres seroient este prinses et delivrees au roy de Portugal que les auroit envoie apres a nostre Sainct pere le pape, et come il fut mande devers sa Sanctite luy demandant sil, ou pourquoy il avoit escript lesdictes lettres, respondit quil les avait escript affin de recouvrer par ce moyen ce que les susdicts marchans luy debuoient a cause de la sollicitation et promesse susdictes, leur donnant a entendre par les susdictes lettres et contre verite avoir donne lesdicts mille ducats, affin quilz luy renvoyassent ladicte somme comme par luy desboursee, considere quil ne pouvoit aultrement parvenir a ce que luy estoit deu par eulx. /f. 2v/

Interrogue quelle chose contenoient plus avant les dictes lettres, veu que pour icelles il fut constitue prisonnier, et quelle chose y avoit prejudiciable au pape ou au Roy, dict que riens et comme nostre Sainct pere vouiloit scavoir pourquoy il avoit donne audict nonce lesdicts mille ducats, respondit quil luy navoit donne riens, ayans seullemnt use de telle invention a la fin que dessus et dict que pour nulle aultre cause il avoit este constitue prisonnier, ny daultre chose avoir este accuse, comme aussi il na eu aulcun proces contre pour ceste matiere, mais quil a este delivre a lordonnance de notre Sainct pere lequel a sa ~~rela~~ relaxation la banny per[pe]tuellement de Rome, sans y adjouster pague en cas de contravention, non scachant que sondict emprisonnement a este faict a la sollicitation du Roy de Portugal.

Dict navoir jamais este aggresse daulcuns serviteurs de lambassadeur dudict Roy en la court de Rome, considere que il qui parle a este tousiours bon serviteur du Roy, mais quil a bien oy dire que Duarte Pays avoit este aggresse et bleses de xx pleines.

Dict estre venu pardeça cincq ou six jours devant la derniere armee de Portugal et ce pour venir trouver jcy sa femme avec tout son mesnaige et tenir en ceste ville son domicile et demeure et que a ceste fin il avoit evocque icy sa mere et femme et aussi escript a sa belle mere et sa propre seur que si elles vouloient venir en compaignie de sadicte femme avec leur mesnaige, quil les favoriseroit pardeça comme a sa propre mere et femme et que ainsi seroient venues a intention de demeurer icy et non passer plus oultre et quil intendoit le mesmes de son beau frere Rederiguo.

Interrogue ou est laultre son beau frere nomme Arias, dict quil est alle de son franc vouloir et sans instigation ou adresse de luy qui parle en Italie ~~po~~ pour chercher sa vie et quil ne luy a donne aulcunes lettres et pense quil est alle au camp de lempereur ou a Venise comme desirant veoir le monde.

Dict aussi que sadicte femme nest partye dudict Portugal pour aulcune crainte de linquisition et quelle ne scet tenue occultement audict Lisbone avant son dict partement, mais quelle est alle les /f. 3r/ dimanches et festes a la messe et que les femmes dudict pays ne sont accoustumees de guaires hanter les rues et principalement en labsence de leurs marys et quil a entendu de sadicte femme quelle est venue publiquement et ainsi aussi embarquee.

Dict que sadicte femme a este prinse a la Vere, non scachant a quelle occasion, si nest au pourchas de quelcun de ses ennemys qui pouroient estre venuz avec ladicte armee et comme il qui parle sest a ceste occasion trouve audict Vere et faict ses plainctes dudict emprisonnement a Monseigneur de Beneres et que sadicte femme avec son assistence a este incontinent delivree et ce le mesme jour de son arrivee audict Vere gratuitement, sinon quil a donne a la seur dudict Seigneur ung verre deaux odorante.

Dict avoir eu une lettre de recomandation du facteur de Portugal a Francisco Pissoa, si daventure il eussist eu affaire de quelque faveur ou assistence et que nulluy de ceste ville estalle avec luy, combien que Jehan Micas est alle ~~en la~~ <a> mesme charrot avec luy, mais pour solliciter ses affaires propres, et dict navoir veu illec Augustin Henrriques sinon quil a bien oy dire quil y estoit venu aussi pour ses affaires.

Dict avoir obtenu certain breve apostolique depuis sa relaxation lequel il a envoye a sa femme en Lisbone, contenant que le pape mandoit a ung chacun de laisser passer sa femme avec sa famille par tous le lieux de la cristiennete pour venir a Rome, sans luy donner aulcun empeschement pour cause que ce fut, mesmement dheresie ou apostasye et a sadicte femme laisse icelluy breve au Ecoutette dudict Vere et est demeure en ses mains pour lequel reavoir apres son emprisonnement en ceste ville a envoie dicy ung jeusne garson momme Andrea Rodrigues estans venu pardeça avec sadicte femme.

Dict que les susdicts motz dheresye ou Judaisme, y estoient contenuz non pour ce que sa femme ou luy avoient de ce leurs consciences chargees mais la voulu avoir ainsi en ample forme, a plus abundante cautele et que telles amples formes sont bien necessaires audict Portugal, veu les cavillations et malveillances que lon y faict audict Portugal aux nouveaux christiens . /f. 3v/

Interroge comment il a peult obtenir ledict bref apres son banissement, lequel comme dessus il a declaire fut fait au temps de sa relaxation, dict quil nestoit banny au temps de sa relaxation mais, estant delivre, que luy furent accordez aulcuns jours pour fer ses affaires, assavoir environ deux mois, pendant lesquelz il a obtenu ledict brief, apres limpetration duquel luy auroit este intime ledict banissement.

Interrogue puis quil est banny de Rome, pourquoy il a envoie a sa femme ledict breve, dict seullement affin que par le moyen dicelluy sadicte femme puist tant plus facilement sortir hors dudict Portugal combien quelle na use dicelluy pour ce quil nestoit besoing, et que tous nouveaux christiens peulvent librement avec femme ou enffans sortir hors dudict royaulme sans congie et principalement quant ils non sont de rien coulpables, dict navoir la copie dudict breve ne sa femme aussi.

Interrogue sil na nul memoire ou instruction pour faire le voyage dicy en Italie, dict que non et quil ne scet que aulcuns de sa famille ayent aulcun en sa maison et en cas que aulcun y soit trouve ne scet a qui il est. Et apres luy avoir monstre ledict memorial et demande sil ne le cognoissoit point ou lescripture, dict que non. Aussi, luy ayant monstre certain petit voire rond de cristallain contenant la figure ou image de diable trouve par le procurateur entre ses secrets et joyaulx et interrogue que chose ne veult estre et sil estoit a luy, dict en soubriant quil la trouve en sa maison esmains dun petit enffant et quil ne sert a rien si non a faire poeur aux enffans …

Dict que a son partement de Lisbone vers Rome na emporte avec luy nulz deniers, sinon autant quil avoit afaire pour son voyage.

Dict navoir aultre breve ou bulles apostoliques que le susdict. Interrogue porquoy il mengeoit indifferement les vendredis et samedis avec tout son mesnaige de la chair, dict nen avoir jamais menge en ceste ville ne ailleurs, ne semblement sa femme, mere ou seur quil sache.

Source:AGR,Bx,OFCB, B.160/1233/2.

[Document 55]
[Official report on the interrogations and depositions of the Portuguese immigrants imprisoned in Antwerp – 1544

Recueil de tout ce que se trouve substantial par information contre le nouveaux christiens detenus prisonniers par le procureur general de Brabant

[1] Le Roy de Portugal a faict publier par tout son Royaulme [un decret] que nulz cristiens [nouveaux] en sortissent avec femme ou enffans sans congie.
> Jl appert de ce, tant que pour souffire, par les depositions de neuf tesmoings, combien quils ne accordent quant au commencement du temps dicelle pubblication.

[2] Prohibition a este faicte par l'inquisition aux capitaines et maistres des navires de ne admettre nulz cristiens [nouveaux] ainsi accompagnez et a ceste fin ont este visitees les naves par les officiers dicelle [inquisition].
> Cest article se veriffie aussi souffisement par plusieurs tesmoings et mesmement bien jusques au nombre de trente et ung.

[3] La cause du partement desdicts nouveaux cristiens est, selon la commune voix et fame, de crainte de l'Inquisition.
> Se veriffie bien par xvi tesmoings et disent alcuns davantaige que cest pour par ce pays passer plus oultre, mesmement vers la Judee. Jl y a aussi alcuns aultres faisant mention de la riguer dont use ladicte jnquisition a present.

[4] Lesdicts nouveaux cristiens sont entrez au temps de leur embarquement sur ou aprez soleil couchier et depuis es grandes navires de nuyct.

Ainsi tous les tesmoings, mesmement plusieurs de ceulx que les ont amenez, concordent en ce et les prisonniers qui sont interroguez ne le nyent en leurs confessions.

[5] Ilz ont paye beaucoup plus pour voiture que les aultres passagiers venuz avec l'armee ou la derniere flote.

De ce deposent assez conformement plusieurs tesmoings bien interrogues au nombre de xj.

/f. 1v/

[6] Et sont entrez secretement et sur le soir apres le son de cloche dedens la ville d'Anvers

Veriffie que les xixe et xxie tesmoings portiers de ladicte ville et adtoustent [sic !] que une compagnie ayt payee jusques a ung ducat pour lentree.

Et a lieu ladicte preuve en general contre tous ceulx qui sont a present detenuz prisonniers combien que aulcuns deulx ont pour eulx preuve davoir este de bonne fame et renommee en Portugal avant le partement et avoir tousiours verse en publique jusque audict temps.

[7] Il y a aulcuns desdicts prisonniers et bien jusques a vii ou viii qui ont fait appareil pour aller a Coulongne et de la en Italye estant dintention d'aller touttefois ver dehors de cristiennette, jusques a trouver lieu commodieux pour gagner leur vye.

Cest article appert par les confessions propres diceulx et cest pardessu ladicte preuve generale de fuyte militante aussi contre eux. Il y a aussi aulcunes lettres contentant le voyage devers ledict quartiers mais nest encoires veriffie es mains desquelz ont este trouvees et confessent plusieurs desdicts prisonniers avoir este ciconsis avant baptisme.

[8] Sebastien Fernandiz avec sa famille et aultres logez en la mesme maison ont depuis leur residence en la ville d'Anvers plus solemnize le

samedi que aultre jours de la sepmaine, usant a tel jour de leurs meilleurs habillements comme aultres cristiens sont accoustoumez de faire la dimences.

Contre iceulx a premierement aussibien ladicte preuve generale de fuyte et pardessu icelle se veriffie le contemu jci par les deposition dune meschine et d'une nourrice ayans servi en la maison ou lesdicts familles ont demeurees depuis leur venue, combien que ledict Sebastien et ung aultre nomme Pierre Loys ont pour eulx plusieurs tesmoings deposant comme jls ont verse en publique avant leur partement et deux ou trois deposent que ledict Sebastien auroit jllec este repute pour homme de bien. Il y a touteffois antre eulx ung appelle Diego Manuel qui confesse avoir este delibere daller jusqua Aix pour son indisposition et dela a [***] avec femme et enffans esperant rencontrer lieu commodieux pour gaigner sa vie.

[9] Diego Fernandis Netto aultrement dict de Roma avec sa famille et compagnie a depuis sa demeure en Anvers menge chair les vendredy et samedy et, pardessus ce, solemnize le samedy comme les precedens.

Pardessus ladicte generalite de fuyte militant contre tous ceulx de cette compagnie (saulf ledict Diego qui vient de Rome) se veriffie le contenu jcy par lesdictes deux femmes. Davantaige aulcunes lettres ont este trouvees es mains d'alcuns de ceste compagnie combien quil nest encores veriffies es mains desquelz, faisans mention du voyage pour aller vers Italie et une aultre par vers Ancone, laquelle ne contient subscription ne superscription. Et quant a la personne dudict Diego il confesse apres son enprisonnement [que a] este banni de Rome par ordre [du] sainct pere le pape combien que la cause pour laquelle il auroit selon sa confession este banni ne sembleroit estre legitime. Le lxiii^e tesmoing depose que ledict Diego ayt este mis en prison audict Rome (y estant lors il deposant) et, comme lon disoit, pour estre coulpe de judaisme et pour avoir envoie en Portugal quelques lettres prejudiciable a nostre Sainct pere et au Roy desquelles lettres ledict Diego confesse assez et mesmement que pour icelles il a este constitue prisonnier mais il nie ledict prejudice. Et a aussi este trouve en son comptoir ou lieu secret une figure de diable en certain voire de cristallain mais nest encores veriffie si cest espert familier ou aultre chose ridicule. La femme dudict Diego a aussi un bref apostolique par luy obtenu pour aller avec sa famille a Rome, sans pouvoir estre detenue ou empeschee en chemin pour cause de crisme quel qui fut, mesmement d'heresie ou judaisme. Et est le dict Diego fort suspect pour avoir sollicite en Rome les affairs des nouveaux cristiens combien quil nappert quil ayt sollicite chose prejudiciable ou altrement contre raison.

[10] Manuel Pignero a este brusle en figure en Lisbone.
Plusieurs tesmoings, et bien jusque au nombre de vingt, deposent de ce par oy dire, et y a ung qui dict avoir veu sa figure comme de brusle en Leglise de Sainct Dominique en Lisbone combien quil adjouste n'oser affirmer que ce soit le dessusdict.

[11] Manuel Fernandiz natif de Porto a este brusle par figure audict Porto.
Le viii^e [tesmoing] dict lavoir veu brusler en figure et se nommer Manuel ou Gabriel et designera son logis en Anvers. Le xe [tesmoing] dict avoir bien cogneu en Portugal Gabriel Fernandiz et avoir veu sa figure en leglise de Saint Dominique et estre ce tout notoire audict Portugal. /f. 2v/

[12] Fernando Galindo orfevre est venu par de ça estant son pere semblement brusle en ~~statue~~ corps.
Le xxiiii^e, xxxvii^e et lvi^e [tesmoings] concordent assez davoir uy dire que ledict pere ayt este brusle ~~par figure~~ <par corps> et le xxvii^e parle de veue.

[13] Henrique Tovar est venu pardeça estant son pere semblement brusle en ~~figure~~ corps
Le lviii^e [tesmoing] dict lavoirr ainsi uy dire

[14] Diego ou Alfonso Ximenes a este brusle en figure avant que venir pardeça. Lequel doibt jcy demeurer aupres de la bourse neufve.
Le lviii^e [tesmoing] le depose par uy dire.

[15] Le docteur Dionisio a este brusle en figure en Lisbone. Mais il est mort, combien qu'il y doibt avoir de ses enffans en Anvers.
Le lviii^e et le lxi^e [tesmoings] par uy dire et le lx^e [tesmoing] lavoir veu ainsi brusler.

[17] La femme de Denys ~~Mendes~~ Gomes a este bruslee en figure et enterree en Anvers aux Carmes en terre vierge, que est la facon d'enterrer les mortes entre les Juyfz. Mais ledict Denis est encores resident en ceste ville.

> Le lx^e [tesmoing] avoit uy dire quelle a este bruslee en figure et le lxi^e [tesmoing] avoir de ce receu lettres de Portugal et tous deux deposent lavoir veu ainsi enterrer. /f. 3r/

[18] Touchant la Synagogue que seroit en ceste ville d'Anvers.

> Le xviii^e [tesmoing] dict avoir uy dire qu'il y en a une [Synagogue], non sachant ou, et que sa femme avoit uy dire le semblable. Le lx^e lavoit semblement uy dire et quelle seroit pret de Carmes aupres la maison de Jehan de Haro. Le ix^e dict que en la maison de Jehan Caldero flameng se font plusieures congregations de nouveaux cristiens, mais ne scet a quel fin.

[19] En la maison de Diego Mendes l'on ne serait accoustume manger poison ou poulletz venuz mortz du marche, mais seroit tousiours fecte envoie et que ledict Diego et les principaulx de sa maison ne seroient accoustumez menger que ce que auroit este tue par ung quidam nomme Rben [*sic* !] Pinto et que les samedi chacuns se seroit tenu secretement en leurs chambres.

> Le lviii^e [tesmoing] l'avoir ainsi uy dire par une femme appellee Marie qui y avoit servie du vivant dudict Diego laffaire dung an et demy. Ceste Marie na este oye pour estre a present a Bruges.

[On the reverse of the sheet:]
Informations prises contre les nouveaux Crispiens.

Source: AGR,Bx, OFB, 160/1233/2.

[Document 56]
Queen Mary to Dom João III, King of Portugal – October 18, 1544]

Serenissimo Rey,

Bien pienso vuestra Serenidad havra entendido la muchadumbre de la gente, assi de casados como solteros, que se dizen christianos nuevos, huydas a ca de sus tierras y regnos de Portugal. Los quales, por la mucha presumpçion que teniamos contra ellos (pues llegaron aqui abscondidamente y de noche) hemos mandados tomar presos a todos y que contra ellos se hiziese informaçion para saber quienes e quales eran. Por la qual y sus proprias confessiones hallamos todos haver se retirados de alla sin liçençia contra la prohibiçion y mandamientos de Vuestra Serenidad y, que pejor es, secretamente y de noche. De que estamos muy maravillada. Y hallandose por la sobredicha informaçion grandissima presumption contra muchos dellos de Judios, apostatas y malos chrispianos, y siendo la provas flacas y no bastantes para condenar los por tales, acuerdamos considerando que de alla podriamos sacar la verdad de todo, avisar lo a Vuestra Serenidad ruegando la fuese servida en fabor de la Justiçia y para que los justos no padescan por los ruynes e pecadores, de mandar tomar en su Reyno informaçion complida sobre los dichos huydos, cuyos nombre y sobrenombres van juntamente con la presente[1], haziendo en en esto toda la diligençia y brevedad que mejor paresçiere a Vuestra Serenidad, hubiando nos las informaçiones selladas por su sello Real y hallende la obra muy meritoria, Vuestra Serenidad nos hara com ello muy singular plazer. La qual nuestro señor guarde y sus reinos prospere y aumente como dessea.

De Bruxellas a xviij° de octobre de 1544 anos.

  Votre humble et bonne […] cousine

  Marie

  De la Torre Verreyhzen (?)

[At the bottom of the sheet:]

Al Rey de Portugal para haver informaçion complida contra los christianos nuevos presos en Enberes

Source: AGR,Bx, OFB 160/1233/2.

1) No copy of this list is preserved in the file.

[Document 57]
[Queen Mary to Prince Henrique, General Inquisitor of Portugal – October 19, 1544]

Ill.mo Jnfante,

Avisamos al serenissimo Rey de Portugal, nuestro muy caro y amado hermano, como de pocos meses a ca han venido huyendo en esta terras muchos christianos nuevos de los de su Reyno, y que contra ellos, por la informaçion que hemos mandado hazer, ay grandissima presumption de Judios, apostatas y malos Xanos, pero que los testigos que dello para aqui ay, son de oyda y no de vista y assi no bastante para condenar les [*sic!*] por tales. Ruegando a Su Serenidad mandase tomar alla otra informaçion mas cunplida contra los sobredichos cuyos nombre y sobrenombres le enbiamos y porque desseamos castigar los malos y sueltar los buenos y sabiendo como Vuestra Ill.ma Señoria era cabeça de la Santa Inquisiçion en el reyno de Portugal, ha nos pareçido avisar le lo mismo, para que con su fabor y assistençia se haga alla la dicha informaçion con tal diligençia y brevedad que en este negoçio vera ser necçesario, y no dudando lo hara assi, hare esta breve remetiendo me a lo de mas a la carta del dicho Serenissimo Rey y reçebir dello singular plazer.

Nuestro señor la persona y estado de vuestra Ill.ma Señoria guarde y aumente come dessea.

Hecha en Bruxelas a xix^e de octubre de 1544 anos.

Votre bonne […] cousine
Marie
De la Torre Verreyhzen

Source: AGR,Bx, OFB 160/1233/2.

[Document 58]
[Queen Mary to the Portuguese Inquisitor Dom João de Melo – October 19, 1544]

Don[1] Juan de Melo

Escrivemos por el presente al Serenissimo Rey de Portugal nuestro muy caro y muy amado hermano y al Ill.mo Jnfante Don Henrique Inquisidor major de la Santa Inquisisçion, como entenderas por nuestra cartas. Requeremos os por el serviçio de dios y fabor de la justiçia que conforme a la neçesidad del negoçio, tomeyes cargo que se haga alla la informaçion contra los nuevo christianos llegados en esta tierra cuyos nombres y sobrenombres enbiamos aldicho Ser.mo Rey y nos hareys en ello mucho plazer. Nuestro señor su persona guarde. De Bruxellas a xix^e de octubre de 1544 anos.

Marie
De la Torre Verreyhzen

Source: AGR,Bx,OFB 160/1233/2.

_____

1. Don (*Spanish*), Dom in *Portuguese*.

[Document 59]
[Queen Mary to the Portuguese Inquisitor Dom Juan de Melo –
October 19, 1544]

Jnstruction et advertissement pour Monsieur Jehan Melo
directeur de la Saincte Inquisition au Royaulme de Portugal

Premierement se tiendra ledict Seigneur Jehan adverti comment tant
en Zeelande que en la ville danvers sont arrivez bon nombre dhommes
femmes avecq leurs enfans et famille venans du dict Royaulme comme il
confessent.

Item que leur partement ~~appointement~~ a este secret et couvert, qui a
donne a la majeste de la Royne douaigiere occasion de suspicion mesmes
a cause de la multiplicite.

Parquoy ladicte majeste sa faict informer de la cause de leur retraicte,
quelles gens ce povoient estre et du movement de se trouver es pays bas.

Que, comme par information sur ce tenue, sont este trouve que
ledictes personnes estoient tous cristiens nouveaux que celeement et
oultre les ordonnances du Roy e de ladicte Inquisition ilz estoient party
dudict Royaulme craindans estre atteintz par par ladicte Inquisition
dappostasie et Judaisme. A ladicte majeste ordonne mectre la main sur
iceulx. /f. 1v/

Et par ce que continuant plus oultre lesdictes informations lon trouve
que linquisition susdicte faisant ses debvoirs a en partye descouvert ceulx
qui audict Royaulme serroient retournez <a Judaisme> ~~en leur prisme
sentiments et credulite~~ appostasiant en notre saincte fois catolique y ayant
trouve grosses faultes de sorte que certain nombre desdict nouveaux
cristiens soyent este executes <par> le feu, plus grant nombre receu a
penitence salutaire et aultres bruslez en estatue ou figure a cause de leur
latitation fuyte et absence de leurs personnes comme convencus dheresie.

Ladicte majeste tenant assez manifeste et certain que lesdictes
personnes arrivez et detenuz, (et lesquellez confessent leur retraict estre
pour crainte de ladicte Inquisition) que ilz se tiennent chargez culpables
comme aultres descouvers, a ordonne que les officiers de lempereur
feront debvoir de se enquester de tant ce que peult duyre en ceste matiere.

Et aussy que la principalle preusve gist sur certains poinctz dont la
certitude se trouvera audict Royaulme de Portugal et mesmement ~~se
pourra trouver~~ par la besoingne de ladicte inquisition, a par sa Majeste

este ordonne de concepvoir cestuy advertissement et instruction et de requerir la Majeste du Roy, linquisiteur de la foy et ledict Seigneur Jehan de envoyer a sadicte Majeste attestation des poinctz qui sen suyvent affin que par faulte de debvoir, ~~lesdicts~~ <telz> appostatz en la saincte foiz ne demeurent impuniz.

Premiers: si par ladicte Majeste du Roy et de semblable de la part de linquisition ne soit este defendu que nulz nouveaulx christiens ne sortiroient du Royaulme du Portugal mesme avecq femmes et <ou> famille sans expres conge de la dite Majeste et inquisition, et quant lesdictes deffences sont advenues.

Item se N.N.N.N. partiz sans conge et licence (come ilz confessent) ne sont estez ou alcuns deulx par alcuns leurs consors accusez de faillir et errer en nostre saincte foy cristienne et destre retournez en leur ancien ~~xyxyxy~~ sentement et <Judaisme> en icelle nostre foiz appostasiant.

Item en avenement que cy, si tous sont chargez ou lesquelz dentre eulx, desquelz lieux ilz sont en Portugal, de quelle parente et dont ilz se soloient mesler.

Item silz ou aucuns deulx ne sont par ladicte Inquisition este attainctz devant leur partement ~~estans~~ <ayans este> receupz en penitence, ou a loccasion de leur latitation et fuge apres <leur fuyte> condempnez et executez em estatue ou figure.

Item si apres leur partement il ny ayt sur eulx ou aulcuns deulx este trouve matiere pour attaindre lesdicts apprehendez et detenuz, combien que ladicte Inquisition encore naye procede a aulcune declaration ou condempnation.

Item en advenement que charge soit trouve sur lesdicts detenuz, soit que condempnation en soit ensuyvye ou non, <desire et prie ladite Majeste> que deue attestation luy en soye envoyee ~~en ladicte matiere~~ tant des declarations et sentences comme ~~de~~ verification des charges dont sentences et declarations ne seroient encores faictes ou donnees.

Item finablement attestation de la reputation que lon a entre les bons chistiens audict royaulme desdicts apprehendez, de leur vie, conduyte et hantise.

Source: AGR,Bx, OFB 160/1233/2.

[Document 60]
[An (incomplete) list of Portuguese immigrants arrested in Flanders in
November 1544]

Henriques Jorge, thirty-three years old, his wife Eleanor Pinhero, and
their three children;
Emanuel Pinhero, a thirty years old man, his wife Beatrix Antunis, his
mother Catharina Gomez, Jorge Pinhero brother of Emanuel;
Francisco Nuñes, his wife Gracia Fernandes and his young daughter
Anna;
Hector Pinhero, 38 years old, his wife Eleanora Rodrigues, their two
children;
Pero Fernandes, Elisabet Bernaldis, Elisabet Nuñes, their niece, their
servant Emanuel.

Source: drawn up by the editor on the basys of documents preserved at
AGR,Bx, OFB, 160/1233.

[Document 61]
[Queen Mary to the Emperor – July 1547]

Quant aux nouveaulx crestiens quj viennent journellement de
Portugal en Anvers, ilz passent continuellement dudit Anvers en France et
dez la, comme lon dit, vuers Ferrare, sans que on scait riens alleguer
contre eulx, entant quilz se disent bons crestiens et sciavent generalement
respondre de la foy crestiene, combien que la presumption soit grande
quilz ne se retirent dudit Portugal en si grand nombre, sans estre
grandement suspectz. Et quant on les interrogue, pourquoy ilz se retirent,
disent quilz le font pour avoir meilleure commodite de vivre, non
saichans gaigner leur vye audit Portugal que nest vraysemblable. Jen ay
par ci devant fait parler au facteur de Portugal pour y remedier, mesmes
que si le roy de Portugal vouloit deffendre leur partement de Portugal et
pourvoir par publication que on se confermeroit de ce coste, mais quil
nestoit de cest advis, et luy sembloit que on les debvoit laisser convenir et
que si par bonne maniere on les scavoit faire demeourer pardeça, que se
fut este bien fait, pour le proufit que les pays en recepvroit, par ce que ce
sont gens industrieulx. Ceulx Danvers se sont doluz du grant nombre qui
y arrive et quant je leur ay demande advis pour y porveoir ilz desiroient

que on leur eust accorde certain lieu vague ou ilz ont ragrandy la ville
pour illec ediffier et pour demeurer en portant une marcque comme font
les Juifz en allemaigne ce que je ne trouvay raisonable, car silz sont Juifz
votre majeste ne les vouldroit tollerer en vos pays mesmes les avoit fait
retirer de gheldres, et silz estoient cristiens on leur feroit tort fer porter
marcque.

Monseigneur, il y a grande presumption contre eulx qui sont vrays
Juifz quy petit a petit se retirent vers la Salonique, vres que on ne les
scait convaincre et pour y pourveoir ne voys autre remede que
entierement leur deffendre la hantize de voz pays. Mais en ce faisant est
a craindre que la negociation de voz pays diminuera entant que aulcun
deulx font grant train de marchandise. Vostre Majeste me pourra
commander son bon plaisir.

Source:AGR,Bx, PEA 1177, f. 90r.

[Document 62]
[The Queen-Regent approves the extra-judiciary settlement proposed by
Nuño Henriques and Henriques Nuñes – Sept. 1, 1547]

L'apppointement fait par la Royne a Nunez Henricx et Henry Nungnes
freres Nouveaulx Christiens

(f. 316) Comme Nunges Henricx et Henry Nungnes freres, chargiez
d'appostasye et de vivre judaicquement et a ceste cause destenuz
prisonniers par le Macrgrave danvers, combien quilz se disoyent estre
christiens nouveaulx vivans selon la foy christienne et les ordonnances et
constitutions de notre mere Saincte eglise, ayant fait faire plusieures
poursuytes devers la Royne Regente, afin destre ouys en justice et que
comme lon avoit prins information a leur charge, que aussy elle fut prinse
a leur descharge, ayant neantmoings depuis offert pour parvenir a la
relaxation de prison afin de povoir garder leur credit Envers les marchans
et eviter longeur de proces, payer au prouffit de lempereur la somme de
cent mil florins de vingt pattar piece, à payer a termes gratieulx,
moyennant que sa majeste leur accorde ensemble à leur femmes enffans,
/f. 316v/ serviteurs et famille, lettre d'abolition de tout ce que lon [a] leur
impose avec seurete et saulfcounduit de povoir continuer leur residence
es pays de pardeça le temps et espace de deux ans, et que au boult

diceulx ilz se pourroyent franchement retirer, ladicte Dame Royne aprez avoir faict veoir en conseil toutes les informations prinses en ceste matiere tant a charge que descharge, a consenty et ordonne que les dessusnommes Nungne Henricx et Henry Nungnes serons relaxez de prison moyennant et parmy ce quilz payeront au prouffit de lempereur ladicte somme de cent mil florins assavoir: ung tiers comptant, un autre tiers à la foire prouchaine et le iiime tiers à la foire froide de Berghes et que de ce il bailleront assignation et seurete daulcuns marchans residens en ceste ville et que oultre ce ilz payeront la somme de mil florins pour payer les despenses de justices. Et furnissant a ce que dessus, sa Majeste leur fera expedier et delivrer lettre dabolition de tous ce quon leur impose avec surete et saulfconduit de pouvoir continuer leur residence es pays de pardeça le temps et espace de deux ans a condition que, sil plaisoit à la Majeste quilz se retirassent plustot, ilz seront tenuz le faire trois mois apres linsinuation qui se fera apres le premier jours de mars et que alors ilz se pourront franchement retirer avecq leurs femmes, enffans serviteurs et familles ensemble leursdits biens bagues et marchandises et silz ne le poroient tous tout retirer avec eulz, quilz pourront lasser ung facteur pour en avoir la charge et administration.

Fe en la dicte ville danvers se premiers jour de septembre de xv^{c} xlvii

Source: AGR,Bx, PEA, Reg. 821, f. 316r–317r.

[Document 63]
[An (unnamed) officer of the Court to the Burgomaster of Antwerp –
August 5 1549]

Monsieur le Bourgmaistre, Estant sur mon partement pour venir. Jay receu lettres de Monseigneur d'Arras[1] qui mescript que lempeurer luy a demande si le placartz et edictz contre les nouveaux christiens estoyent publiez. Et comme il a certiffie a sa majeste que iceulx estoient despeschez et envoyez, ledit Seigneur d'Arras pour ny scavoir si la publication en est faicte ou non, ma de cecy adverti affin de men enquerir et luy escripre ce que en trouveray pour le faire entendre a sa Majeste dont, Messieur le Bourgomaistre, vous advise volentier a ce que me veuillez signiffier se la publication dudict placcart est faicte en Anvers. Et en cas que non, me semble que non obstant les raisons que me alleguastes au lieu de Ryplemonde, ferez bien de tenir main vers Messieurs vos confreres que ladite publication se faice sans ulterieure delation pour non donner mescontentement a sadite Majeste laquelle a laffaire a cueur plus que ne vous scauroye escripre et entend absolutement que lexecution dudict placcart se faice par tous le pays sans faveur ou dissimulation quelconque, a laquelle fin lont despesche les aultres placcarts[2] neantmoins, comme je vous diz, quant la publication sera faict aux Anvers, syl y a aulcuns desdicts nouveaulx christiens y venuz depuis six ans lesquelz y desirent demeurer, estans gens de bonne fame et renommee, vous le pourrez fer remonstrer a sa Majeste, laquelle en pourra dispenser ou aultrement ordonner, comme elle trouvera convenir …

    De Bruxelles ce vme daougst 1549.

Source: AGR,Bx,PEA 1177/1, f. 94.
1) Monseigneur d'Arras: Antoine Perrenot de Granvelle (son of Nicolas, the imperial State Secretary) at the time Bishop of Arras.
2) *les aultres placcarts*: copies of these documents are not preserved in the file.

[Document 64]
[An unsigned letter of a high officer of the Court to the Margrave of Antwerp – August 5, 1549]

Monsieur le Marcgrave,
    ceste sera pour vous advertir que lempereur veult et entend que le placcart des nouveaulx christiens soit pubbliye et estroittement observe, entretenu et execute contre les transgresseurs et desobeissants. Monseigneur le Bourgomaistre danvers et le pensionnaire mesmes se sont trouvez vers moy au lieu de Ryplemonde, remostrant plusieurs causes et raisons pour lesquelles nestoit expedient de faire la dite publlication, mais que pourtant ilz ne la debvoyent differer, affin de non donner mescontentement a sa majeste pour les causes que jescriptz audit Seigneur Bourgomaistre duquel pourrez entendre le surplus, Sur ce, Monsieur le Marcgrave, me r[ecomman]de de bon c[o]eur a vous, priant Dieu avoir en sa grace…
    De Bruxelles le vme daoust 1549.

Source, AGR,Bx, PEA 1177.

[Document 65]

[A Burgomaster of Antwerp informs an unnamed high officer of the Court that the authorities of Antwerp will publish the imperial *placard* – August 7, 1549]

Monsieur, Tres Chier et Honore Seigneur,

Apres mestre humblement recommande en votre bonne grace, … pour response a Vos lettre, quant au placcart mentione esdites votres nous avons differe la publication dicelluy et pour ce que a cause de limportance de laffaire nous sembloit ne le debuoir publier avant avoir remostre a sa Majeste la grand prejudice porte et dommage qui en pourra venir a la ville. A quelle fin avons envoye ung de noz pensionaires vers la court pour poursuyvre la surceance de la dite publication jusques a tant que eussions envoye ung des noz deputez vers sa Majeste pour linformer de tout. Ores, entendant lintention de sa Majeste que a toutte fin veult icelle estre publie, ferons icelle publier ce jourdhuy afin de nencourir lindignation de sadite Majeste et contrevenir a son bon plaisir, combien ne poussions celer que se ne plaist a sa Majeste de laisser avoir cours le train de marchandise en ceste ville, ne voyons le moyen comment la pouvoir tenir comme entendons plus amplement remoustrer et deduyre a sa Maeste. Et comme en ce et autres choses dimportance aurons a faire du poirt et assistence de bons amys, avons ceste confidence en vostre excellence que en ce que nous pourrez favouriser … apres vous avoir offert mon tres humble service, prieray le Createur [etc.]

Danvers ce vij^e daoust lan xv^c xlix. Et ainsi soubzscript E. Drost

Source, AGR,Bx, PEA 1177.

[Document 66]

[An undated (1549–50) list of New Christians presented by Manoel Lopez to the Office Fiscal de Brabant]

Manoel Rodriguez
Fernando Ximenez
Pedro da Veiga
Joan Rodriguez
Gaspar Rodriguez
Jorge Lopez

Viçente Lopez
Rodrigo Mendez
doctor Luis Nuñes
Salvador Nuñez
Duarte Rodriguez
Antonio de Noronha
Pedro Lopez
Duarte Pinel
Lionel Pardo
Dioguo Fernandez – este se chama Pedro Fernandez
Jorge Fernandez
Bernaldo Nunez
Manoel Pirez
Antonio Afonso
Bento Rodriguez – este se chama Pedro Rodriguez
Jeronimo Anriquez
Mestre Alvaro Solorgiao
Jeronimo Lindo
Francisquo Fernandez

[On the reverse of the sheet:]
Touchant l'affaire des nouveaux chretiens

Source, AGR,Bx,OFB, 160/1233/2. The document is composed of two loose, undated leaves.

[Document 67]
[A list of Portuguese New Christians mentioned in an official report to the Court (circa 1550) who were apparently allowed to remain in Antwerp after the 1549 expulsion]

Jeronimo Enriques
Francisco Alvarez
Pero Lopez
Rodrigo Mendez
Licenciado Antonio de Logronho
Lionel Pardo
Jorge Lopez

Mestre Alvaro Solorgiao
Duarte Rodrigues
Gaspar Rodriguez
Manoel Rodrigues
Pero Fernandez
Jeronimo Lindo
Gabriel Jacome
Jorge Mendez
Diego de Camargo
Manoel Manrique
Henrico de Tovar
Lopo Mendez
Fabio and Manoel Rodriguez
Louis Alvarez
Duarte Rodriguez
Christovão Garcia

Source: AGR,Bx,OFB 160/1233/2, compiled from an undated (*circa* 1550) report on the New Christians of Antwerp.

Bibliography[1]

ALVAREZ, M. F., *La España del Emperador Carlos V, 1500-1558, El Hombre, la politica Española, la politica europea* (TOMO XX de la *Historia de España diriga por R. M. PIDAL*) Madrid 1989.

ARBEL, B., *Trading Nations, Jews and Venetian in the Early Modern Eastern Mediterranean*, Brill, Leiden and New York 1995.

AMATUS LUSITANUS, *Amati Lusitani In Dioscoridis Anarzabei de medica materia libros quinque narrationes eruditissimae ...Cum rerum ac vocum memorabilium indice locupletissimo, Venetijs : ex officina Iordani Zilleti, 1557 cum privilegio Ill.mi Senati*, Venice 1557.

———— Curationum medicinalium *Amati Lusitani medici physici praestantissimi centuriae quatuor, quibus praemittitur Commentatio de introitu medici ad aegrotantem, Venetijs Valgrisi ... 1557*

ANSWAARDEN, R., *Les portugais devant le Grand Conseil des Pays-Bas (1460-1580)*, Paris 1991,

AZEVEDO, DE, J.L. *História dos christãos-novos portugueses*, Lisboa 1975.

BAIÃO,A., *A Inquisição em Portugal e no Brasil*, «AHP» IV, Lisboa 1906.

BARON, *A Social and Religious History of the Jews*, XIII: *Inquisition, Renaissance and Reformation*, New York and Philadelphia 1969.

BONAZZOLI, V., "Ebrei italiani, portoghesi, levantini sulla piazza commerciale di Ancona intorno alla metà del Cinquecento" in G. COZZI, ed., *Gli Ebrei a Venezia*, Milano 1987, pp. 727-770.

BONAZZOLI, V., *Una identità ricostruita. I Portoghesi ad Ancona dal 1530 al 15472*, «Zakhor» V, 2001-2002 , pp. 9-38:

BONFIL, R., *Rabbis and Jewish Communities in Renaissance Italy*, Oxford University Press, 1990.

---

1. This list does not include publications cited but once, with full bibliographical references, in the footnotes.

————— *The History of the Spanish and Portuguese Jews in Italy*, in H. BEINART, Edit., *Moreshet Sepharad, The Sephardi Legacy*, pp. 217-39.

BROOKS, Andrée Aelion, *The Woman who defied Kings, The life and times of Doña Gracia Nasi, A Jewish Leader during Renaissance*, St. Paul, Minnesota, 2002.

COOPERMAN, B.D., "Venetian Policy towards Levantine Jews and its broader Italian Context" in G. COZZI,*Gli Ebrei e Venezia, Secoli XIV-XVIII*, Milano 1987.

————— "Portuguese Conversos in Ancona: Jewish Political Activity in Early Modern Italy" in IDEM, Ed., *In Iberia and Beyond, Hispanic Jews between Cultures*, University of Delaware Press 1998, pp. 297-352.

JONGE, De, K. and JANSSENS, G., *Les Granvelle et les anciens Pays-Bas*, Leuven 2000.

DENUCÉ, Jean, *L'Afrique au XVIe siècle et le commerce anversois*, Anvers, De Sikkel, 1937.

FRÉDÉRICK, P., *Corpus Documentorum Inquisitionis Haereticae Pravitatis Neederlandicae*, 5 Vols., Ghent 1897-1902.

FREIRE, A.B. , *Noticias da Feitoria de Flandres*, Lisboa 1920.

GAYANGOS de, P., *Calendar of Letters and Despatches and State Papers relating to the negotiations between England and Spain preserved in the Archives in Simanca Vienna, Brussels and elsewhere under the direction of the master of the Rolls, (Henry VIII, 1542-43)* London 1890-1895.

GÉNARD, P.M.N.J., "Personen te Antwerpen in de XVIe eeuw voor het feit van religie gerechterlijk vervorlgt, lijst en ambtelijke bij-hoorige stukken, in *Antwerpsch Archievenblad* Vol. VII [undated, *circa* 1870], pp. 436-38.

GINZBURGER, E., "Marie d' Hongrie, Charles V, les veuves Mendes et les néo chrétiens", *REJ* 89, 1930, pp. 179-192.

GORIS, J.A. *Étude sur les colonies marchandes meridionales (Portugaises, Espagnoles, Italiennes) à Anvers, de 1488 à 1567. Contribution à l'histoire des débuts du capitalisme moderne*, Louvain 1925.

GOOSENS Aline, *Les inquisitions modernes dans les Pays-Bas Meridionaux 1520-1633, Tome I, La Legislation*, Editions de l'Université de Bruxelles, 1997.

GROTENFEND H. und ULRICHT T., *Taschenbuch der Zeitrechnung des deutschen Mittelalters und der Neuzeit*, Hannover 1960.

GRUNEBAUM BALLIN, P., *Joseph Nasi Duc de Naxos*, Paris 1968.

GUICCIARDINI, L., *Descrittione di tutti i Paesi Bassi*, Antwerp 1567.

HERCULANO, A., *History of the Origin and Establishment of the Inqulisition in Portugal* [transl. by J.C. Branner), New York 1972.

IOLY ZORATTINI, P.C., Edit., *Processi del S. Uffizio di Venezia contro Ebrei e Giudaizzanti, 1548-1734*, 14 Volumes, Firenze, Leo S. Olschki Editore, 1980-2000.

JONGE, De, K. and JANSSENS, G., *Les Granvelle et les anciens Pays-Bas*, Leuven 2000.

KAPLAN, Y., "The Social Function of the Herem in the Portuguese Jewish Comunity of Amsterdam" in J.MICHMAN and T LEVIE Eds., *Dutch Jewish History*, Tel Aviv 1984, pp. 111-156.

LANZ, K., *Coorrespondenz des Kaisers Karl V. Aus dem Königlichen Archiv und der Bibliothèque de Bourgogne zu Brüssels*, Vol. II, 1532-1549, Leipzig 1845

LAURENT, C.H. and LAMEERE, J., *Ordonnance des Pays-Bas, deuxieume série, règne de Carle Quint*, Vol.II, Bruxelles 1893.

LEMOS, M., *Amato Lusitano, A sua vida e a sua obra*, Porto 1907.

LEONI A. DI LEONE, *Gli Ebrei Sefarditi a Ferrara da Ercole I a Ercole II: nuove ricerche ed interpretazioni*:«RMI» LII, 1987 pp. 407-446.

———— *La Nazione Ebraica Spagnola e Portoghese negli Stati Estensi*, Rimini 1992.

———— "La diplomazia estense e l'immigrazione dei cristiani nuovi a Ferrara al tempo di Ercole II", *Nuova Rivista Storica*, 78, 2 1994, 294-326.

————, "Manoel Lopes Bichacho a XVIth century leader of the Portuguese Nation in Antwerp and in Pesaro", *Sefarad* 59, 1999, pp. 77-100.

————, *Per una storia della Nazione Portoghese ad Ancona ed a Pesaro* in Ioly Zorattini, edit. *La identità dissimulata*, Firenze 2000.

————, "Alcuni esempi di quotidiana imprenditorialità tra Ferrara Ancona e Venezia nel XVI secolo", Zakhor, IV, 2000, pp. 57-114.

————, La Nazion Portughesa corteggiata, privilegiata, espulsa e riammessa a Ferrara (1538-1550), *Italia, Studi e Ricerche sulla Storia la Cultura e la Letteratura degli Ebrei d'Italia*, Vol. XIII-XV, Jerusalem, The Magness Press, 2001, pp. 211–247.

MILANO, A., *Storia degli Ebrei in Italia*, Torino 1963

NAHON, G., « Amsterdam, métropole occidentale des Sefarades », *Cahiers Spinoza* III, 1979-80, pp. 15-50.

——, *Les "Nations"juives portugaises du Sud-Ouest de la France (1684-1791), Documents*, Paris 1981,

—— "L'impact de l'expulsion d'Espagne sur la comunauté juive de l'Ancienne France, 1550-1791" *Archives Juives, Revue historique*, 31 Janv. 1980 .pp 94-105.

PIRENNE, H., *Histoire de Belgique des origines à nos jours*, Tome II, *De la mort de Charles le Téméraire à la paix de Munster*, Brusselles s.d. [1950 ?].

RÉVAH, I.-S., "Les marranes portugais et l'Inquisition au XVIe siécle", *in* R. BARNETT, Editor, *The Sephardi Heritage*, London 1972, Vol. I, pp. 479-526.:

REZNIK, Jacob, *Le Duc Joseph de Naxos*, Paris 1936,

ROTH, C. *The History of the Jews of Italy*, Philadelphia 1946.

Roth, C., *Doña Gracia of the House of Nasi*, Philadelphia 1947 [Reprint 1977].

SALOMON, H. P., *Deux études portugaises / Two Portuguese Studies*, Braga 1991.

—— *Portrait of a New Christian, Fernão Álvares Melo, (1569-1632)*, Paris 1882.

SALOMON, H. P. and DI LEONE LEONI, A., "Mendes, Benvenisti, *De Luna, Micas, Nasci, the State of the Art"*, *Jewish Quarterly Review* 88, 1998 pp. 135-211.

SAMUEL, E., "London Portuguese Jewish Community: 1540-1753" R. Vigne and C. Littleto, Eds., *From Strangers to Citizens, The integration of Immigrant Communities in Britain, Ireland and Colonial America, 1550-1750*, Brighton 2002, pp. 239-246.

SEGRE, R., "La formazione di una Comunità Marrana: I Portoghesi di Ferrara" in *Storia d'Italia, Annali*, Vol. XI: *Gli Ebrei*, Torino, Einaudi Editore 1996

SIMONSOHN, S., *The Apostolic See and the Jews*, Toronto 1988-1991.

TAVARES, A.A., Edit., *Estudos Orientais, O Legado Cultural de Judeus e Mouros*, Lisbon 1991.

TAVARES, M. J. FERRO, *Judaísmo e Inquisição*. Lisboa, Editorial Presença, 1987a.

——, *Os Judeus em Portugal no século XV*. Lisboa, Editorial Presença 1987

————, "Para o estudo dos Judeus de Tras o Monte no seculo XVI: a primera geração de cristãos-novos", in *Cultura História e Filosofia*, Universidade Nova de Lisboa, IV, pp. 371-417.

TEIXEIRA PINTO, M.C., *Manuel Dias, um cristão-novo de Fronteira e as vicissitudes do seu tempo*, in A.A. TAVARES, Edit., *Estudos Orientais, O Legado Cultural de Judeus e Mouros*, Lisbon 1991, pp. 267-288.

TOAFF, A., "Nuova luce sui Marrani di Ancona", in E. TOAFF, Edit., *Studi sull'Ebraismo Italiano in memoria di C. Roth*, Roma 1974, pp. 261-80.

TRACY, D., "Heresy Law and Centralisation under Mary of Hungary: Conflict between the Council of Holland and the Central Government over the Enforcement of Charles V's Placards", «ARG» 1982, 284-307

ULLMAN S., *Studien zur Geschichte der Juden in Belgien*, Antwerp 1909

USQUE, SAMUEL, *Consolaçam as Tribulações de Israel Composto por Samuel Usque, Empresso en Ferrara en casa de Abraham aben Usque 5313 da criaçam, am d. 7 de setembro* [Reprint Fundaçâo C. Gulbenkian, Lisbon 1989].

WOLF, Lucien, "Jews in Tudor England", in IDEM. *Essays in Jewish History*, edited by C. ROTH, London 1934, pp. 73-90.

YERUSHALMI, Y.H., *Prolegomenon* to Alexandre Herculano, *History of the Origin and Establishment of the Inquisition in Portugal*, New York 1972.[Original title: *História da Origem e estabelicemento da Inquisição em Portugal*], translated by J.C.BRANNER, Ktav Publishig House New York 1972, New York 1972,

————, *From Spanish Court to Italian Ghetto, Isaac Cardoso, A Study on Seventeenth Century Marranism and Jewish Apologetics*, Columbia University Press 1971, [Reprint 1981].

————, *A Jewish Classic in the Portuguese Language*, preface to SAMUEL USQUE, *Consolaçam as Tribulações de Israel* [Reprint Fundaçâo C. Gulbenkian, Lisbon 1989] vol I, pp. 14-123.

Index of Documents

Document 1 - The Ferrara envoys to the Conference of Bologna report to Duke Alfonso I on their meeting with Monseigneur de Granvelle-December 30, 1529.

Document 2 - The Ferrara delegates to the Conference of Bologna to Duke Alfonso I – January 4, 1530.

Document 3 - Charles V appoints Corneil Scepperus to the rank of General Commissioner "against false and bad Christians" April 4, 1530.

Document 4 - Queen Mary's official statement on the proceedings against Diogo Mendes and instructions for the imperial Commissioners in Antwerp – August 24, 1532.

Document 5 - Queen Mary's instructions for the release of Diogo Mendes upon payment of bail – September 10, 1532.

Document 6 - Antonio Fernandez to Gerolamo Maretta – July 24, 1538.

Document 7 - Duke Ercole II to some (unnamed) Portuguese merchants living in Antwerp- July 29, 1538.

Document 8 - Diogo Mendes to Duke Ercole II d'Este – October 9, 1538.

Document 9 - Gerolamo Maretta to Duke Ercole II of Ferrara – undated fragment of a lost dispatch – 1539.

Document 10 - Duke Ercole II instructs his ambassador in Milan to request the immediate release of Duarte Pinto.

Document 11 - Official report on Loys Garces' accusations against Manuel Serrano, Gabriel Negro, Manuel Manriques, Diogo Mendes and Enrique Pires – July 5 and 6, 1540.

Document 12 - A list of prominent New Christians living in Antwerp in (or around) 1540.

Document 13 - Johannes Vuysting accuses Diogo Mendes and other Portuguese merchants of Antwerp, London and Milan of plotting to have him assassinated – September 21, 1540.

Document 14 - Gaspar Lopes (prisoner in Pavia) states under torture that Diogo Mendes and other Portuguese merchants of Antwerp and London planned to have Johannes Vuysting murdered – September 21, 1540.

Document 15 - Interrogation and deposition of Diego de Redondo, an *Old Christian* merchant living in Antwerp – October 19, 1540.

Document 16 - Charles Boisot's report to the Emperor on the difficult beginning of his mission in Antwerp – November 1540.

Document 17 - Ordinance directing the authorities and the inhabitants of Antwerp to denounce all persons infected by the Judaic fallacy – December 12, 1540.

Document 18 - Deposition of Gaspar Gomes, prisoner in Pavia – December 24, 1540.

Document 19 - Gaspar Gomes, detained in Pavia, discloses under torture the names of several Portuguese Judaizing in London-December 27, 1540.

Document 20 - Queen Mary's instructions to Jerome Sandelin – February 21, 1541.

Document 21 - Queen Mary to Corneille Sceperus, *imperial commissioner against the false Christians* – February 22, 1541.

Document 22 - Queen Mary's explanatory statement to the General Procurator of Brabant and denunciation against the authorities of Antwerp – March 12, 1541.

Document 23 - Bill of credit of 3,000 ducats issued by Diogo Mendes in favour of Duke Ercole II – April 2, 1541.

Document 24 - Juan Rebello to Loys de Schorr, President of the Privy Council – May 13, 1541.

Document 25 - Daniel Bomberg and other merchants in Antwerp to Queen Mary – June 4, 1541.

Document 26 - Duke Ercole II to Nicolas Perrenot de Granvelle – June 20, 1541.

Document 27 - Jeromme Sandelin, *rentmeester* at Bewesterschelt to Loys de Schorr, president of the Privy Council – October 8, 1541.

Document 28 - Queen Mary to Monseigneur de Granvelle – October 15, 1541.

Document 29 - Christovão Garcia' s undated letter to Queen Mary of Habsburg – February/March 1542.

Document 30 - Queen Mary to Eustace Chapuys, the Spanish Ambassador in London, March 3, 1542.

Document 31 - The Emperor reinstates the privileges granted in 1537 to the Portuguese New Christians – March 10, 1542.

Document 32 - Queen Mary To Jerome Sandelin – March 11, 1542.

Document 33 - Charles V to Queen Mary of Hungary (rough draft) – July 15, 1542.

Document 34 - Charles V to the Marcgrave of Antwerp (rough draft) – July 15, 1542.

Document 49 - Deposition of Manuel Fernandiz boatswain of the ship San Salvador – July 16, 1544.

Document 50 - Corneille Sceperus' secret report to Queen Mary on the inquiry against the Portuguese imprisoned in Antwerp, – July 22, 1544.

Document 51 - Deposition of Manuel Bernaldis, cashier of the Portuguese Royal Feitor in Antwerp July 30, 1544.

Document 52 - Judgement issued by Diego de la Torre on the dispute between Diego Fernandiz Netto and Manuel Carneiro, July 30, 1544.

Document 53 - A list of Portuguese immigrants arrested in Antwerp in 1544.

Document 54 - Official report on the interrogations and depositions of Diego Fernandiz Netto – August 1 1544.

Document 55 - Official report on the interrogations and depositions of the Portuguese immigrants imprisoned in Antwerp – 1544.

Document 56 - Queen Mary to Dom João III, King of Portugal – October 18, 1544.

Document 57 - Queen Mary to Prince Henrique, General Inquisitor of Portugal – October 19, 1544.

Document 58 - Queen Mary to the Portuguese Inquisitor Dom João de Melo – October 19, 1544.

Document 59 - Queen Mary to Dom João de Melo, Inquisitor – October 19, 1544.

Document 60 - An (incomplete) list of Portuguese immigrants arrested in Flanders in November 1544.

Document 61 - Queen Mary to the Emperor – July 1547.

Document 62 - The Queen-Regent approves the extrajudiciary settlement proposed by Nuño Henriques and Henriques Nuñes – Sept. 1, 1547.

Document 63 - An (unnamed) officer of the Court to the Burgomaster of Antwerp – August 5, 1549.

Document 64 - An unsigned letter of a high officer of the Court to the Margrave of Antwerp – August 5, 1549.

Document 65 - A Burgomaster of Antwerp informs an unnamed high officer of the Court that the authorities of Antwerp will publish the imperial *placard* – August 7, 1549.

Document 66 - An undated (1549–50) list of New Christians presented by Manoel Lopez to the Office Fiscal de Brabant.

Document 67 - A list of Portuguese New Christians mentioned in an official report to the Court (circa 1550) who were apparently allowed to remain in Antwerp after the 1549 expulsion.

Explanatory Note

In the archival documents personal names and surnames were transcribed in different ways. We adopted the forms which appear most consistently in the sources. In some cases we also indicated the most frequent variants of the same name (in round brackets).

Whenever possible we also provided [in square brackets] the Jewish name used by the Portuguese of Antwerp and London in the privacy of their homes and later, openly, in different Italian cities. We have used the same system to provide the previous "baptismal" name of persons designated by their Jewish name.

In order to better identify the people in question we have stated their family links, academic qualifications, profession, commercial activities, role in the Community and in the Rescue Organization.

Only the names of Authors whose works are directly discussed in our text are included in this index. Authors quoted in the notes are not mentioned.

Index of Names

Abenhini, Benvenida, daughter of Isac Abenhini, wife of Moshe Namias, 120.

Abenhini, Isac: see Jacome, Gabriel.

Abenini, Moshe [*alias* António Lopes], brother of Gabriel Jacome [Isac Abenhini], Portuguese merchant in the Venetian Ghetto, 119-120.

Abendana, Abraham: see Renel, Manuel.

Abraham, the Patriarch, p.75.

Abravanel, Don Samuel, 45.

Abravanel, Family, 77.

Adrian VI, Pope, 8-9.

Adriatic Sea, 42-43, 47.

Affaitati, Giancarlo (Jean Charles), 35, 174.

Afonso V, King of Portugal (1438-1481), 28n.

Agulhar, de, Antonio merchant in London, 163.

Airas (Aires), Master, physician in Lisbon, 143.

Aires (surname unstated) physician in Salonika, formerly secret mohel (circumciser) in Antwerp, 164.

Alaert Isabeau, housemaid of Sebastian Fernandiz, 194–195.

Alfonso I d'Este, Duke of Ferrara (1505-1534), 16-17.

Alps, 37, 75, 184–188.

Altdorf (Alpine village in Switzerland), 186, 188.

Alvares, Emmanuel, physician in Antwerp, arrested in Lierre (1543) while trying to leave the Low Countries, 60.

Alvares, Emmanuel, "conductor" of clandestine emigrants, 60, 118.

Alvares, Katarina, Portuguese immigrant arrested in Middelbourg in 1540, eventually released and expelled from the Low Countries, 167–168.

Alvarez, Francisco, stewart of Antómnio Fernandes, 24.

Alvarez, Francisco, merhant in Antwerp, 77, 237.

Alvarez, Lorenço [Jewish name unknown] merchant in Antwerp, 112, 147.

Alvarez, Luis (or Luys) 112-113, 141, 147.

Alvarez, Pero, merchant in Lisbon, 163.

Alvaro, Gonsales, Portuguese immigrant arrested in Middelbourg in 1540 and eventually released , 166, 168.

Alveres, Fernando, Portuguese Judaizer, officer at the Casa da India in Lisbon, 162.

Alverez Victoria Luis (probably the same as Alvarez Luis, see above) 65 years old merchant in Antwerp (in 1540), 164.

Amato Lusitano, well-known physician, author of famous medical tracts, 3n., 97, 115.

Ancona, 37, 42-43, 48, 99-101, 103-106, 108, 113, 115, 187, 188.

Contarini, Francesco, Venetian Ambassador in Brussels, 31-32.
Council (Grand) of Brabant (Grand Conseil de Brabant), 8, 19n., 20n., 31n., 34n., 35, 63n., 64.
Council (Grand) of Malines (Grote Raad van Mechelen), 6, 24.
Council (Regional) of the Hague, 6.
Coronel, Fernando Perez, Gabriel Negro's son in law, 34-35, 99, 211.
Coronel, Ignacio Lopes, Gabriel Negro's son in law, 99.
 Cremona, 80n., 98, 107, 109, 110, 142.
Cusana, de, Luis merchant in Malines (Mechelen), husband of Elisabet Mendes, sister of Diego Nunes, 162.

Dardero, Salomon, Portuguese merchant in Ferrara, *feitor* of Bernardo Micas, 106.
Dardero, Samuel, nephew of Salomon Dardero, merchant in the Venetian Ghetto, 106.
Dayras, Fernando, husband of Guiomar Dias, Portuguese immigrant arrested in Middelbourg in 1540, eventually released and expelled from the Low Countries, 167–168.
Denmark, 202.
Dias Fernando, Portuguese immigrant arrested in Middelbourg in 1540 and eventually released, 166, 168.
Dias Guiomar, wife of Fernando Dayras, Portuguese immigrant arrested in Middelbourg in 1540 and eventually expelled, 167, 168.
Dias, Hector, Portuguese immigrant arrested at Veere in 1544, 61–62, 198.
Dias, Henrique, husband of Violante Lopes, father of five children, clandestine immigrant imprisoned in Antwerp with his family (1544), 214.
Dias, João, Portuguese merchant in London and in Ferrara, son of Simon Dias, husband of Eleanor Nuñes, 52.
Dias, Margareta, Portuguese immigrant arrested in Middelbourg in 1540 and eventually released, 166, 168.
Diego (Master Diego), Christovão Garcia's factor in London, 55.
Dies, António, merchant in Lisbon, 161.
Dies, Diego, merchant in Lisbon, 161.
Dies, George, merchant in London, 161, 165.
Dies, Manuel, merchant in Lisbon, 161.
Dies, Maria, a poor widow, in London, 163.
Diez, Gonçalo, a young valet in Diogo Mendes' service, 146, 150.
Dionisio, Doctor: see Rodrigues, Denis.
Drago, Gaspar, Portuguese Judaizer, law graduate in Lisbon, 164.
Duardo, Joan, 113, 141, 147.
Dyas (Dayras) Fernando, Portuguese immigrant arrested in Middelbourg in 1540 and eventually released, 166, 168.

Heresy, 5-11, 13–15, 26–27 and passim.
Heresy, Judaizing (*Heresie en Judaïserung, Heresie Judaïque*) 13, 18, 20, 24, 27, 29 n., 32, 47.
Heresy, Lutheran and Anabaptist, 6.

Indian House (Casa da India) in Lisbon, 162, 164.
Inquisition, in the Low Countries (aborted), 8-9, 79, 123.
Inquisition, "Medieval", 79.
Inquisition, Portuguese, 67, 69, 79, 101-102, 106, 189, 210, 219, 223.
Inquisition, Portuguese, *Familiares* of, 67.
Inquisition, Roman, 18, 79.
Inquisition, Spanish, 5, 13.
Ioão III, Dom, King of Portugal (1521-1557), 22, 36, 64-65, 67, 189, 193, 194, 203, 208, 219, 223, 227–228.
Ioly Zorattini, Pier Cesare, Professor of History of Religions at the State University of Udine, Editor of the *Processi* of the Venetian Inquisition, xvii, 127, and *passim*.
Ippolito d'Este, brother of Duke Ercole II, arch-bishop and later cardinal, 106.
Isaac, the Patriarch, 75.
Israel, Jonathan, historian, 45.
Istambul, xvi.
Italy, ix, xiii, xv, 14, 15, 19, 23, 25, 28, 41, 46, 48n., 60n., 66–67, 73, 80, 84, 88n., 90n., 92, 99, 104, 106, 108, 115, 116, 117, 121, 123, 130–133, 149, 151, 158, 197, 203, 221–225.

Jacob, the Patriarch, 75.
Jacome, Gabriel [Isac Abenhini], Portuguese merchant in Antwerp and in Ferrara, 119-120, 238.
Jacome, Maria, mother of Gabriel Jacome [Isac Abenhini] and António Lopes [Moshe Abenini], 119.

Lare de, Guillaume (Wilhelm van Lare), provost marshal of the royal Palace in Brussels, 25.
Larogne: see Ronha.
Leadership, Hebrew, 83-84, 124-125.
Lerma, Juan, Old-Christian Spanish merchant in Antwerp, 209-210.
Levant, xii, 14, 19, 20, 23, 25, 28, 47, 53, 59, 66, 80, 88n., 99, 103, 107, 108, 121.
Levantine Jews, 42, 43, 44, 106, 110.
Lindo, Jeronimo, 116n, 237.
Lisbon, ix, xvi, 2, 15, 18, 22, 36, 44, 53, 67, 69 101-102, 106, 120, 159, 161-165, 181, 204.
Lombardy, xii, 36, 37, 47, 49, 73, 78, 82, 88, 95, 97, 103, 109, 110, 112, 127.

Pinhero, Emmanuel (= Emanuel Navarro), Portuguese merchants in Antwerp and
    Ferrrara, burned in effigy in Lisbon, father of Pero Pinhero [Josef Navarro],
    Lope Pinhero, Salomon Navarro and Christovão Manoel, 67, 94, 114, 162,
    197, 211, 212.
Pinhero, Emmanuel, Portuguese immigrant imprisoned in Antwerp (1544), 64 n.,
    202, 215.
Pinhero, Hector, Portuguese immigrant imprisoned in Antwerp (1544), 64n., 232.
Pinhero, Lope, son of Emanuel, living in Lisbon (1540), 162.
Pinhero, Pero (Petro, Pietro) [Joseph Navarro], son of Emmanuel Pinhero, Jewish
    merchant in Ferrara and in Ancona, Parnas of the Portuguese Nation in
    Ferrara, 114, 162.
Pinta, Anna, sister of Duarte and Bastião Pinto, wife of António de la Ronha, 53,
    160.
Pinto, Alvaro, merchant in London and in Antwerp, 70.
Pinto, Antonio, merchant in Anterp, 160.
Pinto (Rodrigues-Pinto), Bastião (Sebastian), 44, 96-97, 151, 160, 163, 173.
Pinto (Rodrigues-Pinto), Diego 22, 96-97, 142.
Pinto (Rodrigues Pinto), Duarte, brother of Diego, Bastião, Estacio and Anna,
    leader of the Portuguese Nation in Antwerp and Ferrara, 44, 81-82, 141, 147,
    160.
Pinto (Rodrigues Pinto), Stacio (Estacio), brother of Diego, Bastião, Duarte, João
    and Anna, Portuguese merchant in Antwerp and Ferrara, 96-97, 147, 160.
Pinto, (Rodrigues Pinto), João 96-97.
Pinto, Thomas, Portuguese merchant in London and Antwerp, 56.
Pirenne Henry, Belgian Historian, 8–9n.
Pires, Diogo [Isaia Cohen], Portuguese poet, 56, 100-102.
Pires, Estevão (Steven, Stefano) nephew, son in law of Henrique Pires, husband of
    Anna Henriques, member of the Pepper Consortium in Antwerp, commercial
    partner of Duke Ercole II of Ferrara, 44, 100-103, 147, 151, 161
Pires (Pires Coronel), Fernando: see Coronel.
Pires, Henrique [Yacob Cohen], a prominent merchant, partner of the Pepper
    Consortium, leader of the Nation in Antwerp, and Ferrara, Martyr in Ancona,
    144, 147, 161.
Pires, Luis, merchant in Antwerp, 160–161.
Pisa, da Lazarino, banker in Ferrara, second husband of Ora Bichacho, 105.
Placards *(posted edicts)* 7-11 20, 26-27, 32.
Po, River, 37, 45.
Prevost-Marshal of the Imperial Palace (unnamed) dispatched to Antwerp (in
    1540), 30, 156, 170.
Privileged offence (Geprivilegiëerd misdriff) 20, 21.
Privileges of the Portuguese New Christians in Antwerp, 2-3, 178-180.
Privy Council (of Charles V), 28, 35n., 48n.

Rodrigues, Emanuel, Portuguese merchant in London, and Antwerp, arrested in Lierre (1543) while trying to leave the Low Countries, later settled in Ferrara, 60.

Rodrigues, Fabiano [Fabião, Fabio, Fabien], rich merchant, son of Doctor Dionisio, 106-107, 237.

Rodrigues, Felipa, wife of Thomas Gomes da India, 118–119.

Rodrigues, Gaspar, 121, 238.

Rodrigues, Gomes, merchant, founder of the Portuguese Nation in Ancona, 43.

Rodrigues, Gomes, escaped from a prison, 139.

Rodrigues, Hyeronimo, Portuguese merchant in Antwerp and Ferrara, 122.

Rodrigues, Jorge, Portuguese merchant, arrested at the port of Veere and later in Antwerp (1544), 62, 216.

Rodrigues, Manoel, merchant and physician, son of Doctor Dionisio, 106-107, 110, 238.

Rodrigues, Manoel, poor Portuguese émigrés imprisoned in Pavia in 1540, 161.

Rodrigues, de Andrade Antonio, Portuguese immigrant arrested at Veere and later imprisoned in Antwerp (1544), 216.

Rome, 73, 143, 218–220, 222, 225.

Ronchiglium (sic!), merchant in Antwerp, 163.

Ronha (Roña, Rogna, Ronija, Roigne, Loroigne) de la, Family name, xv.

Ronha (Roña, Rogna, Ronija, Roigne, de la, (also spelled: Noronha or Laroigne), António, member of the leadership of the Portuguese Nation and the Rescue Organisation in London and Antwerp, 22-23, 33, 53-54, 83, 94, 118-119, 148, 149–150, 160, 237.

Ronha, de la, Diego, Portuguese Judaizer in London, 54, 94, 163.

Roth Cecil, Jewish Historian, 53, 82, 94.

Rovere, della, Guidobaldo, Duke of Urbino, 103-105.

Rubero, Alphonso, Portuguese immigrant arrested in Middelbourg in 1540, eventually released, deprived of his properties and expelled from the Low Countries, 167–168.

Ruy (Rodrigues), Simon, merchant in London, 163.

Salamanca, de, Andreas, Christian merchant in Antwerp, witness in the 1544 inquiry, 99.

Salonika (Thessaloniki), 18, 28, 46, 98, 99, 143, 159, 161, 164, 233.

Salvaterra (de Salva Terra), Pedro, cloth-shearer in Portugal, clandestine immigrant arrested in Antwerp (1544), 67n., 215.

Samuel, Edgar, historian and litterate, 52-53.

Sandelin Gerôme, Rentmeester (Fiscal receiver) of Bewesterschelt in Zeeland, 33, 51, 166–167, 177, 181.

San Pedro, de, Fray Diego, 19, 143.

San Miguel (S. Michel), Atlantic Island, 218.